SCHOOL

Commendations

This is a truly valuable book. In a collection of outstanding essays, the contributors seek to find firm ground for statements about growth and decline in the Anglican Communion, one of the world's largest religious institutions. At every stage, what they find repeatedly challenges conventional assumptions, and also raises fundamental questions that demand to be applied to other global churches. This is truly eye-opening. I cannot speak too highly of this excellent volume.

Philip Jenkins, *Distinguished Professor of History, Baylor University, USA*

This volume is a veritable goldmine. It contains a huge amount of mostly numerical information on the Anglican Communion in all its fullness. Quite rightly it eschews easy generalizations, probing instead the complex and evolving mosaic that constitutes modern Anglicanism. Almost every reader will be surprised about something. I recommend this book very warmly.

Grace Davie, *Professor emeritus of Sociology, University of Exeter, UK*

To be 'Anglican' once meant to be Christian in a peculiarly Church of England fashion, and the extent of 'Anglicanism' could be neatly mapped onto the boundaries of the British Empire or Commonwealth. This timely and wide-ranging volume demonstrates that, happily, neither of these generalisations any longer applies. It shows how the Anglican Communion since 1980 displays a complex narrative of rise and fall in its different parts, and now exhibits a fascinating range of variations on the historic theme of what it means to be Anglican.

Brian Stanley, *Professor of World Christianity, University of Edinburgh, UK*

Numerical church growth and bolstering congregational numbers continues to preoccupy many mainline denominations in the developed world. As this important study shows, church growth is a complex and nuanced phenomena, and needs to be studied with care if it is to be understood. David Goodhew's continued work in this field offers new perspectives in an arena that is inherently complicated – and he brings to this a clear-sighted vision. For all who research church growth – as theoreticians or practitioners – this major study makes a valuable contribution to a burgeoning field of enquiry that sits between missiology and ecclesiology.

Martyn Percy, *Dean of Christ Church, Oxford University, UK*

This deepening of the analysis of global Anglicanism is refreshing and welcome for its challenge to the popular presentation of declining North versus growing South. This nuanced approach starts outside the North/West and exhibits the range of geo-political contexts and diversity of growth patterns. In so doing it reconfigures and complicates the picture, challenges conceptions of growth and decline, questions projections of secularization, and re-shapes the future Communion.

Kirsteen Kim, *Professor of Theology and World Christianity, Leeds Trinity University, UK*

The Essays in this book invite readers to further discourse on 'growth' and 'decline' within the respective 'Provinces' of Anglicanism in particular, and within Christianity in general. The book is worth reading as a whole, and informative in its wide range of contributions.

Jesse N.K. Mugambi, *Professor of Philosophy and Religious Studies, University of Nairobi, Kenya*

David Goodhew and his diverse team of collaborators have produced a timely, illuminating and comprehensive collection of essays. This landmark volume represents an essential text for students of global Christianity, as well as worldwide Anglicanism, at the turn of the twenty-first century.

Michael Snape, *Michael Ramsey Professor of Anglican Studies, Durham University, UK*

Growth and Decline in the Anglican Communion

The Anglican Communion is one of the largest Christian denominations in the world. *Growth and Decline in the Anglican Communion* is the first comprehensive study of its dramatic growth and decline in the years since 1980. An international team of leading researchers based across five continents provides a global overview of Anglicanism alongside twelve detailed case studies. The case studies stretch from Singapore to England, Nigeria to the USA and mostly focus on non-western Anglicanism. This book is a critical resource for students and scholars seeking an understanding of the past, present and future of the Anglican Church. More broadly, the study offers insight into debates surrounding secularisation in the contemporary world.

Revd. Dr. David Goodhew is Director of Ministerial Practice, Cranmer Hall, St John's College, Durham University, UK. Prior to Cranmer, he was a parish priest in York and before that, Chaplain and Fellow of St Catharine's College, Cambridge. He has published widely in the fields of modern British and South African history. He edited the controversial study *Church Growth in Britain: 1980 to the Present* (Ashgate 2012) and the volume *Towards a Theology of Church Growth* (Ashgate 2015).

Routledge Contemporary Ecclesiology

Series editors:
Martyn Percy, *Dean of Christ Church, Oxford University, UK*
D. Thomas Hughson, *Marquette University, USA*
Bruce Kaye, *Charles Sturt University, Australia*

For a full list of titles in this series, please visit www.routledge.com

The field of ecclesiology has grown remarkably in the last decade, and most especially in relation to the study of the contemporary church. Recently, theological attention has turned once more to the nature of the church, its practices and proclivities, and to interpretative readings and understandings of its role, function and ethos in contemporary society.

This series draws from a range of disciplines and established scholars to further the study of contemporary ecclesiology and publish an important cluster of landmark titles in this field. The series editors represent a range of Christian traditions and disciplines, and this reflects the breadth and depth of books developing in the Series. This series presents a clear focus on the contemporary situation of churches worldwide, offering an invaluable resource for students, researchers, ministers and other interested readers around the world working or interested in the diverse areas of contemporary ecclesiology and the important changing shape of the church worldwide.

Titles in the series include:

The Wisdom of the Spirit
Gospel, Church and Culture
Edited by Martyn Percy and Pete Ward

Practical Theology and Pierre-André Liégé
Radical Dominican and Vatican II Pioneer
Nicholas Bradbury

The Holy Spirit and the Church
Ecumenical Reflections with a Pastoral Perspective
Edited by Thomas Hughson

The Future Shapes of Anglicanism
Currents, Contours, Charts
Martyn Percy

Growth and Decline in the Anglican Communion
1980 to the Present
Edited by David Goodhew

Growth and Decline in the Anglican Communion

1980 to the Present

Edited by David Goodhew

Routledge
Taylor & Francis Group

LONDON AND NEW YORK

First published 2017
by Routledge
2 Park Square, Milton Park, Abingdon, Oxon OX14 4RN

and by Routledge
711 Third Avenue, New York, NY 10017

Routledge is an imprint of the Taylor & Francis Group, an informa business

British Library Cataloguing in Publication Data
A catalogue record for this book is available from the British Library

Library of Congress Cataloging in Publication Data
Names: Goodhew, David, 1965– editor.
Title: Growth and decline in the Anglican communion :
    1980 to the present / edited by David Goodhew.
Description: 1 [edition]. | New York : Routledge, 2017. |
    Includes bibliographical references and index.
Identifiers: LCCN 2016027352 (print) | LCCN 2016038650 (ebook) |
    ISBN 9781472433633 (hardback : alk. paper) | ISBN 9781315585970
Subjects: LCSH: Anglican Communion—History—20th century—Case
    studies. | Anglican Communion—History—21st century—Case studies.
Classification: LCC BX5005 .G76 2017 (print) | LCC BX5005 (ebook) |
    DDC 283.09/04—dc23
LC record available at https://lccn.loc.gov/2016027352

ISBN: 978-1-472-43363-3 (hbk)
ISBN: 978-1-472-43364-0 (pbk)
ISBN: 978-1-315-58597-0 (ebk)

Typeset in Bembo
by Apex CoVantage, LLC

Contents

Contributors

Dr. Barbara Bompani is Director of the Centre of African Studies and Senior Lecturer in African Development, University of Edinburgh.

Dr. Jeremy Bonner is Honorary Fellow, Department of Theology and Religion, University of Durham.

Dr. Richard Burgess is Lecturer in Ministerial Theology, University of Roehampton.

Revd. Dr. John Corrie is Tutor in Mission, Trinity College, Bristol (retired).

Revd. Dr. Daniel Eshun is Chaplain and Lecturer in Theology and Ministerial Studies, University of Roehampton.

Revd. Canon Professor Joseph D. Galgalo is Assistant Professor of Theology and Vice Chancellor of St. Paul's University, Limuru, Kenya.

Revd. Dr. David Goodhew is Director of Ministerial Practice, Cranmer Hall, St John's College, Durham University.

Revd. Dr. Anderson Jeremiah is Lecturer, Department of Philosophy, Politics and Religion, Lancaster University.

Professor Todd M. Johnson is Associate Professor of Global Christianity and Director of the Center for the Study of Global Christianity, Gordon-Conwell Seminary, Mass., USA and Visiting Research Fellow, Boston University.

Professor Andrew Eungi Kim is Professor, Graduate School of International Studies, Korea University.

The Rt. Revd. Dr. Graham Kings is Bishop and Mission Theologian in the Anglican Communion.

Dr. Ruth Powell is Director, National Church Life Survey, Australia and Associate Professor, Australian Catholic University.

The Rt. Revd. Maurice Sinclair is Honorary Assistant Bishop, Birmingham, England and formerly Primate of the Southern Cone.

Professor David Voas is Professor of Social Science and Head of Department, Institute of Education, University College, London.

Revd. Dr. Yossa Way is Academic Dean, Université Anglicane du Congo, Bunia.

Revd. Daniel Wee is Senior Pastor and Vicar, Church of Our Saviour, Singapore.

Dr. Emma Wild-Wood is Lecturer in World Christianities, Faculty of Divinity, University of Cambridge.

Gina A. Zurlo is Assistant Director of the Center for the Study of Global Christianity, Gordon-Conwell Seminary, Mass., USA.

Illustrations

Figures

Tables

Acknowledgements

This volume has taken five years to complete and in that time many people richly deserve thanks for their work towards this project. First and foremost, the contributors, despite being scattered across five continents, have given generously of their time, been endlessly helpful and, often, had to wrestle with highly demanding datasets. This work exists because of their hard work.

David Wilkinson, Principal of St Johns College, Durham, and Mark Tanner, Warden of Cranmer Hall, have consistently supported this research. This book could not have happened without their vision and encouragement. The students and staff of St Johns and Cranmer Hall provide a supportive and stimulating environment, which has shaped this work in many ways. The project was based in Cranmer Hall's Centre for Church Growth Research. The staff of the Centre, especially Ant Cooper, have been a great support during this project. I am grateful to Whitelands College, part of the University of Roehampton, and especially to its principal, Mark Garner, for kindly hosting the conference at which the contents of this book were first made public. As well as supplying a theological 'Afterword' to the volume, Bishop Graham Kings has been a good friend to this project in a wide variety of ways.

Tavis Bohlinger and Clare Bliss provided crucial editorial support and their eagle-eyed work significantly improved the text. David Shervington, Sarah Lloyd, Andrew Weckenmann, Ted Meyer and Eve Mayer from Ashgate and, then, Routledge have been shrewd, helpful and encouraging. As this is the third volume I have worked on with Ashgate, I wish to place on record how deeply grateful I am for the company's readiness to back the hunches of its authors.

Martyn Percy, D. Thomas Hughson and Bruce Kaye, as the editors of the Ashgate Contemporary Ecclesiology series, provided crucial support and advice at the outset of this project. Ed Backhouse, Petrica Bistran, Hannah Frost, Philip Lockley, Jacqueline Stober and Ruth Young were members of the Durham University MA module, 'Growth and Decline in British Christianity since 1945'. As such they were highly stimulating sounding boards for material in this volume. Andrew Brown of *The Guardian*, Daniel Muñoz, David Marshall, Chris Sugden, Vinay Samuel, John Kafwanka, Archbishop Josiah Idowu-Fearon, Peter Lineham and Kevin Ward have kindly shared perspectives and discussed ideas. An anonymous reader from Routledge made stimulating comments which helped in the final editing of the book. But I must stress that responsibility for the judgements within each chapter is that of the author(s) alone.

Thank you to the Revd. Canon Michael Barlowe and Dr. Dale Jones for your help in providing maps in chapter 12. Thank you George Style, Christian Selvaratnam, Ellie Cockayne, Matt Parkins, Ed Thornton and Chris Cox for your help with the cover. In preparing the book for publication Joshua Wells, Jack Boothroyd, Lucy Loveluck, Kevin Kelsey, Denise File and all at Apex CoVantage were extremely helpful – many thanks to you all.

This is the third volume I have edited. And as I look back I am most grateful to my wife, Lindsey, who has provided vast amounts of support, encouragement and good sense to her often distracted husband.

David Goodhew

Introduction

1 Growth and decline in the Anglican Communion, 1980 to the present

David Goodhew

Introduction

The Anglican Communion is one of the largest Christian denominations world-wide. This volume shows how it has grown and declined since 1980, based on the work of an international team of researchers, with the emphasis on the world outside the west. Overall, the Anglican Communion has experienced marked growth in recent decades. In 1970 there were around 47 million Anglicans and by 2010, there were around 86 million.[1] That figure has almost certainly increased since 2010, meaning that the Anglican Communion has roughly doubled in size between 1970 and the present.

But evidence of overall growth needs to be balanced by evidence of decline in parts of Anglicanism. Alongside growth, the Communion has experienced serious divisions and other difficulties in recent years. An understanding of its patterns of growth and decline is crucial to understanding the current and future trajectories of global Anglicanism. As one of the main Christian denominations, an understanding of Anglicanism's growth and decline in recent decades is also significant for wider debates concerning secularisation in the modern world.

This volume starts with this introductory chapter that sets the scene and sum-marises the conclusions of the work. Then follows chapter 2, an overall survey of global Anglicanism by leading religious demographers, Todd M. Johnson and Gina A. Zurlo. Chapters 3 to 14 provide 12 case studies drawn from across the world; five are from Africa (Ghana, Nigeria, Congo, Kenya and South Africa), four from Asia (India, Singapore, South Korea and Australia), two from the Americas (one on the USA and one on parts of South America) and one is from Europe, the Church of England itself. The volume concludes with an afterword by Bishop Graham Kings, Mission Theologian in the Anglican Communion.

Beneath the overall picture are dramatic variations. Different areas have seen growth, decline or have been broadly stable. Some countries have seen a mix of all three. Since 1980 there has been marked decline in areas of previous strength such as England and the USA. There has been major expansion, notably in parts of west and east Africa, but also in areas where Anglicanism had little presence until very recently – such as the Congo, South America and Singapore. Along-side this has occurred the plateauing of areas previously significant, such as South

Africa. The growth and decline which has happened across the Communion since 1980 is as significant as any other time in the Communion's history.

Many assumptions have been made about growth and decline in the global Anglican Communion, despite limited research on the subject. It is widely and rightly stated that Anglicanism has shifted during the last 50 years to being a church predominantly found in the developing world. But it is less recognised that there is great variation *between* different parts of the developing world. There is a right recognition that Anglicanism in many parts of the west has declined, but, again, the variation *within* the west is less well understood. Some parts of western Anglicanism have declined dramatically, some modestly, and in a few areas western Anglicanism has grown. This volume offers detailed research which brings greater clarity to discussions about Anglican growth and decline.

Serious divisions have opened up in recent years between and within parts of the Anglican Communion, which have led to a widening range of ecclesial groups which see themselves as 'Anglican'. This volume focuses only on those churches in full communion with the Archbishop of Canterbury as of 2012.[2] It is alert to other churches which see themselves as Anglican. Such churches deserve research, but that task lies beyond the scope of this volume. The advent of such divisions makes the need for accurate assessments of growth and decline all the more necessary. *Growth and Decline* explores diverse areas and offers a wide-ranging picture of the complexity within contemporary Anglicanism, from Nigeria to the USA, from England to Singapore. It provides encouragements and challenges for all strands of Anglican opinion. The pattern of growth and decline on the ground is often not what has been assumed.

It is widely – and rightly – recognised that the centre of gravity of global Anglicanism has moved decisively towards the developing world in the last 100 years. This process has accelerated since 1980. Consequently the bulk of the book concerns Anglicanism outside of England and outside of the western world, but in a way that is, broadly, representative of the Anglican Communion as a whole. *Growth and Decline* omits many places that deserve consideration. Johnson and Zurlo's chapter offers insights on provinces not covered in this volume, but comprehensive coverage of the entire Communion was not feasible within this project. The volume as a whole seeks, to echo the admirable strapline of Grove Books, not to be the last word on the subject but, in some ways, the first.

The year 1980 has been used as the starting point for the project for the following reasons: first, it allows the survey to look across a substantial period of time, but keeps the focus on the recent past; and second, whilst it would have been helpful to have extended the study back to 1960, the point when many studies see secularisation as taking a marked step forward, this would have been a much larger undertaking and would have produced too unwieldy a volume. It should be noted that the date of 1980 is used flexibly in this volume; the historical context is summarised and where significant developments happened before 1980, these are discussed.

This introductory chapter has four sections.

- The first section explores a series of questions which frame the project: what is church growth and decline and why does it matter? What are the current assumptions within the existing literature and where do they need questioning? How do you measure growth/decline – and what do you do when data does not exist or is of limited quality?
- The second section summarises the overall findings of the book. Whilst all readers are encouraged to read the book in its entirety, those seeking an overview of the volume should read this section.
- The third section discusses how growth and decline within global Anglicanism relates to debates about secularisation.
- The fourth section of this introductory chapter considers what these findings suggest for ecclesiology, how the Anglican Communion 'does church'.

Section one: questioning growth and decline in the Anglican Communion

What is church growth/decline and why does it matter?

The growth and decline of Anglicanism is of as much interest to people who are not Anglicans or, indeed, members of any Christian church as to those who regard themselves as Anglicans. For the former, this volume can be read as a study of the recent history of a major Christian tradition. As such, it contributes both to an understanding of global Anglicanism and to debates about secularisation across the world. For those who see themselves as Anglican, the above questions are important. But there are additional, more theologically based questions which arise. What is the true nature of 'church growth' and 'church decline'? To what extent does the numerical trajectory of a church matter, compared to other aspects of the Christian life such as service to the wider community or the quality of an individual Christian's life?

The Church of England has tended in recent years to describe 'growth' as having three dimensions: growth in service to the community, growth in an individual's holiness and the numerical growth of congregations.[3] This volume focuses on the last of these three aspects of growth – the numerical growth of congregations – but it does so in a way that calls attention to how the three aspects of growth are intertwined and how the growth of congregations *per se* would be of limited significance without parallel growth in service to the community and growth in the lives of individual believers.

Within the developing world, numerical church growth is widely and often enthusiastically sought. However, there is a need to examine the extent and nature of church growth. It is sometimes said that faith can be a mile wide but an inch deep. This needs consideration. But the parallel tendency to see this as a particular problem for Christianity outside the west is highly problematic; there is plenty of inch-deep faith (and unbelief) in the west.

Within the western world, church growth is debated in different terms. Some parts of the western church see it as both desirable and achievable. But in many parts of the western church, where Anglicanism has faced profound secularisation, church growth has been depicted as impossible, unnecessary or even dubious.[4] Some western commentators argue that the greater religiosity of the non-western world is a temporary phenomenon, which will lessen as such areas modernise and 'catch up' with west, or see non-western religiosity as an overstatement of what is a much smaller phenomenon than is often assumed.[5]

More broadly, a significant number of western theologians, church leaders and congregations have asked whether numerical growth is suspect theologically, seeing it as lacking a mandate from the Bible, doctrine or Christian tradition and dangerously close to buying into a secular idolisation of 'success'.[6] Whilst there are dangers, theologically, in a focus on numerical growth, such concerns need to be balanced by a range of theologians from varying traditions who argue that the Bible, the central Christian doctrines and a wide range of Christian traditions view growing churches as a legitimate and desirable goal and that experientially, there is much evidence that being part of a congregation impacts positively on various indicators of well-being.[7]

This more empirical study of patterns of growth and decline since 1980 in world Anglicanism will assist evaluation of such theological debates by offering greater clarity regarding what is happening. No one floats free from their context. The experience of growth or decline within a particular area colours the theology coming from that area. Churches which have historically experienced growth need to question whether such growth comes as much from socio-economic factors as spiritual factors. But churches which have historically experienced decline need to ask whether they have internalised that decline and have assumed that churches cannot, or even should not, grow. Such ecclesiastical pessimism may, on occasion, have less to do with theology than an internalisation of the secularisation thesis. Being theologically supportive of or hostile to congregational growth has an impact. There is substantial evidence that churches that intend to grow tend to grow and churches that do not intend to grow tend not to grow.[8]

What are the current assumptions within the existing literature and where do they need questioning?

The work of William Jacob covers the history of the Communion up to 1960. What is most striking from Jacob's account is the extent to which the leadership of the Communion was dominated by Church of England personnel and culture, even in 1960.[9] This had begun to shift in the postwar period, but the shift only gathered pace in the 1960s and 1970s. This volume shows how the shift away from English hegemony deepened and has been largely completed in the decades after 1980 and how the indigenisation of Anglicanism has impacted on patterns of growth and decline in recent decades.

A range of studies of world Anglicanism have appeared in the last 20 years.[10] Such studies contain much valuable material, but have limitations regarding depiction of patterns of growth and decline. There is awareness of the growth happening in Africa, but little recognition that different parts of African Anglicanism are growing at different rates.[11] Portraits of Anglicanism in South Africa stress, rightly, its many positive elements – especially its resistance to apartheid. One study goes so far as to see it as 'the crucible for Anglicanism in a new century'. But such portraits pass over long-standing evidence of the relative decline of South African Anglicanism.[12]

There is a general awareness of the lack of growth in much of western Anglicanism, but little recognition of the marked variation within western Anglicanism.[13] Conversely, other parts of the Communion deserve greater consideration. Using a quotation from a South American bishop, Ward likens Anglicanism in Latin America to '"a bus desperately needing to be filled"', but parts of Anglicanism on this continent have seen marked growth since 1980.[14] The observations above underline the need for a detailed picture of growth and decline in contemporary Anglicanism.

A recent contribution to debates about Anglican growth and decline is an article by Daniel Muñoz in the *Journal of Anglican Studies*.[15] This article rightly questions the reliability of Anglican data, asking how robust are figures given for the number of Anglicans and asking whether conflicts within contemporary Anglicanism can warp assessment of such figures. But, alongside good questions, this research offers alternative data sources which are themselves problematic. The article concludes that some western provinces of Anglicanism are not declining and that non-western churches are much smaller than is often assumed. A wide range of researchers, including the team behind this volume, offer substantial evidence to the contrary.[16]

How do you measure growth / decline?

> I found (to my horror) in ***** diocese, a proper data collection has not been undertaken since its creation. They have simply added 10% every two years to the numbers.

This startling comment was made by one of the authors in this volume, who, for obvious reasons, must remain anonymous. But the researcher then added, 'My assessment was that they [the diocesan figures] are not far from the target, but not accurate.' This anecdote flags a crucial question for this volume: the quality of the data. There are two key issues: first, there is the issue of what constitutes a valid measure of growth or decline; second, there is the issue of the quality of such data as is available. Beyond this, David Voas points to problems with all religious surveys. Voas coins 'Voas' first law', that a quarter of all responses to any question on religion are unreliable and adds 'Voas' second law', that a quarter of all responses to any question on religion do not mean what they appear to mean.[17] Each chapter in this volume addresses the sobering challenges thrown up by data quality and, at times, conclusions are limited by the limitations of the data. However, it would be a mistake to assume that, when data is problematic, nothing can be said. There *is* a wide range of data available, both quantitative and qualitative and, handled carefully, it can tell us much.[18]

The main quantitative measures are attendance, membership and affiliation. Such measures assess different things and produce different figures. Each of these is needed to make a global assessment of growth and decline in Anglicanism. Attendance is a measure of the number of people at worship, often defined as Sunday worship and is calculated in a variety of ways. Membership is a measure of those who see themselves as church members, however frequently they attend, meaning the membership of a church is usually larger than its attendance.

Affiliation means those who self-identify as Anglicans. Johnson and Zurlo provide an extended discussion of how Anglican affiliation is calculated in chapter 2.[19] Figures on Anglican affiliation come from a range of sources, most importantly: censuses and surveys, polls and statistics from religious communities themselves. The large number of the population of England who have been baptised by the Church of England increases the figure for Anglican affiliation in England in a way not seen in any other province, where nationality and faith do not overlap to the same degree. There is evidence that such vague affiliation to the Church of England is 'softening', with some surveys suggesting that a significant number of those who once called themselves 'CofE' now tick the box marked 'no religion' – although the data is too recent to be secure.[20] Affiliation, being the most general and vague of the measures, is necessarily most problematic. It is therefore important to note that the researchers for each chapter in this volume worked independently. It is striking how, in all but one case, the conclusions of demographers Todd M. Johnson and Gina A. Zurlo chime with the detailed work of the individual case studies.[21] This gives added weight to the figures in chapter 2 produced by Johnson and Zurlo, who have many years of research experience in this field. Whilst calculating religious affiliation is not a precise science, the data in chapter 2 is the best currently available.

Many developing countries do not possess detailed data on attendance, membership and affiliation. In some cases, such as Barbara Bompani's chapter on South Africa, the paucity of the data significantly limited what could be said. Joseph D. Galgalo, speaking of Kenyan Anglicanism, comments wryly that 'available statistics are terribly confusing but not completely useless'. But, his chapter also shows how the dataset can, to a degree, be 'cleaned' and evaluated using a range of metrics.[22] Chapters on Nigeria, Congo and Ghana show how attendance or membership data can be combined with data on the number of dioceses and parishes to test the value of the data.

Moreover, some of the *developed* world data is far from robust. Anglican provinces in the developed world tend to have the more detailed records and to have experimented with a range of measures of growth and decline. Some areas – notably the USA and Singapore – have strong systems of data collection and the chapters on these areas are able to explore the ecclesial landscape in great detail, but this is not true everywhere in the developed world.

This can be illustrated by a discussion of the Church of England itself. This is doubly important as its measures have had considerable influence on other provinces and offer a guide to the possibilities and pitfalls in this area. The Church of England currently has three main measures of congregational growth/decline: electoral roll, usual Sunday attendance and average weekly attendance. For much of the 20th century the main congregational metric was the 'electoral roll', a rough list of adult members. In recent decades, this was supplemented by collection of usual Sunday attendance (uSa), an estimate by leaders of the usual number of people who attend Sunday worship. Around 15 years ago, an additional measure began to be collected: all-age Average Weekly Attendance (aWa). The aWa measure sought to measure more precisely attendance at worship on all days of the week, not just Sundays. It was an average of recorded figures across four weeks – i.e. it was not the estimate of a leader. A fourth measure has been used in recent years, the calculation of the 'worshipping community', meaning all those who worship with some degree of regularity, but thus far it has proved unreliable.[23]

Those who collect this data do excellent work, but these three measures have significant limitations. The 'noise' in all three of the Church of England's measures is sufficient that none of them are reliable when detailed questions are asked of them.[24] For broad-brush issues they have value. It is, for example, certain that all Church of England dioceses have seen net decline since 1980 with the exception of the diocese of London, which shrank in the 1980s but has grown steadily since the early 1990s. It is also clear that the rate of decline varies substantially between dioceses. But the three measures are so flawed that, with specific exceptions (such as the dioceses of London and Lichfield, which have taken particular care over data collection), they are often unreliable when used to answer detailed questions.[25] All religious data has its limitations. The best way forward is to use multiple measures and a wide mix of metrics, testing whether data on membership/attendance/affiliation chimes with other metrics (such as the number of clergy, churches, dioceses and baptisms) and with more qualitative data. A wide mix of measures leads to the most solid conclusions.

Section two: key findings

The research team behind this volume show that the Anglican Communion overall has experienced substantial growth since 1980, but within the Communion there are dramatic variations. The provinces of the Communion stand anywhere on a continuum between rapid growth and rapid decline. This section summarises the main points on that line.

In chapter 2 Johnson and Zurlo provide an overview of Anglican affiliation worldwide, showing how swift and dramatically the centre of gravity has moved towards the non-western world in recent decades. They estimate that in 1970, 62% of all Anglicans were found in Europe. By 2010 this had dropped to 31%. During the same period, African Anglicans grew from 16% of all Anglicans worldwide in 1970 to 58% in 2010. Anglicanism within Asia has also grown rapidly, even though it remains small compared to the rest of the Communion. Anglicanism in South America and Oceania is growing more slowly. But within these vast areas Anglicanism is experiencing both decline and growth. North American Anglicans have shrunk as a proportion of global Anglicanism, constituting 9% of Anglicans worldwide in 1970, but 3% in 2010.[26] It should be remembered that in the early centuries of Christianity it was predominantly a religion of the area sometimes known as the 'Global South', with adherents in the 'Global North' in the minority. So, the recent shift in Anglicanism (mirrored in the rest of Christianity) could be seen, less as a novel development, but, in some ways, as a return to an earlier pattern.[27]

Johnson and Zurlo's chapter offers a means of judging the trends of growth and decline across the Communion and between its member provinces. It should be read alongside the other chapters, which offer more detailed portraits. Yet, whilst these case studies offer more nuance, they are themselves surveys. A province experiencing significant growth may contain dioceses which are experiencing decline. Conversely, a province which is experiencing significant decline may include dioceses which are growing.

Growth

Chapters 4, 5, 6, 9 and 13 depict areas experiencing rapid church growth.

In chapter 4 Richard Burgess shows how the number of Nigerian dioceses rose from 16 in 1979 to 164 in 2011 and the new dioceses have been at the forefront of growth. The diocese of Lagos West, created in 1999, grew from 161 to 240 churches by 2010.[28] Nigeria has seen a high-octane mix of rapidly rising population levels, deep poverty, patchy economic development, erratic governance and much civil strife. In parts of central and northern Nigeria, severe violence has made dioceses shrink rather than grow.[29] But the overall trend is strongly upward. There is some uncertainty as to the size of Nigerian Anglicanism, but the best figures suggest that, in terms of Anglican affiliation, it has grown from under 3 million to around 20 million between 1970 and 2010.[30] A key aspect of Nigerian Anglicanism is its 'pentecostalisation'. Such 'pentecostalisation' is widespread in Nigerian society and has had a significant effect on Anglicanism in the country.[31]

Yossa Way explores in chapter 5 the growth of the francophone province of the Congo, whose socio-economic conditions are similar or worse than much of Nigeria and which has seen greater civil strife. The first Anglican diocese in the Congo came into being in 1972. Then it had 30 clergymen, 25 parishes and 30 churches. As of 2015, Anglicanism in Congo had 545 clergy working in 424 parishes in 9 dioceses. Membership is estimated at around 237,000. Congo became a separate Anglican province in 1992. This happened amidst a backdrop of rapidly rising population levels, deep poverty and frequent warfare. Such turbulence has heavily affected the life of the Church, which struggles to live Christianly amidst huge pressures. The Church itself can be caught up in ethnic strife, as well as engaging in heroic humanitarian work. Civil disorder has led to expansion in unintended ways, as with the extension of Anglicanism from Congo into the neighbouring state of Congo-Brazzaville, partly as a result of the movement of refugees to escape conflicts elsewhere.[32]

Kenya has seen greater political stability than Congo, but similar patterns of demographic expansion. Longer-established than Congolese Anglicanism, Kenyan Anglicanism too has seen rapid expansion since 1980. In chapter 6 Joseph D. Galgalo sifts a range of data and a range of data sources, concluding that Kenyan Anglicanism has expanded by around 400% since 1980, from under one million adherents to around four million. Population growth is undoubtedly a significant motor, but far from the only consideration.[33]

Michael Green, in an earlier work, had flagged the growth happening in Singapore[34] and in chapter 9 Daniel Wee, using a highly detailed dataset, shows how Singaporean Anglicanism grew from an average weekly attendance of 4,100 in 1980 to one of 20,200 in 2012 – a rise of around 500%. This is similar to the growth of some other denominations in that state. The pace of growth has slowed somewhat in recent years, but the Church continues to expand markedly. The diocese of Singapore is also acting as a launch-pad for the planting of Anglican congregations across a wide swathe of South East Asia and beyond – including the nations of Vietnam, Laos, Cambodia, Thailand, Indonesia and Nepal. Long known as a key junction for multiple trade routes, Singapore is becoming similarly strategic as a centre for the expansion of Anglicanism across Asia.[35]

South American Anglicanism looks very different to the Anglicanism of Africa and Asia, but parts of the continent have seen similar levels of growth in recent decades, albeit from a much smaller base. Chapter 13, by Maurice Sinclair and John Corrie, covers Peru, Bolivia, Paraguay, Uruguay, Argentina and Chile which together form the Anglican Province of South America. Across these countries there were around 150 congregations in 1980 and around 400 in 2015. In most of these countries the Anglican Church barely existed in 1980 and the total Anglican community in these countries remains relatively small, but in parts it has grown fast. Peru's first bishop was appointed in 1977, at which point the country had two congregations. In 2015 there were 40. There was no Anglican church in Bolivia in 1979. There are now five congregations with c. 500 worshippers. The first woman priest in South America was ordained in Bolivia in 2015. The globalising nature of the Communion is reflected in Bolivia's three Anglican bishops who have come from the UK, the USA and most recently from Singapore.[36] However, South American Anglicanism is increasingly led by indigenous leaders and is increasingly Spanish speaking. South American, Congolese and Singaporean Anglicanism show the potential for substantial growth in areas where Anglicanism has, historically, been a small force or even entirely absent.

The rapid growth in these areas is echoed in a range of other parts of Anglicanism. Had chapters been written on Anglicanism in, amongst other places, Sudan or Uganda, a similar picture would have been shown. Such growth represents a profound shift. The growth of African Anglicanism has been known for many years, but is now reaching a stage where the largest African church (Nigeria) will be larger than the Church of England in the next few years (or may already be so). A different question is that of strategic shifts within Anglicanism. The marked growth, for example, of the diocese of Singapore, alongside the growth of the province of South East Asia is significant in itself and because it is located at the heart of one of the most globally significant cities. Just as it would have been difficult to predict the growth of African Anglicanism in the century after 1900, so it would be unwise to ignore the potential for Asian Anglicanism to grow in the coming century. To say this is not to suggest that there are no other strategically significant areas of Anglican growth. Rather, it is to emphasise that Anglicanism's dynamism is multi-facetted and diffuse. Conversely, church growth in the past is no guarantee of church growth in the future. What has hitherto gone up could come back down.

Some provinces are not seeing the rapid growth outlined above, but are growing. One example is Ghana, detailed in chapter 3 by Daniel Eshun. Ghana's population has risen dramatically from 8.6 million in 1970 to 24.7 million in 2010. Johnson and Zurlo estimate that the Ghanaian church has grown from around 100,000 to around 269,000.[37] However, such growth is very uneven. The long-established diocese of Accra has grown little, whilst one new diocese, Sefwi-Wiawso, created in 2006, is growing rapidly.[38] Overall, Ghanaian Anglicanism has grown in recent decades, but markedly less than many other African countries and markedly less than many other denominations in Ghana.[39] A range of other countries such as Malawi and Zambia appear to have a similar trajectory to Ghana.[40]

The Church of South India (CSI) came into being in 1947 as India achieved independence. In one sense it is not purely 'Anglican', but an amalgam of several denominations. But it is included in this study as a reflection on an Anglican trajectory on the Indian sub-continent. Chapter 8 by Dr. Anderson Jeremiah shows how the Church then grew from around one million members to around 4.25 million members in the present day.[41] The chapter then focuses on a single diocese, Vellore. This diocese came into being in 1976, when it was estimated to have around 35,000 members. Its current membership is almost treble this figure at 106,320 people. Significant numbers are continuing to join the Church and new congregations are being formed.[42] However, as with Ghana, it is unclear whether, given the rapid rise in the overall population and the rapid rise of other denominations in the area, the growth of Vellore and CSI may be more modest than the numbers suggest at first sight.[43]

Holding steady

Some parts of Anglicanism appear to be holding steady overall, whilst seeing both growth and decline in particular areas. Evidence on South African Anglicanism is limited and does all not point in the same direction.[44] Using a wide range of data, Barbara Bompani concludes that South African Anglicanism has neither markedly grown nor shrunk since 1980. Some newer dioceses have seen a growth in the number of congregations, but the number of new congregations is markedly smaller than in many other African countries.[45] Some rural areas appear to be holding up. Alongside this, with the end of apartheid, there has been a decline in funding from abroad after 1994 and in many areas a considerable sense of stagnation and even decline, with the feeling that the Anglican Church has not discovered a role after the fall of apartheid, in which churches formed a significant strand of opposition.[46] South Africa has seen similar demographic growth to other parts of Africa, but markedly less Anglican expansion compared to countries such as Congo, Kenya and Nigeria. Such comparative lack of growth is echoed in some other Southern African states such as Botswana and Lesotho, although not in all Southern African states.[47] In chapter 10, Andrew Kim explores the recent history of Anglicanism in South Korea. Some strands of Christianity in Korea have seen dramatic growth in recent decades, but Anglicanism stands aside from this – although it has not markedly declined either.[48] South Africa and Korea appear similar to a number of other provinces within Anglicanism such as Japan, Brazil, Hong Kong and the Gambia which are neither markedly growing or declining.[49] Underlying issues vary amongst such diverse areas, but they collectively show that a significant section of the Communion is holding more or less steady.

Decline

Chapters 11, 12 and 14 explore areas which have seen decline in recent decades. Ruth Powell in chapter 11 uses the rich dataset of the National Church Life Survey to show how the Anglican Church in Australia has seen decline, but the picture is varied. There has been dramatic decline in many rural areas, but less decline and some growth in Sydney and other urban areas. The result is moderate decline overall.[50] One diocese which has grown consistently is the diocese of Sydney – although it should be noted that some Australian dioceses, such as the diocese of Canberra and Goulburn, have seen some growth.[51] However, it is harder to form generalisations from Sydney, given the unique dynamics between it and the rest of the Anglican Church in Australia; Sydney being markedly more conservative theologically than the rest of Australian Anglicanism, against which, to a degree, it defines itself.[52]

Anglican congregations in Australia have been aging in recent decades.[53] With high population growth predicted for Australia in coming decades, Anglicanism has a significant opportunity for growth but also faces the possibility of slipping further behind as a proportion of the total population.[54] Other parts of the Communion which appear to share Australia's trajectory of moderate decline include parts of the Caribbean such as Jamaica, Bermuda and Barbados.[55]

Australian Anglicanism faces challenges, but not as great as the challenges faced by a number of other churches in the west. David Voas, in chapter 14, outlines how the Church of England, like Australia, is seeing marked variation between different dioceses, but the balance is more towards decline. Although the diocese of London has seen significant growth across 25 years, the Church of England overall has seen significant decline – shown by the metrics of attendance, membership and occasional offices. The result is that the period between

1980 and 2013 has seen a decline in full-time stipendiary clergy (30%), members on the electoral roll (41%) and usual Sunday attendance (37%).[56] The number of infants being baptised remains large, but is now decidedly a minority of the birth cohort (20%).[57] Like Australia, the dioceses furthest from the largest cities tend to be declining fastest. To a degree there is a 'golden triangle' in England composed of the dioceses of London, Oxford and Ely where growth is more noticeable and decline less pronounced. In the case of the diocese of London, its membership has risen by 70% between 1990 and 2010.[58] But it is unclear to what extent London is an outlier or a harbinger of the future.[59]

The Church of England, due to its deep historical connections with wider English society, has a unique position within the Anglican Communion. Over a third of the English population are baptised as Anglicans (although the great bulk of such members do not attend worship more than occasionally) and the Anglican Church retains a presence within many areas of English society, politics and culture. Nonetheless, such connections are diminishing in general and, in some parts of Britain, have now largely disappeared. There is evidence that vague affiliation to the Church of England is softening, meaning that, whilst rates of Church of England attendance have long been low, now even nominal identification as 'CofE' may be dropping below 50% of the population.[60] At the same time, the dramatic diversification of English society has seen a marked rise in the number of black, Asian and minority ethnic people who identify as Christian. If significant numbers of such Christians were to join the Church of England, that would make a marked difference, but it is, as yet, unclear whether this is happening.[61]

A further, related, question is the wider decline of communal involvement in English society or reluctance to join community groups. Membership of institutions such as political parties and trade unions has declined as much or even more than that of church congregations. To a degree, churches are suffering from a wider decline of communal engagement in English society.[62] To say this is not to airbrush out the reality of congregational decline in the Church of England, but it does indicate that the Church needs to be seen alongside wider societal processes as well as processes specific to Christianity.

In chapter 12 Jeremy Bonner explores the trajectory of the Episcopal Church of the USA. Anglicanism in the USA has seen severe decline, complicated by deep divisions in recent years. The Episcopal Church lost almost a quarter of its members, 1986 to 2011, within the context of a rapidly rising population. However, decline was slower in the 1980s and 1990s and has become much more pronounced since the start of this century, with a number of rural dioceses now barely viable. There has been a wide regional variation. The South grew slightly in this period overall, whilst the East and Mid-West did much worse. That said, all areas have declined in recent years.[63] There has been a steep drop in baptisms, which halved for children and adults between 1980 and 2010. Marriages dropped by over two-thirds from 1980 to 2010.[64] In comparison with other American denominations, the United Church and the Presbyterians are doing worse, but most denominations are doing better and in the case of Roman Catholicism, Baptists and the Assembly of God much better.[65] There is marked variation between dioceses, although most Episcopalian dioceses are now in decline.[66]

It should be noted that similarly severe decline is happening in a number of other churches. The Anglican Church in Canada has seen decline which is similar to or greater than that of the Episcopal Church. Canadian Anglicanism's membership in 1981 was 922,000, but in 2001 was 642,000 and Johnson and Zurlo estimate affiliation alone to have fallen to 590,000 by 2010.[67] Canadian decline is varied. For example, the diocese of Toronto appears to be broadly stable,[68] whereas two-thirds of the parishes of the diocese of Quebec expect to close or amalgamate with others in the next five years.[69] A similar pattern is to be found in Wales. Membership in the Church of Wales has dropped from c. 100,000 in 1990 to 53,000 in 2013.[70]

The chronology of growth and decline varies. The current trajectories in Nigeria, Kenya, Ghana, England and South Africa are a continuation of long-term trends visible well before 1980, though it should be noted that there are exceptions within such areas, whose trajectory has markedly shifted since 1980. Other areas (such as Congo, Singapore, Latin America, the USA). have seen dramatic shifts (whether of growth or decline) since 1980. In every case there are a complex mix of factors at work.

Section three: growth and decline in the Anglican Communion and theories of secularisation

Secularisation theories and contemporary Anglicanism

The findings of this book have significance for more than just Anglicans and offer a contribution to debates about the contemporary history of Christianity and of religion in general. Debates about secularisation frame much discussion of faith in the west and beyond. A significant strand of scholarship sees secularisation as the dominant development of modern religion, with the assumption that it is likely to continue for the foreseeable future. Implicit or explicit in this narrative is the assumption that the secularisation of the west is likely to be the forerunner of global secularisation.[71] The data from this book supports the secularisation thesis – to a degree. In significant parts of the west the decline of Anglicanism chimes with wider evidence that such areas are secularising. The diminution of Christianity's (and Anglicanism's) role in countries such as Canada and Wales is clear.[72] The decline of American Anglicanism mirrors how the USA, often previously seen as a counterweight to the greater secularity of western Europe, is becoming less religious – albeit from a position of far greater religiosity than Europe.[73]

However, the traditional version of the secularisation theory needs to be qualified by an awareness that Anglican decline is not universal across the west[74] and a recognition that, in some parts of the west, many denominations are performing markedly better than Anglicanism.[75] At a different level, Nancy Ammermann's work on American religion points to the ways in which faith continues to weave through daily life in diverse ways.[76] Most importantly, this volume's chapters on Africa, Asia and South America show that non-western Anglicanism is seeing significant growth and usually growing faster than population growth, as is the case for many other denominations.[77] In all this, it is crucial to recognise the agency of those laying hold of faith. As Lamin Sanneh stresses, what people at street level do with Christian faith is often not what educated opinion expects them to do.[78]

A related strand of scholarship argues that greater modernisation leads to greater material security and thus to greater secularity.[79] From this standpoint, the burgeoning church growth in some developing countries in South America and Africa could be the precursor to future decline as those societies modernise. Anglicanism contains some data to support this viewpoint,[80] but the sheer variety of global Anglicanism makes it an insecure generalisation. If, as Davie argues, there are 'modernities' rather than 'modernity' and if the context in which modernisation happens seriously affects the nature of the 'modernisation', then African, Asian and western Anglicanisms will neither 'modernise' nor, necessarily, secularise in the same manner as Europe or the USA.[81]

A different question raised by scholars is the extent to which more conservative forms of religion are able to survive and even thrive in the late modern world. Some researchers have pointed to conservative religion's considerable powers of resilience in parts of the west.[82] An influential strand of thought is 'rational choice theory', which argues that religions which have some measure of monopoly (usually via some form of establishment) are more likely to decline and religions which operate in a pluralist context in which they have no choice but to compete are more likely to be vigorous. Rational choice theory has significant weaknesses as a theory, but some value in discussions of Anglicanism.[83] There is some correlation between establishment and Anglican decline. This is so for England, but US Anglicanism has strong connections with American elites and this may have made some contribution to its decline. A number of the provinces seeing significant growth have stood outside the established order and, sometimes, faced constraints from the state – such as Congo or Singapore. However, it is crucial to note that correlation does not amount to causation. Conversely, the role of the Anglican diocese of London, which, though 'established', works in one of the most pluralist contexts on the planet, is intriguing in this debate, given that it has one of the best records for growth in western Anglicanism. What does matter is to recognise that rational choice theory, which has not been applied to Anglicanism, may have something to offer, if applied with care.

A contrasting line of argument argues that some aspects of modern western society may encourage religious belief, rather than erode it. Affluence has value, but does not invariably lead to a greater sense of well-being.[84] There is substantial evidence from research in the west that those who attend church are markedly more likely to experience well-being by a range of secular indicators. The leading anthropologist, Tanya Luhrmann, speaks of how:

> What one might call an avalanche of medical data has demonstrated that, for reasons still poorly understood, those who attend church and believe in God are healthier and happier and live longer that those who do not.[85]

This 'avalanche' of data is well attested in scholarship, but yet to be properly assimilated by academia, churches and wider society. It is unclear whether it feeds into church growth and/or acts as a buttress against decline.[86]

Demography

Demography is, to a degree, religious destiny. At its most basic, churches in areas experiencing population growth, stability or decline are more predisposed to grow, remain stable or decline. That Kenyan Anglicanism is expanding in a way that Welsh Anglicanism is not is in no small measure due to differing demographic change in those countries, but not entirely due to those changes. It would be a mistake simply to ascribe growth to population change. Johnson and Ross show that in most areas of the world, Anglicanism has been growing faster than population growth, but change on the ground varies markedly.[87]

Ghana, India and Nigeria have seen huge demographic growth as nations and, whilst Anglicanism in all these lands has grown, it has grown at markedly different rates – with much higher growth in Nigeria than in Ghana and India.[88] Despite a similar rise in population, Congolese Anglicanism grew much faster than Ghanaian Anglicanism and, from a much lower base, has outstripped Ghanaian Anglicanism in the years after 1970.[89]

In the case of Singapore, the population has risen markedly, but whereas church growth outstripped the growth of the population in the years up to 2007, population growth has outstripped church growth since 2007.[90] The population of Australia has grown substantially in recent decades and is predicted to grow substantially in coming years. However, such growth is varied, with much population growth in the cities and decline in many rural areas. The Australian Anglican Church has seen marked growth and decline which partly parallels the demographic shifts in the country. The future of Australian Anglicanism is heavily tied to how it responds to the demographic shifts as they continue.[91] There is a parallel process happening elsewhere in the west – England and Wales and the USA are seeing similarly dramatic demographic shifts – with cities mostly expanding combined with some (far from all) rural areas where the population is static or falling.

Eric Kaufman has argued that, since those who espouse a religion tend to have more children than those who are avowedly secular, the future belongs to the more prolific ideologies.[92] Many key countries within the west are seeing rising populations which are diversifying ethnically, in which the white, and increasingly secular, indigenous population is shrinking, whereas those from a migrant background are markedly more likely to practise Christian faith. These changes could fuel decline in the Church of England, as the 'white British' sector of the population shrinks. But the same demographic changes could fuel growth if substantial sections of the migrant Christian population join the Church of England.[93]

A further factor is the way different sections of the population behave differently. American Episcopalians are most concentrated in the more middle class, educated sector which has the lowest birth rate, which feeds into (but does not entirely explain) its large drop in baptisms – halving for children and adults between 1980 and 2010 even as the overall American population is rising significantly.[94] Rates of growth and decline vary markedly across England. But overall, the Church of England's decline combines with a growing population, meaning that the proportionate rate of decline is still greater.[95]

Geography

Whilst more of the west is declining than growing, there is growth within the west. Most important is the diocese of London. This is the only diocese in the Church of England and one of a small number of dioceses in the western world which has grown consistently across recent decades. A further comparison is the marked growth of Anglicanism in Singapore and Sydney. London, Singapore and Sydney are different in obvious ways, but also similar. Each has a rapidly rising, diversifying population. Each has a range of languages, but English is the *lingua franca*. They are 'global cities', with an international profile economically, culturally and politically. These three cities are on key trade routes and are economically highly dynamic. The recent history of Anglicanism in London, Sydney and Singapore suggests that globalising cities offer particular possibilities for Anglicanism and they show that it cannot be assumed that western Anglicanism is 'bound' to decline. The three Anglican dioceses are varied in terms of theological tradition. Their respective bishops and archbishops have, in recent years, been anglo-catholic, charismatic and evangelical respectively. But each diocese has grown significantly in recent decades. There seems to be a potential correlation between church growth and globalising 'anglosphere' cities. Beyond this, there is a broad correlation between Anglican growth and 'trade routes' and between areas distant from trade routes and decline.[96]

It is startling to realise how global Anglicanism was dominated by the English until the recent past. In 1960 much of the Anglican Communion still had English-born bishops but in the present day this is a rarity. However, whilst domination by English personnel has ceased, the significance of the English language and English-speaking culture remains a key resource to contemporary Anglicanism. Part of what links London, Singapore and Sydney is that they are part of what is sometimes called 'the anglosphere'.[97] This term is used mainly in political/cultural debates, but it expresses not only politico-cultural realities, but something about religious networks too. The power of the English nation may have waned, but the potency of the English language and English-speaking cultures is fundamental not only to the modern world, but to modern religion – a factor which will influence significantly the future trajectory of the Anglican Communion. That said, it should be noted that recent decades have seen growing elements of the Anglican Communion which are francophone or Spanish-speaking – as the chapters on Congo and South America show.

Grace Davie has questioned whether highly secular Europe, rather than the 'norm' to which other parts of the world will conform, constitutes an 'exceptional case', in a world which is, for the most part, markedly more religious.[98] Philip Jenkins goes further by focusing on the world outside the west and argues that we are seeing the emergence of 'the next Christendom', based largely in the non-western world, in which non-western Anglicanism plays a significant role.[99] The evidence of this volume supports Davie's formulation – with some caveats. First, Anglicanism is growing in many parts of the non-European world, but not in all parts. Second, secularity is as much a socio-cultural-political phenomenon as something that can be measured by numbers. An Anglicanism which appears numerically vigorous may be secularising in other, less visible, ways.

Nonetheless, the way global Anglicanism has roughly doubled in size between 1970 and 2017 casts doubt on the idea of secularisation as an inevitable process. Western Anglicanism has become increasingly exceptional within Anglicanism as a whole and, having exercised such a strong influence on other parts of the world, is increasingly influenced by non-westerners living in the west. Afo Adogame has charted the formation of an African Christian 'diaspora', which is becoming more significant within the west. But in that development both the west and African Christianity are changed.[100] Whether, in the decades to come, the main development is that western Anglicanism becomes more non-western, or non-western Anglicanism becomes more western, remains to be seen.

More widely, growth and decline in many areas correlate with 'trade routes'. David Bebbington has pointed to the way religious movements diffuse along the same networks by which other aspects of culture permeate wider society.[101] This chimes with the recent history of Anglicanism. The contrast between urban and rural Australia or between Anglicanism in London and Wales, suggests that in the west growth has a significant connection with a concentration of transport networks, population growth and diversification and economic dynamism (noting that 'economic dynamism' is *not* the same as wealth – the East of London is economically dynamic, but often very poor). However, the correlation between 'trade routes' and non-western Anglicanism may be more complex. Growth in areas such as the eastern Congo and southern Sudan and more limited growth in Ghana does not neatly map onto trade routes and reflects a broad range of factors.

More generally, economics has a relationship with Anglican Church growth and decline. There is some correlation between affluence and decline. At its crudest, many of the Anglican provinces where there is the most growth are in the less affluent parts of the world and many of those where there is much decline are in the most affluent parts of the globe.[102] But the correlation is far from exact. Singapore, Sydney and London contain much affluence and much Anglican growth, whilst growth is patchy in parts of African Anglicanism which face much greater economic challenges.

A further wild-card is the trajectory of Chinese Christianity. It has been argued that just as the 20th century was dominated by America politically and economically, so Christianity in the 20th century was dominated by American forms of Christianity. It can be argued that just as the 21st century may be dominated by China politically and economically, so Christianity in the 21st century may be increasingly influenced by Chinese forms of Christianity.[103] Anglicanism has had hitherto a small role within Chinese Christianity. That role may or may not grow, whilst Anglicanism could itself be impacted by the growing Chinese Church.

Peter Berger and David Martin are senior scholars of religion in the modern world. One of the many insights they bring is a rich global awareness, helping to sensitise academics and church leaders who often work from a western mind-set.[104] David Martin offers this cautionary tale regarding the way such a mindset can act as a set of blinkers when it comes to faith:

> The power of the ruling paradigms came home to me most forcibly on a bus full of Western academics in Guatemala. When told that 66 per cent of the population was Catholic they asked no questions about where the rest might be, even though the answer shouted at them from texts on huts in remote El Peten, store-house churches called 'Prince of Peace', and buses announcing 'Jesus is coming'.[105]

Section four: ecclesiology and global Anglicanism

Alongside theoretical questions, the data from this book on Anglican growth and decline raises a range of explicitly ecclesiological questions, some of which are discussed below.

'Pentecostalisation' and Anglican traditions

The Pentecostal tradition can be seen as the main innovation within 20th century Christianity and has spread swiftly across highly diverse contexts.[106] Anglicanism has been and remains a diverse mosaic of Christian traditions, which includes almost every aspect of global Christianity from the most liberal to the most traditional, from the lowest of low church to the highest reaches of anglo-catholicism. But one of the most striking shifts since 1980 is the 'pente-costalisation'[107] of Anglicanism, which is a persistent theme across many of the chapters in this volume.[108]

Burgess notes how strands of early 20th century Nigerian Anglicanism had Pentecostal elements, but how the bishops, all English, sought to counter them.[109] Later the growth of Pentecostalism spliced with the Nigerian civil war to help 'pentecostalise' the country, in ways which have substantially impacted upon Nigerian Anglicanism.[110] Thus, one of the most important leaders, Benjamin Kwashi, Archbishop of Jos, was originally converted through the Deeper Life Church – one of the fastest growing Pentecostal churches in Nigeria.[111] Sinclair and Corrie discuss how the vigorous strains of Latin American Pentecostalism have influenced Latin American Anglicanism. What is striking is how, whilst Anglican congregations can be 'pentecostalised', Anglicanism can also mould Pentecostal spirituality – symbolised by congregations which have left the Anglican Church and then subsequently rejoined the Anglican Church.[112] Bompani and Jeremiah note the phenomenon of South African and Indian Anglicans, respectively, attending both Anglican and Pentecostal churches.[113]

Singapore offers a very different context from either Nigeria, South America or South Africa and a different sort of 'pentecostalisation'. Singaporean Anglicanism has been deeply shaped by the charismatic movement from the 1970s onwards. Wee sees the growth of the diocese of Singapore as deeply linked to charismatic renewal, which has brought growth and vitality, but also, at times, division. One of the ongoing challenges for Singaporean Anglicanism is how it relates to such renewal both within Anglicanism and as found in burgeoning churches outside Anglicanism.[114]

Ghanaian churches have been as 'pentecostalised' in a similar way to those of Nigeria, but the interaction with Anglicanism has been different. Eshun notes how in the 1980s mainline Christians spoke derogatively of the Pentecostals as 'mushroom churches', which, they believed, sprang up quickly then faded just as fast. Eshun argues that, in fact, they have proved to be 'boabab trees', showing greater staying power than the mainline and that many former mainliners have joined the Pentecostal churches, especially the young and well-educated.[115] Eshun raises the issue of witchcraft and how elite Anglicans do not wish to discuss it, but how ordinary Ghanaian Christians often believe in it.[116] This complex issue, which can have deeply dubious pastoral consequences, raises the problems with as well as the potential of 'pentecostalisation'.[117]

The wider 'pentecostalising' of the Anglican Communion puts into context the well-known ministry of Holy Trinity, Brompton ('HTB') and the Alpha Course which originated there, a major strand of 'charismatic' Anglicanism. HTB, especially via church planting, has had a marked effect on the growth of the diocese of London, although a wide range of other factors have fed into London's growth.[118] The Alpha Course has had a significant impact across many parts of the Communion. However, it should be noted that the 'pentecostalising' of the Anglican Communion was happening before the growth of HTB's ministries. HTB has played a key role, but should be seen as part of a wider movement, rather than as unique. It has, on occasion, been influenced by currents of spirituality which arose elsewhere.[119] A study of global Anglicanism since 1980 shows that the most substantial and widespread innovation and the one which has added most significant impetus for growth is the 'pentecostalising' impulse within the Anglican Communion. Johnson estimated that there were 18.6 million Anglicans influenced by the Pentecostal/charismatic tradition in 2010 (about 22% of all Anglicans). However, it is extremely difficult to establish such a figure with certainty.[120]

Whilst 'pentecostalisation' is a key development in recent years, it is crucial to recognise that there continue to be a wide range of other traditions which operate vigorously within Anglicanism. Whilst significant parts of the Communion have 'pentecostalised', there is much overlap between that strand of spirituality and evangelicalism and the latter continues to be a highly significant component in growth within global Anglicanism.[121] The anglo-catholic and liberal traditions are prominent in parts of the Communion which have seen more decline and less growth, such as North America and parts of South Africa. However, there is growth happening within areas which are deeply influenced by the anglo-catholic tradition, such as Papua New Guinea and Melanesia.[122] Moreover, the anglo-catholic and liberal traditions had and continue to have a profound cultural and intellectual influence within Anglicanism. Many of Anglicanism's leading theologians come from its anglo-catholic and liberal wings and exercise a deep influence, even though this strand of Anglicanism is less numerically strong than it was in the mid-20th century.[123] Moreover, tradition is far from a fixed quantity; some Anglicans start 'low' and end up 'high'/liberal.

A related factor are centres of higher education emerging outside the west such as Trinity College, Singapore, St Paul's University in Limuru, Kenya, and the Alexandria School of Theology. These institutions are relatively recent in foundation, highly dynamic and offer distinctive theological voices. They have significantly contributed to the theological and missiological trajectory of Anglicanism in recent decades. Such colleges have often acted as significant carriers of tradition and innovation within Anglicanism. The future of Anglicanism will look markedly different, depending on whether such institutions continue to grow and how their respective theological stances develop in comparison to theological developments within western Anglicanism.[124]

Church growth and church structures

A different ecclesiological issue is the role that structures have played in growth and decline within the Communion. In Congo, one of the fastest growing parts of the Communion, located in a highly unstable political and economic context, the structures of Anglicanism have played a crucial role by giving organisational 'spine' to the church. Way highlights the importance of what Congolese Anglicans call *utaratibu* – order – both structural and liturgical, for health and growth of the Congolese Church. In part this ensures solidity within a wider church context where church splits are common.[125]

Congo is a context in which the number of dioceses has multiplied. Sinclair and Corrie note how in a South American context the founding of new dioceses and other structures has been important in fostering growth.[126] Burgess' study of Nigeria shows the correlation between some of the most marked growth in the Anglican Communion and the most dramatic proliferation of dioceses. This said, a recent moratorium on the founding of new dioceses may indicate that such a policy has its limits – or it may simply indicate a drawing of breath prior to further proliferation.[127] Burgess sees the missionality of bishops as key to the growth of their dioceses:

> Taking into account other variables such as geographical location and financial capacity, the fastest-growing dioceses tend to be those that are led by bishops with conservative evangelical credentials, receptivity to charismatic spirituality, administrative skills, and a strong commitment to mission and evangelism.[128]

In the missionary bishops of contemporary Anglicanism, there is an intriguing echo of missionary bishops such as Chad and Cedd in early English Christianity, notwithstanding the somewhat different spirituality of the latter.[129]

In general, the new dioceses created in Nigeria, South America, Ghana, South Africa and India correlate with growth. Conversely, the amalgamation of dioceses in England and the USA correlates with decline. However, correlation is not proof of causation. Eshun argues that 'establishment mindset' has limited growth.[130] Certainly, the structures of Ghana and South Africa have been markedly less fluid that other African provinces which have seen greater growth.

Powell notes the way a high level of diocesan autonomy in Australia has proved problematic, particularly in preventing united action across the Church.[131] Australia's dioceses see things differently from each other, most markedly in the contrast between the strongly conservative diocese of Sydney and some other parts of the Australian Church. However, it is unclear whether such autonomy has hampered, or even sometimes helped, church growth.

Laicisation, indigenisation and generation

Whilst structures matter, so does the space for lay members to exercise ministry and take initiatives. Burgess notes how the growth of the Nigerian Church has seen a growth in the number of clergy alongside vigorous lay organisations such as the Mothers' Union, the Anglican Youth Fellowship and the Evangelical Fellowship in the Anglican Communion. In Congo and South India unsalaried evangelists are central to the work of the Church.[132]

A range of chapters reflect on the importance of transmitting faith to the next generation. David Voas sees this as both critical and as a critical failing in much English Anglicanism. Similarly, there has been a dramatic fall in US baptisms. In Australia, the evidence is more mixed, with evidence both of an aging church and some evidence of growth amongst those in their 20s.[133] Generational dynamics are different in other cultures, but concern is no less deep. Nigerian Anglicanism has seen education as a key part of mission strategy. A similar emphasis is found in Congolese Anglicanism, including the foundation of an Anglican University in 2010.[134]

The Gambian scholar Lamin Sanneh has argued for the importance of translation in the development of churches and Ashley Null sees translation as central to Anglicanism through its centrality in the work of Thomas Cranmer.[135] It is possible to view Anglicanism's recent decades as a story of attempted indigenisation, in which structures, liturgy, theology and mission have to be translated into a plethora of global contexts. This indigenisation entailed a shift, for the most part, away from an English episcopate. This volume charts the growth of significant communities of French and Spanish-speaking Anglicans. There is a significant correlation between indigenisation and growth. Sinclair and Corrie note how the Anglican Church in Uruguay went from 1 to 11 congregations between 1980 and 2015 and from an English-speaking church to one that is mainly Spanish-speaking.[136] A parallel example is the growth of Anglicanism in the Congo, which is closely related to its embrace of Congolese culture which is, overall, francophone.[137]

Politics and church growth and decline

The word 'politics' embodies a huge variety of realities, but impacts significantly on church growth and decline. Independent Ghana's first president, Kwame Nhrumah, rephrased the New Testament with his adage 'Seek ye first the political kingdom.' However, as Ghanaian politics post-independence turned sour, this made the Pentecostal slogan of the 1980s/90s 'Only Jesus can Save' all the more credible and Ghanaians did the opposite of Nkrumah's adage, seeking a religious 'kingdom', in the face of temporal uncertainty.[138] In Nigeria, political upheaval impacted on Anglican growth and decline. The work of Richard Burgess has shown how the Nigerian civil war of the 1960s helped 'Pentecostalise' the country, which has impacted on Anglican Church growth. At the same time, more recent violence between Muslim and Christian communities in the northern and central parts of Nigeria has led to decline in some areas.[139] In Congo, the Anglican Church has had to live with dictatorship, civil war and, at times, significant restrictions on religious life. In 1970s the then president Mobutu only allowed three churches officially to exist, meaning Anglicanism was officially amalgamated with other churches, but the Church continued to grow. Yossa Way has shown how in such a context Anglican churches can be caught up in ethnic tension but also contribute significantly to reconciliation and humanitarian aid.[140] Indian Christianity intersects with a society that is highly dynamic, but also struggling with serious issues around the questions of caste and corruption – issues which are affecting the Church of South India.[141]

Social action and church growth and decline

The Anglican 'five marks of mission' are in part an attempt to balance between congregational growth and service to the world. The studies in this volume have much to say on this subject. There is no sense that churches which seek actively to grow numerically sideline service to the community. Nigeria and Singapore are examples of fast growing areas of Anglicanism where service to the community is a high priority.[142] Daniel Wee notes that the Singaporean Anglican Church's active work in medical welfare and education improves the standing of the church with wider society – a significant factor in a society where Christianity is a minority faith which has to earn the right to be heard.[143] Data from Australia shows the high value Australian Anglicans put on service to the community in terms of humanitarian work, care for creation and advocacy of those seen as oppressed. Powell notes how Australian Anglicans are markedly more likely to engage in such acts of service than in evangelism.[144] At the same time the Australian National Church Life Survey – one of the most sophisticated and long-standing surveys of church life – shows that such social action on its own does not tend to feed into numerical growth. Ruth Powell has surveyed for NCLS a wide range of factors and how they correlate with church growth. She concludes: 'previous research based on NCLS data across all Australian churches has found that high levels of service is the quality least associated to outcomes such as attracting newcomers, or numerical growth.'[145] However, a Church of England study argues that social action does correlate with numerical growth, albeit from a more limited evidential basis.[146] The conclusion from the NCLS data does not, in any way, invalidate the importance of service to the community, which matters hugely for its own sake, regardless of any other consequences. Equally, it does suggest western churches which focus on social action and make minimal efforts in evangelism may struggle to grow.

Church growth and decline across the denominations

Anglicanism's rates of growth and decline need to be compared with other denominations. This question is not always straightforward to answer, but some comments can be made. In the case of Nigeria, Anglicanism has often outpaced other denominations in a religious world where there is much expansion – although Roman Catholicism and some Pentecostal groups have seen similar growth.[147] By contrast, Ghanaian Anglicanism is growing less quickly than similar denominations such as Methodism.[148] Data from South Africa and India paints a similar picture to Ghana.[149] In Singapore, Anglicanism appears to have been ahead of other churches, but the latter are catching up in recent years.[150] In the USA, the Episcopal Church has declined less than the United Church and Presbyterians. However, most others have been doing better, and in the case of Roman Catholics, Southern Baptists and the Assemblies of God much better.[151] In England, the trajectories of different strands of Christianity are very varied. Methodism and Presbyterianism have declined faster than the Church of England. Baptist churches have, in general, performed better than Anglican churches. Pentecostal, Orthodox churches and many newly founded denominations have grown markedly, as the Church of England has shrunk overall.[152] Sinclair and Corrie speak of the province of South America as a setting where Anglicanism has grown, but remains much smaller than Catholicism or the burgeoning Pentecostalism, yet feel it has something unique to offer:

> In a region where Catholicism and Evangelicalism are expressed in other ways, this Anglican identity may have no immediate recognition or appeal. Yet paradoxically a biblical combination of evangelical and catholic traditions is what the Latin American Church most needs and which Anglicanism, the product of the moderate 'Cranmerian' Reformation, can demonstrate and offer.[153]

The notion of the Anglican 'via media' was coined with regard to 16th century England, but continues to have currency in the 21st century far beyond England.

Conclusion

The dramatic shifts within Anglicanism since 1980 are so recent that caution is needed in assessing what such shifts signify. Few would have predicted the growth and decline outlined in this volume and it is legitimate to ask what future shifts in world Anglicanism will surprise observers looking from the vantage point of the present. However, some trends are emerging. Anglicanism is growing, not shrinking, overall. The recent trajectory of the Anglican Communion calls into question the narrative that sees secularisation as inevitable in the modern world. Numerically, the Communion is expanding faster than ever and it has in recent decades grown markedly in highly strategic areas of the world such as London and Singapore, from which further growth is being seeded. Equally, overall rise should not obscure major decline in some areas, nor the possibility that other areas may decline in the future.

It is easy to forget how recent much of the 'Anglican Communion' is. Until the mid-19th century, it was confined to England and a small number of countries to which the English had migrated, most in what is now seen as 'the west'. It began seriously to move beyond these areas in the 19th century. But even by the end of the 19th century it had little or no presence in areas which now have very large communities of Anglicans. In particular, Anglicanism in sub-Saharan Africa and Asia has dramatically expanded in the 20th century. The research in this volume shows that the pace of change has not slackened in the 21st. Significant new centres of Anglicanism have arisen since 1980 and others are in the process of formation. In all this, the centre of gravity continues to shift towards the developing and non-western world, a shift which is currently accelerating.

How western and non-western Anglicanism are seen and see one another matters greatly. The temptation, in a context where church life and wider social life are liable to polarise, is to see one as 'good' and the other as 'bad'. This can be manifest as an assumption that developing countries need to, and will eventually become, more western, or, on the other hand, the assumption that western Christianity is 'dying'. As this volume shows, the realities on the ground are much more complex. Anglicanism outside the west has shown substantial and growing agency and is unlikely simply to sing to a western hymnsheet. Anglicanism within the west has struggled in recent decades, but has significant life within it. This volume provides significant insights into the nature of the Anglican Communion, but there is much more research to be done and the conclusion of this volume offers ideas on fruitful future projects.

Notes

1 These figures represent affiliation, those who self-identify as Anglicans. They come from: T. Johnson and G. Zurlo, 'The Changing Demographics of Global Anglicanism, 1970–2010', in D. Goodhew (ed.), *Growth and Decline in the Anglican Communion, 1980 to the Present* (Abingdon: Routledge, 2017): 38.

2 Within this, the volume includes the Church of South India, a church formed from a union of Anglicans and other denominations and which is regarded as in communion both with the Archbishop of Canterbury and with other denominations.

3 *From Anecdote to Evidence: Findings from the Church Growth Research Programme* (London: Church Commissioners for England, 2014): 3. This understanding is similar to the 'five marks of mission', widely used across Anglicanism.

4 For a survey of such assumptions, inside and outside of Anglicanism, see: D. Goodhew, 'Towards a Theology of Church Growth: An Introduction', in D. Goodhew (ed.), *Towards a Theology of Church Growth* (Farnham: Ashgate, 2015): 27–36.

5 P. Norris and R. Ingelhart, *Sacred and Secular: Religion and Politics Worldwide* (Cambridge: Cambridge University Press, 2004); S. Bruce, *Secularization: In Defence of an Unfashionable Theory* (Oxford: Oxford University Press, 2011); A. Brown, 'Dissolving the Anglican Communion Would Simply Be a Recognition of Reality', *Guardian*, 17 September 2015, available at http://www.theguardian.com/commentisfree/2015/sep/17/dissolving-anglican-community-archbishop-canterbury-anglicanism accessed 29 February 2016.

6 J. Hull, *Mission-Shaped Church: A Theological Response* (London: SCM Press, 2006): 2; D. Runcorn, *The Road to Growth Less Travelled: Spiritual Paths in a Missionary Church* (Cambridge: Grove, 2008). See also: M. Percy, 'It's Not Just about the Numbers', *Church Times*, 28 February 2014; G. Fraser, 'Christianity, When Properly Understood Is a Religion of Losers', *Guardian*, 3 April 2015.

7 See: D. Goodhew (ed.), *Towards a Theology of Church Growth* (Farnham: Ashgate, 2015). For empirical data on the effect of Christian faith on well-being, see: H. Koenig, D. King, and V. Carson, *Handbook on Religion and Health* (New York and Oxford: Oxford University Press, 2012).

8 *From Anecdote to Evidence*: 8–9; M. Threlfall Holmes, 'Growing the Mediaeval Church: Church Growth in Theory and Practice in Christendom, c.1000 to c.1500', in D. Goodhew (ed.), *Towards a Theology of Church Growth* (Farnham: Ashgate, 2015): 195.

9 W. Jacob, *The Making of the Anglican Church Worldwide* (London: SPCK, 1997): 292–8; echoed by K. Ward, *A History of Global Anglicanism* (Cambridge: Cambridge University Press, 2006): 296.

10 W. Sachs, *The Transformation of Anglicanism from State Church to Global Communion* (Cambridge: Cambridge University Press, 1993); Ward, *History of Global Anglicanism*; B. Kaye, *An Introduction to World Anglicanism* (Cambridge: Cambridge University Press, 2008); I. S. Markham, J. B. Hawkins IV, J. Terry, and L. N. Steffensen (eds.), *The Wiley-Blackwell Companion to the Anglican Communion* (Chichester: Wiley-Blackwell, 2013); M. Chapman, S. Clarke, and M. Percy (eds.), *The Oxford Handbook of Anglican Studies* (Oxford: Oxford University Press, 2015); A. Day (ed.), *Contemporary Issues in the Worldwide Anglican Communion* (Abingdon: Routledge, 2015).

11 See, for example: Sachs, *Transformation of Anglicanism*: 336. Chapters 3, 4, 5, 6 and 7 of this volume show how African Anglicanism has grown at diverse rates since 1980.

12 I. Markham, 'The Anglican Church of Southern Africa', in I. S. Markham, J. B Hawkins IV, J. Terry, and L. N. Steffensen (eds.), *Companion to the Anglican Communion* (Chichester: Wiley-Blackwell, 2013): 198; Sachs, *Transformation of Anglicanism*: 314–19; Kaye, *Introduction to World Anglicanism*: 247–53. For evidence of South African Anglicanism's limited growth in recent decades, see: B. Bompani, 'South Africa', in D. Goodhew (ed.), *Growth and Decline in the Anglican Communion* (Abingdon: Routledge, 2017): 134–5.

13 See, for example, the discussion of the USA in: Ward, *Global Anglicanism*: 63–7; Kaye, *World Anglicanism*: 47–50. J. Barney Hawkins IV notes Anglicanism's recent decline in the USA but does not consider its magnitude, speed or variation across the country – 'The Episcopal Church in the USA', in I. S. Markham, J. B. Hawkins IV, J. Terry, and L. N. Steffensen (eds.), *Companion to the Anglican Communion* (Chichester: Wiley-Blackwell, 2013): 514. Likewise, a discussion of England notes decline, but not the wide variation between different parts of England: M. Chapman, 'The Church of England', in I. S. Markham, J. B. Hawkins IV, J. Terry, and L. N. Steffensen (eds.), *Companion to the Anglican Communion* (Chichester: Wiley-Blackwell, 2013): 424–5.

14 Ward, *Global Anglicanism*: 109. But a number of Latin American countries – such as Peru, Chile and Argentina – have seen significant growth in recent decades. See: M. Sinclair and J. Corrie, 'The Anglican Province of South America', in D. Goodhew (ed.), *Growth and Decline in the Anglican Communion* (Abingdon: Routledge, 2017).

15 Daniel Munoz, 'North to South: A Reappraisal of Anglican Membership Figures', *Journal of Anglican Studies* 14, no. 1 (2016).

16 The evidence offered by 'North to South' runs counter to the bulk of the work in this volume, but also to many of the findings of other researchers, who, mostly, view contemporary Anglicanism in terms of a marked shift from western to non-western Anglicanism. See: Markham, Hawkins IV, Terry, and Steffensen (eds.), *Companion to the Anglican Communion*; Sachs, *Transformation of Anglicanism*; Kaye, *Introduction to World Anglicanism*. For a detailed review of 'North to South', see: http://community.dur.ac.uk/churchgrowth.research/research/new-research-project-growth-and-decline-in-the-anglican-communion-1980-to-the-present.

17 D. Voas, 'Afterword: A Reflection on Numbers in the Study of Religion', *Diskus* 16, no. 2 (2014): 117.

18 For an example of similar debates regarding Pentecostalism, see: T. M. Johnson, 'Counting Pentecostals Worldwide', *Pneuma* 36 (2014).

19 For a more detailed discussion, see: Johnson and Zurlo, 'Changing Demographics': 37–9. See also: T. M. Johnson and B. J. Grim, *The World's Religions in Figures: An Introduction to International Religious Demography* (Oxford: Wiley-Blackwell, 2013): 163–89.

20 S. Bullivant, *Contemporary Catholicism in England and Wales* (London: Benedict XVI Centre for Religion and Society, 2016), available at http://www.stmarys.ac.uk/benedict-xvi/docs/2016-may-contemporary-catholicism-report.pdf.

21 Chapter 13 shows that Peru and Uruguay have seen significant growth in recent years, albeit from a very small base. This is not echoed in the data from chapter 2 by Johnson and Zurlo. However, these countries represent a small part of the overall picture and such growth has been recent, so may have yet to register in wider datasets.

22 J. Galgalo, 'Kenya', in D. Goodhew (ed.), *Growth and Decline in the Anglican Communion* (Abingdon: Routledge, 2017): 118.

23 For an evaluation of the problems with this measure, see: M. Wigglesworth, 'A Critical Evaluation and Theological Reflection on "Worshipping Community"' (MA Dissertation, Durham University, 2014). Available at http://community.dur.ac.uk/churchgrowth.research/research-outputs/conference-papers-dissertations.

24 A major example of the 'noise' present across the different measures used by the Church of England is the confusion created by parishes with more than one church in them. This has caused major distortions in the data and the Church of England has recently sought to eliminate the problem by collecting figures for each individual church, rather than for each parish. This reform is a significant advance, but is only of help with new

data. In existing data such 'noise' remains a serious problem. For a detailed discussion of the range of problems within Church of England data, see: section one of the report, 'Amalgamations and Team Ministries', Strand 3c of the Church of England's Church Growth Research Programme, available at http://www.churchgrowthresearch.org.uk/progress_findings_reports.

25 An example of the consequences of problematic data quality is a report by the Church of England on 51 'greater churches' (churches which are not cathedrals, but have a substantial civic role). The report found that two-thirds of the data from such churches was so poor as to be unusable, severely limiting analysis of such 'greater churches'. See: J. Holmes and B. Kautzer, *Cathedrals and Greater Churches* (Durham: Cranmer Hall, 2014): 65–7, available at http://www.churchgrowthresearch.org.uk/findings.

26 Johnson and Zurlo, 'Changing Demographics': 2.

27 Wonsuk Ma, 'A "Fuller" Vision of Mission and Theological Education in the New Context of Global Christianity' (a presentation at the 50th anniversary celebration of the School of Intercultural Studies, Fuller Theological Seminary, Pasadena, CA, October 2015).

28 R. Burgess, 'Nigeria', in D. Goodhew (ed.), *Growth and Decline in the Anglican Communion* (Abingdon: Routledge, 2017): 86.

29 Ibid.: 91.

30 Johnson and Zurlo, 'Changing Demographics': 48.

31 Burgess, 'Nigeria': 81–4.

32 Y. Way, 'Congo', in D. Goodhew (ed.), *Growth and Decline in the Anglican Communion* (Abingdon: Routledge, 2017): 107, 109–11.

33 Galgalo, 'Kenya': 117–25.

34 M. Green, *Asian Tigers for Christ: The Dynamic Growth of the Church in South East Asia* (London: SPCK, 2001).

35 D. Wee, 'Singapore', in D. Goodhew (ed.), *Growth and Decline in the Anglican Communion* (Abingdon: Routledge, 2017): 159, 161. See also: http://www.anglican.org.sg/index.php/directory_s/deaneries, accessed 3 November 2015.

36 Sinclair and Corrie, 'South America': 255–8, 262–4.

37 Johnson and Zurlo, 'Changing Demographics': 47.

38 D. Eshun, 'Ghana', in D. Goodhew (ed.), *Growth and Decline in the Anglican Communion* (Abingdon: Routledge, 2017): 65–6.

39 Ibid.: 63–4.

40 Johnson and Zurlo, 'Changing Demographics': 48, 50.

41 A. Jeremiah, 'The Church of South India', in D. Goodhew (ed.), *Growth and Decline in the Anglican Communion* (Abingdon: Routledge, 2017): 152.

42 Jeremiah, 'South India': 153–4.

43 Ibid.: 155–6. Comparative data from Sri Lanka suggests that South Asian Anglicanism is growing, but growing moderately: Johnson and Zurlo, 'Changing Demographics': 49.

44 Census data gives evidence of decline in the number of Anglicans in recent decades, see: D. Goodhew, 'Growth and Decline in South Africa's Churches, 1960–91', *Journal of Religion in Africa*, 30 (2000): 3. However, Johnson and Zurlo argue that the aggregate number of Anglicans in South Africa has grown, although such growth has not kept pace with population growth: Johnson and Zurlo, 'Changing Demographics': 49. It should be noted that political upheaval prior to 1994 had a marked effect on data collection. It made such collection more difficult and the apartheid state's granting of a spurious 'independence' to certain areas complicates assessment of the numbers for South Africa as a whole.

45 The new diocese of Christ the King grew from 22 to over 40 congregations between 1990 and 2015: http://www.christthekingdiocese-anglican.org/index.php accessed 3 November 2015. The website of a major growth initiative within South African Anglicanism does not suggest that many new Anglican churches are arising overall in South

Africa: http://www.growingthechurch.org.za/site/home.aspx accessed 15 October 2015.

46 Bompani, 'South Africa': 130, 134–6.

47 Johnson and Zurlo, 'Changing Demographics': 46–50.

48 A. Kim, 'South Korea', in D. Goodhew (ed.), *Growth and Decline in the Anglican Communion* (Abingdon: Routledge, 2017).

49 Johnson and Zurlo, 'Changing Demographics': 46–50. Brazil, like South Africa, has seen a numerical rise, but this is broadly in line with population growth and has not included foundation of significant numbers of new churches.

50 R. Powell, 'Australia', in D. Goodhew (ed.), *Growth and Decline in the Anglican Communion* (Abingdon: Routledge, 2017): 198.

51 Data from http://www.anglican.org.au/home/about/students/Pages/how_big_is_the_anglican_church.aspx accessed 23 July 2015.

52 M. Porter, *Sydney Anglicanism and the Threat to World Anglicanism: The Sydney Experiment* (Farnham: Ashgate, 2011).

53 Powell, 'Australia': 217–18.

54 Ibid.: 200.

55 Johnson and Zurlo, 'Changing Demographics': 46–50.

56 D. Voas, 'The Church of England', in D. Goodhew (ed.), *Growth and Decline in the Anglican Communion* (Abingdon: Routledge, 2017): 269.

57 Ibid.: 279.

58 J. Wolffe and B. Jackson, 'Anglican Resurgence: The Church of England in London', in D. Goodhew (ed.), *Church Growth in Britain, 1980 to the Present* (Farnham: Ashgate, 2012): 32.

59 Voas, 'Church of England': 285.

60 S. Bullivant, *Contemporary Catholicism in England and Wales* (London: Benedict XVI Centre for Religion and Society, 2016), available at http://www.stmarys.ac.uk/benedict-xvi/docs/2016-may-contemporary-catholicism-report.pdf.

61 Church of England Council for Christian Unity, *Changes in the Ethnic Diversity of the Christian Population of England between 2001 and 2011, North East Region* (London: Church House, 2014).

62 G. Davie, *Sociology of Religion* (London: Sage, 2007): 92–3.

63 J. Bonner, 'USA', in D. Goodhew (ed.), *Growth and Decline in the Anglican Communion* (Abingdon: Routledge, 2017): 234.

64 Ibid.: 236–7.

65 Ibid.: 238–9.

66 Ibid.: 239–44.

67 For data on Canada, see: http://www.anglican.ca/wp-content/uploads/2011/07/National-Statistics-2001.pdf; http://www.anglican.ca/wp-content/uploads/2011/07/National-Statistics-1981.pdf accessed 13 September 2015; Johnson and Zurlo, 'Changing Demographics': 18.

68 For data on Toronto diocese, see: http://www.toronto.anglican.ca/about-the-diocese/profile-of-the-diocese/; http://www.anglican.ca/wp-content/uploads/2011/07/National-Statistics-2001.pdf accessed 13 September 2015.

69 For data on Quebec diocese, see: http://www.province-canada.anglican.org/synod%202015/Quebec%20Diocesan%20Report.pdf accessed 13 September 2015.

70 For data on Wales, see: http://www.lphparish.org.uk/mf_2013.pdf; http://www.arthurrankcentre.org.uk/lfirc/item/download/1861 accessed 15 October 2015.

71 Norris and Ingelhart, *Sacred and Secular*; Bruce, *Secularization*.

72 M. Noll, 'What Happened to Christian Canada?', *Church History*, 75 (2006); P. Chambers, *Religion, Secularisation and Social Change* (Cardiff: University of Wales Press, 2005).

73 M. Chaves, *American Religion: Contemporary Trends* (Princeton: Princeton University Press, 2011): 110–14.

74 There is substantial evidence that the church, overall, in London has been growing for several decades. See, for example: P. Brierley, *Capital Growth: What the 2012 London Church Census Reveals* (Tonbridge: ADBC, 2013).

75 Bonner, 'USA': 238–9.

76 N. Taton Ammerman, *Sacred Stories, Spiritual Tribes: Finding Religion in Everyday Life* (New York: Oxford University Press, 2014).

77 P. Jenkins, *The Next Christendom: The Coming of Global Christianity* (Oxford: Oxford University Press, 2007).

78 L. Sanneh, *Translating the Message: The Missionary Impact on Culture* (Maryknoll: Orbis Books, 2009).

79 Norris and Ingelhart, *Sacred and Secular*.

80 South Africa has modernised further than most parts of sub-Saharan Africa, but research would be needed before answering the question as to whether Anglicanism has been less dynamic there than in many other parts of Africa due to its greater degree of modernisation or other causes.

81 Davie, *Sociology*: 106.

82 D. Kelley, *Why Conservative Churches Are Growing: A Study in the Sociology of Religion* (Macon, GA: Mercer University Press, 1995); R. Stephen Warner, *New Wine in Old Wineskins: Evangelicals and Liberals in a Small Town Church* (Berkeley: University of California Press, 1988).

83 Davie, *Sociology*: 67–88.

84 For example, the chronic loneliness that afflicts many in the west is a mounting concern. See: J. Cacioppo and W. Patrick, *Loneliness: Human Nature and the Need for Social Connection* (New York: W.W. Norton & Co., 2008).

85 T. Luhrmann, *When God Talks Back: Understanding the American Evangelical Relationship with God* (New York: Vintage Books, 2012): 331.

86 For a guide to wider debates on this issue, see: Koenig, King and Carson, *Handbook on Religion and Health* and the report, *Religion and Well Being* (London: Theos, 2016).

87 T.M. Johnson and K.R. Ross, *Atlas of Global Christianity* (Edinburgh: Edinburgh University Press, 2009): 75.

88 Eshun, 'Ghana'; Burgess, 'Nigeria'; Jeremiah, 'South India'.

89 Johnson and Zurlo, 'Changing Demographics': 46–7.

90 Wee, 'Singapore': 164.

91 Powell, 'Australia': 198, 201.

92 E. Kaufmann, *Shall the Religious Inherit the Earth? Demography and Politics in the 21st Century* (London: Profile 2010); E. Kaufmann, A. Goujon, and V. Skirbekk, 'The End of Secularization in Europe? A Socio-Demographic Perspective', *Sociology of Religion* 73, no. 1 (2012): 69–91; E. Kaufmann and W. Bradford Wilcox (eds.), *Whither the Child? Causes and Consequences of Low Fertility* (Colorado: Paradigm Press, 2013).

93 These movements can be seen in a recent study of the north-east of England which shows English Christianity diversifying rapidly, but showing that diversification as happening mostly outside of Anglicanism. See: D. Goodhew and R. Barward-Symmons, *New Churches in the North East* (Durham: CCGR, 2015).

94 Bonner, 'USA': 227, 236–7.

95 Voas, 'Church of England': 274.

96 Ibid.: 15. For a further discussion of 'trade routes', see: D. Goodhew, *Church Growth in Britain, 1980 to the Present* (Farnham: Ashgate, 2012): 8–9, 224–6, 255.

97 For a discussion of the anglosphere as a concept, see: A. Roberts, *A History of the English-Speaking Peoples Since 1900* (London: Weidenfeld & Nicolson, 2006) and the debate between Robert Conquest and Michael Ignatieff in *New York Review of Books*, http://www.nybooks.com/articles/archives/2000/may/11/the-anglosphere/ accessed 5 November 2015.

98 G. Davie, *Europe: The Exceptional Case: Parameters of Faith in the Modern World* (London: DLT, 2002).

99 Jenkins, *The Next Christendom*.

100 A. Adogame, *The African Christian Diaspora: New Currents and Emerging Trends in World Christianity* (London: Bloomsbury Academic, 2013).

101 D. Bebbington, 'Evangelicalism and Cultural Diffusion', in M. Smith (ed.), *British Evangelical Identities Past and Present* (vol. 1; Bletchley: Paternoster, 2008).

102 H. McLeod, *The Religious Crisis of the 1960s* (Oxford: Oxford University Press, 2007): 102–23.

103 H. McLeod, 'Being a Christian at the end of the Twentieth Century', in H. McLeod (ed.), *World Christianities, c. 1914–2000* (Cambridge History of Christianity, vol. 9; Cambridge: Cambridge University Press, 2006): 646–7. See also: D. Bays, *A New History of Christianity in China* (Chichester: Wiley-Blackwell, 2012).

104 P. Berger, *The Desecularisation of the World: Resurgent Religion and World Politics* (Grand Rapids: W.B. Eerdmans, 1999); D. Martin, *On Secularisation: Towards a Revised General Theory* (Aldershot: Ashgate, 2005).

105 David Martin, quoted in Davie, *Sociology of Religion*: 247.

106 Davie, *Sociology of Religion*: 18.

107 'Pentecostalisation' refers both to influences from 'classic' Pentecostalism and from the more diffuse 'charismatic movement'. For a discussion of these traditions, see: A. Anderson, *An Introduction to Pentecostalism* (Cambridge: Cambridge University Press, 2004).

108 See also: D.S. Parsitau, 'From the Periphery to the Centre: The Pentecostalisation of Mainline Christianity in Kenya', *Missionalia* 35, no. 3 (2007); J. Zink, '"Anglocostalism" in Nigeria: Neo-Pentecostalism and Obstacles to Anglican Unity', *Journal of Anglican Studies* 10 (2011): 2.

109 Burgess, 'Nigeria': 80.

110 Ibid.: 81–4.

111 Ibid.: 87.

112 Sinclair and Corrie, 'South America': 253.

113 Bompani, 'South Africa': 140; Jeremiah, 'South India': 155.

114 Wee, 'Singapore': 159–61, 165–9, 171, 174.

115 Eshun, 'Ghana': 57–8, 62–4, 68–71, 73. Bompani notes a similar unease about the 'pentecostalising' of Anglicanism in South Africa: Bompani, 'South Africa': 137.

116 Eshun, 'Ghana': 69.

117 For evidence of the troubling consequences of allegations of witchcraft, see: http://www.bbc.co.uk/news/magazine-19437130 accessed 5 November 2015.

118 Wolffe and Jackson, 'Anglican Resurgence': 35.

119 Leaders from HTB have been at pains to stress these points. It should be noted that the first splicing of Anglicanism and Pentecostalism happened in the north-east of England, via the remarkable ministry of the Revd. Alexander Boddy, vicar of an inner city parish in the industrial city of Sunderland, see: G. Wakefield, *Alexander Boddy: Pentecostal Anglican Pioneer* (London: Paternoster, 2007).

120 Johnson, 'Counting Pentecostals Worldwide': 281.

121 Those areas described as 'pentecostalising' in this section could also be located within the evangelical tradition. Significant sections of evangelical Anglicanism have not 'pentecostalised' to any great degree but are growing. See, for example: Powell, 'Australia': 198, 204; Bonner, 'USA': 242.

122 For example, the marked growth in areas such as Papua New Guinea and Melanesia is largely within the anglo-catholic tradition, whilst the liberal catholic tradition in North America shows sustainability in places. See: Johnson and Zurlo, 'Changing Demographics': 46–50; Bonner, 'USA': 240–1.

123 The following works illustrate the academic and cultural strength of the Anglo-Catholic and liberal traditions of Anglicanism: Sachs, *Transformation of Anglicanism*; Ward, *History of Global Anglicanism*; Kaye, *Introduction to World Anglicanism*; Markham, Terry, and Stefferson

(eds.), *Wiley-Blackwell Companion to the Anglican Communion*; Chapman, Clarke, and Percy (eds.), *Oxford Handbook of Anglican Studies*; Day (ed.), *Contemporary Issues in the Worldwide Anglican Communion*.

124 A sense of these institutions can be obtained via: http://www.ttc.edu.sg/english/ and http://www.spu.ac.ke/home/spu.html accessed 9 March 2016. See also: http://www.anglicancommunion.org/mission/theology/theological-colleges.aspx accessed 9 March 2016.

125 Way, 'Congo': 98, 108.

126 Sinclair and Corrie, 'South America': 262.

127 Burgess, 'Nigeria': 80–1, 85–7.

128 Ibid.: 87.

129 Bede, *The Ecclesiastical History of the English People*, J. McClure and R. Collins (eds.) (Oxford: Oxford University Press, 1994): 146–9, 164, 174–9.

130 Eshun, 'Ghana': 67.

131 Powell, 'Australia': 203.

132 Burgess, 'Nigeria': 88; Way, 'Congo': 101; Jeremiah, 'South India': 154.

133 Voas, 'Church of England': 285–7; Bonner, 'USA': 236–7; Powell, 'Australia': 218.

134 Burgess, 'Nigeria': 189; Way, 'Congo': 107–8.

135 Sanneh, *Translating the Message*; A. Null, 'Divine Allurement: Thomas Cranmer and Tudor Church Growth', in D. Goodhew (ed.), *Towards a Theology of Church Growth* (Farnham: Ashgate, 2015): 207, 215. This finds an echo in Ward, *Global Anglicanism*: 16–17.

136 Sinclair and Corrie, 'South America': 262.

137 Way, 'Congo': 103.

138 Eshun, 'Ghana': 63.

139 Burgess, 'Nigeria': 81–2, 90–2.

140 Way, 'Congo': 105, 110–11.

141 Jeremiah, 'South India': 155.

142 Burgess, 'Nigeria': 89–90; Wee, 'Singapore': 175.

143 Wee, 'Singapore': 175.

144 Powell, 'Australia': 215–16.

145 Ibid.: 216.

146 Benita Hewitt, *Growing Church Through Social Action: A National Survey of Church-Based Action to Tackle Poverty* (London: Church Urban Fund, 2012).

147 Burgess, 'Nigeria': 77–8.

148 Eshun, 'Ghana': 64.

149 Bompani, 'South Africa': 134–6; Jeremiah, 'South India': 153–6.

150 Wee, 'Singapore': 171–2.

151 Bonner, 'USA': 238–9.

152 See: P. Brierley, *UK Church Statistics 2: 2010–2020* (Tonbridge: ADBC, 2014): 1.1, 1.2, 1.3.

153 Sinclair and Corrie, 'South America': 264.

Overview

2 The changing demographics of global Anglicanism, 1970–2010

Todd M. Johnson and Gina A. Zurlo

The Church in England, by some accounts, stretches back to the first centuries but was largely confined to the British Isles until the modern period. Although global expansion of the Church occurred during the nineteenth century, it was in the twentieth century that Anglicans experienced profound changes in their demographic make-up. According to the Atlas of Global Christianity, the statistical centre of gravity of Anglicanism shifted from France in 1910 to Chad by 2010.[1] This movement to the south was also experienced by the other Christian traditions (Catholic, Orthodox, Protestant) and was the result of two simultaneous trends: (1) the growth of churches of all kinds in the global South and (2) the decline of Christianity (by percentage) in the global North.

In the twenty-first century global Anglicanism continues its shift to the south. While the number of Anglicans nearly doubled from 47 million in 1970 to 86 million in 2010, the concentration of Anglicans in Africa grew (see Table 2.1). In 1970, 62% of all Anglicans were found in Europe. By 2010 this had dropped to just 31%. During the same period, Africa grew from 16% of all Anglicans worldwide in 1970 to 59% in 2010. In essence, Europe and Africa changed positions over the 40 years. Northern America fell from 9% of global Anglicans in 1970 to 3% in 2010. The two pie charts also illustrate changes in the continental shares of Anglicans in 1970 and 2010, and also clearly show the decline in Northern America and Oceania (see Figures 2.1 and 2.2).

The discipline of counting Anglicans (and adherents of any religious tradition) is fraught with many challenges and problems. If the findings are to be useful in examining trends in global Anglicanism, then they must stand up to methodological scrutiny. Therefore, this chapter considers definitions, methods and unique obstacles in counting Anglicans.

Who is an Anglican?

The central tenet in counting all religionists is self-identification. The starting point in any analysis of religious adherence is the United Nations' 1948 Universal Declaration of Human Rights, Article 18:

> Everyone has the right to freedom of thought, conscience and religion; this right includes freedom to change his religion or belief, and freedom, either alone or in community with others and in public or private, to manifest his religion or belief in teaching, practice, worship and observance.[2]

Table 2.1 Anglicans by continent, 1970 and 2010

	Anglicans 1970	% of all Anglicans	Anglicans 2010	% of all Anglicans
Africa	7,728,000	16.3%	50,398,000	58.6%
Asia	361,000	0.8%	855,000	1.0%
Europe	29,367,000	61.9%	26,436,000	30.7%
Latin America	775,000	1.6%	915,000	1.1%
North America	4,395,000	9.3%	2,527,000	2.9%
Oceania	4,781,000	10.1%	4,843,000	5.6%
Global total	47,407,000	100.0%	85,974,000	100.0%

Source: Todd M. Johnson and Gina A. Zurlo, eds., *World Christian Database.* Leiden/Boston: Brill, accessed July 2015.

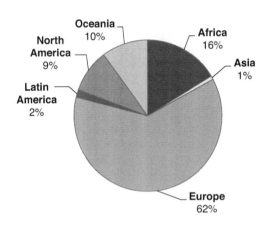

Figure 2.1 Anglicans by continent in 1970

Source: Todd M. Johnson and Gina A. Zurlo, eds., *World Christian Database.* Leiden/Boston: Brill, accessed July 2015.

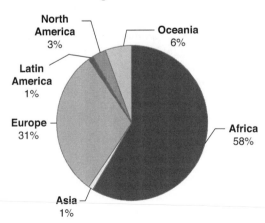

Figure 2.2 Anglicans by continent in 2010

Source: Todd M. Johnson and Gina A. Zurlo, eds., *World Christian Database.* Leiden/Boston: Brill, accessed July 2015.

This means that, in simple terms, all people who consider themselves Anglicans are Anglicans.

However, Anglicanism is more than individual self-identification. As historian Kevin Ward states, 'The Anglican communion describes itself as a 'fellowship' or 'communion' of autonomous Christian churches, united by a common history, confessing a common faith and (traditionally) a common liturgy'.[3] The 1662 Anglican Catechism describes Anglicanism not in terms of individuals but in terms of a global whole, describing a family of churches, united by doctrine and order, that are in full communion with one another and the See of Canterbury.[4] Therefore, Anglicanism includes individuals who self-identify as Anglicans and who retain a very strong corporate global identity. Despite its lack of complete centralisation (in comparison to, for example, the Roman Catholic Church), Anglicanism is characterised by significant global connections, with room for interpretation of what this dynamic looks like. Historian Bruce Kaye prefers the metaphor of a 'conversation' in describing Anglicanism. He states:

> I will be treating Anglicanism as a tradition. By this I do not mean a set of fixed habits from the past, but rather the more dynamic sense of being a conversation over time amongst a community of people held together by sets of practices and beliefs.[5]

Anglicans tend to prefer language of communion, community and family as motifs for self-understanding.

A related challenge in studying Anglicanism involves its name, which describes a worldwide church based on its English roots. Originally, 'Anglican' was another word for 'English', which potentially raises questions of whether this 'parochial' name can really be appropriate for a global communion.[6] However, the unique local character of Anglican communities is a central feature of the global communion. Global Anglicanism, then, represents a mixture of the Anglican tradition (with its English characteristics) and local customs.[7] Traveling the Anglican world, one would expect to encounter great local diversity while recognising common themes between churches. Indeed, variation in music, liturgy, dress, ordination and other areas of church life exists side-by-side a common set of beliefs, theological foundations and history.[8]

Sources

Figures on religions in general and Anglicans specifically come from a number of different sources.[9] The three most important are (1) censuses; (2) surveys and polls; and (3) statistics from religious communities themselves. Each of these is needed to make a global assessment of the demographics of Anglicanism.

Censuses

Censuses are one of the most comprehensive ways in which people are counted. About half of the national censuses in the world include a question on religion. A major problem for religious demographers has been the use of non-standardised terms and categories, which makes comparison between censuses (whether within a single country or between multiple countries) difficult or impossible. Nonetheless, national censuses are the best starting point for the identification of religious adherents, because they generally cover the entire population. Some censuses, such as South Africa's, even provide information on subgroups of major religious traditions (such as Protestant/Catholic or Shia/Sunni). Governments typically conduct major population censuses around the end of every decade and then take three to five years to publish complete datasets.

Whether respondents feel free to be completely truthful in answering census questions can be affected by methodological decisions, political biases and social concerns over how the data will be managed. In addition, problems with comparability of census data can arise when the methods of collection vary (even – and perhaps especially – within a single census). Seemingly mundane issues, like the time of the year when the census is taken, are not irrelevant, because environmental and social factors (such as the weather on enumeration days) can influence the results.

The United Kingdom's 2001 census was the first time in the UK since 1851 that a religious question was asked outside of Northern Ireland.[10] Unfortunately (for demographers), the question was not asked consistently across the countries of the UK. The censuses in Northern Ireland and Scotland included options for response relating to various Christian denominations, but this was not the case in England and Wales, making comparisons difficult. In England, the Church of England was one of the available responses in both 2001 and 2011. In an effort to addresses criticisms of the 2001 questions on religion, officials made changes for the 2011 census,[11] thus complicating comparisons between the two. In some smaller countries, such as the Bahamas, census results offer detailed age–sex breakdowns. The 2010 census reported 3,772 females between the ages 5–14 identified as Anglicans.[12] But in many other countries with an Anglican presence (such as Australia, Uganda and the United States), either no religion question is asked or, if it is, no specific question on Christian tradition is included.

Surveys

In the absence of census data on religion, large-scale demographic surveys, such as the MEASURE (Monitoring and Evaluation to Assess and Use Results) Demographic and Health Surveys (DHS), often include a question about the respondent's religious affiliation. In some instances, demographic surveys by groups such as UNICEF (United Nations Children's Fund) include a religious affiliation question, as UNICEF's 2005 Multiple Indicator Cluster Survey did.[13] Demographic surveys, though less comprehensive than national censuses, have several advantages over other types of general population surveys and polls. As with most reputable general surveys, a demographic survey bases its sample on population parameters from the most recent census. In contrast to other general surveys, a demographic survey completes sufficient household interviews to produce an accurate demographic profile not only of the country as a whole but also of its major states, provinces, and/or regions. To provide this coverage, demographic surveys have larger sample sizes and choose more random locations for samples.

General population surveys also provide valuable information on the percentage of the population belonging to major religious groups. Such surveys include the Pew Global Attitudes Project,[14] the World Values Survey,[15] the Gallup World Poll,[16] the European Social Survey,[17] the International Social Survey Programme,[18] the Afrobarometer[19] (as well as other regional Barometer surveys)[20] and occasional cross-national surveys by the Pew Research Center's Religion and Public Life Project,[21] as well as single-nation surveys such as the Pew Forum's US Religious Landscape Survey.[22] However, because general population surveys typically involve only 1,000 to 2,000 respondents, they cannot provide accurate detail on the sizes of smaller religious groups.[23]

Surveys are sometimes conducted only in urban areas or areas that are easily accessible to pollsters, and therefore they might present a distorted picture of the country's religious composition. Religious adherence can differ significantly by age and gender, and surveys that are not truly representative of the demography of the target population can provide only limited data to researchers. Given these criticisms and uncertainties, the limitations of polling must be taken seriously[24] and poll results measured against other data sources when possible.[25] The major limitation of surveys in relation to Anglicans is that only occasionally is 'Anglican' an option for self-identification. One notable exception is the National Church Life Survey in Australia, where denominational identification is combined with opinion polls. This produces fascinating results, such as that 50% of Anglicans believe that climate change is caused by humans, the highest percentage for any denomination in Australia.[26]

Religion statistics in yearbooks and handbooks

Religious communities keep track of their members, using everything from simple lists to elaborate membership reports. The most detailed data collection and analysis is undertaken each year by some 45,000 Christian denominations and their 4.7 million constituent churches and congregations of believers.[27] The latter invest more than USD 1.1 billion annually for a massive, decentralised and largely uncoordinated global census of Christians. In sum, they send out around 10 million printed questionnaires in 3,000 different languages, covering 180 major religious subjects reporting on 2,000 socio-religious variables. This collection of data provides a year-by-year snapshot of the growth or decline of Christianity's diverse movements, offering an enormous body of data from which researchers can track trends and make projections.[28]

The Roman Catholic Church does the most extensive of these inquiries. Parallel to the obligation of many other religious leaders, all Roman Catholic bishops are required to answer, by a fixed date every year, a 21-page schedule in Latin and one other language asking 140 precise statistical questions concerning their work in the previous 12 months. Results are then published the following January.[29]

At least seven varieties of religious statistics are compiled and kept by religious communities, mainly at the national level. These are (1) demographic and sociographic statistics on religious populations in particular areas and among particular peoples; (2) statistics of religious behaviour and practice; (3) statistics of religious and ecclesiastical jurisdiction and structures; (4) statistics of personnel and lay workers; (5) statistics of social and cultural institutions (such as schools and hospitals); (6) statistics of prosperity and finance; and (7) statistics of religious psychology, beliefs, motivation and attitudes.

There currently is no annual handbook on global Anglicanism that includes membership figures. On its website, the Anglican Communion calls itself 'one of the largest Christian faith communities, comprising 85 million people in over 165 countries'.[30] While a directory of all national churches (or provinces) in the Communion is found on the website, membership statistics by country or province are not presented. Instead, links from the directory send visitors to the national websites, which often do not have membership figures. One must track down individual yearbooks, statistics in annual reports and other websites to fill out the demographic profile of the Communion. In addition, various scholarly books publish estimates for the national churches and sometimes offer a global estimate.[31]

Analyzing data

In summary, amassing any large collection of data for tracking religious demographics (such as for Anglicans) poses two practical challenges. First, no data source includes every country in the world, which means researchers must use multiple sources to cover the entire globe. Second, the ways religion is categorised in the different data sources that are available are often incompatible, and some reconciliation is required to make them suitable to be combined. For instance, some general population surveys might estimate religious affiliation only for the country's adult population, requiring inferences to be made about the religious affiliation of children. Other surveys may have data only on women, requiring inferences to be made about men. Still others might miss certain parts of a country or be representative only of the primary urban centres. For Anglicans it is necessary to use every source available, keeping in mind these limitations.

Counting Anglicans

In order to offer a comprehensive assessment of the global Anglican population, it is necessary to situate Anglicans within a global taxonomy of religion, which includes at least three major considerations: (1) Anglicans in the context of other Anglicans; (2) Anglicans in the context of other Christians; and (3) Anglicans in the context of other religionists. Creating a global taxonomy of Anglican membership must address consistency of data between the groups in order to provide a more accurate and comprehensive picture.

With other Anglicans

First, any data collected need to be comparable between different Anglican communities, particularly from one country to the next. Even at this foundational level, counting Anglicans presents several challenges. Individual churches report membership figures to national headquarters, but this reporting can be uneven from congregation to congregation. Some represent very detailed membership lists kept by church secretaries, while others are rough enumerations. Also, some congregations have strict requirements as to who can be considered a member, while others have much looser definitions of what constitutes membership. Rules for inclusion as a member can differ based on a range of issues, including baptism, confirmation and active membership.[32] Thus, all sources need to be analyzed for comparability. A national census, for example, asks for self-identification whereas a church membership roll could be based on baptisms and therefore might not match exactly. For instance, in Grenada in 1990–91, the census reported that 13.9% of the population identified as Anglican. That same year the Anglican Church reported 14,600 members (or 16.0% of the population). Several reasons for the difference are possible: (1) baptised Anglicans considered themselves something else; (2) the census did not properly identify children of Anglicans as Anglican; (3) people who refused to answer, or checked 'don't know' or 'none', were actually baptised Anglicans. Regardless, comparing with earlier census and church statistics, either of the figures reflects a steep decline in Anglicanism in Grenada (from 35% in 1900 to 11% in 2015).[33]

With other Christians

Second, who is counted as an Anglican needs to be consistent with how other Christian traditions are counted. That is, the data collected need to be counting the same population – for example, including both men and women and children and adults. One of the fundamental areas of comparison relates to the counting of children. Groups that practise infant baptism, like Anglicans, tend to count all children as church members, while those who practise adult ('believer's') baptism do not. Most membership figures from Anglican churches do include children, though surveys and polls normally include only adults. If adults only are included then special formulas based on a demographic profile of the community (or, lacking that, of the general population) are needed to add children to the adult figures.[34]

With other religions

Finally, the method of counting Anglicans should be consistent with those used for other religions. It should make sense when someone reports figures for, say, Muslims and Anglicans in the same country. Both should include children and comprise individuals who self-identify with that tradition. One way in which this does not happen is when counting Anglicans relates to practice, such as church attendance, while counting Muslims is based on self-identification (instead of comparable mosque attendance). For example, while it is interesting that one million Anglicans are in church every Sunday in England, this figure cannot be compared with the 2.7 million self-identified Muslims in England.[35] A more accurate comparison would be how many self-identified Anglicans vs. self-identified Muslims live in a country, or how many church-attending Anglicans and mosque-attending Muslims there are.

Considerations

One unique consideration in counting Anglicans is the impact on Anglican numbers of union churches that Anglican dioceses or provinces have joined. Examples include the formation of the Church of South India (1947), Church of North India (1970), Church of Pakistan (1970) and Church of Bangladesh (1970). In each of these cases, Anglicans joined with Christians from other traditions (including Methodists, Presbyterians, Congregationalists and sometimes others) to form united churches. Technically, members of these united denominations are not 'Anglicans' (or Methodists, etc.), despite the long and rich histories of Anglicanism in each and the fact that each retains an affiliation with the Anglican Communion (affiliations are simultaneously maintained with other international bodies such as the World Alliance of Reformed Churches).

Another surprisingly complex task is determining the number of people affiliated with the Church of England. This question appears to have at least three answers. Using church attendance as a guide, approximately one million people participate in a Church of England service each week.[36] Using surveys as a guide, 8.5 million identify with the Church of England.[37] Finally, using the Church's figures of baptised members gives a figure of approximately 25 million in the Church of England.[38] As stated earlier, if comparability with the demographics of other Anglicans, Christians and religious adherents is indeed important, then it is highly plausible that the larger number represents the wider reality of the Church of England (baptism and self-identification). Note that the figure of 25 million is also used by the Anglican Communion to arrive at their global total of 85 million.[39] At the same time, stricter measures of participation and involvement are useful in examining the health and vitality of the tradition.

Results

The two tables below utilise the sources and the methods described above to arrive at estimates for the number of Anglicans in each country of the world. Seven of the ten countries with the most Anglicans in 2010 (Table 2.2) are found in the Global South (Asia, Africa, Latin America). Most of these were former British colonies, such as Nigeria, Uganda, Kenya and South Africa. Over the 40-year period the countries in the Global North with the most Anglicans – the United Kingdom, United States, and Australia – have seen their Anglican populations either decline or barely grow. At the same time, the Anglican churches of the Global South continued to grow, and some at extremely high rates, such as in Uganda (averaging 5.83% annually 1970–2010) and Tanzania (5.52%).

Table 2.3 offers a complete assessment of Anglican churches around the world for the years 1970 and 2010. Globally, Anglicans averaged a growth of a modest 1.5% annually, similar to global population growth over the same period. Overall the tradition grew fastest in Africa, averaging 4.8% per year. This growth is astounding considering British colonial history in many parts of Africa, and was encouraged by the adaptation of Anglicanism to African cultures and communities.

The table shows a great variety of demographic trends across global Anglicanism. Anglicans experienced decline (negative rates of growth) in many countries in which they have a long history, including the United Kingdom (–0.27%) and the United States (–1.26%). Anglicans in many Western Asian countries also experienced significant losses (Lebanon, –6.19%; Kuwait, –6.12%; Iraq, –2.39%), which could be due to overall Christian persecution in these places. It has already been noted that in Bangladesh, India and Pakistan, Anglicans were incorporated into church unions and are represented with zeros because there is no longer a distinct 'Anglican' identity. Yet, Anglicans have grown rapidly in Africa (Cameroon, Mauritania), Asia (Thailand, Yemen) and Latin America (Honduras,

Table 2.2 Largest Anglican communities, 2010

Country	Pop. 1970	Pop. 2010	Growth % p.a. 1970–2010
United Kingdom	29,059,000	26,109,000	–0.27%
Nigeria	2,941,000	20,100,000	4.92%
Uganda	1,291,000	12,450,000	5.83%
Kenya	583,000	5,000,000	5.52%
Australia	3,777,000	3,800,000	0.02%
Tanzania	386,000	3,318,000	5.52%
South Africa	1,236,000	2,798,000	2.06%
United States	3,196,000	1,923,000	–1.26%
South Sudan	210,000	1,554,000	5.13%
Rwanda	162,000	1,240,000	5.22%

Source: Todd M. Johnson and Gina A. Zurlo, eds., *World Christian Database*. Leiden/Boston: Brill, accessed July 2015.

Table 2.3 Anglicans by country, region, continent and globe, 1970 and 2010

Country	Pop. 1970	Pop. 2010	Growth % p.a. 1970–2010
Afghanistan	100	50	−1.72%
Algeria	800	100	−5.07%
American Samoa	100	60	−1.27%
Angola	2,000	37,800	7.62%
Anguilla	2,800	3,900	0.82%
Antigua & Barbuda	29,500	25,100	−0.40%
Argentina	13,200	23,000	1.40%
Aruba	300	850	2.64%
Australia	3,777,000	3,800,000	0.02%
Austria	2,000	3,200	1.18%
Azerbaijan	0	1,800	13.86%
Bahamas	30,000	48,700	1.22%
Bahrain	2,500	5,600	2.04%
Bangladesh	0	0	0.00%
Barbados	89,600	75,600	−0.42%
Belgium	12,000	10,900	−0.24%
Belize	16,000	10,000	−1.17%
Bermuda	22,000	14,000	−1.12%
Bolivia	200	1,500	5.17%
Botswana	7,000	10,200	0.95%
Brazil	45,000	109,000	2.24%
British Virgin Islands	1,500	3,400	2.07%
Brunei	4,000	4,000	0.00%
Burundi	45,000	850,000	7.62%
Cambodia	200	530	2.47%
Cameroon	0	1,600	13.53%
Canada	1,177,000	590,000	−1.71%
Caribbean Netherlands	60	250	3.63%
Cayman Islands	100	3,400	9.22%
Channel Islands	68,400	71,000	0.09%
Chile	4,000	18,200	3.86%
China	100	700	4.99%
Colombia	2,000	3,200	1.16%
Congo DR	100,000	500,000	4.11%
Cook Islands	100	90	−0.26%
Costa Rica	1,900	1,300	−0.90%
Cuba	12,000	3,400	−3.10%
Curacao	900	1,800	1.68%
Cyprus	6,000	2,600	−2.07%
Czech Republic	200	2,200	6.18%

Country	Pop. 1970	Pop. 2010	Growth % p.a. 1970–2010
Denmark	6,000	2,900	−1.80%
Dominica	1,000	1,400	0.84%
Dominican Republic	3,100	6,300	1.77%
Ecuador	510	11,900	8.19%
Egypt	1,000	3,900	3.46%
El Salvador	160	580	3.35%
Ethiopia	3,000	700	−3.57%
Falkland Islands	1,000	810	−0.53%
Fiji	6,500	6,600	0.04%
Finland	270	100	−2.44%
France	15,000	15,000	0.00%
French Guiana	50	90	1.48%
Gambia	2,000	2,900	0.93%
Germany	20,000	29,200	0.95%
Ghana	100,000	269,000	2.50%
Gibraltar	1,900	1,800	−0.07%
Greece	3,000	3,500	0.39%
Grenada	20,000	12,300	−1.21%
Guam	500	1,000	1.75%
Guatemala	750	2,400	2.95%
Guinea	2,000	1,400	−0.89%
Guinea–Bissau	200	280	0.84%
Guyana	100,000	55,000	−1.48%
Haiti	38,500	122,000	2.93%
Honduras	210	49,900	14.66%
Hong Kong	23,200	23,700	0.05%
India	0	0	0.00%
Indonesia	2,000	3,800	1.62%
Iran	2,600	1,000	−2.36%
Iraq	500	190	−2.39%
Ireland	97,500	90,000	−0.20%
Isle of Man	28,000	38,200	0.78%
Israel	900	1,500	1.29%
Italy	10,000	10,300	0.07%
Jamaica	100,000	90,000	−0.26%
Japan	49,100	58,000	0.42%
Jordan	3,500	7,100	1.78%
Kenya	583,000	5,000,000	5.52%
Kiribati	150	150	0.00%
Kuwait	1,500	120	−6.12%
Laos	300	200	−1.01%
Lebanon	1,800	140	−6.19%

(Continued)

Table 2.3 (Continued)

Country	Pop. 1970	Pop. 2010	Growth % p.a. 1970–2010
Lesotho	80,000	111,000	0.82%
Liberia	11,000	38,100	3.15%
Libya	380	80	−3.82%
Luxembourg	200	500	2.32%
Macao	200	150	−0.72%
Madagascar	50,400	386,000	5.22%
Malawi	76,500	288,000	3.37%
Malaysia	69,600	240,000	3.14%
Malta	3,000	1,000	−2.71%
Mauritania	0	1,100	12.47%
Mauritius	8,000	5,600	−0.89%
Mexico	8,900	27,500	2.87%
Monaco	450	280	−1.18%
Montserrat	4,000	1,400	−2.60%
Morocco	600	1,600	2.48%
Mozambique	45,000	135,000	2.78%
Myanmar	27,000	63,900	2.18%
Namibia	20,000	70,000	3.18%
Nauru	150	350	2.14%
Netherlands	8,000	8,500	0.15%
New Caledonia	50	270	4.31%
New Zealand	876,000	630,000	−0.82%
Nicaragua	3,200	9,700	2.81%
Nigeria	2,941,000	20,100,000	4.92%
Niue	30	40	0.72%
Norway	2,000	2,000	0.00%
Oman	1,100	6,400	4.50%
Pakistan	0	0	0.00%
Palestine	1,400	5,500	3.48%
Panama	15,000	24,800	1.26%
Papua New Guinea	60,000	197,000	3.02%
Paraguay	3,000	19,600	4.80%
Peru	2,500	2,000	−0.56%
Philippines	63,300	145,000	2.09%
Portugal	4,500	2,700	−1.27%
Puerto Rico	9,700	5,700	−1.31%
Qatar	700	8,300	6.38%
Romania	200	550	2.56%
Russia	500	3,700	5.13%
Rwanda	162,000	1,240,000	5.22%
Saint Helena	4,000	3,400	−0.41%

Country	Pop. 1970	Pop. 2010	Growth % p.a. 1970–2010
Saint Kitts & Nevis	17,500	16,600	−0.13%
Saint Lucia	3,000	3,300	0.24%
Saint Vincent	30,000	18,700	−1.17%
Samoa	350	340	−0.07%
Saudi Arabia	2,000	19,000	5.79%
Senegal	100	220	1.99%
Serbia	400	310	−0.64%
Seychelles	3,900	5,400	0.82%
Sierra Leone	25,000	23,800	−0.12%
Singapore	10,000	58,000	4.49%
Sint Maarten	40	500	6.52%
Solomon Islands	49,000	173,000	3.20%
Somalia	200	220	0.24%
South Africa	1,236,000	2,798,000	2.06%
South Korea	32,400	80,100	2.29%
South Sudan	210,000	1,554,000	5.13%
Spain	12,000	11,800	−0.04%
Sri Lanka	46,200	54,200	0.40%
Sudan	90,000	520,000	4.48%
Suriname	1,000	770	−0.65%
Swaziland	3,600	24,800	4.92%
Sweden	3,000	3,100	0.08%
Switzerland	10,000	13,800	0.81%
Syria	50	5,100	12.26%
Taiwan	2,100	950	−1.92%
Tanzania	386,000	3,318,000	5.52%
Thailand	700	19,500	8.67%
Tonga	800	1,600	1.75%
Trinidad & Tobago	150,000	80,400	−1.55%
Tunisia	150	80	−1.56%
Turkey	2,000	23,000	6.30%
Turks & Caicos Is	1,100	2,400	1.97%
Uganda	1,291,000	12,450,000	5.83%
United Arab Emirates	1,700	8,400	4.07%
United Kingdom	29,059,000	26,109,000	−0.27%
United States	3,196,000	1,923,000	−1.26%
United States Virgin Is	9,700	14,200	0.96%
Uruguay	1,000	1,500	1.02%
Vanuatu	10,000	32,200	2.97%
Venezuela	1,100	910	−0.56%
Viet Nam	2,200	3,900	1.44%
Yemen	170	2,200	6.61%

(Continued)

Table 2.3 (Continued)

Country	Pop. 1970	Pop. 2010	Growth % p.a. 1970–2010
Zambia	85,000	264,000	2.87%
Zimbabwe	153,000	381,000	2.31%
Africa	7,728,000	50,398,000	4.80%
Eastern Africa	3,102,000	25,878,000	5.45%
Middle Africa	102,000	539,000	4.25%
Northern Africa	92,900	526,000	4.43%
Southern Africa	1,347,000	3,014,000	2.03%
Western Africa	3,085,000	20,440,000	4.84%
Asia	361,000	855,000	2.18%
Eastern Asia	107,000	164,000	1.06%
South Asia	48,900	55,300	0.31%
South–eastern Asia	179,000	539,000	2.79%
Western Asia	25,800	97,000	3.36%
Europe	29,367,000	26,436,000	−0.26%
Eastern Europe	900	6,500	5.05%
Northern Europe	29,264,000	26,316,000	−0.27%
Southern Europe	34,800	31,400	−0.25%
Western Europe	67,700	81,400	0.46%
Latin America	775,000	915,000	0.42%
Caribbean	554,000	542,000	−0.06%
Central America	46,100	126,000	2.55%
South America	175,000	247,000	0.88%
Northern America	4,395,000	2,527,000	−1.37%
Oceania	4,781,000	4,843,000	0.03%
Australia/New Zealand	4,653,000	4,430,000	−0.12%
Melanesia	126,000	409,000	3.00%
Micronesia	800	1,500	1.58%
Polynesia	1,400	2,100	1.09%
Globe	47,408,000	85,973,000	1.50%

Source: Todd M. Johnson and Gina A. Zurlo, eds., *World Christian Database*. Leiden/Boston: Brill, accessed July 2015.

Cayman Islands). Note, however, that small populations report very high growth rates even if they experience only modest numerical changes, so these figures should be taken with caution.

The demographic future of Anglicanism

By 2050 Anglicans could number 165 million globally. Nigeria likely will be the country with the most Anglicans (50 million) and Uganda second (38 million), with Britain falling to a distant third.[40] At the same time, whether the Anglican

Communion will hold together that long is a question of increasing importance. The Communion is currently embroiled in debate over a series of theological issues that calls into question the common doctrinal unity of belief and practice. While Anglicans have avoided major splits so far, there is no guarantee that this will continue into the future.[41] The shifting demographics outlined above likely will have a profound impact on the future as African, Asian and Latin American Anglicans have a stronger voice in the discussions. Regardless, Anglicans will continue to navigate the global and local features of their communion, where none of the churches exist in isolation from each other but, at the same time, no global body makes decisions for those local churches.[42] How tens of millions of Anglicans around the world work though their differences in the coming years will be either a model for other Christians or a path to avoid.

Notes

1 The statistical centre of gravity is the geographic point at which equal numbers of Anglicans can be found to the north and south and to the east and west. It does not reflect the Anglican population of the country in which it lies.

2 The full text of the UN resolution can be found in P. M. Taylor, *Freedom of Religion: UN and European Human Rights Law and Practice* (Cambridge: Cambridge University Press, 2005): 368–72.

3 K. Ward, *A History of Global Anglicanism* (Cambridge: Cambridge University Press, 2006): 1.

4 Cited in J. Rosenthal (ed.), *The Essential Guide to the Anglican Communion* (Harrisburg, PA: Morehouse Publishing, 1998): 79. It should be noted that there are dozens of self-identified Anglican groups that are not in communion with the See of Canterbury.

5 B. Kaye, *An Introduction to World Anglicanism* (Cambridge: Cambridge University Press, 2008): 3.

6 Ward, *Anglicanism*: 2.

7 Rosenthal, *Guide*: 136.

8 On varieties, see I. S. Markham, J. B. Hawkins IV, J. Terry and L. N. Steffensen (eds.), *The Wiley-Blackwell Companion to the Anglican Communion* (Chichester: Wiley-Blackwell, 2013). On commonality, see P. Avis, *The Identity of Anglicanism: Essentials of Anglican Ecclesiology* (London: Bloomsbury, 2008).

9 This section is adapted from T. M. Johnson and B. J. Grim, *The World's Religions in Figures: An Introduction to International Religious Demography* (Oxford: Wiley-Blackwell, 2013): 163–89.

10 P. Weller, 'Identity, Politics, and the Future(s) of Religion in the UK: The Case of the Religion Questions in the 2001 Decennial Census', *Journal of Contemporary Religion* 19 (2004): 3–21.

11 'Census: How Religious Is the UK?', *BBC News Magazine*, 21 February 2011, available at http://www.bbc.co.uk/news/magazine-12507319.

12 The Commonwealth of the Bahamas, *2010 Census of Population and Housing*, Nassau, August 2012, Table 7.0 'Total Population by Sex, Age-Group and Religion': 78.

13 United Nations Children's Fund, Childinfo: Monitoring the Situation of Children and Women, 'Multiple Indicator Cluster Surveys/MICS3', March 2012, available at http://www.childinfo.org/mics3_surveys.html.

14 Pew Forum on Religion and Public Life, *17-Nation Pew Global Attitudes Survey* (Washington, DC: Pew Research Center, 2007), available at http://pewglobal.org.

15 Available at http://www.worldvaluessurvey.org.

16 Available at http://www.gallup.com/consulting/worldpoll/24046/About.aspx.

17 Available at http://www.europeansurvey.org.

18 Available at http://www.issp.org.

19 Available at http://www.afrobarometer.org/. 'The Afrobarometer is an independent, nonpartisan research project that measures the social, political, and economic atmosphere in Africa'.

20 Available at http://www.globalbarometer.net.

21 Available at http://pewforum.org.

22 Pew Forum on Religion and Public Life, 'U.S. Religious Landscape Survey', 2007, available at http://religions.pewforum.org/.

23 Pew Forum on Religion and Public Life, 'Tolerance and Tension: Islam and Christianity in Sub-Saharan Africa', April 15, 2010, available at http://www.pewforum.org/executive-summary-islam-and-christianity-in-sub-saharan-africa.aspx.

24 K. A. Frankovic, 'Reporting "the Polls" in 2004', *Public Opinion Quarterly* 69 (2005): 682–97; S. Igo, *The Averaged American: Surveys, Citizens, and the Making of a Mass Public* (Cambridge, MA: Harvard University Press, 2007).

25 R. P. Daves and F. Newport, 'Pollsters Under Attack: 2004 Election Incivility and Its Consequences', *Public Opinion Quarterly* 69 (2005): 670–81.

26 *NCLS Research Fact Sheet 14020*, 'Attenders' climate change attitudes', Strathfield, NSW, 2014: 2, available at http://www.ncls.org.au/default.aspx?sitemapid=7216 accessed July 2015.

27 D. B. Barrett and T. M. Johnson (eds.), *World Christian Trends, AD 30–AD 2200: Interpreting the Annual Christian Megacensus* (Pasadena, CA: William Carey Library Publication, 2003): xiii.

28 One attempt to organise a variety of source material for researchers is the website www.adherents.com, which offers thousands of figures for adherents of hundreds of religions. However, there is no attempt by its organisers to reconcile the numerous contradictions in the source material. Nonetheless, it offers an invaluable look at the amount of data researchers have at their disposal.

29 See the yearly publication: *Annuario Pontificio* (Citta del Vaticano: Tipografia Poliglotta Vaticana).

30 Available at http://www.anglicancommunion.org/identity/about.aspx accessed July 2015.

31 Such as country articles in Markham, Hawkins IV, Terry, and Steffensen, *Companion*.

32 Ward, *Anglicanism*: 1.

33 See 'Grenada', in D. B. Barrett, G. T. Kurian and T. M. Johnson (eds.), *World Christian Encyclopedia* (second edition; New York: Oxford University Press, 2001): 321–3.

34 See 'Enumerating Global Christianity', in T. M. Johnson and K. R. Ross (eds.), *Atlas of Global Christianity* (Edinburgh: Edinburgh University Press, 2009): 343.

35 A more nuanced piece comparing Christian practice with Muslim practice by D. Thompson, editor of *Telegraph* blogs, can be found at http://blogs.telegraph.co.uk/news/damianthompson/100073809/practising-muslims-will-very-soon-overtake-weekly-churchgoers-in-britain/.

36 M. Chapman, *Anglicanism: A Very Short Introduction* (Oxford: Oxford University Press, 2006): 9.

37 NatCen's British Social Attitudes survey, May 2015, available at http://www.natcen.ac.uk. See also, RT News, May 31, 2015, https://www.rt.com/uk/263693-anglican-church-decrease-believers/.

38 This is the figure the Church of England reports to the World Council of Churches. See https://www.oikoumene.org/en/member-churches/church-of-england.

39 See 'What Is the Anglican Communion?', available at http://www.anglicancommunion.org/identity/about.aspx.

40 T. M. Johnson and G. A. Zurlo (eds.), *World Christian Database* (Leiden: Brill, accessed July 2015).

41 Ward, *Anglicanism*: 317–18.

42 I. T. Douglas and J. Tengatenga, 'Anglicans, 1910–2010', in T. M. Johnson and K. R. Ross (eds.), *Atlas of Global Christianity* (Edinburgh: Edinburgh University Press, 2009): 73. One of the most significant issues facing Anglicanism is homosexuality (ordination of gay clergy and same-sex marriage). Episcopal churches in the United States have split over this issue, creating new off-shoots that are not in communion with the See of Canterbury, such as the Anglican Church in North America, which has around 100,000 members. Other Episcopal parishes have left the American church and aligned themselves with more conservative bishops in other parts of the world, especially Africa.

Africa

3   Ghana

Daniel Eshun

Introduction

When it comes to numerical church growth and decline in Ghana, the Anglican Church is an enigma. On the one hand, the Church has increased the number of dioceses since 1980, which seems to suggest that there is growth. On the other hand, there are no clear national statistics of membership to show that the creation of more dioceses is an indication of overall numerical growth. Whilst some dioceses seem to have declined in activity, others are flourishing so the whole national picture is a mosaic. Furthermore, the Anglican Church is the oldest mainline Protestant Church in Ghana, but she has been outgrown by other mainline Protestant Churches – Methodist and Presbyterians – and the Pentecostal/Charismatic movements that recently appeared in terms of numerical growth, infrastructure and other resources. This chapter attempts to explain this enigma: the ambiguities, ironies and paradoxes that surround the Anglican Church.

We will start by giving a very brief history of the Anglican Church in Ghana to set the scene.[1] Secondly, to get a measure of how the Anglican Church is faring in the Ghanaian religious marketplace in comparison to the Methodists, Presbyterians, and other Churches (particularly the Church of Pentecost and International Central Gospel Church), we shall consider the population explosion and the general growth of Christianity in Ghana since the 1960s. This is really important because the Anglican Church like all other Churches in Ghana is 'fishing' or 'competing' for men and women in the same religious 'pond' or 'market' so her performance can only be measured and explicated by observing other Churches alongside her. We shall then discuss Anglican growth and decline in comparison with other Churches. Finally, I shall attempt to offer explanations that account for growth and decline, and make some suggestions for hope in the future.

Before we proceed, we need to flag up some data and methodological issues. It appears that the national malaise of not effectively documenting events and keeping statistics has affected the Anglican Church more than the other mainline Churches and well-run, business-like Charismatic and Pentecostal Churches. Commenting on the documentation of the Anglican Church in Ghana, J. S. Pobee, an illustrious son of Church, points out: 'One of the banes of the Anglican Church in Ghana is constant failure to document things, leading to loss of resources.'[2] Pobee suggests, even when one takes into account that there is a large number of non-literates in the Anglican Church, we should still insist that keeping accurate records is a necessity.

> It has been depressing to see that record keeping of the Anglican Church in Ghana, whether at the Provincial or the Diocesan or the Parish levels leave much to be desired. It has been a wounding sorrow to see that that Joint Anglican Diocesan Council's (JADCs) offices have no up-to-date records of statistics of numbers. It has been further wounding to see that parishes have kept no up-to-date-log book of principal service.[3]

The present writer encountered the same difficulties and frustrations in writing this chapter. We will come back to this lack of data when discussing the numerical growth and decline of the Anglican Church.

Owing to the lack of clear national statistics and other documentation, we have relied on figures that the Anglican Church has provided at the websites of the World Council of Churches, Diocesan websites, where figures of growth have been made available, the Ghana national census, national newspaper reports, and Bishops and other Church leaders' public comments on growth and evangelism in media. In addition, we have found J. S. Pobee's *The Anglican Story in Ghana* very helpful. Furthermore, the writer is a Ghanaian priest, though selected, trained, and ordained within the Church of England in the United Kingdom. He has maintained close links with the Anglican Church in Ghana, visiting every other year. The writer also, between 1996 and 1998, conducted extensive fieldwork in the country examining the mainline Churches' (Catholics, Anglicans, Methodists and Presbyterians) responses to the Ghanaian traditional religion, African Independence Churches and the Charismatic Movements. The observations, experiences and the data collected during these periods have informed the analysis of this chapter.

A brief history of Anglican Church in Ghana

The Anglican Church in Ghana is the oldest Protestant Church in the country. It began on May 13, 1751, in the person of the Revd. Fr Thomas Thompson, an Englishman from Yorkshire, Fellow and Senior Dean of Christ's College, University of Cambridge, who accepted the post of a Chaplain to the European traders at the Gold Coast and to be a missionary for the Society for the Propagation of the Gospel. Thompson's ministry lasted only four years and did not make any impact on the indigenous population for two reasons: Thompson did not have command over the indigenous language and his commitment as the Chaplain to the Europeans took much of his time.[4] However, Thompson learnt from his little engagement with the indigenous peoples that it would be easier for them to communicate the gospel to their own people than for Europeans to do so.

To follow up this vision he sent three people – Cudjoe, Coboro and Quaque – to England in 1754 to be educated for the priesthood (Quaque was the only one who survived).[5] The Revd. Philip Quaque was the first black African to be ordained into priesthood in the Anglican Church in 1765. He returned to the Gold Coast in 1765 in the employment of SPG as Chaplain to European traders and missionary to the indigenous population. We shall argue later that the ministry did not bear much fruit for many reasons that still have a bearing on the situation of Anglicanism in Ghana today. Ghana was given an Episcopal See in 1904, the Diocese of Accra, with Nathaniel Temple Hamlyn as the first Bishop. After a succession of colonial Bishops, the diocese came under the first Ghanaian Bishop, Ishmael Samuel Mills Lemaire, in 1968. Since then eight more dioceses have been created. It is interesting to note that the SPG appointed Thomas Thompson, Philip Quaque, and subsequent priests primarily as Chaplains, and that there was no clear mandate for their missionary work.

Ghana's population explosion and the growth of Christianity from post-independence to the present

The growth or the decline of the Anglican Church ought to be understood against the backdrop of Ghana's population explosion. In 1960, Ghana's population three years after independence was 6.7 million. This figure increased to 8.6 million in 1970.[6] For whatever reason, the 1970 census of Ghana did not include the religious affiliations of the population but the 1960s did as follows:

Table 3.1 Religious affiliation in Ghana in the 1960s

Total population: 6.7 million	Religious affiliation in percentages
Christian	41
Muslims	12
Traditionalists	38
Others	9

The Ghana Statistical Service breakdowns of the total percentage of Christians were as follows:[7]

Table 3.2 Christian denomination percentages in Ghana in the 1960s

Total percentage of Christians: 41	Representation of Christian denominations in percentages
Catholic Church	13
Mainline Protestant Churches	25
Pentecostals	2
African Independent Churches (AICs)	1

A few observational comments need to be made here. First, the percentage of Christians in comparison to traditional religion was not very high (41% and 38% respectively). This was partly due to Nkrumah's attempt to protect Ghanaian traditional religions within the religious market for the sake of national identity and pride. During the colonial period, Britain did not declare the Gold Coast as a Christian nation although all the institutions established were modelled on the European style and on Christianity. 'All the state functions in the colonial period began and ended with Christian prayer.'[8] Christianity was given a privileged position over traditional religions and Islam.[9] After political independence, Nkrumah was of the view there should be a 'new political order as well as religious order',[10] and he declared Ghana a pluralistic society, where no one religion had an advantage over others. Paradoxically, though, traditional religion was given a privileged position. Nkrumah wanted Ghana to forge her national identity on the Ghanaian traditional religion and culture rather than on Western values.[11]

For example, to demonstrate to the whole world that a new identity was being created, all Nkrumah's cabinet ministers wore the Ghanaian traditional Kente clothes, libation was poured to ancestors instead of Christian prayers, and the traditional drums were played accompanied by traditional religious dance at the Independence Day ceremony held on 6 March 1958. During the colonial period, European missionaries banned the use of traditional drums in the Church, as they were perceived as 'satanic' and 'pagan', and the Anglican Church in Ghana embraced the Book Common Prayer, as the only proper way of being an Anglican.[12]

The Christian Council of Ghana initially resisted Nkrumah's new religious policies but the autocratic government and its oppression made the Church leaders bow to political pressure. For example, in June 1961 Nkrumah had a private meeting with the Reverend Professor Christian Baeta (a Ghanaian Presbyterian), the Head of the Department of Theology at the University of Ghana and the Chairman of Christian Council of Ghana. Hitherto the department had focused on Christian Theology, Biblical Studies and Church History. Nkrumah said:

> You know that I do not want to interfere with the teaching of Theology or Christianity or anything, but this is a secular university. . . . If you are going to teach Christianity, then you are also going to teach African Traditional Religions and Islam seriously.[13]

The political pressure brought to bear on Christians leaders led Baeta to stress in a paper he wrote in the 1960s that the continuous Christian denunciation of traditional beliefs and practices as mere 'superstition and false' did not address the national aspiration. He argued that whereas officially the Church condemned traditional religious rite as 'pagan and false', even members of the Church resorted to traditional religion in times of crisis.[14] He recommended that 'instead of Church condemning traditional religious beliefs and practices as superstition, the Church should adopt these practices and Christianise them'.[15] We will deal with the link between Anglican growth and need for a proper response to traditional religion later in this chapter.

Due to political instability, severe drought, famine and economic hardship there was no census in the 1980s. However, the Ghana Statistical Service report estimated that the total population was 10.8 million;[16] the religious affiliations were as follows:

Table 3.3 Religious affiliation in Ghana in the 1980s

Total population: 10.8 million	Religious affiliation in percentages
Christian	62
Muslims	14
Traditionalists	21
Others	1

Christian percentage of the population in denominations in the 1980s was as follows:[17]

Table 3.4 Christian denomination percentages in Ghana in the 1980s

Total percentage of Christians: 62	Representation of Christian denominations in percentages
Catholic Church	15
Mainline Protestant Churches	25
Pentecostals	8
African Independent Churches (AICs)	14

The 1980s figures were speculation but they roughly pointed to the trajectories of church growth. For example, they indicated a decline of traditional religion. Those who claimed to be traditionalists and non-believers were 38% and 9% in 1960. These numbers dramatically declined to 21% and about 1% respectively. Whereas the Catholic Church grew 2%, the mainline Protestant Churches – Anglicans, Methodists and Presbyterians – did not grow. The real growth occurred among the Pentecostals and African Independent Churches (AICs). As Asamoah-Gaydu observes, the phenomenal growth of the Pentecostals and African Independent Churches caused panic among the Presbyterian and Methodist Churches. These church leaders realised that many of their members were leaving their sort of Christianity for the Pentecostal and AICs. The Methodists and Presbyterian Churches observed that 'practices unusually unfamiliar in the churches' such as speaking in tongues, healing and deliverance, the holding of all-night vigils, the use of indigenous traditional choruses took place in the Pentecostal and AIC Churches. Mainline Church members who left their denominations 'complained that mainline Churches' style of worship and liturgy are dull and not spiritual enough'.[18] Whereas the Methodists and the Presbyterians were making every effort to make sense of the impressive growth of the Pentecostal, the Charismatic and the AICs, there is no evidence on record, verbally or written, that the Anglican Church responded in the same way.[19] If the Ghana Statistical Service's projection of the Pentecostals and the AICs' growth in the 1980s caused terror among the mainline Churches, the 2000 and 2010 actual census and the continued growth of Pentecostal/Charismatic Churches was a real shock.

On 26 September, 2010, the Ghana Statistical Service announced that the total population on that very day stood at 24,658,823. The Ghana Statistical Service mentioned that the results indicated a population increase of 30.4% over the 2000 population figure of 18,912,079 (Ghana Statistical Service, 2010). In the 2000 census there were 68.8% Christians whereas in 2010 this was 71.2%. The Ghana Statistical Service (2010) breakdown of the religious and Christian denominational affiliation was:

Table 3.5 Religious affiliation in Ghana in 2000 and 2010

Religious affiliation	Population at 2000: 18,912,079	Population at 2010: 24,658,823
Overall Christian population	68.8%	71.2%
Pentecostal/Charismatic	24.1%	28.3%
Mainline Protestants	18.6%	18.4%
Catholic	15.1%	13.1%
Muslims	15.1%	17.6%
Traditionalist	8.5%	5.2%
None	6.1%	5.2%
Other	0.7%	0.8%

The phenomenal growth of Christianity was a surprise to many academics, Church leaders and missionary organisations. For with the erosion of Christianity in Western society and Nkrumah's autocratic leadership and manipulation of Church leaders in post-colonial Ghana, many Westerners were pessimistic about the future of Christianity in the country and perhaps the whole of Africa. Yet, as Adrian Hastings observed in the 1990s, 'Black Africa today is totally inconceivable apart from the presence of Christianity, a presence which a couple of generations ago could still not be unreasonably dismissed as fundamentally marginal and a mere subsidiary aspect of colonialism.'[20] What no academician, diviner or prophet foresaw was the pace of growth of the Pentecostal/Charismatic growth in Ghana. When the present writer was growing up in the 1980s, as a teenager in a Catholic Boarding School, the mainline Churches including the

Anglican Church referred to Pentecostal/Charismatic and the AICs derogatorily as 'mushroom Churches'. Presumably this image of 'mushroom' was chosen with the dismissive assumption that these Churches were springing up very fast so they would have an ephemeral lifespan. What they did not anticipate was that they were growing to become baobab trees that would transform the religious landscape of Ghana!

As Paul Gifford, the former Ghanaian Anglican, observes:

> Mensa Otabil's International Central Gospel Church in Accra is the biggest church, bigger than the Catholic, Anglican or Methodist churches. Although there is no reason to believe these figures any more than those for most other churches in Africa, there is no denying that it is an enormous enterprise, with branches in sixteen different countries.[21]

Gifford continues:

> It is clear that most of the members of the Charismatic Churches were formerly members of mainline churches. The many of the members of the Pentecostal/Charismatic churches are young graduates, well-educated and professional and seem to attract the poor and well-off in equal measure.[22]

It is important to note that the number of Ghanaian traditionalists have significantly reduced from 38% in 1960 to 5.1%. Why? Nkrumah, who used Ghanaian traditional religions to project the new independent nation's identity, told the new nation, 'Seek ye first the political kingdom and all else shall be added unto you.'[23] Ghanaians sought the political kingdom but all the other material things were not added. Post-colonial Ghana experienced political instability, unemployment, economic decline, corruption, mismanagement and the dilapidation of national infrastructure. One of the big hits of the Pentecostal/Charismatic choruses in the 1980s and '90s was 'Only Jesus Can Save'. With the failure of the state to enable individuals to fulfil their dreams and aspirations, Jesus became the only hope. Charismatics and Pentecostals have repackaged the Christian message of hope in a way that resonates with the Ghanaian traditional religious, cultural, social and economic experiences. After all, the traditional religion was about fecundity and well-being and this is what the Pentecostals/Charismatic Churches are offering within the context of the Christian faith.

The Anglican Church in Ghana: is she is growing or declining?

The Ghanaian religious market is booming one. A Ghanaian lorry driver wrote on his vehicle, with his tongue in his cheek: 'Christianity is good business in Ghana.' So how the has the Anglican Church fared within the competitive religious market in Ghana from 1980 to the present? We have already noted the lack of overall national statistical data to give information on Church membership, baptism, confirmations, clergy numbers and so on. However, the Church leadership insists that the Church is 'growing in leaps and bounds!'[24] For example, when Bishop Daniel Sarfo, the Archbishop of the Internal Province of Ghana, was interviewed at the USPG's (US) office in London, he told his audience: 'The Anglican Church started with one diocese in 1752. Now we have 12 bishops team. This is something to celebrate! We are a growing in leaps and bounds! There's a bright future for the church in Ghana.'[25] This resonates with the writer's own observation of the Anglican Church in Ghana, that there is a considerable number of young members, despite many of the youth flocking to Charismatic and Pentecostal Churches. It may be that the Church is growing, but the lack of hard evidence makes these claims of growth provisional at best.

If one were to measure growth by the creation of more dioceses alone one could argue that the Anglican Church has 'grown in leaps and bounds!' Until 1980, there were two only dioceses in the country – Accra and Kumasi. Since 1981 seven more dioceses have been created – Cape Coast, Koforidua, Sekondi-Takoradi, Sunyani, Tamale, Ho and Wiaso.[26] The creation of these new dioceses has led the Church to declare herself an Internal Province of West Africa. The argument is that 'the advantage of forming a Province is to enable them to find appropriate expression in the worship and effectively influence national life'.[27] So the Church has high aspirations and hopes. However, creating more dioceses cannot be used to measure the overall numerical growth of people attending the Church. For example, many of these dioceses are not financially viable or self-supporting and have to rely on other sister churches within the Anglican Communion for financial support and partnership.[28] From the present writer's experience it is not uncommon for an Anglican clergy to wait for over four months to receive a stipend because the diocese or the parish is struggling with her finances.

It is interesting to compare the Anglican Church with the experience of the Methodist Church over the same time span. The Methodist Church adopted the episcopal structure at their National Conference in August 1999. Before then there were eight districts (Methodist equivalents of dioceses). From 1999 to the present day, eight more dioceses have been created, all financially viable. Furthermore, between 2003 and 2008, the Methodist Church planted 406 new churches in Ghana and has started new missionary ventures in Burkina Faso. So even if one assumes that the creation of the seven new dioceses in the Anglican Church signifies growth, it has not been as successful as the Methodist Church.[29]

According to the figures accessed on 17 June 2015 at the World Council of Churches' website, there are 300,000 Anglicans in Ghana but as there are no previous records it impossible to use this figure to measure growth.[30] Even if we take this figure on face value, compared to other mainline Protestant Churches, the Anglican Church is lagging behind. According to the same sources, there are 800,000 Methodists and 565,637 Presbyterians in Ghana.[31] It is equally significant to mention that the Methodists and the Presbyterians provide the number of clergy as 700 and 538 respectively, whereas the Anglican Church is eloquently silent.

Perhaps to get a picture at the diocesan level it is worth comparing the growth of the Accra Diocese with the development of the International Central Gospel Church (ICGC) in the Accra area. This comparison is very relevant to this discussion as the founder of the ICGC Pastor Mensah-Otabil was an Anglican who decided to form his own Church. ICGC was officially inaugurated on the 26 February 1984; their first meeting was held in small classroom with an initial numerical membership of twenty people. From February 1984 to April 1986, the membership grew in Accra to 180 adults at their regular Sunday Service.[32] Within a ten-year period, from 1986–1996, the membership rose to over 4,000 at the main central church in Accra. The ICGC have planted forty 'parishes' or 'assemblies' out of the original main congregation in Accra-Tema metropolis alone within this period. Each 'assembly' or 'parish' has her own team of pastors and is financially independent from the central administration. ICGC claim that

> they are socially conscious Christian church which upholds the philosophy of Human dignity and Excellence. They do engage in promoting and staging events whose impact have reached to the depths of the Ghanaian society and brought Christ to the doorsteps of the people.[33]

Comparing the ICGC to the Anglican Diocese of Accra is very instructive. The Anglican Diocese of Accra was established in 1904 and after a succession of colonial Bishops she came under first Ghanaian Bishop, Ishmael Samuel Mills Lemaire, in 1968. We do not have clear statistics of the whole membership of the Anglican Diocese of Accra. But in 1996 it was stated that the Anglican Diocese of Accra has twenty-three parishes and in 2006 it was recorded that she has grown into twenty-eight parishes.[34] So within nearly ten years the diocese only grew by five parishes. We will attempt to account for the massive growth of ICGC in comparison to the fortunes of the Anglican Diocese of Accra later in this chapter.

Whereas the Accra diocese has not done well in comparison to the ICGC, the newest Anglican diocese, Sefwi-Wiawso, created in 2006, has grown tremendously and there are statistics and figures to demonstrate this. The first Bishop of the diocese, the Rt. Revd. Abraham K. Ackah, himself from the episcopal area, was consecrated and enthroned on 11 June, 2006. The Diocese is made of twenty parishes with four Archdeaconries and the Cathedral and has a total membership of 15,000 on the electoral roll.[35] According to USPG (US) reports, Sefwi-Wiawso has seen enormous growth since 2006: 'In his first two years in the post he confirmed 900 people, and he oversaw the planting of 15 new Anglican churches in his first seven years.'[36] Under the leadership of Bishop Abraham the new diocese has planted seventy other churches that they are nurturing to grow to become viable parishes in their own right.[37]

In Bishops Abraham's own words: 'When I arrived I found many people had drifted from Anglican churches, so I took on the task of bringing people together.'[38] To reverse the decline of the Church he put an emphasis on healing ministry – using the Anglican Clinics within his diocese to provide medical care but also training lay people who have the appropriate gifts to pray with the sick. For Jesus said, the Church should heal the sick.[39] One of the three clinics, Bodi Clinic, serves a catchment area of around 30,000 people and sees approximately 700 out-patients per month. Key health concerns include HIV, malaria, nutrition, cholera and typhoid. The second clinic, Boinzan Clinic, serves approximately 8,000 people, and sees around 1,000 out-patients and 250 in-patients per month. The third clinic, Subiri Clinic, sees up to 500 out-patients per month, with a focus on mother and child health, malaria, nutrition, TB and HIV.[40] The present writer visited all three clinics in 2010. Not all who go to the clinic will convert to Anglicanism. However, the fact that lay people have been trained to offer prayers for those who wish to receive has made Anglicanism popular and attractive to many people who hitherto would have gone to one of the new churches for these prayers. We will visit this theme again in our attempt to explain what contributes to growth and decline. Bishop Abraham's biggest problem as he puts it relates to growth: 'We need more clergy and lay people who are equipped and able to minister to the people. The work is not easy. We need people to pray so the Lord will show us the way and support us.'[41]

Before we attempt to explain the causes of growth and decline of the Anglican Church in Ghana, we need to make a few remarks about the meaning of statistics in the Ghanaian religious market. Within church growth discourses one often hears that it is the quality not the quantity that counts. A case in point is Anderson's argument that

> numbers and growth are important in God's arithmetic: not necessarily large and increasing numbers, but representative numbers and growth in grace. The representative few stand for all, the key question is not how churches can grow numerically, but how they can grow in grace and so become God's representative number.[42]

This may be true: the quality is always vital. However, we need the quantity before we can measure the quality. How could one measure anything when there is nothing tangible and substantial to evaluate? As Pobee has argued, 'a Church that ignores raw data is not going anywhere.'[43] It is very sobering that in the book of Acts we read the writer's interest in statistical growth of the Church. As the writer puts it, 'So the churches were strengthened in the faith and grew daily in numbers' (Acts 16:5). On the one hand the lack of statistics and documentation may simply suggest a lackadaisical attitude to Church administration, but at a deeper level this also sheds light on attitudes to church evangelism and growth.

Even if we concede that the Anglican Church in Ghana has many illiterate people within her membership at the grassroots level this cannot fully account for the lack of documentation and statistical figures at the national level. At the national level, the Anglican Church is manned by many competent people with graduate and postgraduate degrees. And if we take the example of the Church of Pentecost in Ghana, which has more non-literates than any other Protestant denomination in Ghana, at the national level it has a glossy website giving statistics of growth. The Church of Pentecost claims a membership of 2.1 million and 12,238 branches in Ghana and it has built a private Pentecost University.[44] The Church had 400 members in the mid to late 1950s. This astonishing growth overshadows any talk of growth within the Anglican Church with twelve bishops and 300,000 members. As the Archbishop Sarfo told his interviewers, the Anglican Church has been in Ghana since 1752 so one would have expected growth that trumps that of the Church of Pentecost because of the number years of the presence of Anglicanism in Ghana.

It is possible to argue that the Anglican Church in Ghana is displaying self-deprecation and living out the theology of modesty by failing to provide actual figures of her growth at a national level. The irony, however, is that the new diocese of Sefwi-Wiawso is growing fast and, because it has to be accountable and transparent to her sister churches and other organisations overseas that provide financial support, gives clear information on websites including reports and statistics, trumpeting successes and achievements as well as noting challenges.[45] Similarly, the Methodists and Presbyterians who are members of the World Council of Churches provide statistics of their clergy and pastors, but the Anglican Church does not.[46] We argue that in the Ghanaian competitive religious market, statistics are not mere representation of mathematical figures and numbers, they are public religious testimonies about what the Lord Jesus is doing in our Church, statements of witness saying our 'brand of Spirituality' has worked for 'x' number of people, so we invite you to 'taste and see that the Lord is good' (Psalm 34:8). Bearing this argument in mind, what makes one church shout from the roof top about their growth and another movingly silent about how well their church is doing at the national level? One possible explanation for the Anglican silence is that the Church has an establishment mind-set. The Church has always had most of the Ghanaian elite as members, including cabinet ministers, lawyers, parliamentarians, and the Asante royals. In fact, one of her own clergy before ordination was Commissioner for Trade and Commerce. There seems to be complacency that the Anglican Church has a monopoly within the Ghanaian religious market. As Pobee observes, 'the Anglican Church in Ghana have tended to have an Establishment mentality complex, though officially the Church was never established in the Gold Coast or Ghana.'[47] This mind-set has influenced the Anglican attitude to numerical growth and indicates a complacency that the Church does not need to pay attention to the religious 'marketplace'.

Explanation of lack of growth/decline and the need for 'contextualisation' of Anglicanism

Any statement about growth or decline of the Anglican Church in Ghana ought to be tentative because, apart from the figures that have been provided at the World Council Churches website, there are no other clear national statistics available for analysis. As we have seen, the creation of seven new dioceses could be argued as growth, but they are not financially viable. We have seen that there are clear indications of growth in Sefwi-Wiaso, whilst Accra diocese is not growing in the same way, and certainly not in comparison to the ICGC. The picture of the Anglican growth or decline in Ghana is, therefore, patchy.

Recent scholarship on the subject has indicated that the other mainline Protestants and the major Pentecostal and Charismatic Churches have performed better in areas of growth than the Anglican Church.[48] As Pobee makes clear:

> Anglicanism was the second Christian denomination to have appeared in Gold Coast in 1751. Before Anglicanism, Roman Catholicism appeared 15th Century in Elmina; after Anglicanism came the Basel Mission of Germany, now Presbyterian Church in 1828 and Methodism in 1835. Today numerically speaking, Anglicanism is the least of all the Historic Churches a hint that Anglicanism has not done what it takes to capture the natives of Ghana.[49]

And we have seen that the Church of Pentecost, which emerged in the mid-1950s, and the International Central Gospel Church, which emerged in the 1980s, have both surpassed the Anglican Church in numerical growth.

There have been many diagnoses for the Anglican Church's failure in comparison to other Churches. Pobee suggests that the lack of growth could be attributed to the very name 'Anglican'. He argues

> it is my conviction and proposal that the very name 'Anglican' which means English needs to be revisited and changed. It is odd for a bone fide African to carry the description 'Anglican' (English) such situation reveals something of an English captivity of the Anglican Church in Ghana.[50]

This is an interesting point but one could argue that the Catholics, the Methodists and the Presbyterians are all using the very names of their founding mission agencies and they all doing very well numerically. As the Ghanaians say, 'The cat will still meow even when you call her tiger.' Besides, Sefwi-Wiawso, the newest diocese, still bears the name 'Anglican' and is growing. The fact Sefwi-Wiawso is flourishing means that Anglicanism still has something distinctive to offer Ghanaians. The ministry offered at the health clinics, when lay men and women offer prayers that the spiritual root causes of people's ailments will be removed in Jesus' name, is a case in point. So it is not so much about the name 'Anglican' or the spirituality or the ethos of Anglicanism but how the Church contextualises her message to meet the needs and aspiration of Ghanaians within a competitive religious market.

The Anglican Church attracts intellectuals but has an equally high proportion of illiterate and semi-literate people within her congregations. For a church that operates within a context where many people do not have access to secondary and university education the use of the English language as the principal medium of official business and liturgical practice has already excluded the majority of her semi-literate and illiterate membership. This will contribute to a lack of understanding of her message and a lack of engagement. Presbyterians, Methodists and, since Post-Vatican II, the Catholics have made their liturgies, hymns and their discipleship books accessible in indigenous languages to a greater degree than Anglicans. At Presbyterian or Methodist gatherings illiterate members can choose a hymn translated into their own language that they have memorised and can have a sense of belonging that you scarcely see among Anglicans. Interestingly, at the fastest-growing diocese of Sefwi-Wiaso, the writer witnessed people praying for the sick in their indigenous language.

Furthermore, it seems the Anglican Church is not flourishing because, in the words of the novelist Edith Wharton, 'they all lived in a kind of hieroglyphic world, where the real thing was never said or done or even thought, but only represented by a set of arbitrary signs'.[51] Why am I making this reference? The Anglican Church has able theologians and competent leaders who are aware that, despite the scientific and technological advancements, Ghanaians still believe that human misfortunes are caused by the malevolent spiritual forces – the gods, witchcraft, sorcerers and demons. As Phillip Jenkins has pointed out, Ghanaians, like many southern Christians, are quite at home with Biblical notions of the supernatural'.[52] When Ghanaians read the Bible translated into their indigenous languages and encounter verses like, 'You shall not suffer a witch to live' (Exodus 22:18) they are actually reading their traditional religious ideas within the Christian context. As Meyer has demonstrated, through Biblical translation into indigenous language 'witchcraft beliefs have become part of Ewe (Ghanaian) Christian ideas . . . it is structural element of their Christian faith'.[53] For many Ghanaians,

> Bible translation is faithfulness to the word of God, not loyalty to one or another worldview, and certainly not to the elitist account of the matter. The task itself is guided by the view of God's interest in all peoples and their cultures, not by whether or not these peoples accede to our standard of progress.[54]

It may be very embarrassing for the Anglican Ghanaian elite to theologise or to do appropriate biblical exegesis that engages with belief in witchcraft in the twenty-first century, but as Meyer and Gifford have both observed, the subject of witchcraft deserves far more scholarly attention than it has so far received.[55] But 'how can one write about politics and sorcery in Africa without evoking an image of the continent as hopelessly backward, fundamentally different and exotic?'[56] It is not uncommon for Anglicans in Ghana to attend church services and then to seek solutions to their problems that they believe to be caused by witchcraft in a Charismatic/Pentecostal Church or an AIC. Typically, they leave the Anglican Church to find a spiritual home where their concerns are taken seriously and addressed. Anglican Church growth and decline is, therefore, more closely linked with her contextualised theology and biblical interpretation than many Anglican leaders care to admit.

Pobee (the leading Ghanaian Anglican theologian), with his equally able and intellectually nuanced Ghanaian colleagues, K. A. Dickson (Methodist) and Kwame Bediako (Presbyterian), were among the early advocators of contextualisation of Christianity in Africa. Yet the Anglican Church continues to struggle to present and articulate biblical exegesis, theology and liturgical expressions in ways that echo with the Ghanaian indigenous worldview. This has negatively affected her evangelistic overtures.

In the current competitive religious market, evangelism involves public proclamation of the word, open lively worship, openly praying for the sick with sense of expectation of being healed and engaging in deliverance and casting out demons and witches, which reverberate with the traditional Ghanaian religious understanding.[57] In practice, Ghanaian Anglican clergy are reluctant to do this sort of evangelism, though they recognise its effectiveness, and frequently call on Pentecostal and Charismatic evangelists and prophets for support. A case in point was the effort made by the present Bishop of Accra, the Right Reverend Dr. Daniel Sylvanus Mensah Torto, who told the Ghana News in an interview on 9 May 2013 that he was making an effort to 'rebrand Anglicanism', to revive the Anglican's mission and evangelism by organising a three-day 'crusade' at the Black Star Square in Accra on the theme 'Only Jesus Can Save'. The Bishop said, 'Our vision is to build the Anglican Diocese of Accra . . . equipping and empowering church agents, clergy, to deliver excellence; deepening spirituality; growth based on integrity and discipline; financial sustainability, and social impact'.[58]

The 'crusades' took place in May 2013 and it was crowned with a Thanksgiving Service on Sunday 19 May 2013 at the cathedral. Bishop Torto relied on his Pentecostal/Charismatic friends as speakers including Dr. Lawrence Tetteh, President and Founder of World Miracle Outreach; Dr. Richard Roberts, President of the Oral Roberts Ministries at Oklahoma, USA; Dr. Stephen Mwiluki, a UK-based Kenya Pastor of the Charismatic Church; Mr. Richard Shakarian, International Head of the Full Gospel Businessmen's Fellowship; and Reverend Paul Naughton, Chairman of Benny Hinn Ministries in the UK.[59] In the usual Ghanaian Anglicanism 'establishment mind-set complex' manner,[60] the special guests of honour invited to the crusade were the national President, John Dramani Mahama and his wife, Lordina (both members of the Assemblies of God), and Mrs. Georgina Theodora Wood, the Chief Justice.[61]

There are complex issues that surround the question of crusades that illustrate the point we are articulating about Anglican growth and decline in Ghana. There is the question of why the Anglican Church that wishes to have distinctive Anglican public witness in a competitive religious marketplace would rely on Pentecostal and Charismatic Preachers and Prophets for her witness? Whilst we recognise that there are good reasons for ecumenical relationships in mission, the question still remains that if the Anglican Church was confident in her message, couched in a language that was responsive to the demands and needs of the Ghanaian context, why should she be reticent about proclaiming it in an 'unashamedly Anglican' way to the next generation?[62]

The truth is the Anglican Church has always relied on her schools, hospitals, and other charitable works as a means of evangelism and missionary outreach into the community. The assumption is that once an individual has been to an Anglican school, the person will automatically become a loyal son or daughter of the Church, identify with the Church's mission and vision. Whereas this approach has merits and did significantly contribute to the growth of all the mainline Churches in the past, the Ghanaian religious climate has now completely changed. There is the emergence of the Charismatic Churches (who themselves are building primary and secondary schools in addition to well-equipped private universities), the government taking control of Church schools, the increasing influence of electronic communications, and many Charismatic/Pentecostal Churches advertising themselves on TV and radio stations, which means that choosing one's church membership does not simply depend on one's loyalties to the school attended or to family denominational affiliation. The choices people make depend on how a particular brand of theology and liturgical expression addresses the various spiritual and material concerns of the individual religious consumer. It is often assumed that the 'paradigm shift' within the contemporary Ghanaian religious market is new and due to outside influence.[63] This may be true as a result of advancement of Western technology particularly in the new form of media, as the consumerists' attitudes are vividly portrayed in electronic media. However, Ghanaian traditional attitudes to religion have always been consumerist. Ghanaian traditional religion is transactional. Traditional worshipers made their offerings to the deities and ancestors' shrines in anticipation that they will meet their material and spiritual needs.[64] When the gods, the ancestors and the various shrines receive all the cultic attention and fail to meet the emotional, psychological and material needs of their devotees they go into oblivion.[65] By implication a church that fails to meet the spiritual and emotional needs of her devoted members becomes irrelevant. This point is significant in understanding the current lack of Anglican Church growth and her financial viability.

It appears that the lack of growth in comparison to other mainline Protestant Churches is linked with the Church's self-understanding and her history: 'in the Anglican mission history in Ghana there has been a tendency and, perhaps a temptation to confuse mission and chaplaincy.'[66] Anglicans in Ghana tend to opt for a chaplaincy approach which 'is more like a maintenance operation and not necessarily mission which is a dynamic search after transformation and renewal'.[67] Human and institutional histories are messy and complex, and judgements made with hindsight can sometime be very unfair and cruel. However, the fact still remains that the Society for the Propagating of the Gospel appointed Philip Quaque without any clear mandate for mission. Quaque worked as 'a Chaplain to the Cape Coast Castle' for nearly fifty years. Intriguingly, Quaque even claimed that after over ten years in England, he had forgotten how to speak his own native language of Fanti.[68] So how could he proclaim the Gospel in his own indigenous language for his fellow Ghanaians to understand? This initial appointment 'set a tone' for an approach to church growth and mission that seems to have remained to the present day.

In contrast, Samuel Ajayi Crowther, a Yoruba ex-slave, was trained in England, made a deacon in 1843 and priested a year later at St Paul's Cathedral (the second black African in the history of the Anglican Communion to be ordained). In 1864, through Henry Venn's 'three-selfs' formula in mission – 'Self-supporting', 'Self-propagating' and 'Self-governing' – Crowther was consecrated in the Canterbury Cathedral as Bishop of the West Africa countries beyond British Jurisdiction (the first black bishop in the Anglican Communion).[69] Unlike Quaque, Crowther was given a clear mandate for mission – not only to preach the gospel to his fellow Nigerians but also to establish churches that would be self-supporting and self-governing. Crowther engaged with the Yoruba Traditional Religion, particularly the Yoruba worshippers of Ogun (the god of Iron) and Sango (the god of thunder), and Islam beyond the Niger Delta, what we now call Northern Nigeria.[70] Whereas Quaque claimed that he could not speak or preach in his native Fanti language, Crowther translated parts of New Testament and the Church of England Prayer Book into his Yoruba language.[71] It is the case that the two great Anglicans in West Africa lived in two different centuries and in very different contexts. However, the point here is about two different models of evangelism and how they have shaped the two sister Anglican Churches in Ghana and Nigeria respectively. Without evoking missionary rivalries between USPG and CMS, it would perhaps be missiologically and theologically informative to explore how the different approaches influenced later growth of Anglicanism in West Africa.

Perhaps closely linked with the point just made is financial independence. What accounts for the massive expansion ICGC and what could only be described as the limited growth of Anglican Diocese of Accra? In 1968, the Anglican Diocese of Accra, and for that matter the whole of the Anglican Church of Ghana, was in debt to the tune of £38,893 as at December 1968.[72] The Church financially depended on USPG and incurred debt. Even today, the Anglican Church has the general perception that that money for her mission and ministry should come from overseas, so the Church is constantly looking for overseas partners, rather than becoming self-supporting, self-proclaiming and self-governing. In contrast, Pastor Mensah-Otabil, the ex-Anglican, claims that one of the reasons for his calling into ministry was to challenge the Church in Africa to be financially self-sufficient. He wrote:

> When the Lord called me to pioneer a church, He impressed on me strongly to found a church that would not be tied to the apron-string of foreign mission board. The Lord called me to teach my congregation to stop looking to Europe or America as their source of supply but to cultivate a new spirit and ethic of national development. . . . As a result of the conviction, our Church has pursued a vigorous policy of indigenous financing and government.[73]

Asamoah-Gyadu observes that Mensah-Otabil has taught all the mainline Churches the importance of financial giving and self-sufficiency in Christian missions and evangelism.[74] Mensah-Otabil and the experience of the Nigerian

Anglican Church have demonstrated that a church that is financially independent has a better chance of growth than one that is constantly looking overseas for resources.

This brings us to the extraordinary growth the Anglican Diocese in Sefwi-Wiawso. Sefwi-Wiawso diocese is in partnership with sister Anglican Churches within the Anglican Communion. However, Sefwi-Wiawso diocese is under episcopal leadership of Bishop Abraham Ackah who comes from the area. As a result he has taken the laity within his diocese with him; there is a shared vision between the leadership and the laity. As Pobee put it:

> the Sefwi-Wiawso people are proud to have their own man at the helm. The pride has already been translated into deeds. As soon as the creation of the Diocese was announced, a native [one person] built a Cathedral at Sefwi-Wiaso. It was a rebuilding of the earlier Church of the Ascension in manner befitting a Cathedral.[75]

The present writer attended an ordination service that Bishop Abraham presided over in July 2010 at Sefwi-Wiawso Anglican Cathedral, and Pobee's observations resonates with the writer's experience: there was no doubt that not only members of his flock but the whole population of the region is behind him. So it may be that there is something to be said for indigenous leadership and church growth. Another factor for growth appears to be the prayer ministry that is offered at local health clinics: it takes both a scientific and traditional cosmological understanding of illness seriously.

Finally, one can attribute the slow growth in the Anglican Church to a lack of women in leadership roles. Many of the flourishing mainline and Pentecostal and Charismatic Churches have women in leadership positions. For some reason the Anglicans have not taken women's ministry seriously – and this is in a culture where women have traditionally exercised religious leadership. The Anglican presence would have been very negligible had it not been for the work of women and catechists who often had no former theological education but displayed a passion for mission and evangelism. An example is the story of Tabitha Quaye of All Saints Parish in Sekondi-Takoradi whose zeal for the Lord Jesus led her to be first woman to attend the six-week special lay training course at the St. Nicholas Seminary, Cape Coast, and to found an Anglican Church at Shama, which has now grown to be a parish with a congregation of over a hundred in the late 1980s.[76] Paradoxically, 'the Anglican Church in Ghana rooted in the High Church Tradition, has not been only clergy-centred but also male dominated. But everywhere women have made significant contributions in cash and kind and in leadership and mission'.[77] This clergy-centred approach to ministry has deprived the Anglican Church of many talented women and other laity who did not feel called to priesthood but had gifts for evangelism. Many of the Anglicans who left the Church to join the Charismatic and Pentecostal movements in 1980s and 1990s were laity who felt their gifts were not being recognised and used for the mission of the Church.

Conclusion

In conclusion, an absence of sound data indicates a lack of confidence in the Anglican witness in shouting what the Lord is doing in their midst. It also means that the analysis and conclusions drawn must be provisional. If the Church begins to take the collection of data seriously, as part of their Christian witness, it would be fascinating to revisit this subject in five years' time.

Whilst the Anglican Church in Ghana appears to have lost ground in the Ghanaian religious market in comparison to other Churches, there are areas of growth which defy this trend. The hope for the future lies in how the Anglican Church contextualises her theology and biblical interpretation, finds a language that resonates with people's religious experiences and takes her laity – particularly women's ministry – seriously.

Notes

1 For the history of Anglican Church in Ghana, see J.S. Pobee, *The Anglican Story in Ghana: From Mission Beginnings to Province* (Accra: Amanza, 2009); F. L. Bartels, *The Roots of Ghana Methodism* (Accra: Amanza, 1965); H. W. Derbrunner, *History of Christianity in Ghana* (Accra: Presbyterian Press, 1967).

2 Pobee, *The Anglican Story in Ghana*: 369.

3 Ibid.

4 T. Thompson, *An Account of Two Missionary Journeys by the Appointment of the SPG* (London: SPCK, 1758): 36.

5 Ibid.

6 S. K. Gaisie, *Ghana Population Analysis, Accra* (Ghana Statistical Service, 2005).

7 *Ghana Statistical Service, Population and Housing Census* (1981): 196:24.

8 K. Bensti-Enchil, 'The Quality of Ghana Response to the Impact of Western Civilisation', in A. W. Kayper-Mensah and H. Wolf (eds.), *Ghanaian Writing* (Federal Republic of Germany, 1964): 69.

9 G. M. Okafor, *Christianity and Islam in West Africa: The Ghana Experience* (Accra: Asempa Press, 1979).

10 A. Mazuri, 'Towards a New International Order: African Perspective', in *Christianity and Islamic Contribution Towards Establishing Independent States in Africa South of Sahara* (Papers and Proceedings of the African Colloquium, Bonn-Bad Godesberg, 2–4 May, 1979): 24.

11 J.S. Pobee, *Kwame Nkrumah and the Church in Ghana 1949–1960* (Accra: Christian Council of Ghana, 1989): 18

12 Interview with Revd. Dr. J. K Agbeti, Cape Coast Diocese, 3 April 1999.

13 C. G. Baeta, *The Relationship of Christians with Men of the Other Living Faith* (Accra: Christian Council of Ghana, 1971): 14.

14 Ibid.

15 Ibid.

16 *Ghana Statistical Service* (1985): 26.

17 Ibid.: 24.

18 J. K. Asamoah-Gyadu, *Contemporary Pentecostal Christianity Interpretations from an African Context* (Oxford: Regnum Books International, 2013): 12.

19 Interview with Revd. Fr. Quaye, Sekondi Diocese, 8 July 1998.

20 A. Hastings, 'Christianity in Africa', in Ursula King (ed.), *Turning Points in Religious Studies* (Edinburgh: T. and T. Clark, 1990): 208.

21 P. Gifford, *Ghana's New Christianity: Pentecostalism in a Global Africa Economy* (London: Hurst and Company, 2004): 53.

22 Ibid.: 528.

23 E. O. Addo, *Kwame Nkrumah: A Case Study of Religion and Politics in Ghana* (Lanham, MD: University Press of America, 1977): 102.

24 'Anglicans in Ghana: "We Are Growing in Leaps and Bounds!"', available at http://www.weareus.org.uk/news/daniel/ accessed 29 June 2015.

25 Ibid.

26 Pobee, *Anglican Story in Ghana*: 70.

27 Ibid.: 75.

28 Ibid.

29 *Ghana Methodist National Report* (2009).

30 World Council of Churches, available at http://www.oikoumene.org/en/member-churches/church-of-the-province-of-west-africa/ accessed 17 July 2015.

31 Ibid.

32 International Central Gospel Church, available at http://icgcedmonton.com/icgc accessed 8 July 2015.

33 Ibid.

34 Pobee, *Anglican Story in Ghana*: 382.

35 'Annual Report of the Us Trustees', available at http://www.weareus.org.uk/docstore/97.pdf accessed 28 January 2015: 1.

36 Available at http://www.weareus.org.uk/worldwide/ghana/ accessed 14 March 2015.

37 'Annual Report': 1.

38 Available at http://www.weareus.org.uk/worldwide/ghana/ accessed 14 March 2015.

39 'Annual Report': 4

40 Available at http://www.weareus.org.uk/worldwide/ghana/ accessed 14 March 2015.

41 Ibid.

42 G. H. Anderson et al., *Mission Trends No. 2: Evangelization* (New York: Paulist Press and Grand Rapids: Eerdmans, 1975): 66.

43 Pobee, *Anglican Story in Ghana*: 369.

44 Available at http://www.thecophq.org/ accessed 20 July 2015.

45 Available at http://www.stjosephqv.org/diocese-of-wiawso.html accessed 24 May 2015.

46 Available at http://www.oikoumene.org/en/member-churches/presbyterian-church-of-ghana accessed 17 June 2015.

47 Pobee, *Anglican Story in Ghana*: 104.

48 Gifford, *Ghana's New Christianity*; Asamoah-Gyadu, *Pentecostal Christianity*.

49 Pobee, *Anglican Story in Ghana*: 384.

50 Ibid.: 385.

51 E. Wharton, *The Age of Innocence* (New York: Appleton Company, 1921): 34.

52 P. Jenkins, *The New Faces of Christianity: Believing the Bible in the Global South* (Oxford: Oxford University Press, 2006): ix.

53 B. Meyer, *Translating the Devil: Religion and Modernity among the Ewe in Ghana* (Edinburgh: Edinburgh University Press, 1999): 130.

54 L. Sanneh, *Whose Religion Is Christianity? The Gospel beyond the West* (Cambridge: Eerdmans Publishing, 2003): 115.

55 Jenkins, *The New Faces of Christianity*: 110

56 Gifford, *Ghana's New Christianity*: 22

57 Ibid.

58 *Ghana Chronicle*, 10 May, 2013.

59 Ibid.

60 Pobee, *Anglican Story in Ghana*: 104.

61 *Ghana Chronicle*, 10 May, 2013.

62 S. Sykes, *Unashamed Anglicanism* (Oxford: Abingdon Press, 1995).

63 Gifford, *Ghana's New Christianity*: 38.

64 C. R. Gaba, 'Sacrifice in Anlo Religion, Part 1', *Ghana Bulletin of Theology* 3 (1969): 16–42.

65 K. Baber, 'How Man Makes God in West Africa: Yoruba Attitudes towards Orisha', *Africa* 51 (1981): 725–45.

66 Pobee, *Anglican Story in Ghana*: 26.

67 Ibid.
68 Derbrunner, *History of Christianity in Ghana.*
69 S. A. Crowther and Schon, *Journals of the Expedition Up the Niger* (London: C.M.S., 1841): 32.
70 S. A. Crowther, *Observation on the Niger Delta* (London: C.M.S., 1861): 28.
71 S. A. Crowther, *Experiences with Heathens and Mohammedans* (London: C.M.S., 1859): 54.
72 Pobee, *Anglican Story in Ghana*: 379.
73 M. Otabil, *A Biblical Revelation on God's Purpose for the Black Race* (Accra: Altar Media, 2004): 64.
74 Asamoah-Gyadu, *Pentecostal Christianity*: 94.
75 Pobee, *Anglican Story in Ghana*: 384.
76 Ibid.
77 Ibid.: 354.

4   Nigeria

Richard Burgess

Introduction

The Anglican Church has experienced fluctuating fortunes in Nigeria. Generally regarded as the fastest-growing and largest Member Church in the global Anglican Communion,[1] it has also suffered periods of stagnation and decline. This chapter explores the factors that account for this growth and decline. According to the World Christian Database, in 2005, Anglicans in Nigeria numbered 18 million, compared to 10.1 million in Uganda, 3.4 million in Kenya, 3 million in Tanzania and 2.8 million in South Africa.[2] These figures must be understood against the backdrop of the overall number of Christians in Nigeria. According to Pew Research Center, in 2011, Nigeria was rated sixth in the list of countries with the largest number of Christians (behind the USA, Brazil, Mexico, Russia and the Philippines), with an estimated 80.5 million.[3]

National population and religious demography are also important factors that need to be taken into account when considering Anglican Church growth. Nigeria is currently Africa's most populous nation with an estimated 167 million people in 2011.[4] The country is evenly divided between Christians and Muslims, though estimates of the exact balance vary. The situation is complicated by the geographical distribution of the two faiths. Of the three main ethnic groups, the Northern Hausa-Fulani are predominantly Muslim, the Eastern Igbo are predominantly Christian, and the Western Yoruba are divided between the two faiths. Northern Nigeria as a whole has a majority Muslim population. The Middle Belt, which is roughly the lower half of northern Nigeria, has a large number of Christians while the 'core north' has only a small percentage of Christians. Regional variation in religious demography is partly responsible for differential rates of Anglican Church growth in the country, as we will see later.

Anglican Church growth in Nigeria has far outpaced that of other Protestant mainline denominations. For example, the Baptist denomination, which was introduced to Nigeria in 1850 by the American Southern Baptist Convention, claimed a membership of about 6.5 million in over 10,000 churches in 2013.[5] The Methodists, who entered Nigeria in 1841, have a membership of about 2.6 million, according to the website of the World Methodist Council.[6] The only mainline denomination to keep pace with the Anglican Church is the Catholic Church, with approximately 18 million members in 2005.[7] However, the major challenge has come from the Pentecostals. According to the World Christian Database, there were over 7.6 million mission-related Pentecostals and 27 million independent Charismatics in Nigeria in 2011.[8] The fastest-growing Pentecostal denomination in Nigeria is the Redeemed Christian Church of God, led by former Anglican Enoch Adeboye, which has close to 24,000 congregations.[9] Living Faith Church, founded in 1983 by former Anglican David Oyedepo, owns the largest church auditorium in the world, the 50,400-seat Faith Tabernacle in Lagos. Its headquarters church numbers in the region of 150,000 members.[10] As we will see later, the Anglican Church in Nigeria has suffered both losses and gains through its interactions with the Pentecostal/ Charismatic movement.

Anglicanism in West Africa has been influenced by two approaches to mission, represented by the evangelical Church Missionary Society (CMS) and the 'High Anglican' Society for the Propagation of the Gospel (SPG).[11] In Nigeria, the Anglican Church was influenced by the CMS and the mission theology of Henry Venn, who became CMS Secretary in 1841. Venn anticipated the formation of self-governing, self-supporting and self-propagating indigenous churches through the adoption of African customs and the promotion of local agency.[12] This vision was based on his belief in the fundamental equality of humankind and his confidence in the capacity of indigenous peoples to rule in secular as well as ecclesiastical positions. Two key ideas emerged, according to Peter Williams, which it was hoped would shape missionary work in Africa. The first was the development of indigenous pastors under European supervision as a preparation for leaving the work entirely in their hands. The second was a direct consequence of this: the so-called 'euthanasia' of missions.[13] Venn's vision was radically different from the mission strategy of the SPG, which worked in Ghana.[14] The SPG 'believed bishops should be sent as pioneer missionaries who would then build a church around themselves'.[15] Venn's hopes were pinned on Samuel Ajayi Crowther, who became the first black Anglican bishop in 1864. Significantly, the three-self formula has continued as a salient factor in the growth of the Anglican Church in Nigeria and remains part of its official discourse up to today.[16]

Venn's indigenous church policy figures prominently in the account of Anglican Church growth outlined in this chapter. The chapter begins by giving an overview of Anglican Church history in Nigeria. The Anglican Church in Nigeria became an independent Province in 1979. The main focus of the chapter is an analysis of factors that have influenced the growth of the Church since 1980. The concept of contextualisation is a key to understanding the Church's fluctuating growth in Nigeria. Grant LeMarquand suggests that there are four ways in which Anglican communities can measure whether they are becoming appropriately contextualised. Three of these go back to Venn's indigenous church principles of self-governance, self-support and self-extension. However, he suggests that the fourth 'self', self-theologising, 'may be the most crucial of all of the various aspects of contextualization'.[17] As we proceed, we will pay attention to the way adherence to these principles has influenced Anglican Church growth in Nigeria. Research for the chapter is based on interviews with Anglican and other Nigerian church leaders, participant observation and information obtained from diocesan websites.

An overview of the Anglican Church in Nigeria

From the 1830s, freed slaves from Sierra Leone, mostly of Yoruba and Igbo descent, began to return to Nigeria as traders. As the Yoruba returnees formed church congregations, they invited missionaries in Sierra Leone to join them.[18] The present-day Church of Nigeria (Anglican Communion) traces its origins to 1842 when the CMS established a mission in Abeokuta in Western Nigeria under the supervision of CMS missionary Henry Townsend. Townsend was joined by the freed slave, Samuel Ajayi Crowther, in 1845. The Yoruba Mission subsequently spread to Lagos, which became a British colony in 1861. The major missionary role was undertaken by Sierra Leone Yoruba and by converts from the indigenous population.[19] The explorations on the River Niger (1830–57) laid the foundations for the evangelisation of eastern Nigeria. In 1857, CMS opened the first permanent missionary base at Onitsha, and until 1885, it remained the only missionary organisation within Igboland. As was the case with the Yoruba Mission, the bulk of missionary work in eastern Nigeria was undertaken by indigenous agents.[20]

During the high imperial period (1880 to about 1920), there was a partial reversal of Venn's indigenous church approach in Nigeria, as European missionaries, influenced by Keswick holiness spirituality, gradually replaced local leaders. Interdenominational rivalry was an important theme, a development which intensified missionary efforts and contributed to Anglican Church growth in Nigeria. The purge of the Niger Mission and the humiliation of its head Bishop Samuel Ajayi Crowther precipitated the first wave of Nigerian independency, as 'African' or 'Ethiopian' churches were founded in Western Nigeria as a response to white discrimination of African agents.[21] In eastern Nigeria, Anglican congregations of the Niger Delta became an independent self-supporting Pastorate within the Anglican Church. From 1892 until their reunion in 1931, there were two Anglican bodies, the CMS and the Niger Delta Pastorate (NDP), in eastern Nigeria.[22]

Anglican Church growth received a significant boost from the 1890s through mass conversion movements affecting both Protestant and Catholic churches. In the case of the Yoruba, the surge in church growth followed the colonial conquest of the Ijebu Kingdom in 1892. Prior to this, the Ijebu, who inhabited the hinterland of Lagos, had resisted Christianity. The mass movement, which was strongest among the Ijebu, was not directly organised by the CMS, but the Lagos Church Missions, an arm of the pastorate serving the indigenous population. It was the catechist, with limited education, who bore the brunt of evangelism and teaching.[23] All missions made progress in Yorubaland during the period 1890 to 1960, and all used the school as an instrument of evangelisation. However, it was the CMS, the largest mission in Western Nigeria, which succeeded more than the others in forming an indigenous ministry and this aided its growth. A similar mass movement occurred among the Igbo in eastern Nigeria, this time from 1906, and involved Protestants and Roman Catholics.[24] This rapid expansion followed the British conquest of the Igbo interior and was precipitated by the arrival of CMS missionaries at Owerri in central Igboland.[25]

From 1914, Anglican Church growth in Nigeria was influenced by a series of revivals with Pentecostal overtones. The first was associated with Garrick Sokari Braide, who was from the Niger Delta and a member of the Anglican Niger Delta Pastorate. Local response in eastern Nigeria was spectacular, partly due to Braide's healing gifts and crusade against idolatry, and the NDP churches were the main beneficiaries. Kevin Ward suggests that the movement was an appeal for a more 'indigenised form of Christianity than Anglicanism was at that time ready to accept'.[26] Unfortunately, the assistant Bishop of the NDP, James Johnson, who had initially approved of Braide, later rejected the movement due to his faith-healing practices, mass baptisms and the use of the title 'prophet' by his followers.[27] The second wave of revival was the Aladura movement in western Nigeria which posed a serious challenge to Anglican Church growth. Some of the pioneers of the movement, such as Josiah Oshitelu and Joseph Babalola, had an Anglican background, and there was strong resistance from Anglican authorities to the movement's rejection of infant baptism and reliance on divine healing. Consequently, many participants and converts left the Anglican Church to join the new Aladura churches.[28]

Although these movements contributed to the indigenisation of the Anglican Church, episcopal leadership remained in the hands of the missionaries. Little attention was given to the formation of African clergy, and by 1950, no African Anglican diocesan bishop had been appointed since the death of Crowther. The first diocese (Lagos) was created in 1919 with F. Melville Jones as Bishop, followed by the Diocese on the Niger in 1920, presided over by Bishop H. Tugwell. The Province of West Africa, consisting of the dioceses of Sierra Leone, Accra, Lagos, On the Niger and Gambia, was inaugurated in 1951 with Leslie Gordon Vining as the first Archbishop.[29] As independence loomed and missionary recruitment levels declined following World War II, there was a growing awareness of the need to increase the number of ordained Africans. Yet despite the granting of a level of autonomy to the Anglican Church in Nigeria, there was only limited transfer of ecclesiastical authority. By 1960, when Nigeria became independent, there were Nigerian diocesan bishops in Lagos, Ibadan, Ondo-Benin and the Niger Delta, but Igboland remained under the authority of the British Archbishop C. J. Patterson in Onitsha.[30]

In 1979, the Province of Nigeria was inaugurated with Timothy Olufosoye, the Bishop of Ibadan, as the first Primate (1979–87). At its inception, it consisted of 16 dioceses including the Diocese of the North created in 1954. A further ten were created between 1980 and 1987, including the dioceses of Kano, Kaduna and Jos out of the former Diocese of the North. During the tenure of the second Primate, Joseph Adetiloye (1988–99), 49 dioceses were created, beginning with the diocese of Abuja in 1989. The multiplication of dioceses reached a climax during the tenure of the third Primate, Peter Akinola (2000–10), when 88 dioceses were created, bringing the total to 164 in 2011.[31]

In 1997, the Anglican Church in Nigeria was split into three provinces to facilitate effective management. Province One consisted of the dioceses in the west and was headed by Archbishop Adetiloye; Province Two consisted of the eastern dioceses, with Benjamin Nwankiti of Owerri and after his retirement in 1998, Jonathan Onyemelukwe, Bishop on the Niger, as Archbishop; while Province Three consisted of the northern dioceses with the Bishop of Abuja, Peter Akinola, as Archbishop.[32] Subsequently, during Archbishop Akinola's tenure, a ten-province structure was created in 2003: Lagos, Ibadan, Ondo, Bendel, the Niger, Niger Delta, Owerri, Abuja, Kaduna and Jos. Four more were subsequently created (Lokoja, Kwara, Aba, Enugu), making a total of 14.[33]

In the remainder of the chapter, we examine the factors that have influenced Anglican Church growth in Nigeria from 1980 to the present, paying particular attention to the twin processes of indigenisation and contextualisation.

Evangelical revival and the 'Pentecostalisation' of the Anglican Church

The emergence of the modern Charismatic movement in Nigeria during the 1970s has had a significant impact upon the growth of the Anglican Church. The movement had its roots in an evangelical revival which occurred in the aftermath of the Nigerian civil war (1967–70), initially among students and young people belonging to the mission churches (both mainline and Pentecostal) and interdenominational groups such as Scripture Union, the Fellowship of Christian Students and university Evangelical Christian Unions. It produced a new generation of indigenous leaders and provided the impetus behind the emergence of a multiplicity of new Pentecostal denominations.[34]

A series of crises following Nigerian independence exposed the deficiencies of the mainline churches, including the Anglican Church, and created a favourable environment for the revival. During Nigeria's First Republic (1960–66), hopes were raised due to the improving economy and the growth in secondary and tertiary educational institutions. Oil had taken over from agriculture as the mainstay of the economy, and by 1966, Nigeria ranked thirteenth among the world's crude-oil producers.[35] However, optimism gave way to disillusionment due to pervasive corruption, the collapse of the parliamentary democratic system in 1963, the contested 1964/5 elections and the growth of regional and ethnic antagonisms. In 1966, a military coup, followed by a counter-coup, left General Yakubu Gowon in charge. Meanwhile, a series of violent pogroms in the north, largely directed against easterners, resulted in a mass exodus of a million or so Igbos from all over Nigeria back to their crowded homeland. The series of crises reached their climax with the civil war (1967–70), described by Toyin Falola as 'Africa's first and most costly modern war', when an estimated three million Igbos died (over a quarter of the population).[36] Many Nigerians found the dominant brand of Christianity, represented by the mainline churches, lacked the power to help them fulfil their deep-seated aspirations, cope with the stresses engendered by political and economic instability, and engage effectively in mission. The revival was a response to the crisis generated by decolonisation and civil war, but received significant impulses from external sources and was part of the larger global Charismatic movement.

During the 1970s and early 1980s, as the religious marketplace expanded, the Anglican Church experienced significant numerical losses to the new Pentecostal churches. This was because those from an Anglican background constituted the largest proportion of members of these churches.[37] One reason for the exodus of young people in particular was the opposition they encountered from church leaders and family members due to their aggressive evangelistic style, their promotion of Holy Spirit baptism and exercise of charismatic gifts, their interdenominational stance and their radical holiness ethic. In some cases, the young revivalists were literally driven out and branded as fanatics. Many felt so alienated from the Anglican Church that they left to form new churches or transferred to other denominations more sympathetic to the revival. The perception of those caught up in the revival was of an Anglican Church dominated by nominal Christianity and liberal clerics, and unable to respond to the felt needs of its members. However, from the perspective of the Anglican authorities, the young revivalists were guilty of indiscipline and non-Anglican practices.[38] Resistance to the revival impeded the indigenisation process and especially the development of younger leaders. It also hindered the development of a contextual theology more in keeping with African religious sensibilities.

Since the mid-1980s, the Pentecostal impulse which originated in revival has now spread to the mainline churches whose leaders once rejected it. In the case of the Anglican Church, there were several reasons for this. Firstly, the Church hoped to stem the flow of young people leaving to join the new churches in a quest for a more meaningful and practical spirituality. This exodus challenged the churches to emulative action as a means of retaining their members. Secondly, some former revivalists, who embraced Pentecostal spirituality during the revival but chose to remain in the Anglican Church, have since attained positions of influence. These include a number of senior bishops.[39] They have been joined by younger clergy, equally open to Pentecostal spirituality and eager to spread it among their members.[40] Today, the majority of bishops are open to Pentecostal spirituality and actively encourage its expression within their dioceses.[41] Thirdly, some Pentecostals are either returning to the Anglican Church or joining it for the first time, and an increasing number are becoming ordained.[42] Together these groups are labelled 'Reformists' by Matthews Ojo in his typology of African Charismatics because they seek to precipitate revival and renewal within their existing non-Pentecostal denominations.[43] Their Pentecostal experience has been sustained and renewed by their membership in the Evangelical Fellowship in the Anglican Communion (EFAC) and their participation in the activities of parachurch organisations like Scripture Union and the Fellowship of Christian Students.[44]

EFAC in particular helped to stem the exodus and stimulate revival within the Church of Nigeria.[45] EFAC was founded in 1961 by the British Anglican John Stott and other evangelical Anglican leaders from around the world to foster fellowship between evangelical groups and defend evangelical belief within the worldwide Anglican Communion.[46] By 1962, some Nigerian Anglicans had become members of EFAC. However, the Nigerian branch of EFAC was officially inaugurated in 1978 at the University of Ife (now Obafemi Awolowo University) during the post-civil war revival, with Yemi Ladipo, the then Vicar of St. Piran's Anglican Church (Jos), as the first National Secretary. An important influence was the veteran Pentecostal missionary Sydney Elton, based in western Nigeria. During the 1970s, Elton predicted a revival in the Anglican Church and encouraged the pioneer members of EFAC facing persecution from Anglican authorities to remain within the Church.[47] From 1981 to 1990, the General Secretary of EFAC was Josiah Idowu-Fearon, the recently retired Bishop of Kaduna Diocese and current Secretary General of the Anglican Communion worldwide.

The development of EFAC Nigeria shows how local religious actors can adapt global resources to suit their own agendas and satisfy community demands. In contrast to EFAC in Britain, which has no connections with the Charismatic renewal and is a relatively inconsequential force within the Church of England today, EFAC Nigeria is an overtly Charismatic organisation with branches in most dioceses. EFAC Nigeria has also added to the original objectives of the worldwide organisation in response to local contingencies by emphasising the need to check the 'exodus of born-again brethren from the Anglican Church', to pray for the 'revival and renewal of the Anglican Church' and to 'mobilize Anglicans for evangelism within and without the church'.[48] In 1992, the EFAC annual convention in Nigeria was attended by 12,000 people, and today it is a predominantly lay movement within the Anglican Church.[49]

The Pentecostal impulse within the Anglican Church has been a significant factor behind church growth in recent decades. Firstly, there is now a greater emphasis on personal conversion and openness to the work of the Spirit as a conscious experience, even if this is not always articulated in terms of a formal doctrine of Spirit baptism subsequent to conversion. Linked to this are receptivity to spiritual gifts, such as speaking in tongues, prophecy and healing, and a determination by some to integrate them into the life of the church. This has made the Anglican Church more appealing to ordinary Nigerians and resonates with the pragmatic nature of indigenous spirituality. Secondly, Pentecostal spirituality has affected the worship and ministry styles of many Anglican congregations. A growing number of churches now engage in worship using modern electronic instruments and contemporary songs of Western and local origin. 'Gospel bands', similar to those found in Pentecostal churches, are employed alongside more traditional choirs during Sunday worship. Hand-clapping, drumming and dancing, simultaneous audible prayer, 'night vigils' and communal 'praise and worship' sessions are now regular features of many congregations. This has helped to stem the flow of young people leaving the Anglican Church for the newer Pentecostal churches and encourage those who have left the Church to return. One example is the Contemporary Anglican Church within Kaduna diocese, started by former Bishop Josiah Idowu-Fearon to cater for younger members agitating for more Charismatic and non-liturgical forms of worship. Contemporary Anglican churches have been introduced in all the major congregations within Kaduna metropolis.[50]

Finally, the Pentecostal impulse has challenged the Anglican Church in the area of mission and evangelism. Members of renewal groups like EFAC and the Anglican Youth Fellowship are often those most committed to evangelism. Revival meetings, open-air 'crusades' and healing and deliverances services are becoming popular within the Anglican Church and, as with the Pentecostal churches, are being advertised through electronic and print media. Particularly significant is the recognition now given to lay ministries. Some Anglican congregations have teams specialising in intercessory prayer, evangelism, deliverance, counselling, prison and hospital visitation, and youth work. As a result, lay members are discovering their gifts and an increasing number are entering the ordained ministry.

Openness to Pentecostal/Charismatic spirituality has contributed towards the Church becoming a self-governing and self-propagating institution which augurs well for its future growth. It has also assisted the self-theologising process by giving greater prominence to pneumatological themes more in keeping with African idioms of spiritual power, and by contextualising Anglican practices of worship and mission. This has contributed to its appeal among ordinary Nigerians. The phenomenal growth of the Anglican Church in Nigeria compared to its counterpart in Ghana can partly be explained by the receptivity of Nigerian bishops and priests to Pentecostal beliefs and practices.

The decade of evangelism and the 'diocesanisation' of the Church of Nigeria

Anglican Church growth gained considerable momentum during the tenure of the second Primate, Joseph Adetiloye (1988–99). This was partly because Adetiloye's primacy coincided with the Decade of Evangelism, launched in 1991. The response of the Anglican Church in Nigeria to the Decade of Evangelism is another example of how cultural flows through global religious networks can influence African Christianity without stifling creativity and over-riding local concerns. In 1988, the Lambeth Conference issued a call to every province and diocese in the global Anglican Communion 'to make the closing years of this millennium a "Decade of Evangelism" with a renewed and united emphasis on making Christ known to the people of his world'.[51] Significantly, the Anglican Consultative Council (ACC) appointed Cyril Okorocha as Director of Mission and Evangelism for the Anglican Communion, with responsibility for coordinating the Decade throughout the world. Okorocha was one of the leading protagonists during the post-civil war revival and is currently Bishop of Owerri Diocese in eastern Nigeria. The Decade of Evangelism represented a shift from maintenance to mission within the worldwide Anglican Communion,[52] and provided a boost to the evangelistic and church-planting endeavours of the Anglican Church in Nigeria, particularly in the predominantly Muslim north.

During the colonial era, the British had entered into an agreement with the Muslim rulers of the Northern Protectorate to limit Christian missionary activity. Hence, the Christian presence in the north prior to independence consisted largely of southern populations who had migrated for economic purposes. Following independence, the new government 'relaxed the restrictions on evangelism', providing new opportunities for evangelism, especially in the Middle Belt.[53] However, initially the Anglican Church made little progress in attracting indigenous populations in the core northern states where Islam was more entrenched. In 1990, at a service marking the beginning of the Decade, Archbishop Adetiloye performed a special ceremony in Lokoja intended to stimulate Anglican missionary activities in the north. Soon afterwards, he consecrated nine missionary bishops and charged eight of them to plant missionary dioceses in parts of northern Nigeria where Islam was the dominant religion.[54] A missionary diocese is one created out of an existing diocese specifically to extend the Church's impact in areas where there is little or no Anglican presence. Most receive financial support from an older diocese for an initial period of three years.[55] The Church historian J. A. Omoyajowo referred to this development as the 'diocesanisation' of the Church of Nigeria.[56] Stephen Fagbemi describes it as a paradigm shift in mission because it meant that the bishop was 'placed firmly at the head of local mission' and became the 'chief missionary and evangelist of the diocese' rather than an 'arm-chair bishop preoccupied with administration'.[57] It also contributed to the development of indigenous leaders and provided opportunities for younger clergy to be appointed to the episcopate.[58]

One of the missionary dioceses inaugurated in 1990 was the Diocese of Kafanchan, created out of the Diocese of Kaduna. By 2012, the Diocese of Kafanchan had grown to 112 congregations organised in 12 archdeaconries with 28 rural deaneries. The total Anglican membership in 2012 was 12,213. According to Markus Dodo, the incumbent Bishop of Kafanchan, most of the new churches were founded through evangelism in areas where there was no previous Anglican presence. Since its inception, Kafanchan diocese has itself given birth to two missionary dioceses (Zonkwa and Kwoi).[59] However, some dioceses in the far northern states have yet to make significant progress in attracting indigenous members and consist largely of members from southern populations. For example, over 95 percent of members belonging to the missionary diocese of Damaturu in Yobe State are of southern (mainly Igbo) descent. The diocese was created out of the Diocese of Maiduguri in 1996 and is currently made up of 30 churches. The introduction of Sharia has seriously hindered evangelism and church-planting in the state, as we will see later.[60]

As noted previously, the creation of dioceses, and the attendant numerical growth of churches and members, has escalated since 1990. This is partly due to Nigeria's deteriorating socioeconomic situation. The rapid expansion of the petroleum sector made Nigeria the wealthiest country in Africa during the 1970s. However, as Toyin Falola and Matthew Heaton note, rather than contributing to national development and improved conditions for Nigerian citizens, this wealth was distributed unequally, mainly benefitting those who had access to state power.[61] Since the mid-1980s, neoliberal economics, associated with Structural Adjustment Programmes (SAPs) and diminished public sectors, has taken its toll, resulting in increased levels of unemployment, poverty and violent conflict. Despite recent economic reform and government attempts to diversify the economy, most Nigerians remain poor, lacking basic necessities and social services.[62] In this context, Anglican Church communities are important sources of sustenance and social security, offering hope and support through networks of relationships, welfare provision and access to prayer for divine intervention.

By 2011, when Nicholas Okoh became the fourth Primate, the Anglican Church in Nigeria consisted of 164 dioceses and 14 provinces. This is a remarkable statistic considering there were just 16 dioceses in 1979. His predecessor, Peter Akinola, must take some credit for the proliferation of dioceses and the emphasis on mission and evangelism among Anglican priests and laity. However, an important question is to what extent the proliferation of dioceses has translated into sustainable church growth, given that most new dioceses are carved out of existing ones. The multiplication of dioceses has certainly assisted administration by reducing the number of congregations in each diocese and enabling closer contact between bishops, priests and church members. It has also encouraged the planting of new congregations, especially in rural areas and places with little or no Anglican presence.[63] One example is the Diocese of Lagos West, arguably the fastest-growing dioceses in Nigeria. When it was created in 1999 it inherited six archdeaconries and 161 churches from the original Diocese of Lagos. The first bishop of the new diocese was Peter Adebiyi (1999–2012) who adopted a three-point agenda: aggressive evangelism, church-planting and youth development. By January 2010, the Diocese of Lagos West had grown to 23 archdeaconries and 240 churches, despite having lost churches through the creation of two new dioceses.[64] Another example is the Diocese of Ife, formerly Ife archdeaconry within the Diocese of Ibadan. At the time of its transition to diocesan status in 1990 it consisted of seven districts with 101 churches. Between 1990 and 2015, it planted 35 new churches and currently consists of 13 archdeaconries.[65]

However, lack of funds has sometimes hampered the missionary activities of the newer dioceses. This has raised the question of whether the creation of new dioceses is appropriate while existing ones are not self-supporting.[66] Archbishop Akinola sought to address the issue of diocesan self-reliance by establishing a one-billion-naira Endowment Fund shortly after his election as Primate in 2000. The main purpose of the Endowment Fund was to support rural dioceses, mission and evangelism.[67] More recently, the incumbent Primate, Archbishop Nicholas Okoh, introduced the St. Matthias Fund specifically to support missionary dioceses struggling to survive financially.[68] Individual dioceses have also engaged in fund-raising activities. For example, the Diocese of Lagos West established the Covenant Seed Scheme as a means of generating funds for evangelism and church-planting.[69] These initiatives have helped to address the third of Venn's indigenous church principles, the development of self-supporting dioceses and congregations. Recently, Archbishop Okoh imposed a five-year embargo on the creation of dioceses because it was recognised that some of the newer missionary dioceses are not financially viable.[70]

Leadership, laity and mission

The calibre of Christian leaders can either stimulate or hinder church growth. Due to the strongly hierarchical nature of Anglican ecclesiology, bishops play an important role in shaping the missionary vision of individual dioceses in Nigeria. Taking into account other variables such as geographical location and financial capacity, the fastest-growing dioceses tend to be those that are led by bishops with conservative evangelical credentials, receptivity to Charismatic spirituality, administrative skills and a strong commitment to mission and evangelism.

One example is Benjamin Kwashi, Bishop of Jos Diocese (Plateau State) and Archbishop of the Ecclesiastical Province of Jos, which covers northeastern Nigeria. Jos diocese was inaugurated in 1980 with Samuel Ebo as the first elected Bishop (1980–84). Bishop Ebo was succeeded by Bishop Timothy Adesola (1985–91) and subsequently by Bishop Kwashi (1992 to present). An indigene of Plateau State, Benjamin Kwashi was converted through the ministry of Deeper Life Bible Church in Lagos, one of the first Pentecostal denominations to emerge from the post-civil war revival.[71] He subsequently chose to return to the Anglican Church and was ordained as an Anglican priest in 1982. According to one of my informants, Kwashi has encouraged the expression of Charismatic spirituality and instilled a strong focus on evangelism and mission throughout the diocese. What is relatively unusual for an Anglican bishop is that he leads by example by actively engaging in missions himself.[72] Soon after his consecration as Bishop, Kwashi organised a meeting of clergy and outlined the three main areas he felt that God was asking him to work in: evangelism, community building (schools, hospitals, community development and building relations between Christians and Muslims) and community leadership. At the time of his consecration in 1992, the Diocese of Jos covered Plateau, Benue and Gongola States. In Jos town itself, there were just four Anglican churches in 1992. By 1997, this had increased to 18 churches. For example, St. Michael's Anglican Church in Jos town started with 12 people in 1993, and by 1997 had grown to over 800 members.[73] Within the first six years, the diocese as a whole had grown from 85 to 195 churches, including churches with indigenous congregations and clergy, and the number of clergy had increased from 17 to 88. Over the next eight years, the diocese had established over 300 congregations.[74] Due to the proliferation of dioceses in Nigeria, Jos diocese covers a much smaller geographical area today. In 2012, it consisted of seven archdeaconries and 50 congregations.[75]

There are now a significant number of bishops of northern descent in Nigeria, an outcome of the indigenisation policy of the Church. However, while bishops are largely responsible for shaping the missionary vision of individual dioceses, the major ministry and missionary role is undertaken by priests and evangelists. With the proliferation of dioceses and parishes in recent decades, the number of non-episcopal clergy has multiplied. In the southern states, the Anglican Church has gone some way towards achieving the goal of self-governance by raising indigenous leaders. However, this remains a challenge in northern Nigeria where the majority of ordained priests are of southern (mainly Igbo or Yoruba) origin.[76]

An important aspect of organisational culture that has contributed to Anglican Church growth in Nigeria is the capacity of leaders to mobilise lay volunteers for mission and ministry. While ordained clergy are largely responsible for planting churches, lay members are actively engaged in mission through such groups as the Mothers' Union, the Anglican Youth Fellowship and EFAC. During Akinola's tenure as Primate, various Directorates were introduced at the National Church and diocesan levels to assist administration and harness the Church's human resources, each with their own directors and lay members.[77] For example, the Diocese of Lagos has a Directorate of Church Planting, a Directorate of Youth and a Directorate of Missions, Evangelism and Disciple-ship.[78] Recently, the Diocese of Ife trained 20 lay members of EFAC and sent them to lead some of its newly planted churches. Subsequently, 15 decided to seek ordination as priests.[79]

Individual dioceses employ a variety of strategies to mobilise their members and evangelise local communities. These include mission awareness weeks, discipleship programmes, urban and rural neighbourhood outreaches, street evangelism, evangelistic 'crusades' or 'revival' meetings and church-planting. For example, in August 2012, Jos diocese held a mission conference, attended by about 600 participants, aimed at 'stirring the church workers to their responsibil-ity as co-ministers' and training them in 'ways of doing mission strategically'.[80] Each archdeaconry in Jos diocese organises 'revival' meetings and regular neighbourhood outreaches, involving house to house and street evangelism. The diocese has also adopted the 1+1+3 church growth strategy introduced by Archbishop Akinola in 2004, which encourages each person to lead one person to Christ and disciple them for three years so that they in turn can disciple someone else.[81] The rationale behind Kaduna diocese's urban church-planting strategy is twofold: to cater for members in Kaduna metropolis who often have to travel long distances to attend church, and to finance church-planting among rural communities in Kaduna State.[82] The diocese organises bi-annual mission outreaches which engage ordained clergy in evangelism and church-planting in rural areas. During Josiah Idowu-Fearon's tenure as Bishop of Kaduna (1998–2015), 96 Anglican congregations were planted among the indigenous people groups in rural areas of Kaduna State.[83] The diocese of Ibadan North has established a mission training college called the Nigerian Intercultural College of Missions to train missionaries for cross-cultural ministry within and beyond Nigeria. The college is affiliated with Bethany International University, Singapore.[84]

In 1994, following a Provincial Missions Conference held in Jos, a recom-mendation to establish a mission body was sent to the Episcopal Synod for consideration. The Church of Nigeria Mission Society (CNMS) was inaugurated in 1996 as an independent and indigenous mission agent of the Anglican Church in Nigeria, with Ken Okeke (now Bishop of the Niger) as the first Chairman.[85] Okeke was one of the leaders of the post-civil war revival who subsequently returned to the Anglican Church. The CNMS was set up to raise awareness of missions through the media, to train and send mission partners to unreached areas of Nigeria and beyond, and to coordinate the missionary effort of the Church. Since its inception, the CNMS has sent mission partners to work in dioceses within Nigeria as well as in other African countries such as Cote d'Ivoire.[86] However, its work has suffered through lack of funds, which has made it difficult for it to support its mission partners. In 2001, it began to rethink its mission strategy. Responding to local diocesan demands, it decided to assist individual dioceses to train their own missionaries who they would then deploy locally.[87]

Education is another important mission strategy adopted by some dioceses, especially in northern Nigeria, echoing the schools' approach to evangelism of the early CMS missionaries. This has been the strategy employed by the diocese of Jos since its inception because it was believed that the education of both adults and children would hasten the spread of the gospel.[88] For example, by 1984, Makurdi district of Jos diocese had opened three secondary schools, and by 1987, it had established 29 primary schools and four nursery schools.[89] The emphasis on education has continued during the tenure of Benjamin Kwashi as Bishop of Jos diocese. Kwashi regards Christian education as an essential key to sustainable church growth and development.[90] Kaduna diocese has also opened primary and secondary schools in Kaduna metropolis and recognises the importance of education for nurturing new converts, especially in rural areas where there are high levels of illiteracy.[91] Kaduna diocese has benefitted from its links with the Anglican Alliance, a global religious development agency which hosts the Commonwealth Professional Fellowship Scheme. The scheme is aimed at building capacity in Anglican education by equipping 'those running church education services to take on leadership, trainer and mentor roles'.[92] In 2015, Martin Odidi, the diocesan education secretary in Kaduna diocese, spent seven weeks in the UK participating in the scheme.[93] Significantly, Anglican schools in Kaduna and Jos dioceses cater for both Christian (including non-Anglican) and Muslim students.

Social welfare projects are also an important aspect of the Church's mission outreaches at both national and diocesan levels. This is in keeping with one of the five marks of mission of the global Anglican Communion, the call 'To respond to human need by loving service', as well as the vision of the Church of Nigeria adopted in 2000 during the primacy of Archbishop Akinola which includes a commitment to social welfare.[94] The provision of social welfare programmes, geared towards addressing the needs of local communities, is an example of how Anglican dioceses and congregations are contextualising their mission strategies in a context where neoliberal economics has created conditions of increasing poverty. A case in point is Egba diocese in southwestern

Nigeria which has a medical outreach to rural areas, a HIV/AIDS ministry, a social ministry for the elderly and orphans and a legal aid ministry offering free legal advice and assistance.[95] The social arm of Osun diocese is called the Social and Economic Development Commission, which consists of four departments: 'Agriculture and Rural Development', 'Vocational Training of Women and Youths', 'Micro Credit Loans' and 'Welfare and Visitation'. One of its aims is to establish economic empowerment programmes and activities for youths, women and the disabled in society.[96] Healthcare provision in particular is regarded as an opportunity to spread the gospel. This is reflected in Kaduna diocese's Rural Health Ministry established in order to support its ministry of rural evangelism. The ministry includes a health centre, a mobile clinic, and a free annual medical outreach. A report of the 2014 annual medical outreach records that 5,600 people received medical consultations and treatments, and more than 5,000 individuals received 'spiritual counselling, of which 466 accepted Christ as their personal Saviour, and 437 received deliverance ministrations'.[97] Kaduna diocese has benefitted from its partnership with Trinity Episcopal Church in the USA, which has contributed financially to its medical outreaches and to the payment of staff salaries and the purchase of drugs for its health centre.[98] The Anglican Alliance has also sponsored Anglican healthcare projects in Nigeria. One example is a community healthcare project run by Jos diocese which provides health information and improved access to healthcare in Plateau State.[99]

Ethno-religious violence and discrimination in Northern Nigeria

In northern dioceses such as Kaduna and Jos, external hardships caused by ethno-religious violence and violation of religious rights have had a detrimental effect on Anglican Church growth. One contributory factor is the application of Sharia to criminal law which has affected the status of Christian communities in the north. Currently, Sharia has been introduced in 12 northern Nigerian states: Zamfara, Sokoto, Kebbi, Katsina, Kano, Niger, Jigawa, Yobe, Borno, Bauchi, Kaduna and Gombe.[100] Many Anglican bishops in the north participated in protests against the adoption of Sharia.[101] Since its introduction, existing discrimination against indigenous and non-indigenous Christian minorities in relation to employment and access to public services has increased.[102] Churches are also denied certificates of occupancy, preventing them from owning land and restricting the construction of church buildings, and existing church buildings are routinely demolished for alleged infractions or when land is seized for 'development' projects.[103] Another factor is the Boko Haram terrorist insurgency, undoubtedly the most significant threat to religious freedom in Nigeria today.[104] Boko Haram (meaning 'Western education is forbidden') is a Salafi-jihadi group which is seeking to eliminate all 'western influences' and create a 'pure' Islamic state ruled by Sharia. As well as attacks on moderate Muslims and government institutions, the group targets Christian communities and churches in northern Nigeria. In northeastern Nigeria, Boko Haram is involved in a systematic campaign of 'religious cleansing' through suicide bombings, violent attacks on church services, destruction of church buildings, murder of Christian businesspeople, assassinations of church leaders and house-to-house killings in Christian suburbs.[105]

Anglican dioceses in Sharia states report significant decline in church attendance in some congregations due to the mass relocation of members to safer environments.[106] In Kaduna State, which has a history of ethno-religious violence stretching back to the 1980s, the proposed introduction of Sharia in 2000 generated a fresh wave of inter-religious riots.[107] In view of Kaduna's large Christian population, the introduction of Sharia in the state was likely to attract more controversy and protest than in other northern states. Christian anxieties emanated, largely, from concerns over restrictions to religious freedom and the perception that their full citizenship rights would be denied them.[108] The 2000 crisis was associated with a march on Government House organised by the Christian Association of Nigeria to protest the introduction of Sharia. Fighting erupted as marchers clashed with groups of Muslims. The violence spread to poorer areas of the city, resulting in the killing of close to 5,000 people and the injuring of many more. A further bout of fighting broke out two years later when Nigeria was to host the Miss World contest, and most recently in the aftermath of the 2011 presidential elections, when, following the defeat of Muhammadu Buhari, supporters of his Congress for Progressive Change party engaged in violent attacks on churches in Kaduna.[109] More recently, Kaduna State has become a prime target for Boko Haram. During his tenure as Bishop of Kaduna diocese, Josiah Idowu-Fearon responded to the violence by advocating peaceful dialogue between Christians and Muslims which made him unpopular with some of his fellow bishops.

Jos is the capital of Plateau State, which has become one of the centres of ethno-religious violence in Nigeria over the past decade. In contrast to Kaduna, Plateau is a non-Sharia state with a Christian majority. Analysts of the crisis have mainly focused on the indigene–settler issue and the politics of participation in government involving the 'indigenous' Plateau peoples and the Hausa-Fulani 'settlers'.[110] The issue of indigeneity is relegating many Nigerians to the status of second-class citizens in states other than their own.[111] Despite the constitutional provisions guaranteeing citizenship rights, many states refuse to employ non-indigenes in their state civil services and deny them access to academic scholarships. Non-indigenes also face other discriminatory practices, such as barriers to admission to state universities, political participation and access to basic amenities. In Plateau State, Hausa-Fulani Muslims tend to be defined as 'settlers', whereas the mainly Christian Plateau peoples are recognised by the state government as 'indigenous'. There are also large Christian (mainly Igbo and Yoruba) populations from the south who have been settled in Jos just as long as the Hausa-Fulani and have also been excluded from the benefits of indigeneship. However, unlike the Hausa-Fulani, they are not contesting with the indigenes for political control of Jos. When violence ensues, the Hausa-Fulani often count themselves with the indigenes, and communities from the south have incurred significant losses as a result.[112] According to Adam Higazi, the indigene–settler issue has served to exclude the Hausa-Fulani from governance.[113]

One consequence of the violence in Kaduna and Jos dioceses has been the segregation of communities, an indication of deepening polarisation in what were once genuinely mixed populations. Kaduna city is divided between the predominantly Muslim Kaduna North and the predominantly Christian Kaduna South. The city of Jos has also experienced increasing segregation along religious lines between Jos North, which is predominantly Muslim, and Jos South, which is predominantly Christian. There are now certain parts of the city that are off-limits for members of the 'wrong' religion. Both dioceses have reported a significant decline in attendance in some congregations due to increased security measures on Sunday mornings, which make travel difficult; the destruction of church buildings and killing of church members; the relocation of members; and fear of terrorist attacks.[114] The Bishop of Jos diocese, Benjamin Kwashi, has had his church and home burned down by Muslim extremists. They have also threatened his life and the lives of his family members.[115] Another effect of the growing mistrust between Christians and Muslims, as well as Christian complicity in acts of violence against Muslims, is the difficulties churches now face in evangelising their Muslim neighbours.[116]

Conclusion

This chapter has discussed the factors behind the growth and decline of the Anglican Church in Nigeria from 1980 to the present and related this to the concepts of indigenisation and contextualisation. Initial resistance to Charismatic spirituality and to the missionary zeal of post-civil war revivalists within its ranks led to a haemorrhaging of members and hindered the achievement of self-propagation and the development of younger leaders. The subsequent 'Pentecostalisation' of the Church is a remarkable turnaround and has hastened the contextualisation of its theology and its practices of worship and mission. This has contributed to its appeal in a context where neoliberal reforms have resulted in increasing levels of poverty and inequality. The Decade of Evangelism delivered a boost to the Church's evangelistic and church-planting endeavours, resulting in an escalation in the number of dioceses. This has assisted the achievement of self-governance and self-propagation by developing indigenous leaders, providing opportunities for younger clergy to be appointed to the episcopate, and mobilising the laity to engage in mission. However, many Anglican dioceses are not yet self-supporting, lacking funds to pay the salaries of their clergy and finance their mission activities. The efforts of Primates Peter Akinola and Nicholas Okoh to encourage the introduction of investment schemes and economic empowerment programmes are a welcome development as is the recent embargo on the creation of new dioceses. In terms of church growth, the future of the Anglican Church in Nigeria remains bright in the run-up to the next Lambeth Conference. However, what is less certain is its relationship with other Member Churches of the Anglican Communion in view of recent debates over the authority of Scripture and human sexuality.

Notes

1 The Church of Nigeria (Anglican Communion) is listed as the second largest Member Church of the Anglican Communion after the Church of England but its number of regular churchgoers is far higher.

2 World Christian Database, cited in Pew Forum on Religion & Public Life, 'Global Anglicanism at a Crossroads', available at http://www.pewforum.org/2008/06/19/global-anglicanism-at-a-crossroads/ accessed 19 June 2008.

3 Pew Research Center, 'Global Christianity – A Report on the Size and Distribution of the World's Christian Population', available at http://www.pewforum.org/2011/12/19/global-christianity-exec/ accessed 19 December 2011.

4 National Population Commission, Nigeria, 'Nigeria over 167 Million Population: Implications and Challenges', available at http://www.population.gov.ng/index.php/84-news/latest/106-nigeria-over-167-million-population-implications-and-challenges accessed 8 August 2013. This figure is a projection from the last national census (2006), when the estimated population was 140 million.

5 J.F.A. Ajayi, *Christian Missions in Nigeria 1841–1891* (Harlow: Longman, 1965), available at http://www.nigerianbaptist.org/.

6 Available at http://worldmethodistcouncil.org/about/member-churches/statistical-information/.

7 D. Cheney, 'Statistics by Country, 20 Nov 2005', available at http://www.catholic-hierarchy.org/country/sc1.html.

8 World Christian Database, June 2011, cited in D. Miller, K.H. Sargeant and R. Flory (eds.), *Spirit and Power: The Growth and Global Impact of Pentecostalism* (Oxford: Oxford University Press, 2013): 324–7.

9 A. Ukah, 'Roots and Goals: Nigeria's Redeemed Christian Church of God', available at http://pulitzercenter.org/reporting/africa-nigeria-lagos-pentecostal-church-religious-mission-RCCG-Asonzeh-Ukah accessed 13 January 2014.

10 R. Burgess, *Nigeria's Christian Revolution: The Civil War Revival and Its Pentecostal Progeny (1967–2004)* (Carlisle: Paternoster, 2008).

11 B.C.D. Diara, 'Anglican Church and the Development of Pentecostalism in Igboland', *Journal of Educational and Social Research* 3 (2013): 44.

12 A. Hastings, *The Church in Africa 1450–1950* (Oxford: Clarendon Press, 1994): 290.

13 P. Williams, '"Not Transplanting": Henry Venn's Strategic Vision', in K. Ward and B. Stanley (eds.), *The Church Missionary Society and World Christianity 1799–1999* (Grand Rapids: Eerdmans, 2000): 147–72.

14 See Eshun in this volume.

15 S. Spencer, *SCM Guide to Anglicanism* (London: SCM Press, 2010): 70.

16 This is evident from the following diocesan websites: Diocese of Ibadan North, 'Vision & Mission', 2012, available at http://www.ibadannorthdiocese.org/missions-cont.html; Diocese of Ife, 'About Us', 2012, available at http://dioceseofife.org/about.php; St. Christopher's Anglican Church, Kaduna Diocese, 'The New Church Catechism', 2014, available at http://stchristopherschurchkaduna.org/our-beliefs/the-new-church-catechism/.

17 G. LeMarquand, 'Globalization of the Anglican Communion', in I.S. Markham, J.B. Hawkins IV, J. Terry and L.N. Steffensen (eds.), *Wiley-Blackwell Companion to the Anglican Communion* (Chichester: Wiley-Blackwell, 2013): 669–70.

18 O.T. Olumuyiwa, *A History of Anglican/Methodist Collaboration in Nigeria within the Yoruba Socio-Cultural Context* (Frankfurt am Main: Peter Lang, 2013).

19 K. Ward, *A History of Global Anglicanism* (Cambridge: Cambridge University Press, 2006).

20 F.K. Ekechi, *Missionary Enterprise and Rivalry in Igboland 1857–1914* (London: Frank Cass, 1972); Burgess, *Revolution*.

21 Ward, *Anglicanism*.

22 Burgess, *Revolution*.

23 J.D.Y. Peel, *Religious Encounter and the Making of the Yoruba* (Bloomington & Indianapolis: Indiana University Press, 2000): 242–3.

24 Hastings, *Church in Africa*: 252, 443–53.

25 Ekechi, *Missionary Enterprise*; E. Isichei, *A History of the Igbo People* (London and Basingstoke: The Macmillan Press Ltd., 1976); C. C. Okorocha, *The Meaning of Religious Conversion in Africa: The Case of the Igbo of Nigeria* (Aldershot: Avebury, 1987).

26 Ward, *Anglicanism*: 120.

27 G.O.M. Tasie, *Christian Missionary Enterprise in the Niger Delta (1864–1918)* (Leiden: Brill, 1978): 166–86. In the Niger Delta churches, the number of baptised Christians rose from 900 in 1909 to 11,700 in 1918.

28 M. Ojo, *The End-Time Army: Charismatic Movements in Modern Nigeria* (Trenton, NJ: Africa World Press, 2006); Ward, *Anglicanism*.

29 Church of Nigeria, 'About Us', 2015, available at http://anglican-nig.org/about-us/.

30 Burgess, *Revolution*.

31 B. A. Kwashi, 'The Church of Nigeria (Anglican Communion)', in I.S. Markham et al. (eds.), *The Wiley-Blackwell Companion to the Anglican Communion* (Chichester: Wiley-Blackwell, 2013): 165–83.

32 O. Adebogun, 'The Anglican Church of Nigeria and the New Testament Church', available at http://users.accesscomm.ca/theadeboguns/anglican_church_of_nigeria.htm accessed December 2002.

33 Kwashi, 'Church of Nigeria': 175.

34 See Ojo, *End-Time Army*; Burgess, *Revolution*.

35 E. W. Nafziger, 'The Economic Impact of the Nigerian Civil War', *Journal of Modern African Studies* 10 (1972): 233–4.

36 T. Falola, *Violence in Nigeria: The Crisis of Religious Politics and Secular Ideologies* (Rochester, NY: University of Rochester Press, 1998): 1.

37 Ojo, *End-Time Army*: 233, 177; Burgess, *Revolution*; A. O. Nwoka, 'Pentecostalism and the Anglican Communion in Nigeria', in D.O. Ogungbile and A. E. Akinade (eds.), *Creativity and Change in Nigerian Christianity* (Lagos: Malthouse Press Limited, 2010): 79–94.

38 Burgess, *Revolution*; Nwoka, 'Pentecostalism and the Anglican Communion'; C. Okorocha, *The Cutting Edge of Mission: A Report of the Mid-Point Review of the Decade of Evangelism* (London: Anglican Communion Publications, 1996).

39 Examples include Bishops Cyril Okorocha (Owerri), Raphael Okafor (Ihiala), Ken Okeke (the Niger), Peter Onekpe (Ika), E. A. Awosoga (Ijebu), G. L. Lasebikan (Archbishop of Ondo) and Gideon Olajide (former Bishop of Ibadan).

40 One example is James Odedeji, recently consecrated Bishop of Lagos West diocese.

41 Interview with Dapo Asaju, 11 October 2011; interview with Solomon Akanbi, 24 July 2015.

42 Interview with Martin Odidi, 11 June 2015. Martin Odidi, a former Pentecostal evangelist, is currently an archdeacon in Kaduna diocese. He joined the Anglican Church in 2000 and was priested in 2007. Another example is Dapo Asaju, Bishop Theologian, Professor of Theology at Lagos State University, and Rector of Crowther Graduate Theological Seminary in Abeokuta. Asaju was the former General Overseer of a Pentecostal denomination called the Evangelical Church of Yahweh.

43 Ojo, *End-Time Army*.

44 Burgess, *Revolution*.

45 Nwoka, 'Pentecostalism and the Anglican Communion'.

46 A. Chapman, *Godly Ambition: John Stott and the Evangelical Movement* (Oxford: Oxford University Press, 2012); H. R. Gough, 'The Evangelical Fellowship in the Anglican Communion: Message from the President', *The Churchman*, no date: 39–44, available at http://churchsociety.org/docs/churchman/076/Cman_076_1_Gough.pdf.

47 Interview with Ken Okeke, 17 December 1998.

48 EFAC Nigeria, 'Our History', 2013, available at http://efaclz.org/us/history/.
49 C. Okorocha and R. Kew, *Vision Bearers: Dynamic Evangelism in the 21st Century* (Ridgefield, CT: Morehouse Publishing, 1996): 88–9.
50 Interview with Martin Odidi, available at http://anglicandioceseofkaduna.org/blog/the-presidential-address-from-the-1st-session-of-the-20th-synod-of-the-diocese-of-kaduna/ accessed 11 June 2015.
51 Available at http://www.anglicancommunion.org/ministry/mission/commissions/missio/b_doc.cfm.
52 Anglican Consultative Council, *Mission in a Broken World: Report of ACC-8 Wales 1990* (London: Church House Publishing, 1990).
53 For Anglican mission in northern Nigeria, see Ward, *Anglicanism*; Kwashi, 'Church of Nigeria'.
54 Okorocha and Kew, *Vision Bearers*; Kwashi, 'Church of Nigeria'; S. A. Fagbemi, 'Territorial Expansionism or Passion for the Lost? A Reflection on 21st-Century Mission with Reference to the Anglican Church of Nigeria', *Transformation* 31 (2014): 69–78. The missionary dioceses created in 1990 were Minna, Kafanchan, Katsina, Sokoto, Makurdi, Maiduguri, Bauchi and Yola.
55 'Provincial Bishops Missionary Conference 2008', 2008, available at http://dioceseoflagoswest.org/Archive/MissionaryConference/index.html; Kwashi, 'Church of Nigeria'.
56 J. A. Omoyajowo, *The Anglican Church of Nigeria* (Lagos: Macmillan Nigerian Publishers, 1994), cited in Fagbemi, 'Territorial Expansionism': 74.
57 Fagbemi, 'Territorial Expansionism': 74.
58 Ibid.
59 M. M. Dogo, 'Anglican Diocese of Kafanchan', available at http://anglicankafanchan.blogspot.co.uk/p/assistance-project.html accessed 20 July 2015.
60 O. Ekpewu, 'Introducing the Missionary Diocese of Damaturu (Anglican Communion)', 2014, available at http://www.anglicandiocesedamaturu.com/our-history.html.
61 T. Falola and M. Heaton, *A History of Nigeria* (Cambridge: Cambridge University Press, 2008): 181.
62 Ibid.: 236–42.
63 Interview with Solomon Akanbi, 24 July 2015.
64 '10 Years of DLW: The Future Starts from Here', *Kerygma*, January 2010: 8–9, available at http://www.dioceseoflagoswest.org/Download/kerygma%20January%202010.pdf.
65 Interview with Solomon Akanbi, 24 July 2015; Diocese of Ife, 'Archdeaconries', 2012, available at http://dioceseofife.org/archdeaconries.php; Diocese of Ife, 'History of the Diocese', 2012, available at http://dioceseofife.org/history3.php.
66 Interview with Solomon Akanbi, 24 July 2015; Fagbemi, 'Territorial Expansionism': 15.
67 Interview with Solomon Akanbi, 24 July 2015; P. Onwubuariri, 'Nine New Missionary Dioceses for Nigeria', *Church of Nigeria News*, 5 October 2004, available at http://www.anglicannews.org/news/2004/10/nine-new-missionary-dioceses-for-nigeria.aspx.
68 Bishop P. Adeyemo, 'Bishop's Charge Delivered to the First Session of the Second Synod', Cathedral Church of St. Paul, Omu-Aran, Kwara State, 11–13 October 2012.
69 '10 Years of DLW: The Future Starts from Here', *Kerygma*, January 2010, 8–9, available at http://www.dioceseoflagoswest.org/Download/kerygma%20January%202010.pdf.
70 Interview with Solomon Akanbi, 24 July 2015; Fagbemi, 'Territorial Expansionism': 77.
71 Interview with Martin Odidi, 11 June 2015.
72 Ibid.
73 B. Kwashi, *The Mission of Evangelism* (Jos: Pastoral Publications of the Anglican Diocese of Jos, 1997), available at http://anglicandioceseofjos.com/new/files/2713/5151/9903/Mission_of_Evangelism.pdf.
74 A. Sanusi, *Gloria! The Archbishop's Wife* (Lakewood: Hippo Books, 2014).
75 Information available at http://anglicandioceseofjos.com/new/.
76 For example, clergy in the Diocese of Jos are largely of Igbo and Yoruba descent.

77 Interview with Solomon Akanbi, 24 July 2015; G. Onayiga, 'Akinola's Primacy: The Journey So Far', *Nigeria Guardian*, 30 August 2009, available at http://anglicanmainstream. org/akinolas-primacy-the-journey-so-far/.

78 Diocese of Lagos, 'Directorates', 2013, available at http://www.dioceseoflagos.org/?/ page/directorates/.

79 Interview with Solomon Akanbi, 24 July 2015.

80 'The Diocesan Commission on Foreign and Local Missions', available at http:// anglicandiocesejos.org/missions/local-missions/.

81 'Diocesan Mission Team', Jos diocese, available at http://anglicandioceseofjos.com/ new/index.php/about/; 'NIGERIA: Anglican Province Now Over 25 Million in Unique Discipleship Program', *Orthodox Anglicanism*, 16 April 2008, available at http:// orthodoxanglicanism.blogspot.co.uk/2008/04/113.html.

82 J. Idowu-Fearon, 'Rural Church Planting and Urban Church Growth', 1 October 2012, available at http://www.anglicandioceseofkaduna.org/news03.php; J. Idowu-Fearon, 'The Presidential Address from the 1st Session of the 20th Synod of the Diocese of Kaduna', 3 June 2015, available at http://anglicandioceseofkaduna.org/blog/ the-presidential-address-from-the-1st-session-of-the-20th-synod-of-the-diocese-of-kaduna/.

83 J. Idowu-Fearon, 'The Presidential Address'.

84 Dioceses of Ibadan North, 'Missions College (NICOM)', 2012, available at http://www. ibadannorthdiocese.org/missioncollege.html.

85 Adebogun, 'Anglican Church of Nigeria'.

86 K. Okeke, 'Church of Nigeria Missionary Society (CNMS) – Mission Arm of the Church of Nigeria', 4 February 2010, available at http://www.anglicancommunion. org/ministry/mission/ecgi/documents/church _of_nigeria_missionary_society.pdf.

87 Ibid.

88 Sanusi, *Gloria*.

89 'The Anglican Missions in Jos Diocese, 1980 to 1992', available at http://anglicandiocesejos. org/about-us/history-2/.

90 C. Cox and C. Butcher, *Cox's Book of Modern Saints and Martyrs* (London: Continuum, 2006): 107.

91 J. Idowu-Fearon, 'Rural Church Planting'.

92 'Commonwealth Fellowship Shares Education Skills and Experience across the Communion', 19 June 2015, available at http://www.anglicanalliance.org/news/20284/ commonwealth-fellowship-shares-education-skills-and-experience-across-the-communion.

93 Interview with Martin Odidi, 11 June 2015; I. Sabera, 'Anglican School in Nigeria More Welcoming towards Muslim Students', *ACNS*, 4 June 2015, available at http:// www.anglicannews.org/news/2015/06/anglican-school-in-nigeria-more-welcoming-towards-muslim-students.aspx.

94 Onayiga, 'Akinola's Primacy'.

95 '2015 Synod Church', available at http://egbaanglicandiocese.org.ng/2015-synod-charge, no date.

96 S. Awoniyi, 'Poverty and Christian Welfare Scheme: Evidence from the Church of Nigeria (Anglican Communion) Osun State, Nigeria', *Journal of Arts and Humanities* 4 (2015): 74–91.

97 J. Idowu-Fearon, 'News from Kaduna Diocese', 27 June 2011, available at http:// anglicandioceseofkaduna.org/blog/news-from-kaduna-diocese/.

98 Idowu-Fearon, 'News from Kaduna Diocese'.

99 'Improving Community Health', Plateau State, Diocese of Jos, available at http://www. anglicanalliance.org/projects/project/62.

100 Nine states have instituted full Sharia. Three states (Kaduna, Niger and Gombe) have instituted Sharia in areas with large Muslim populations.

101 C. Imo, 'Evangelicals, Muslims, and Democracy: With Particular Reference to the Declaration of Sharia in Northern Nigeria', in T. O. Ranger (ed.), *Evangelical Christianity and Democracy in Africa* (Oxford: Oxford University Press, 2008): 37–66.

102 Christian Solidarity Worldwide, 'Universal Periodic Review – 17th Session, CSW (Joint Submission) – Stakeholder Submission, Federal Republic of Nigeria', March 2013: 1–7. Available at: http://www.stefanus.no/filestore/Rapporter_notater_blader_etc/NigeriaCSWreport2013.pdf.

103 Interview with Kefas Tangan, 17 July 2013; interview with Dr. Khataza Gondwe, London, 16 July 2013.

104 A. Adesoji, 'The Boko Haram Uprising and Islamic Revivalism in Nigeria', *Africa Spectrum* 45 (2010): 95–108.

105 Christian Solidarity Worldwide, 'Universal Periodic Review'; interview with Kefas Tangan, 17 July 2013.

106 'Church of Nigeria Anglican Communion Fact Finding Report of Some Dioceses', Report of committee set up by the Primate in 2013.

107 C. Harris, 'Transformative Education in Violent Contexts: Working with Muslim and Christian Youth in Kaduna, Nigeria', *IDS Bulletin* 40 (May 2009): 34–40.

108 Imo, 'Evangelicals'.

109 Human Rights Watch, '"They Do Not Own This Place": Government Discrimination against "Non-indigenes" in Nigeria', *Human Rights Watch* 18, no. 3 (April 2006): 1–65; C. Harris, 'Gender and Religion in Conflict and Post Conflicts: The Cases of Tajikistan, Northern Uganda, Northern Nigeria', Paper presented at the DSA-EADI joint conference, 'Rethinking Development in an Age of Scarcity and Uncertainty: New Values, Voices and Alliances for Increased Resilience', University of York, 20 September 2011.

110 A. Higazi, 'The Jos Crisis: A Recurrent Nigerian Tragedy', Discussion Paper, No. 2, January 2011; P. Ostien, 'Jonah Jang and the Jasawa: Ethno-Religious Conflict in Jos, Nigeria', *Muslim-Christian Relations in Africa* (August 2009): 1–42, available at http://www.sharia-in-africa.net/media/publications/ethno-religious-conflict-in-Jos-Nigeria/Ostien_Jos.pdf; Human Rights Watch, 'They Do Not Own This Place'.

111 J.B. Ejobowah, 'Ethnic Conflict and Cooperation: Assessing Citizenship in Nigerian Federalism', *Publius* 43 (2013): 728–47.

112 Ostien, 'Jonah Jang': 10–11.

113 Higazi, 'Jos Crisis': 9.

114 Interview with Martin Odidi, 11 June 2015; 'Jos East Archdeaconry Synod Report Presented to the Third Session of the Eleventh Synod of the Anglican Diocese Of Jos', available at http://anglicandioceseofjos.com/new/files/7613/5468/6803/Jos_east.pdf; Chris Sugden, 'The Church of Nigeria – The Martyr Church of the Anglican Communion in the 21st Century', 28 December 2012, available at http://www.anglican-mainstream.net/2012/12/28/the-church-of-nigeria-the-martyr-church-of-the-anglican-communion-in-the-21st-century/.

115 Cox and Butcher, *Cox's Book of Modern Saints*; Kwashi, 'Bearing Witness to the Love of Christ with People of other Faiths', available at http://anglicandioceseofjos.com/new/files/6713/5151/9573/BEARING_WITNESS_TO_THE_LOVE_OF_CHRIST.._WITH_PEOPLE_OF_OTHER_FAITHS_XXX.pdf.

116 Interview with Kefas Tangan, 17 July 2013.

5   Congo

Yossa Way with Emma Wild-Wood

Introduction

This article examines the growth of the Anglican Church of Congo (EAC) which experienced significant growth from 1992 as an independent province, aided by having the correct structures in place and a political situation more conducive to church growth. Indeed, the appeal to utaratibu (order) as a valued attribute of Anglican worship and structure aided expansion in a number of ways both locally and nationally. The Church has grown in a situation of chronic poverty and instability, exacerbated by a series of wars from 1996 and local conflicts in the Democratic Republic of Congo (DRC) that continue until the present day. War has taken its toll on the infrastructure of the Church and challenged its mission and pastoral care. It has also been instrumental in its spread, through refugees, into neighbouring countries.

Taking an historical and dialectical approach, we use written documents, photographs, films and video cassettes. Interviews provide data unobtainable from other sources. Africans often prefer to express themselves verbally than to commit their opinions to writing, as Rachid Yakani said, '. . . rather give me a hoe to cultivate a field than give me a pen to compose a letter'.[1] Participant observation has played a role since the author is a member of the Anglican Church. Church structure and institutions are both instruments in church growth in Congo and, in a country where statistics are often unrecorded or unreliable, markers of that growth. The development of parishes in new areas is the surest marker of growth, since membership statistics are not always accurate. In Congo parishes are spread over large areas and are composed of several sub-parishes and chapels. To establish a university or a diocese demands a certain provincial or regional capacity. Whilst resources often appear inadequate, the establishment of institutional structures can be read as points of pride, signs of hope in God's provision and signals of missionary intent to serve the country alongside the many other denominations that operate in DR Congo.

The article explains a number of elements deemed to promote the Church's spread from a small area on the eastern border across the vast country and into Congo-Brazzaville. It starts by delineating the origins of the Church in the DRC, and concludes by reflecting on the present situation of the Church.

The origins of the Eglise Anglicane du Congo

Congo has experienced successive waves of evangelisation from Anglican churches in the neighbouring countries of Uganda, Zambia and Rwanda, of which the former two were British colonies. The missionary activity, trade and colonisation of the nineteenth century led to the creation of Anglican churches in many areas of the world. The political and economic position of Great Britain in this époque encouraged the expansion of its established church, not only in its own colonies but in other corners of the world. Britons across the world influenced the adoption of the title 'Anglican' for those churches who pastorally and canonically connected with Canterbury. Whilst British missionaries were often at work before the development of an imperial presence, colonial power made England a significant centre for the radiation of Christianity. The Ugandan influence on Congo is the oldest and most significant. Whilst Anglicans came from Zambia to Lubumbashi in the 1950s and from Rwanda to the Goma area about 1975, Ugandan evangelists brought Anglicanism to the Boga area in 1896. Uganda had embraced Christianity from 1877 and both Anglican and Catholic Christians spread their faith rapidly through the region.

The Anglican Church in Boga

The Boga area is about 120km south of Bunia, the centre of the Ituri province. The Semiliki plain to the east and south-east of the region acts as a natural border between Congo and Uganda. The natural frontiers insisted upon by the Berlin conference separated related ethnic groups into different colonial polities, with religious, economic and cultural consequences.[2] Some ethnic groups were divided across two or more countries. The inhabitants of Boga, the Banyamboga, were originally Bahuma pastoralists from the Kingdom of Bunyoro Kitara, Uganda, who migrated into the region probably towards the end of the sixteenth century, although the mixing of peoples over centuries has obscured a detailed history of their settlement.[3] Boga became part of Congo in 1910 and the convention of London of 3 February 1915, definitively fixed the border between eastern Congo and Uganda. Political frontiers were also religious frontiers: Roman Catholicism was ascendant in the Belgium Congo; in Uganda, despite a large Catholic presence, the Anglican Church was politically influential.[4]

The first evangelism of Boga

Anglican evangelisation of Boga took place in two waves. In 1894 the second king of the dynasty of Boga, Paulo Tabaro II, crossed the Semiliki River to visit his colleague, Kasagama of Toro, Uganda, intending to solicit the protection of Britain over his territory.[5] Kasagama spoke to him of the new religious practices in Toro and which encouraged literacy in his population. Enthused by this information, Chief Tabaro invited Ugandan evangelists to come to work in Boga. Immediately, two evangelists, Petero Nsubuga and Sedulaka Makwata, were sent. These pioneers of Anglicanism were warmly welcomed by Chief Tabaro and they constructed a chapel near to the royal court. However, within the year they were forced to leave the area and return to Uganda. According to Tibenderana Yakobo, they were proud and unwilling to work in the fields, a task reserved in Buganda for the lower classes, women and slaves. The strangers also refused to drink the local brew that everyone was expected to take at the royal court. So the chief commanded that his subjects should not provide food to the catechists until they left the area. Another hypothesis suggests that these first missionaries were obliged to turn back because the chief became hostile, anxious that the new religion swept away ancestral customs and consequently made his kingdom fragile. As Pirotte says, 'the encounter between Christianity and the diversity of cultures and religions is sometimes seen as a rupture. . . . Because mission is a (disturbing) announcement, and also a conflict (which necessitates opponents) for the kingdom of God'.[6] The chief may have invented excuses to make the visitors leave, a view Titre Ande supports.[7]

These pioneers were obliged to leave the mission field because they were unable to adapt to the culture of the area. They considered themselves to be superior to those they were evangelising. They adopted an evangelisation model that Pirotte calls 'the importation–imposition model'.[8] Effectively they brought the Gospel and their culture. They created a monolithic and centralised church without appreciating Christian experiences nourished by the riches of local traditions. Constructing the chapel in the royal court indicates the intention, common among other Ganda evangelists, to prioritise the conversion of the chief and then benefit from his influence to gain adherences among his subjects for the new religion. Perhaps they also thought that their role consisted only of preaching the Gospel and that the follow-up should be left to other Christians, an expectation that is often evident in the African church today. Despite the departure of the evangelists, the Gospel had touched the hearts of some in Boga and the church was born in that place. More enterprising catechists were able to continue the mission. Apolo Kivebulaya, today considered the founder of the EAC, was the next choice.

The second evangelism in Boga

Church Missionary Society (CMS) missionary A. B. Fisher saw in Apolo a faithful and steadfast catechist so, with Sedulaka Zabunamakwata, he was sent to continue the work abandoned by his predecessors. Apolo had been working amongst the Konjo in the foothills of the Rwenzori and had seen the Semiliki escarpment from afar and the dense forest beyond. His biographer suggests that he was nervous of working in the forest.[9] In December 1896 he crossed the Semiliki with a different evangelistic strategy in mind. In his luggage he had some books, a Bible and a hoe. The journey was made on foot and even in the dry season took at least four days from Fort Portal to Boga.[10] When he arrived in Boga the chief saw his hoe and declared 'here comes a man who is going to conquer'.[11] He was content that Apolo was not going to be a burden on the community. He happily told his subjects to provide for Apolo's needs, saying that they would feed him until his own field was ready.[12] Apolo immediately set about cultivating his field and building a house.

The expectation of unsalaried ministry continues until today in the Anglican Church of Congo. From its inception the EAC has not wanted to talk about ministerial stipends. Apart from the bishops and certain department directors who receive their monthly stipend from abroad, the pastors of the Church are rarely remunerated and this remains a challenge for the Church. They occasionally receive what is called 'soap', a financial aid received when possible. As Etsa Lombomba says, they work because of their vocation, it's not a lucrative employment for them; he signs a contract with God, his employer.[13] The pastors seem resigned to this situation; Mbabiri Zunguluka says, 'we don't have a salary, but we live in peace more than other people'.[14] Pastors in the EAC are generally in good health, especially in rural locations. There is some consolation in the fact that they are living similarly to the majority of the Congolese population who have little or no regular income.

The ecclesiological approach of Apolo was different from his contemporaries Simon Kimbangu and William Wade Harris, who founded African churches in particular African circumstances. They led huge crowds in their movements. Apolo's commitment to the Church of Uganda and beyond that to the Church of England, through CMS, meant that he did not act like the founders of African Initiated Churches. Yet Apolo felt responsible for the EAC and had a large vision of Anglican evangelisation through what is now the DRC.

After a ministry of about 40 years Apolo was diagnosed with a heart problem and advised that he should take three months of rest. Apolo, feeling that death was close, asked that he be taken straight away to Boga, so that he would amongst his own and receive a good burial. He died there on the 30th May 1933 at 20.45. Before he died, he requested that he be buried with his head towards the west, contrary to the custom of the area, which expected that the dead be buried with the head eastwards. In insisting on this cultural change, Apolo was predicting that the mission he had inaugurated at Boga would progress westwards, among the pygmies of the forest and beyond, in order to win the extent of the DRC. Perhaps that is what he understood by well-buried.[15]

This missionary vision is already accomplished. The EAC has spread across the length of the country and has gone beyond the prophecy of the missionary because she has crossed the river Congo and from 1996 has been planted in Congo-Brazzaville. Rwandan Hutu refugees established their own Anglican congregations in Congo-Brazzaville from 1996 and then made contact with the EAC in Kinshasa. Ven Banzunzi, a priest in Kinshasa but originally from Congo-Brazzaville, was sent as archdeacon to organise the church there. He and a few other native Congolese worked with the Rwandans to develop the Anglican Church in the country. The first indigenous priest, Emmanuel Nimbi Loubassou, was ordained in 2012 after completing a theological degree at the Institut Supérieur Théologique Anglican (ISThA). He works well with the Rwandais priests. His ministry gradually inspires confidence in other Congolese whose numbers grow each year. There are now four parishes spread throughout the country. Since 2013 an assistant bishop has been working in Congo-Brazzaville to prepare a diocese there.

The period of stagnation

Anglicanism remained for many years in the Boga and its environs. It spread in a radius of only 80km from the centre. There were three main reasons: first it was impermissible to act beyond the mission field accorded to CMS during the conference of Edinburgh in 1910; secondly, the Belgium colonial administration, whilst proclaiming freedom of religion, was often hostile to missions that were not Belgian and Catholic; thirdly, the Banyamboga considered Anglicanism as part of their own heritage and the adherents of other ethnic groups like the pagans adhering to Judaism.[16] The catechism and the Book of Common Prayer had been translated into Kihema (Nyoro) and had to be used by neighbouring ethnic groups until 1973 when the prayer book was translated into Swahili, the regional trade language.

To these three principles one can add two others: first there was a lack of indigenous leaders who were prepared to go beyond the mission centre of Boga; secondly, because of the name 'Anglican' the Church was understood as something specifically English, and therefore a foreign thing. When Anglicanism arrived in Aru district in the far north-east of the country evangelists of other confessions did not hesitate to call Anglican evangelists the 'false prophets to whom Christians would follow in the last days'.[17] It's one of the reasons why some countries preferred to use the word 'episcopal'. However, in DRC the appellation 'Anglican' remained out of habit.

The period of expansion

The single parish of Boga, created by Apolo in 1897, had many sub-parishes but it was 40 years before it was divided into two posts, Boga and Kainama, in 1938. Boga was led by Nasani Kabarole and comprised of Boga, Walendu/Bindi and Walese. Limenya Yusufu was posted to Kainama which includes the areas of Wanande, Wanyali, Watalinga, and Mbuti pygmies.[18] Kabarole and Limenya had taken an accelerated theological formation at the college at Mukono, Uganda. They were the first to be ordained deacon, and then priest in 1940. As the number of local clergy grew so did the number of new parishes, like that of Bukiringi parish among the Walendu/Bindi created in 1946, and of Bundingiri among the Walese Vonkutu created in 1947, and Ofayi in 1955, and Kamango among the Amba in 1956.

One of the key figures of the EAC's expansion in DRC is Theodore Lewis. This American employee of the International Development Agency (USAID) in Kinshasa went to Boga in 1969 and found a well organised Anglican church. Returning to Kinshasa, he wrote a report that was widely diffused in Anglican circles. One of the principle complaints in the report was the lack of a diocesan bishop for the church. The question was discussed during a conference of African Anglican archbishops held in Zambia in February 1970. The delegates recommended to the Archbishop of Uganda Erica Sabiti, who was at the same time bishop of the diocese of Rwenzori of which Boga was a part, to proceed with the creation of an Anglican diocese in Congo. Returning to his diocese, the bishop submitted a proposal to the diocesan synod. He then interested CMS in the project and requested an expatriate missionary to take charge of the first diocese. The CMS sent missionary Philip Ridsdale to lead the first Congolese diocese. The inauguration took place on the 9th July 1972. At that time there were 30 clergymen, 25 parishes and 30 chapels. The church of Boga depended upon the Church of Uganda for 84 years until 1980 when a francophone province was created. Whilst all decisions of the church were taken during synods held in Uganda, not only was the administration burdensome because of the distance and lack of communication, but also the concerns of the Congolese Christians were not given priority in the objectives of the diocese.[19]

Events which promoted the spread of the EAC

Francophone autonomy

Developing structures which allowed the Church to operate nationally – rather than in a larger regional group that crossed international boundaries and significant linguistic divisions – was significant in promoting a confident church that was able to attend to its development westwards, across DRC, rather than concerning itself with the affairs of its eastern neighbours.

The EAC had long been part of the Ugandan diocese of Rwenzori with the Anglican churches of Burundi, Rwanda and Congo being part of the single Province of Uganda, inaugurated on 16th April 1961. Leslie W. Brown was the first archbishop. The official language of meetings was English so francophone delegates felt unable to communicate effectively. Sometimes they used an interpreter or relied on local languages like Nyoro or Ganda. To avoid the marginalisation of French speakers a francophone council was created in 1976, but it did not have decision making powers, nor could it cater for the different foci of the French speaking Christians. Thus on 11th May 1980 a francophone province was created, and Ndahura Bezaleri, from Boga, was consecrated first archbishop at Bukavu by Robert Runcie, Archbishop of Canterbury, and Silvanius Wani, Archbishop of Uganda. The new province was called the Province of Burundi, Rwanda and Boga-Zaire.

The formation of a new province encouraged its members to develop Anglicanism in their respective countries. There appears to be a correlation between appropriate macro-structures of Anglicanism and grassroots growth. A separate province gave greater impetus and attention to the appearance of local congregations and permitted their organisation into parishes with an Anglican structure. In Congo churches were planted in Mahagi and Aru in the far north-east of the country. Towards the centre the diocese of Kisangani, which stretches to

Kinshasa, was inaugurated in 1980 under the leadership of its first bishop, Tibafa Mugera. In the south of the country, Katanga diocese, inaugurated in 1986, under the leadership of the first bishop, Mbona Kolini, opened new parishes across the Province of Katanga.

Ndahura died suddenly on Christmas Day 1981 and was replaced by Justin Ndandali on 6th June 1982. As soon as he was inaugurated the new archbishop moved the seat of the province to Butare, Rwanda. Ndandali's tenure was controversial.[20] The third archbishop, enthroned on 9th June 1987, was a Burundian, Samuel Sindamuka. Despite making strides in evangelisation in each of the three countries, relations between them were strained, so during the archiepiscopacy of Sindamuka the province was divided in two: one branch composed of the dioceses of Boga-Zaire, Bukavu, Kisangani and Butara, the second branch composed of the diocese of Buve, Shyira, Gittega, Shaba and Bujumbura.[21] Finally in 1992 the Province of the Church of Burundi, Rwanda and Boga-Zaire split into three new provinces, one for each country. The inauguration of the Congo Province took place in Bunia on 30th May 1992 with the enthronement of Njojo Byankia as the first archbishop. At that point there were five dioceses: Boga, Bukavu, Kisangani, Katanga and Nord-Kivu.

Political independence and the awakening of indigenous missionaries

Structures were in place to maximise growth from 1992. However, long before then a sense of confidence and commitment generated in the post-independence era paved the way for growth. Congo gained its independence from Belgium on 30th June 1960. Noting the departure of expatriates and driven by a sense of freedom, Anglicans felt the need to spread their Church into other regions of the country under the direction of Festo Byakisaka, a Munyamboga and Dean of the Church in Boga, replacing Ugandan E. Waluggyo and CMS missionaries Charles and Beryl Rendle. At the same time Byakisaka solicited the official state recognition of the Church by the Congolese state. This personalité civile was granted by the Presidential Ordinance on 1st December 1960. From now on the Congolese themselves took control of their church. The Belgian regime had not permitted the indigenous church to take control of its affairs; now it was required by the independent state that Congolese run their own churches. On the 30th January 1967 CMS officially transferred its authority and responsibility in matters of finance, administration, medical work and education and the pastoral to the indigenous church in Boga.[22]

When the Church was controlled by expatriates its development was very slow but when the indigenous people took over it saw spectacular expansion. Throughout Congo western missionaries had established a system of dividing geographical areas between them which was intended to avoid competition but which limited denominational growth and sometimes re-enforced tribalism. Even though the Anglican Church in the Boga area was still incorporated into the Rwenzori diocese of Uganda, the majority of the work was done by the church of Boga, herself. In the southern Ituri region new parishes were established, like those of Geti in 1964, Bwakadi in 1965 and Bunyagwa in 1967, where there had only been small chapels before. In 1968 the deanery of Boga became an archdeaconry and Byakisaka, a Munyamboga who had become a canon of the diocese of Rwenzori one year earlier, was made archdeacon. In 1970 other new parishes were created, including Bunia, the Ituri district capital, and Beni, the Beni district capital. In 1970 Butembo Parish was created among the Nande, Vuhozi among the Yira, and Mulobya among the Amba.

Political regimes favourable to evangelisation

The period of 1980 until today is marked by a succession of three different political regimes, that of Mobutu, Laurent Désiré Kabila and the latter's son, Joseph Kabila Kabange, which aided the Church by giving it the freedom to exercise its activities in the country.

On 24th November 1965, Lieutenant-Général Joseph Mobutu, commander in chief of the army, took power and claimed himself President of the Republic, with the help of the USA.[23] Mobutu reinforced his power and legitimacy by gradually dismantling the institutions of the old Republic. All the political parties were dissolved and political activities forbidden. Mobutu continually insisted that African tradition did not permit two chiefs. Thus the Congolese state would have a single national party, the Mouvement Populaire de la Révolution (MPR).

With power centred on one individual Mobutu could rule with impunity. Between 1966 and 1971 a number of cities were renamed, as was the country: it became the Republic of Zaire. In 1973 Mobutu declared that only three churches could exist: the Roman Catholic Church, the Eglise du Christ au Zaire (ECZ) and the Kimbanguist church. All the Protestant confessions, including the Anglican Church, had to incorporate themselves into the ECZ as communautés and not churches.[24] Reuniting all Protestant confessions into one church was intended by Mobutu to give him control over them. There was to be a single legal representative for all the communautés with whom he could cooperate. He also desired a strong Protestant church as a counter-balance to the strength of the Catholic Church which sometimes challenged the regime. For Protestants Mobutu was a necessary evil: his regime permitted them to form an organic unity under the leadership of a single head; furthermore, Protestant numbers increased because all congregations had to belong to state registered communauté. The Communauté Anglicane du Congo (CAC) welcomed a number of denominations who were unable to gain membership of the ECZ as separate entities. This was the case, for example, for the Eglise Libre Protestante au Congo (ELPC) of Kindu, which formed the basis of the present Anglican diocese there, and numerous little revivalist churches in Katanga who became Anglican members around 1972. Thus the Anglican Church grew where there had been little or no prior Anglican presence.

Rural exodus, the internally displaced and the influx of refugees to the country

The migration of the village populations towards the towns has greatly contributed to the expansion of the EAC. It is the same in regard to the internally displaced who leave their area because of war. Refugees from neighbouring countries have also aided the Church's growth in Congo, as Emma Wild-Wood confirms:

> Migration is one of three significant factors in the growth of the Anglican Church throughout Congo. Many Anglicans took advantage of the economic opportunities of the 1960s and moved to urban areas to establish small businesses. They established Anglican chapels as they went. Anglicans from neighbouring Sudan, Uganda, Rwanda and Burundi brought their church tradition with them when they fled conflict in their own countries and influenced the villages in which they settled. A number of the migrants were influenced by the East African Revival and placed great emphasis on evangelism.[25]

Commercial activities, a succession of wars and insecurity in certain places provoked internal migration. Very often such people did not abandon their religious identity. This is the case, for example, of the implantation of Anglicanism at Aru and Mahagi, two territories in the very north-east of Congo. The share 200km of border with Uganda and the same ethnic groups – Kakwa, Lugbara and Alur – live on both sides and move freely across the national boundary. Anglicanism was already being introduced to the area through a passive diffusion, well before its official implantation. Protestant Congolese who went to Uganda would pray in the Church of Uganda and Ugandans who came to Congo prayed in one or other member of the ECZ, particularly the largest communauté of the area, the Communauté Evangélique au centre de l'Afrique (CECAC 20), installed by the African Inland Mission (AIM).

Many Congolese Kakwa, Lugbara and Alur had emigrated to Uganda in search of employment or to escape the yoke of the Belgian colonists. The fall of dictator Idi Amin Dada in 1979 caused the rapid return of these Congolese migrants in large numbers. The returnees, who were already members of the Church of Uganda, joined local Protestant churches, especially CECA 20, because there was no Anglican church in the area. However, the relationship between the new-comers and the CECA 20 faithful was not good. The terms 'them' and 'us' were frequently used to distinguish one from the other. Also liturgical practice, admission to the sacraments and the ecclesiological system were different. Yonatana Mandela said, 'I could not put up with the way in which we were treated by CECA20 members, especially the insistence on rebaptising all those who had been baptised by aspersion'.[26] It took some time before the returnees realised there was an Anglican church in Congo. Eventually, they invited the Bishop of Boga diocese to open the Anglican church in the area. The church in Mahagi was formally opened on 24th December 1979 and Aru church was opened on 13th March 1982. It is noticeable that Anglicanism entered Aru and Mahagi territories through the initiative of lay people who had become Anglicans in Uganda. Their church now has its own diocese.

The creation of dioceses

The creation of the first diocese in 1972 detonated evangelistic efforts to develop the Church still further. Among the principal actors of the expansion of Anglicanism in Congo is the first bishop of Boga, Philip Ridsdale, with the financial and material support of the Church Missionary Society, UK. Bishop Ridsdale greatly contributed to the growth of the Church until his death. His work continues through the UK-based Congo Church Association (CCA) which he created and which remains the main partner of the EAC. The diocese of Boga is the progenitor of all the other dioceses in the country. The chronology of their creation is as follows: Bukavu diocese in 1976, Kisangani in 1980, Katanga in 1986, North-Kivu in 1992, Kindu in 1997, Kinshasa in 2003, Aru in 2005 and finally Kasai in 2012. The diocese of Katanga has already sent an assistant bishop to Kalemie near Lake Tanganyika with the intention of creating another diocese here. The diocese of Kinshasa has similarly sent an assistant bishop to Congo-Brazzaville with the same vision. As the statistical tables below show, the Church continues its expansion in Congo and the number of new members continues to grow.

The creation of the Anglican University of Congo

The need to form pastors has been important since the beginning of the Anglican mission in Congo. The number of western missionaries of CMS was insufficient to train leaders of the Church. Under the inspiration of Archbishop Ndahura Bezaleri, the National Council of the Church created an Interdiocesan Theological Institute (ITI) in 1980. The ITI was established in Bukavu and only manage to train a single in take. In October 1981 Bezaleri created the Institut Supérieur Théologique Anglican (ISThA), which functioned from the archbishop's garage. The same garage served as chapel, dormitory and canteen for the students. ISThA suffered a number of difficulties in Bukavu: many of the academic and administrative staff came from other churches, especially the Communauté Baptiste au Centre de l'Afrique (CBCA) and the Roman Catholic Church. The full-time staff were overburdened holding several posts, teaching and carrying out administration. This over-working continues today as Anglican employees wear many hats. This modus operandi, which appears less costly for the Church, often has unsatisfactory results. After only a year the institute closed because of the lack of finances, the sudden death of Ndahura and the transfer of the site of the legal representative of the Church from Bukavu to Bunia.

Concerned for the formation of the leaders of the Church, the National Council of the Church, which met in Lubumbashi, in 1986 decided to reopen ISThA at Bunia. Thus ISThA was re-established in 1988 and has functioned for over 20 years, providing the undergraduate course in theology as well as a Centre for Biblical formation for those without the qualifications for higher education. However, because of financial constraints ISThA only produced about ten graduates in theology every year: a drop in the ocean when compared with the need! In order to respond better to the needs of the population the Administrative Council of ISThA decided to transform the institute into a university, named the Anglican University of Congo (UAC). In October 2010 the university opened its doors with six faculties: Theology, Psychology and Educational Science, Engineering, Economy and Management, Sciences and Development. With the transformation of the college into a university the number of students, which was always about 30, rose to 300 and keeps rising. UAC is one of the significant universities of the town of Buna; she is also an instrument for the mission of the Anglican Church of Congo. She contributes to the growth of the Church.

Utaratibu

'Bila Utaratibu hatutaendelea', declared the Archbishop, 'without order we won't progress'.[27] Utaratibu is Swahili for 'order', or 'respect for instructions, directives and for established structures'. It can be understood as the opposite of laissez-faire or disorder. The notion of utaratibu is as applicable to the liturgy as to the general administration of the Church. As an example, on 17th June 2013, Revd. Munganga Kyamulesere, coordinator of schools of Boga Diocese, was invited to speak at Gbanday sub-parish, Bunia, about the utaratibu of the Church. After his talk the discussion turned to the necessary elements of the service, respect for the start time of the service (the end time was ignored!) and the need to stay until the final benediction.

The EAC interprets the notions of utaratibu as a strategy to conserve unity. Other Protestant churches of Congo split frequently to create new denominations; but this is not the case for the EAC because the administrative structure is cemented by utaratibu. Dirokpa Balufuga noted that it was not possible for a member of the EAC to create another Anglican church in the country because it would be outside the structure of the Anglican Communion. 'Our church is a church of order'.[28] Thus for the leaders of the Anglican Church, utaratibu guarantees not only the unity of the Church but also ensures the survival of ecclesiastical structures at all levels. Archdeacon Bezaleri Kahigwa, speaking to the church leaders of his archdeaconry, reminded them that 'the submission to hierarchical order is a characteristic of a good collaborator'.[29] Emma Wild-Wood has also noted this trait: 'the EAC attempted to preserve unity through respect for utaratibu of the Prayer Book and the hierarchy of church workers'.[30] Respect for utaratibu in church administration is a form of protection and a way of encouraging expansion of Anglicanism in Congo.

The present situation in the Anglican Church of Congo

The Church has nine dioceses, spread across Congo and also covering a large part of Congo-Brazzaville. There is an archbishop who is also Bishop of Kinshasa and Primate of the Province. There are eight diocesan bishops and two assistant bishops. The bishops are as follows: for Boga, William Bahemuka Mugenyi; for Bukavu, Sylvestre Bahati Bali-Busane; for Kisangani,

Lambert Funga Botolome; for Katanga, Corneille Kasima Muno; for Nord-Kivu, Adolphe Isesomo Muhindo; for Kindu, Zacharie Masimango Katanda; for Kinshasa, Henri Isingoma Kahwa; for Aru, Dr. Georges Titre Ande; for Kasai, Marcel Kapinga

It is likely that the number of members has decreased in the east of the country because of the long years of conflict in this area. Below are the statistics for the dioceses in tabular form:

Table 5.1 Membership and structure of the Anglican Church in Congo

N°	Diocese	Established	Archdeaconry	Parishes	Clergy	Members
01	Boga	1972	06	28	52	34,000
02	Bukavu	1976	08	88	89	75,388
03	Kisangani	1980	12	62	65	16,520
04	Katanga	1986	08	34	32	9,545
05	Nord-Kivu	1992	15	64	143	42,672
06	Kindu	1997	09	49	57	20,000
07	Kinshasa	2003	02	10	26	2,244
08	Aru	2005	04	24	41	31,000
09	Kasai	2012	09	65	40	5,339
	Total		73	424	545	236,708

Source: Figures come from L' Eglise Anglicane du Congo

The table (5.1) shows that for 236,708 members there are 545 pastors, and about 434 members per pastor. Some dioceses have more pastors than others relative to the number of members. The general image of the province is one of inequality in organisation. Because of the autonomy of each diocese there is little mechanism for changing this, although the Church should be capable of sending missionaries from one diocese to another as interdiocesan missionaries if it could contemplate such a missional strategy.

Another table (5.2) suggests that in five years the province has added 100 new parishes, ordained 100 new pastors and has received 81,383 new members (about 16,276 a year). So, despite difficulties, the Church continues to develop.

Table 5.2 Growth in church numbers between 2007 and 2012 in Congo

Year	Parishes	Clergy	Members
2007	324	445	155,325
2012	424	545	236,708
Growth in 5 years	100	100	81,383

Source: Figures come from L' Eglise Anglicane du Congo

The main challenges

As Mushila Nyamankank has noted, Africa has experienced injuries of all kinds: the slave trade, colonial and post-colonial violence, unjust use of resources, unequal development of societies and so on.[31] In Congo there are complaints from the colonial era, from the second Republic and the present daily complaints, one against another. The 1990s saw a change in the political landscape in central Africa with the wave of democratisation, the disappearance of the one-party regimes and the development of competitive, multi-party political systems. For Congo it also saw prolonged war. And today, the democratic transition in Africa is being eroded. Cunning leaders pass themselves off as democrats whilst in reality they are intolerant dictators who regard their own interests above everything.[32] Congolese society continues to stagnate in misery: she faces a general deterioration of quality of life, insufficient means for the education of young people, deficiency of health services ensuring the persistence of endemic disease, fear of war, sexual violence and rape, the daily spectacle of refugees and displaced people, murder and theft, especially in the eastern region.

According to Beni Bataaga, the Church has not known how properly to play its role as a source of healing for individuals and societies. Indeed, it is sometimes part of the problem instead of bringing a solution. Many of the leaders of the Church show indifference when faced with current issues in Congolese society and are considered to contribute to the perennial national misery and to comply with the oppressive regime.[33] To give one example, during the ethnic conflict in Ituri in 2002–2003, the Church planted in the heart of an ethnic group the tendency to see the Church on its side. One pastor told us that the militia confessed before the church leaders and asked for prayer before going to attack the other ethnic group. During services there was a tendency to pray that God would grant victory to the militia who defended them. If they heard that members of the enemy group were massacred it was considered good news by everybody, including the local church.[34] The language was destructive: the declarations of the members of the ethnic groups were partial, each one demonised the other and justified the actions of their own group against the other. Kabona Kairu noted how lies abounded during the war.[35]

Conscious of its mission in the world and in contrition for its often uncertain stance during the wars from 1996, the EAC created in 2004 a department for Evangelisation, Peace and Reconciliation. Through this department the Church was actively involved in the reconciliation process at all levels. Masimango Katanda cites as an example the role played by the EAC to bring to an end the ethnic war between the Hema and Giti in Ituri.[36] The first meeting was held in Nairobi 17th–18th August 2004, bringing together ten delegates: five Ngiti representatives led by Archdeacon Move Karabutege, and five Hema representatives led by Bishop Njojo Byankia. This first meeting opened the door for a larger meeting held in Bunia on 19th September 2004 with the support of Eben-Ezer

Ministry and brought together 105 delegates from the two warring ethnic groups and certain neutral mediators including myself. Since this encounter, relations between the two groups have returned to normal, which confirms the affirmation of John Paul II who said that the best method for peace is dialogue and solidarity rather than the battle to destroy one's enemy by war.[37]

Despite the continuing insecurity, particularly in the east of the Congo, churches, local and international NGOs have attempted to aid the victims of war, violence and illness. In Butembo, for example, the Anglican Church has supported Compassion Orphanage, which was started by Mbambu and her husband Emmanuel, who adopted 40 children in their own home. Another 40 children have been adopted by concerned families. The parents of these children were killed in the war or died from AIDS. A school and health centre were built to care for the orphans, and another 100 extremely vulnerable children and women in the local community. It also supports many women victims of violence.[38]

On 1st December 2013 leaders of the Anglican and Roman Catholic churches in DR Congo, Rwanda and Burundi gathered in Goma, to launch a Campaign for Peace in the Great Lakes Region. The campaign works at every level, with local populations, especially youth, and also with the respective governments, in initiatives that promote peace, justice and reconciliation and bring transformation to the region. This collaboration between Anglican and Catholic churches and the three countries is unprecedented, and there is the hope that other churches will join in too. Micah 6 v 8 is a key text in the campaign: 'He has showed you, O man, what is good. And what does the Lord require of you? To act justly and to love mercy and to walk humbly with your God'.[39]

There is always more that can be done. The acceptance of self and a proper perception of reality are important attributes:[40] often Africans pretend that all is well. One greets 'How are you?' and the reply is 'Fine' even when it's far from fine. It's with difficulty that one discovers that the person hadn't eaten the previous day, or their child is ill, or they haven't been paid for two months, and so on. Even if nothing is working well in the business of the Church, often Congolese prefer to hide the reality and give false report. This inhibits the growth of the Church. The development offices in each diocese aim to assess real needs and provide skills and resources. Claudaline Mukanirwa in Goma, for example, runs a tailoring workshop for female victims of violence (often rejected by their partners) in order that they might regain their dignity and gain a livelihood. Claudaline also employs nine women in her own sewing workshop. Work ennobles yet working well is one of the biggest challenges for the improvement of life in Africa in general and DRC in particular. By working, the expectations of foreign aid will steadily disappear. By their own efforts Africans will be autonomous, free from dependence, able to make their own decisions and engage in interdependent relationships. On a macro-level Claudaline and her husband, Revd. Desiré, facilitate this interdependence by counselling couples affected by sexual violence.[41]

Conclusion

The EAC started in 1896 and was under the jurisdiction of the Ugandan Church for 84 years. In 1980 it became a province with the Church in Rwanda and Burundi. Since that date the development of the Church has accelerated, and even more so since 1992 when it became an autonomous province. However, the challenges are innumerable and may hinder its growth. In order to meet these challenges, the EAC must develop a new paradigm of spirituality, an emancipatory, humane spirituality for every human being.

Notes

1　Interview with development worker and water engineer Bureau de Développement Communautaire (BDC) de Boga, Kumuru, 25 September 1989.

2　Yossa Way's own ethnic group, the Kakwa, are found in Congo, South Sudan and Uganda.

3　J. Ki-Zerbo, *Histoire de l'Afrique noire, d'hier à demain* (Paris: Hatier, 1978): 181.

4　Y. Way, 'La pensée sociale de l'Eglise Anglicane du Congo. Approche missiologique, Mémoire de DEA, Kinshasa, Université Protestante au Congo', 2008: 11–12.

5　Eglise Anglicane du Zaire, *Kwa Imani Apolo: Maisha ya Apolo Kivebulaya* (Gateshead, Tyne and Wear: Paradigm Print, 1986): 4.

6　J. Pirotte, *Résistances à l'évangélisation. Interprétations historiques et enjeux théologiques* (Paris: Karthala, 2004): 29–39 (translation ours).

7　T. Ande, *Leadership and Authority: Bula Matari and Life-Community Ecclesiology in Congo* (Oxford: Regnum, 2010).

8　Pirotte, *Résistances*: 15–22.

9　Eglise Anglicane du Zaire, *Kwa Imani Apolo*: 4.

10　Revd B. Tito, sermon delivered on St Apolo's day, 30 May 1990.

11　A. Luck, *African Saint: The Story of Apolo Kivebulaya* (London: SCM Press, 1963): 71.

12　Eglise Anglicane du Zaire, *Kwa Imani Apolo*: 6.

13　Interview with the Diocesan Secretary of Kinshasa, 30 May 2012.

14　Pastor of Boga parish, in conversation with J. Acheson, Boga, 3 November 1990.

15　E. Wild-Wood, *Migration and Christian Identity in Congo (DRC)* (Leiden: Brill, 2008): 203–5.

16　D. Balufuga, 'Liturgie anglicane et inculturation hier, aujourd'hui et demain, regard sur la célébration eucharistique en République démocratique du Congo' (PhD thesis; Laval University, Quebec, 2001): 36.

17　K. Baguma, Archdeacon of Aru, quoted in Wild-Wood, *Migration*: 118.

18　Interview with D. Balufuga, Archbishop of PEAC, Kinshasa, 31 January 2008.

19　Interview with N. Byankia, second bishop of the Diocese of Boga and first Archevêque of the PEAC, 30 May 1992.

20　'Pendant les cinq ans de règne de Mgr Ndandali nous avons eu de problèmes durant toutes nos réunions, tant au collège des évêques qu'au conseil exécutif. Le climat dans lequel nous avons travaillé ne nous a pas permis de collaborer dans un climat d'amour et de compréhension mutuelle' ('Province Francophone de l'Eglise du Burundi, Rwanda et Boga-Zaire; Rapport préparatoire pour la consultation des partenaires en mission [Kigali, September 1989]: 21).

21　Ibid.: 20.

22　N. Bezaleri, *Mémoire*: 99.

23　G. Nzongola-Ntalaja, *The Congo from Leopold to Kabila: A People's History* (London: Zed Books, 2002): 141–6.

24　At this stage Islam was not large enough to gain attention from the political system.

25　Interview with N. Byankia, 30 May 1992.

26 Interview with Y. Mandela, member of Aru parish, Aru, 25 June 2013.
27 Spoken by I. Kahwa, Archbishop of the Province de l'Eglise Anglicane du Congo, during the Provincial Synod, Kinshasa, 24–29 June 2012.
28 Interview with D. Balufuga, former Archbishop of the PEAC, Kinshasa, 10 February 2008.
29 Interview with B. Kahigwa, Bunia, 6 July 2013.
30 Wild-Wood, *Migration*: 113.
31 M. Nyamankank, 'Fondements théologique et éthique des droits humains', *RCTP* 14–15 (2001–2002): 279.
32 E. C. Goma-Foutou, 'Construire un nouveau paradigme de paix dans la sous région d'Afrique Centrale, séminaire organisé à l'Institut Vie et Paix, Brazzaville, du 13 au 15 septembre 2007': 2.
33 Interview with Beni Bataaga, Bunia, 27 December 2012. Similar accusations have been levelled at church leaders in Haiti in 1991 and Rwanda after 1994. P. Russ, *Healing Wounded History: Reconciling Peoples and Restoring Places* (Cleveland: Pilgrim Press, 2001): 78–9.
34 Anonymous, Bunia, 5 January 2006.
35 Interview with K. Kairu, Pastor of Kasenyi Parish, Bunia, 19 December 2011.
36 Interview with M. Katanda, Bishop of Kindu, Dean of PEAC, Kinshasa, 12 February 2008.
37 Jean-Paul II, *Encyclique Centesimus Annus* (Kinshasa: Saint Paul Afrique, 1991): 45.
38 Available at http://www.semiliki-trust.org.uk/projects/butembo/compassion-orphanage/ accessed 23 March 2015.
39 Available at http://www.congochurchassn.org.uk/ accessed 23 March 2015.
40 A. Maslow, *Devenir le meilleur de soi-même: Besoins fondamentaux, motivation et personnalité*, L. Nicolaieff (trans.) (Paris: Groupe Eyrolles, 2008): 212.
41 Available at http://www.semiliki-trust.org.uk/projects/bukavu/goma-centre-for-women-and-children/ accessed 23 March 2015.

6   Kenya

Joseph D. Galgalo

A humble beginning

The Anglican Church of Kenya is guided by the mission 'to bring all people into a living relationship with God through Jesus Christ, through preaching, teaching, healing and social transformation and enabling them to grow in faith and live life in its fullness'.[1] True to this commitment, the Anglican Church of Kenya has continued to grow in leaps and bounds, both spiritually and numerically. The beginning, which stretches back over 170 years is credited to the work of Church Mission Society (CMS) and is as humble as it can get.

The foundation of what today is a robust Church commanding over 4 million members was laid in great toil and sacrifice. The first missionary, a German CMS recruit, the Revd. Johann Ludwig Krapf arrived in Mombasa in May of 1844 accompanied by his wife, Rosina. The wife and their new born baby girl succumbed to malaria, dying shortly after their arrival in Mombasa. The tragic loss did not deter Krapf, who himself barely survived his first bout of malaria. He soon settled down and prioritised learning the local language and establishing contact with potential converts. His biggest challenge soon proved to be the difficulty to 'sell' Christianity to a people deeply steeped in their traditional culture and religious practices. This was a virgin field for Christianity to claim but it was not going to be easy.

In 1846, Krapf was joined by the Revd. Johannes Rebmann, another CMS missionary to the region. Together the pair established a mission base at a place called Rabai Mpya, some 12 miles into the interior from the coastal town of Mombasa.

The initial efforts to evangelise the local people did not bear much fruit. The locals were said to be extremely hospitable and friendly. Accepting foreign missionaries, however, did not necessarily translate into acceptance of the gospel. Although many became regular attendants at prayer meetings, perhaps for most part out of curiosity, it took many years before any of the locals made a serious commitment to the Christian faith. The first record of baptism is of a dying cripple called Mringe, a longtime acquaintance of Krapf. He was baptised on his deathbed by Rebmann in 1851. Today, the Anglican Church of Kenya has one of the largest followings, second only to the Roman Catholic Church, and commands a comprehensive geographical spread in Kenya. This chapter maps the growth trajectory of the Church from the early days of its beginning but with particular emphases on the decades from 1990 to the present day.

Method

We here attempt to document the story of the Church's sustained growth. We begin with a sketch of the earliest years, gleaning through available reports and church records with special attention to the numerical growth of the Church. Beside the use of available records, we also attempted to gather information on Anglican population from each of the dioceses, although with limited success. To give us a sense of specific examples of growth, we also examined records of baptism from ten selected diocesan cathedrals from different parts of the country.

One caution with regard to our task needs to be sounded right from the onset. As observed by Grant LeMarquand, 'accurate church growth statistics are hard to come by'.[2] We make an observation that statistical records were kept with great care and consistency in the early years of the Church. Missionaries were particular about numbers and meticulously kept records of various categories of followers as communicants, adherents and seekers, to use their distinctions. An actual head count of attendants would be taken at every service and updated statistics were maintained by use of a simple service register with appropriate fields to be filled at every service. Records of baptisms and first admittance to Holy Communion following confirmations by the bishop were also kept by every church. These practices slowly died out as the Church grew, and notably as the leadership slowly changed hands from the missionaries to local leaders over time. Today, available data is based on an informed guess at best, and most dioceses do not have accurate records regarding the population of their followers. Even where good attempts have been made at record keeping, gaps are plenty and are not always easy to fill.

We interviewed the leaders, specifically the Administrative Secretary or the Diocesan Bishop, from a total of 31 dioceses. Simple questions regarding the number of their congregations, total number of parishes, ordained clergy in active service and the total number of their Christians were put to them. Only 24 dioceses were able to respond. The dioceses that did not respond either asked for time to complete an 'on-going' census or promised to consult their records and submit updated numbers. A cursory observation revealed that the majority of the Parishes no longer stock copies of the Confirmation and Baptismal Register or the Sunday Service Register, and those who do, hardly update their records with any consistency. It is also worth noting that a number of factors, unfortunately, seems to influence the acceptance and use of old and outdated data or skewed statistics for varied reasons as we shall see later.

The early days

The early days, needless to say, were extremely hard for the pioneers. The progress to inch forward geographical expansion and numerical growth of the Church was painfully slow. The baptism of Mringe predates the formation of any formal congregation. Years later, two adult adherents, a father and a son, were baptised. The father was named Abraham and the son Isaac, to signify perhaps a new dispensation, envisioning the two as the founding family of a new community of faith. The two were baptised in 1860 but they had to wait for nine more years till 1869 before they were confirmed and admitted to the Holy Communion because there was no bishop to confirm them. Eight (8) more converts were baptised in 1861.

In spite of the slow growth, and the small number of converts, the first diocese in the region was established in 1884, some 50 years after the arrival of Krapf. It was called the Diocese of Eastern Equatorial Africa, which comprised a vast region that today consists of the three East African countries of Kenya, Uganda and Tanzania.

In 1899, the diocese of Mombasa, comprising Northern Tanganyika and the then British East Africa (present-day Kenya, excluding until 1920 some western regions, which then were part of Uganda), was born out of the diocese of Eastern Equatorial Africa. The new diocese of Mombasa was placed under the charge of Bishop Peel, who was consecrated in June of 1899 in London and immediately thereafter sent to his new diocese.

Bishop Peel inherited a poorly resourced diocese with only three ordained clergy and with no particular mission strategy. By the close of the 1890s, the earliest of the mission stations were, however, registering impressive growth, attracting new congregants faster than ever before. Bishop Peel was keen on collecting figures and keeping track of the numerical growth of each congregation. In almost all his reports, he always included a section on the growth in numbers. By the year 1900, about four of the earliest coastal mission stations including Mombasa (based in Frere town), Rabai Mpya, Sagalla and Taveta had, between them, a total of about 5000 regular attendees at the Sunday Services.[3] In the same year, a worship centre was established in Nairobi, and soon followed by the opening of the first major inland mission station at Kabete, on the southern edge of the populous Kikuyu region.

Bishop Peel was keen to put in place a workable mission strategy to strengthen and grow the Church in a structured and a more effective way. Notable amongst these strategies was training and general promotion of literacy through basic education; and also, the establishment and strengthening of a pastoral oversight council for each congregation. The councils were tasked to spur and manage a structured growth. In one of his numerous reports he writes, 'I cannot convey to the committee, how serious I consider the need to be preparing and providing African clergy, readers (evangelists) and catechists, school-masters and school matrons'.[4]

Under Peel, the number of mission stations increased and so did the congregations and the number of those presented for baptism and confirmations. By 1916, the year in which Bishop Peel died, there were well over 15 mission stations mainly established in the central and western parts of the British East Africa. A good foundation had been laid but not strong enough for Peel's dream of African leadership to be realised as fast as he would have wished. It was not until 1955 when the first Africans, Festo Olang' and Obadiah Kariuki, were consecrated as bishops of the Church to assist the then diocesan missionary bishop. In 1960, the province of East Africa, comprising Kenya and Tanzania, was formed with

Leonard James Beecher as the first archbishop. Festo Olang' became the first African archbishop of the province of Kenya in 1970, when Kenya and Tanzania became two separate provinces. The birth of the province, coinciding with the consecration of the first Kenyan archbishop in 1970, marks the proper beginning of the Anglican Province of the Church of Kenya. With this transition, the long gestation period was over, and the 'growing up' stage began.

The growth of the Church proved steady but generally remained slow mainly on account of inadequate personnel, especially in the period before the 1970s. At the beginning of 1938 there were 19 fully established mission stations in addition to 449 sub-stations that conducted regular worship services. Each sub-station would remain under the supervision of the mother station until it qualified for elevation to a fully-fledged congregation status. The personnel, at the time, comprised 73 CMS missionaries assisted by a total of 38 African clergy, between them serving 67,712 congregants on record at the close of 1937.[5]

The years immediately preceding Kenya's independence from British rule was not easy for the Church. Leadership wrangles and political and doctrinal differences prompted some serious splits especially in the regions with substantial Anglican following. This notwithstanding, at the time of becoming a province in 1970, the Church of the Province of Kenya (now Anglican Church of Kenya – ACK) had a 742,300 strong membership with about 200 clergy.[6] This steady progress was maintained and the Church had a following of about 910,000 by 1980.[7] The available data from this year onwards is confusing and unreliable. It seems not much attention was given to proper record keeping of the Church's numerical growth from around 1990 onwards.

Current growth trajectory

Based on a number of carefully examined sources, Dickson Nkonge gives the estimate of Anglican congregants as 1,858,200 by the year 1990.[8] Surprisingly, four years later, the ACK official figures recorded in the 1994 issue of the Church Directory has not changed one way or another, also giving 1,858,200 as the total number of congregants in 1993.[9] The estimates on record from this time on are generally conservative giving the impression of a shrinking church. The evidence on the ground, however, makes one doubt the reliability of the figures that are in circulation. The continuous establishment of new congregations across the dioceses is sure evidence of a robust growth. In 2008, for example, there were 29 dioceses, up from 20 in 1993. The number of dioceses currently stands at 34 (including three diocesan missionary areas – Lodwar, Maralal and Garissa). The increase in the number of dioceses is not a sure indicator of a definite overall numerical growth. This is because dioceses have often been subdivided on the basis of other considerations such as vast geographical expanse of the see, language considerations and sometimes for the avoidance of conflict or on the basis of a special consideration. There is no denying, however, that most dioceses, especially so the rural dioceses, have over the years continued to register visible increase in the number of their parishes, number of congregations and human resource capacity. Dioceses are regularly building and consecrating new churches, establishing new congregations, ordaining more clergy and creating more parishes year after year, sure evidence of a sustained growth.

The Anglican Church enjoys visible and active presence in every part of the country. Notably, church planting and efforts to increase the number of congregants continue to be a major focus for all the dioceses. It seems the Anglican Church simply stopped 'counting' and chose to fervently concentrate on sparing no effort to 'multiply' its membership. Up to date records of numbers may not be available, but the evident numerical strength is a story so clearly told by the imposing presence of the Church in every corner of this vast country.

Crunching the numbers

Making sense of the available statistics is not easy. We shall examine a few sources before we draw conclusions regarding the numerical size of the Anglican Church of Kenya. The official ACK website records that 'Today the church has grown tremendously from a few members scattered around the coastal region to over 5 million across the country'.[10] The same website provides partial data of the statistical records from some dioceses. The numbers provided there, although incomplete, do not add up to coming anywhere close to the declared figure of 5 million (see Table 6.1 below). The other problem with this data is that it is rather dated, going back to 2009 although it was posted in 2014. This means that the Church has not been able to update its records and old statistics have been quoted and passed as official figures as if growth has remained static.

Table 6.1 gives the estimated number of Christians in 19 out of the total of 31 dioceses (excluding three missionary areas) as 1,389,096. Data for 12 dioceses out of 31, which translates to 38.7%, is missing. Possible differences of numerical strength of the 12 dioceses notwithstanding, 38.7% translates to approximately another 860,800 additional Christians. This places the value of Table 6.1 roughly at 2,258,896 as the estimation of Anglicans as of 2010. We also note that this data was already five years old by the time it was posted in September 2009. It does not, therefore, capture an accurate and up-to-date numerical size of the Church.

Another pertinent observation needs to be made. The figures (Table 6.1) provided by the dioceses, even though incomplete, gives an indication that either the official estimate of 5 million is highly exaggerated or else the estimates provided by the dioceses are grossly inaccurate. We are persuaded that the assumption of inaccuracy makes a more convincing case because of reasons we shall elaborate a little later. Before we make our conclusions, however, it is worth looking at a few other sources, which give varied statistics. Table 6.2 below presents a comparison of at least three other sources. Unfortunately the sources capture statistics from different periods (2008, 2009 and 2014) and except for source 1 (Nkonge's Source) the other two are incomplete. The comparison is meant to show how available statistics are terribly confusing but not completely useless

Table 6.1 Parishes, congregations/churches and estimated number of Anglicans in Kenya

#	Diocese	No. of parishes	Fulltime clergy	No. of churches (congregations)	Estimated no. of congregants
1	All Saints Cathedral	Not listed	–	–	–
2	Bondo	21	29	155	192,000
3	Bungoma	50	68	750	149,200
4	Butere	43	33	160	Not provided
5	Eldoret	46	117	536	29,490
6	Embu	44	70	122	45,000
7	Kajiado	20	31	100	8,000
8	Katakwa	Not listed			
9	Kericho	10	Not provided	78	5,846
10	Kirinyaga	102	213	221	70,000
11	Kitale	38	76	204	20,000
12	Kitui	57	Not provided	136	40,800
13	Machakos	96	46	200	40,800
14	Makueni[11]	–	–	–	
15	Marsabit	Not listed			
16	Maseno North	46	45	175	12,000
17	Maseno South	35	50	270	60,000
18	Maseno West	43	54	258	380,000
19	Mbeere	30	52	125	50,000
20	Meru	44	70	122	45,000
21	Mombasa	Not listed			
22	Mt. Kenya Central	107	135	372	159,960
23	Mt. Kenya South	115	146	220	90,000
24	Mumias	33	40	206	Not provided
25	Nairobi	Not listed			
26	Nakuru	Not listed			
27	Nambale[12]				
28	Nyahururu	Not listed			
29	Southern Nyanza	Not listed			
30	Taita Taveta	Not listed			
31	Thika	Not listed			
32	3 missionary areas (Garissa, Lodwar and Maralal) are not listed and their numbers are not included in that of the mentoring dioceses.				
	Total				**1,398,096**

Source: ACK official website (2010)

Table 6.2 Comparison of statistics from three different sources of numbers of Anglicans by diocese in Kenya

#	Diocese	Source 1 (Dickson Nkonge)[13]		Source 2 (Provincial survey 2009)[14]	Source 3 (Interviews conducted in 2014)[15]
		Active members	Adherents		
1	All Saints Cathedral	8,900	39,000	17,600	11,500
2	Bondo	12,915	78,915	66,000	59,000
3	Bungoma	–	90,000	352,300	–
4	Butere	54,000	125,000	29,700	25,000
5	Eldoret	250,000	340,000	–	130,200
6	Embu	55,000	145,000	28,050	25,000
7	Kajiado	9,282	34,282	16,620	15,000
8	Katakwa	99,000	169,100	145,885	85,383
9	Kericho	–	–	6,000	5500
10	Kirinyaga	150,000	350,000	–	140,607
11	Kitale	29,386	79,846	110,000	24,362
12	Kitui	9,883	44,883	88,670	–
13	Machakos	56,000	125,000	–	7,000
14	Maseno North	35,000	115,000	48,000	33,000
15	Maseno South	55,000	142,500	109,900	70,000
16	Maseno West	61,000	153,000	41,290	140,800
17	Mbeere	51,131	121,976	67,200	35,729
18	Meru	12,972	43,972	8,200	–
19	Mombasa	50,100	141,600	34,190	22,000
20	Mt. Kenya Central	150,000	372,000	157,600	170,000
21	Mt. Kenya South	81,093	161,095	51,800	90,000
22	Mt. Kenya West	27,600	48,600	35,200	31,000
23	Mumias	34,000	69,000	41,300	–
24	Nairobi	22,060	67,290	31,200	49,000
25	Nakuru	32,457	98,457	19,700	13,000
26	Nambale	90,000	191,000	46,700	–
27	Nyahururu	21,000	77,200	–	–
28	Southern Nyanza	15,000	47,250	20,770	18,257
29	Taita Taveta	64,500	164,500	21,570	25,840
30	Thika	27,324	78,324	23,800	27,000
	Total	**1,565,056**	**3,711,890**	**1,619,245** (Note: data for 2 new dioceses not available)	**1,261,178** (Note: data from 7 dioceses and 3 missionary areas are not available)

to help us make a realistic estimation of the possible numerical strength of the Anglican Church of Kenya.

Before getting into the analysis of Table 6.2 above, it is worth mentioning that one other source, a baseline survey conducted in 2012 by the Anglican Provincial Directorate of Social Services, gives an estimated population of Anglicans as 1,987,432. One puzzling thing to note is that this figure is only slightly higher than the figure of 1,858,200, which we quoted above given as the official population of Anglicans in the 1994 Provincial Directory. If these figures are correct, it means that the Church grew only slightly by 129,232 members between 1993 and 2012, translating into an increase in membership by only about 6400 (0.3%) per year over 18 years, a share of about 213 members per year per diocese.

We also note that the figure from the baseline survey is in the range of Nkonge's category of what he called active members in 2008; and also roughly compares to source 2, that is, the Provincial Survey conducted in 2009. Also, the data we obtained from 24 dioceses (in 2014) through our interviews confirm that the estimation of Anglicans in Kenya is in the range of 1,261,178 (actual total received from 24 out of 31 dioceses) and approximately 1.8 million (based on our projection of what if all dioceses had submitted their data). Do we then, based on these estimates, conclude that the numerical strength of the Anglican Church in Kenya is in the range of 2 million or thereabout? Is it possible that although the Church was 1.9 million strong in 1994, it only barely grew to about 2 million by 2010? What about the gap from 2010 to 2015 for which no data seems to be available? Could the Anglican Church of Kenya (ACK) be a case of a stunted growth, or even worse a church on the decline?

A casual observation can attest to the vibrant growth of the Church, evidenced particularly by continued planting and consecration of new churches, creation of new dioceses and increasing number of parishes and places of worship in all the dioceses throughout the country. Given that figures from the 1990s are in the range of 2 million members, and that there is evidence, based on observation, of continuous growth being registered across all the dioceses, it is difficult to affirm the veracity of the estimates currently in circulation. It is also to be noted that the whole idea of counting is generally counter cultural, and explains why the churches are not so keen on keeping records or getting accurate figures. Sadly, it is good enough, so it seems, for one to pass on a number given to them some ten years ago, without thinking twice about the obvious changes that continues to take place over the years.

In the absence of credible statistics and with plenty of confusing data on our hands, we now make a reasonable estimation, informed partly by insider knowledge as one who has served in the ACK since the early 1990s and partly based on available estimates and records from the early '90s. Our opinion is that it is possible to make a reasonable estimate of the Church's numerical strength based on earlier records because these were kept with greater accuracy and can be used to inform a reliable annual growth projection to date. It is also possible, based on a sample of churches and dioceses with complete data, and by considering the comparative strength of some churches with incomplete data, to arrive at a plausible annual percentage growth rate. We shall use a combination of these approaches to arrive at a sound conclusion.

Based on CMS archival records, the authors of *Rabai to Mumias* give the following progressive comparative figures of growth between 1937 to 1994: 1937 (67,712 members); 1962 (200,000 members); 1980 (910,000 members); and 1994 (1,858,200). We note that the growth between 1937 and 1962, spanning 25 years, is understandably low. Poorly resourced, the missionaries were able to increase outreach and establish more mission stations only at a very slow pace. In the next 15 or so years, the population of the Church more than quadrupled, registering an enormous average growth rate of more than 30% per annum up to the year 1980. Number of factors – including an increase in the number of clergy, mission support, increased levels of literacy, improved access to most parts of the country and Christianity's sustained presence in and penetration into hitherto largely African traditional societies and consequently mass movements into churches – combined to make possible this exceptional growth.

By 1994, the total population of Anglicans in the country increased from 910,000 in 1980 to 1,858,200 over a period of about 15 years. This figure, based on the Provincial Directory record, can be trusted because the records going back to the early 1990s are fairly accurate and were based on actual censuses and records were updated with reasonable consistency. The cumulative growth during this period stood at over 100%, translating to an average growth rate of about 7.2% per annum.

Dickson Nkonge observes that this phenomenal increase drastically dropped to about 'an annual average growth rate of 2 per cent in the years between 1990 and 2000 and [went up again to] 6.7 per cent from the beginning of . . . the year 2000'.[16] Nkonge contends that some of the factors to blame for the slow growth in the 1990s were the rising influence of Pentecostalism (highly vibrant during this decade and particularly attractive to the youth), coupled with other challenges such as a church liturgically unresponsive to the needs of the faithful, as well as leadership wrangles that around this time resulted in numerous subdivisions of several of the Anglican dioceses.

Accepting the argument that the Church grew by an annual average of about 2% or only slightly higher during this period, means that the membership increased by a total of 222,984 from 1994, bringing this to a total of 2,081,184 in the year 2000. Anecdotal evidence shows that the growth of the Church really picked up again from the year 2000 onwards. The reasons for this change of fortune are numerous. The most significant development is that the Church managed to deal with matters of conflict, comprehensive liturgical reforms and renewal were undertaken, and congregational driven responses to Pentecostalism helped stem the loss of membership.

To test the specific level of turn of fortunes, and also to provide specific examples of growth, we sampled 10 diocesan cathedrals out of 29, and analyzed their baptismal records from 1990 to 2015. The ten sampled cathedrals are from different regions of the country, deliberately chosen in order to attain wide regional coverage. Surprisingly, although there is no regular membership registration drive, or records of congregational census, records of baptisms were meticulously kept. This has been possible because clergy are required by law to issue baptismal certificates to the candidate. Also, given that each certificate is issued at a cost, the clergy have no option but to record it for ease of accounting.

The baptismal data from the cathedrals is very revealing. All the sampled cathedrals show a similar pattern of depressed growth in the number of those baptised from the year 1990 to the year 1998. Some show a real annual increase from this year onwards, with about three cathedrals out of ten returning only a marginal increase of baptised numbers per year. Most important to note, the numbers of the baptised on average increased by about 6.46% per annum for almost all the cathedrals that were sampled. We note that this is in congruence with Dickson Nkonge's overall congregational average annual growth of 6.7% per annum realised from 2000 onwards. We contend that, the cathedral being the mother church in the diocese, its growth pattern is a reflection of the diocesan growth pattern. We also reasonably assume that the annual number of baptisms is proportionately comparable to the overall growth, especially of active members. It is plausible to concede, therefore, that the province in general and the dioceses in particular grew on average by around a similar percentage of between 6–7% per annum from the closing years of the 1990s onwards.

We also take cognizance that the figures collected through our interviews are grossly understated across the board and are based on old statistical records or dated estimates. Seen in this light and in comparison with the data from the sampled cathedrals, we agree that Nkonge's annual average growth rate of 6.7% per annum from 2000 is reasonable. We can use this rate to arrive at a reasonable estimate of ACK's numerical strength. Given that we had 2,081,184 members in 2000, and with an average of 6.7% annual growth rate, we estimate that the numerical strength of ACK in the year 2014 stood at 4,033,334. There is one other important source we can use to support this conclusion. This is the government of Kenya's national population census results of 2009.

Kenya has conducted a physical head count of all its citizens every ten years since 1969. Enumerators move from house to house as they register everyone. The last census was conducted in 2009 – with total population recorded as 38,412,088. Pertinent to our study is the 2009 Census volume 2, Table 12, which lists population numbers according to citizens' religious affiliation.[17] Anglicans are not listed separately but included in the Protestant category, a group with a total population of 18,307,466. The Catholics are listed separately as 9,010,684. The Pentecostals are grouped together in a category simply designated 'Other Christians', and stands at 4,559,584. Of interest to us is the Protestant category with a population of 18,307,466 and in this group is included Anglicans alongside Presbyterians, Methodists, Reformed Church, Mennonites, Lutherans, Friends, the Adventists, African Inland Church, the Baptists and a host of African Instituted Churches. None of these churches, going by their own estimation, except the Anglican Church, claim a following of more than 4 million faithful.[18] Only a few, including the African Inland Church, the Presbyterian Church in East Africa and the Methodist Church in Kenya, record a membership of more than 3 million. The rest usually give a much lower estimate of their population.

By a long stretch, the population of these Protestant Churches excluding the Anglican Church would not exceed 14 million, leaving us with an estimation of Anglican membership of at least 4.3 million. This is in agreement with our estimate of 4.03 million and also in line with Nkonge's 6.7% as the annual average growth rate realised year by year since 2000. Based on available figures as incomplete and at times as confusing as these are, comparative numerical strengths of the Protestant Churches in light of the 2009 government census, and specific examples of growth patterns of the sampled cathedrals, it is reasonable to conclude that the Anglican Church in Kenya currently has a membership approximately between 4 to 4.5 million.

Explaining the data challenge

This conclusion brings us to the most difficult question regarding the credibility of available statistics. Why, then, do the diocesan estimates add up to a much lower number than 4 million, even when the official declaration records a number of 5 million strong?

There are a number of possible explanations to the question of the accuracy of numbers that are provided by the dioceses. The major reason is simply lack of proper records, and in its absence, churches tend to keep quoting old statistical records and uncritically pass these on as if they are current. A quick glance through any diocesan bishop's annual or quarterly programmes reveals that, on average each diocesan bishop is scheduled to conduct confirmation services at least six times in the year. Unfortunately, records of the number of believers confirmed are hard to get because most parishes do not bother to keep a compiled report, especially where joint confirmation services were held at deanery or archdeaconry levels. The practice of joint services at a deanery or archdeaconry level is very common in most dioceses for events where the bishop presides.

We also observed that there is a general tendency to provide numbers of adult communicants only, at the exclusion of the members of the youth services and the children (even though they may be baptised and form the bulk of the congregations). Kitui diocese, for example, in the data provided for the Provincial Survey in 2009, submitted that their total number of Christians is 28,400 and that separate from this, they had a total of 57,700 children registered in their Sunday School Services. Taita Taveta gave their population as 15,680 excluding 3,142 children in Sunday school. Thika diocese recorded their adult population as 11,964 and the children were accounted for separately as 6,044. This seems to be the trend with all the dioceses, where baptised children or even confirmed young adults are left out of the official estimates.

An interesting reason why figures are often understated and sometimes even deliberately skewed is because of an established link between numbers and how the dioceses raise their funding. The Anglican Church of Kenya's dioceses use a quota system where each parish is allocated a certain amount to be paid as its financial contribution to the diocese. The amount allocated is arrived at based on the numerical strength of each parish. This is informed by the assumption that cumulative financial strength is in numbers. The quota allocation using this system is simple. The total diocesan budget less other income is divided by the total number of Christians so as to arrive at the amount to be allocated to each parish. If the quota allocation per Christian is, for example, Kenya Shillings 3,000/-, then a parish of, let us say 300 Christians would pay 300 Christians × 3,000/- totaling to Kenya Shillings 900,000/- and a parish with twice as many Christians would pay double that amount. The diocesan quota is a financial obligation that the parish carries in addition to all other financial obligations of the parish. It is interesting to note that for most parishes, the declared number to be used for the purpose of quota allocation has remained constant year after year.

Not totally unexpected, most parishes also declare a conservative number to minimise the amount allocated to them. In any case, for the purpose of quota allocation, it is only the total number of adult congregants that is required from the parishes. Numbers may also be understated or manipulated for selfish political reasons. Parish churches are the financial backbone in support of diocesan development projects and the ministry of the bishop. If a clergyperson is unhappy with the one in authority, withholding quota payment has often been used as a tool to 'frustrate' the work of the one in authority. Numbers in the Anglican Church of Kenya, therefore, often have huge political or financial implications and could be understated or manipulated for such reasons.

We also observed that although most dioceses conduct a census from time to time, the exercise is largely left in the hands of individual parishes with minimal diocesan or provincial supervision. Most dioceses design a form to be filled and returned by individual Christians through their parish churches. A high percentage of these forms are not returned due to poor follow-up. Most Christians also are not motivated enough to return the form because of fees chargeable per number of family members that one lists on the form. In the circumstances, it is not surprising that some families hardly include every member of the family on the form; children are especially left out if that would save them some cost. Others simply miss out on filing and returning the form, or even for genuine reasons would miss a few Sundays in a row, and all together miss out picking up or returning the form.

Conclusion: where do we go from here?

There is no denying that 'accurate church growth statistics are hard to come by'. We, however, have shown that it is possible to make a reasonable estimate of the numerical strength of the present-day Anglican Church of Kenya. The Church has continued to register impressive growth over the years. The numerical expansion is faster and more impressive in some decades than in others. We noted, for example, how conflict related to subdivision of some dioceses, phenomenal growth of Pentecostalism, and the Church's lack of comprehensive programmes for its most vibrant segments such as youth, and lack of liturgical and pastoral innovativeness, negatively affected the growth especially in the 1990s.

In the more recent decade, an upward numerical growth has sustainably continued to be realised. This can be credited to a leadership that has largely proved responsive to the Church's changing needs and a firm commitment to the vision and mission of being a growing and gospel centred church. To sustain this growth, the Church needs to strengthen a few areas of weaknesses.

A key imperative in this regard is the need for a practical mission strategy that embraces and supports effective evangelism, seeks social and economic justice and supports a robust and relevant theological education, as well as implementing and sustaining a transformative pastoral service system. With the increasing 'Pentecostalisation' of the Church, incipient secularisation, doctrinal challenges and numerous competing loyalties, it is also imperative for the Church to strengthen its theological and liturgical traditions. With these key imperatives in mind, and if workable strategies are formulated and implemented with diligence, there is no doubt that the Church will continue to realise even greater and faster growth for the foreseeable future. The humble beginning, comparable to the parable of the mustard seed, has surpassed expectations, confidently marching on with its light held high for all to see.

Notes

1 The vision and mission of the church is always reproduced in the annual issue of the *Church Pocket Book and Diary*, a diary with a lectionary guide published every year by Uzima Publishing House (the official publishing house of the Anglican Church of Kenya).

2 Quote from E. Wabukala, 'Charge of the Fifth Archbishop of Kenya', Presented at the Service of His Enthronement, All Saints Cathedral Church, Nairobi, Kenya, 5 July 2009, *Anglican and Episcopal History* 80 (2011): 284–95, available at http://www.jstor.org/stable/42612607 accessed 13 November 2014.

3 Provincial Unit of Research of the Church of the Province of Kenya, *Rabai to Mumias: A Short History of the Church of the Province of Kenya 1844–1994* (Nairobi: Uzima Press, 1994): 19.

4 Ibid.

5 CMS Report, 1937/1938.

6 These figures, using various sources, are provided by D. Nkonge, 'Equipping Church Leaders for Mission in the Anglican Church of Kenya', *Journal of Anglican Studies* 9 (2011): 154–74.

7 Provincial Unit of Research, *Rabai*: 26.

8 Ibid.: 163.

9 Ibid.: 187.

10 Available at http://www.ackenya.org/ack/history.html accessed 13 September 2014.

11 The same figures provided for Machakos are also entered for Makueni. We note that the figures are from 2009, long before Makueni was curved out of the larger Machakos diocese to become a diocese on its own in 2013.

12 The same figures provided for Mumias are also entered for Nambale. The duplication is most likely a mistake.

13 Nkonge, 'Equipping': 163.

14 This survey was conducted by the ACK Provincial office in February 2009. We had access to raw data from the Provincial Mission Desk.

15 I personally conducted these interviews through telephone conversations, email communication and face-to-face meetings, July–December 2014. Respondents answered questions on the number of clergy, number of congregations, number of parishes and an estimated or actual number of Christians in the diocese. Note that although these figures are estimates, they are not current. Most dioceses submitted figures that they have had for a while now. I received from the Diocese of Katakwa, for example, figures based on the Diocesan Statistical Directory compiled in 2007 and not updated since.

16 Nkonge, 'Equipping': 164.

17 Available at https://www.opendata.go.ke/-Environment-And-Natural-Resources/2009-census-volume-2-table-12-Population-by-Religi/jrmn-krnf accessed 13 November 2014.

18 See, for example, J. Kibor, 'The Growth and Development of the Africa Inland Mission and the Africa Inland Church in Marakwet, Kenya', *African Journal of Evangelical Theology* 24 (2005): 107–28; https://www.en.wikipedia.org/wiki/Presbyterianism; Worldwide Ministries, Africa PC (USA), available at http://www.presbyterianmission.org/ministries/global/kenya/.

7 South Africa

Barbara Bompani

Introduction

The Anglican Church of Southern Africa (ACSA) presents an interesting narrative that reflects many interconnections with the religious and socio-political history of South Africa and the way Christianity developed, expanded and was transformed across several decades due to the influence of international and global trends as well as national and local specificities.

The chapter provides an analysis of the Anglican Church in South Africa from the final years of the apartheid regime in the mid-80s to the present day with the intention of highlighting trends in and drivers of the growth and decline of its membership over the last thirty years. In doing so, the chapter shows how the ACSA has struggled to find its way in the post-apartheid era, experiencing a decline in membership and public influence, much like other mainline churches. This does not, however, reflect broader secularisation processes in South Africa, but rather a general shift towards more charismatic and evangelical Christian denominations. In the post-apartheid era the Anglican Church has suffered from a lack of vision and strong central leadership, which is reflected at a local level in issues such as a lack of basic record keeping (see section 2) and lack of a strong sense of community within parishes (with parishioners acting within a multi-denominational marketplace). In a certain way a local organisational deficit and a lack of coordination reflects the central Church's lack of a core strategy, which has been an ongoing issue for the Anglican Church in South and Southern Africa, especially in the face of new competition or changing contexts.

Following a note on methods and the limits of data sources (section 2), a brief historical account of the origin of the Church in the country will follow (section 3). The chapter will turn to investigate data on Anglican members (section 4) and it will then offer an explanation (section 5) of changes within its own membership and the institutional reactions to them. These shifts will be investigated through an analysis of broader economic, political, social and religious changes that are transforming the country. Findings for this work are based on research conducted on archival sources (Historical Papers archive, the University of the Witwatersrand),[1] and material collected in parishes and through interviews with Anglican clergy in the country, especially in Johannesburg and in Pietermaritzburg, between February and March 2014.[2]

A note on methods, data and numbers

It is necessary to acknowledge a limitation that influenced the research process for this chapter and that is the lack of detailed records on members kept by Anglican parishes.[3] Until 2001 religious membership data could be understood and analyzed in comparison with data collected by Statistics South Africa for the national census (then published and made available in 2004). However, in the latest national census in 2011 (then published in 2014) the question on religious belonging was, for the first time, not included in the questionnaire.[4] While informal discussions with religious leaders seemed to indicate a perception that the question on religious belonging was intentionally omitted from the questionnaire with the precise top-down intent of further separating public matters from religious ones in light of a reaffirmation of the secularity of the South African state,[5] the Stats South Africa website provided a different explanation, affirming that

> in 2008, Stats South Africa embarked on a series of user consultations, to get advice as to what questions should be asked in the questionnaire. The question on religion was low on the list of priorities as informed by the users of census data, and it therefore did not make it onto the final list of data items for the 2011 census.[6]

In the parishes under analysis and from interview data, it emerged that the membership figures collected exhibit a large discrepancy between the official statistics reported by the Church nationally (data from Cape Town Bishop's Office) and the statistics recorded by dioceses and local parishes. This is mainly due to the fact that at a national level the Church reports numbers based on actual registers collected from parishes while at a local level the idea of membership is interpreted differently and with a more inclusive understanding. Many local parishes would consider churchgoer numbers in attendance on a weekly basis and in weekly activities and not just those recorded in the parish register. In urban churches it is quite common, for example, to report membership of people who are also recorded as members in their rural birthplace parishes:

> Have you heard of ploughing back? It means bringing back to the community and this is what many Anglicans coming from townships or the rural areas do. They attend service in the urban church but then they would send money to the birthplace church. Their sense of membership lies there.[7]

Similarly: 'It is very frustrating for the clergy when a lot of the community is loyal to the township. Their contributions go to their township church where they only go a couple of times a year'.[8]

The issue of accuracy in parish questionnaires and data collected was also questioned in interviews. A reverend, for example, stated that

> it is well known that people filling the questionnaire tend to exaggerate; numbers are more or less accurate. We [Anglican priests] are supposed to keep records of people attending but not all the parishes do that. Some dioceses do not even produce returns on their income![9]

Most of the clergy also lamented the lack of administrative capacity in collecting precise information about their membership due to scarce resources and limited time available.[10] From the interviews it emerged that most of the leaders shared the impression that the Anglican Church was holding up well in rural areas while in urban contexts the Anglican membership was weakened and challenged by the dynamic proselytising work of Pentecostal Charismatic churches.

This research project found out that generally the clergy were quite demoralised for their work conditions in the post-apartheid context.[11] The message usually was that the Anglican Church had a strong public vision, position and articulated action in the struggle against apartheid, but after that churches and leaders have started to work in isolation although the post-apartheid context presents many challenges (like social division, economic disparity, crime and injustice) that should be addressed collegially and cohesively. The lack of funding from abroad after 1994, both from Anglican and interfaith groups, was also highlighted as a huge problem that badly reflected on churches and parishes.[12] These themes, and others, will be explored in the remainder of this chapter.

An overview of the Anglican Church of Southern Africa (ACSA)

Until 2006 the Anglican Province was known as the *Church of the Province of Southern Africa* (CPSA) but the name was changed to 'ACSA' by the Southern African Provincial Synod held on 8 and 9 September 2006 with the intent to better highlight the regional scope and define a stronger presence within the Worldwide Anglican Communion.[13] ACSA is extremely widespread and it comprises six countries of Southern Africa and two islands. The six countries are Namibia, Swaziland, Lesotho, Angola, Mozambique and South Africa, along with the islands of St Helena and Tristan Da Cuna. The Episcopal area is divided into twenty-eight dioceses with a bishop at the head of each diocese. The head of the Church is the Archbishop of Cape Town, who is also the Metropolitan of the Anglican Church in Southern Africa. The number of Anglican parishes in the Southern African area recorded by the Church is 1,404 with an estimated 3,000 congregations in the region. There are more than 2,000 trained clergy, including bishops, listed in the Anglican Church of Southern Africa's clerical directory.[14] From an analysis of the clerical directory of the Anglican Church in Southern Africa, in which all the clergy and parishes in the country are represented, it is possible to verify that every single municipality in South Africa (226 local municipalities in total according to *The Local Government Handbook*[15]), has an Anglican presence, with certain areas having more than one parish and at least three fulltime priests.[16]

ACSA is not the only form of Anglicanism in South Africa. We can also find the Church of England in South Africa (CESA) that represents a more evangelical and biblically conservative Anglicanism.[17] CESA is amongst the most theologically conservative evangelical denominations in the country. In the South African context this is somewhat ironic because its origins are associated with John William Colenso, first Church of England Bishop of Natal, theologian and mathematician known for his liberal views of the Bible and radical views of politics who was supportive of the Zulu cause during the Anglo-Zulu War in 1879. Because of his unconventional theological views, he was tried for heresy and excommunicated from the Anglican Church. CESA was established by his supporters. Yet CESA and its biggest congregation, St James Church Kenilworth, could not be more theologically and politically distant from Colenso. According to Balcomb's analysis, members and clergy of the Church describe the beginnings of CESA as a 'struggle for survival'. Through the myth of this struggle the denomination ultimately emerged as a locus of conservative theological and political convictions. As the ex-Presiding Bishop Frank Retief has said, it started 'as a small group of people . . . committed to the evangelical, Reformed and Protestant convictions of its forbears'.[18] As Balcomb puts it, CESA has profound significance for at least three reasons: (1) it adopts a theological position opposed to that of its more 'liberal' counterpart, the Church of the Province of South Africa (CPSA) or the 'Anglican' Church; (2) it has its own history of 'struggle' centred on issues of theology and political practice; (3) it was able to attract the white alienated community that did not approve of the Anglican Church's political involvement during the 1970s and 1980s and the role that the black Anglican leadership was playing at the time.[19] Therefore CESA became an island for conservative whites opposing the 'liberal' positions of Desmond Tutu and others in the CPSA and the vocal South African Council of Churches (SACC).[20] The denomination is not as large as the Anglican Church in South Africa but indications are that it is growing faster. It extends from South Africa to Namibia, Zimbabwe and Malawi. Its total membership is around 100,000 members with an overall average Sunday morning attendance at St James of 1,800 and an average Sunday evening attendance of 1,000.[21] Mid-week Bible studies attract about 600 people. Membership is roughly 70% White and 30% Coloured,[22] with a very small number of Black people. The high income of the Church (probably around 3 million rand a year, or about $300,000) makes it the richest church in the denomination.[23] Official Anglicanism in South Africa has been, historically and in the present, associated with ACSA. CESA is not part of the Anglican Communion as confirmed by the fact that it does not take part in the Lambeth Conference although there have been several attempts from the CESA side to be included in the international conference of the Communion.[24]

The Anglican Church came to the Cape and was originally established in South Africa to minister to the army and the first British settlers. The first Anglican ministry in Southern Africa was initiated to deal with the needs of the British militia at Cape Town during the second British occupation in 1806.[25] However, it was not until 1848 with the appointment of Robert Gray as Bishop of Cape Town that a proper institutional Church was established in the region. In 1848, when Robert Gray arrived in South Africa, there were ten churches, sixteen priests and no more than 10,000 churchgoers but at the time of his death in 1872 there was a whole province, five dioceses, a synodical structure and a strong corporate identity (the Church of the Province of Southern Africa – CPSA). At the time of his appointment as the first Bishop of Cape Town, the Anglican Church was not a very visible Church, had little prestige compared to the Reformed Church and could not even claim a majority of the English settlers who were based in the Eastern Cape. For example, in the first half of the 19th century Methodists had a much stronger presence across English-speaking settlers.[26] 'From their arrival English-speaking communities reproduced the parochial life of Great Britain. Anglican Parish churches coexisted with Baptist, Congregational, Methodist and Presbyterian congregations as did their emerging denominational structures'.[27] Presbyterians, suspicious of the Anglican episcopacy because of the historic conflicts in Scotland, found more affinity with the Dutch Reformed churches, aligned by their common Calvinist theology.[28]

The first attempt to give the Anglican Church an administrative system occurred while Robert Gray was Bishop of Cape Town; until then Anglican buildings and churches were built by shareholders of joint stock corporations – these include St George's Church in Cape Town. Unlike free churches, the Anglican Church in South Africa was ruled and organised by the clergy and this can be explained not only by theological reasons, but also by the ambition of using the Cape as the starting point of expansion of Anglicanism in Southern Africa, where, in fact, between 1848 and 1924 it expanded from the Eastern Cape, to Rhodesia, St Helena and Damaraland.[29]

Links with the motherland remained strong and this was evident in the liturgy, religious architecture, music and hymns and the fact that the great majority of the ministers were trained in Britain. Overall, English-speaking churches were united in their loyalty to the British Empire and their missionary societies, consciously or not, were embedded into the colonial project and the consolidation of the British Empire and declarations of loyalty to the crown were regularly sent to the British monarch's representative in South Africa, the Governor-General, until 1948 (and perhaps even later) when the National Party came to power and the regime of apartheid was formally established in the country.[30] The constant complaint from the South African government was that the Anglican Church leadership represented discredited imperial British values; this was linked to the fact that clearly and particularly its leaders were predominantly of British origins. The first South African-born bishop was Bill Burnett proclaimed in 1974. The clergy of the Anglican Church were overwhelmingly expatriate and ministered primarily to English-speaking white congregations composed of European settlers.[31] The Anglicans treasured episcopacy and the Book of Common Prayer and eventually produced their own South African revision only in 1954 and again in 1989.[32] The first provincial Missionary Conference of the CPSA was held in October 1892 in Queenstown in the Eastern Cape.

Christian missionary activities have been extremely active in South Africa in the 19th century and in the first half of the 20th century. Associated with each denomination were missionary societies who sought to evangelise the indigenous peoples of the sub-continent.[33] Missionary churches grew constantly in the first half of the 20th century and they kept growing in the 1960s and in the 1970s at a lower rate and with differences between ethnic groups, but from the 1980s mainline Christianity[34] started to suffer a considerable decline.[35] The literature on the growth and development of the Anglican Church from the arrival of Bishop Robert Gray indicates that the early understandings of 'mission and welfare' for the Anglican Church in Southern Africa was an intervention that sought to care for the needs of the English first, conversion of the indigenous people second and social outreach to indigenous people third.[36] While in its initial life the Church mainly concentrated on administering the interests of British settlers, through the years and up to this stage there was a significant African membership (in 1970 there were 982,000 African Anglicans; in 1980 there were 815,000; in 1991 there were 646,000; in 2011 there were 1,007,808). By the 1970s there was a significantly sized Anglican Church in Southern Africa, which had by this stage contributed to the development of the country through the creation of schools, hospitals and mission stations. With the election of Desmond Tutu as Archbishop of Cape Town in 1986,[37] the Anglican Church became increasingly perceived as a 'black church' that in South African terms would translate into a Church careful to the needs and aspirations of the African population.

Anglican presence in South Africa from 1984 to 2014

The wider context for the South African Church has changed hugely in the past two decades with the passage from apartheid to democracy. Transition to democracy in South Africa has meant different things for various religious communities and the Christian spectrum has varied dramatically in the past thirty years.

While the African Independent movement has experienced a constant level of growth in membership since the end of the 1980s, mainline churches went through the opposite process.[38] Mainline denominations kept growing until the 1960s, then started to shrink or remained static in the 1970s, and after that they started a steady decline,[39] with a marked drop between the 1996 and 2001 censuses when mainline churches decreased their share from 36.5% to 32.6% of the entire South African population.[40] The decline in mainline churches' membership since the 1970s reflects a global and continental trend framed in the success of less institutionalised religions with more vibrant expressions of spirituality;[41] even though in South Africa that was the time in which mainline Christianity was particularly active in the public sphere and a time in which mainline Christianity played a very significant role in the democratisation of South Africa.[42]

Even the ecumenical movement that brought together Christian denominations and other religions and whose identity was closely knit to the anti-apartheid era has emerged considerably weaker. This has happened in part because senior leadership was lost to new institutions of State or other secular organisations including business, in part because the shift from the register of resistance to the key of cooperation with government has proven very difficult, and in part because the identity of these organisations (once the apartheid regime had been defeated) could not remain the same and their reason for existence was no longer obvious, such as was the case of the South African Council of Churches (SACC). Cuts in funding, especially from abroad, also contributed to the weakening of interfaith and ecumenical synergies.[43] As an Anglican reverend articulated:

> the post-apartheid affected churches and our theologians were caught in the government and aligned with it. In the last 20 years the Anglican Church did not have a public voice, a prophetic voice, and people are wondering why they should stay in the Church.[44]

Mainline churches grew constantly in the first half of the 20th century and they were uncontestably dominant in the Christian landscape. They kept growing in the 1960s and in the 1970s at a lower rate and with differences within different ethnic groups, but in the 1980s Protestant Christianity started to suffer a considerable decline.[45] Statistics from 1911 until 2001 indicate that Christianity increased from 45.7% of the population in 1911 to 79.8% in 2001 while affiliation to 'no religion' decreased from 50.7% to 16.4% in 2001.[46] Figures from the 1980s onwards suggested that the long-term proportional decline among white mainline Christians was now becoming an absolute decline. This is confirmed by examining the denominations as a proportion, not of the total white population, but of those who expressed a religious affiliation. Thus, the proportion of Anglicans amongst whites who expressed a religious preference dropped from 10% in 1980 to 7% in 1991.[47] As Kritzinger explained, the 1991 census forms stated explicitly that the furnishing of information on religious affiliation was voluntary while no other information was classified as such.[48] The regulation of confidentiality may have been in force at the time of the previous censuses, but the voluntary nature of the survey was never stated so clearly, with the result that only 3% of the people did not provide this information in the 1980 census. A large number of people (almost 30% of the total) in 1991 decided not to furnish any information on their religious affiliation and there is no information available on this percentage of the population.

In the decades between 1970 and 1990 mainline Protestantism suffered a serious decline but overall Christianity was not in retreat. Catholicism for example experienced growth. However, the most striking data across the Christian spectrum in these years was the fact that African Independent Churches and charismatic forms of Christianity were re-emerging.[49] By the 1991 census this trend affected the Catholic Church as well – it registered a marked drop as per the other Protestant mainline churches,[50] passing from 12.3% in the 1980 census to 11.4% in 1991,[51] and down again to 8.9% by the 2001 census.[52]

White Catholics decreased from 388,000 in 1980 to 315,000, but the drop for white Anglicans was even worse, from 462,000 to 292,000.[53] To put this in context, in 1996 approximately 30 million people were classified as belonging to a Christian religious group of one kind or another, compared to 35.8 million in 2001. Approximately 4.6 million people reported having no religious affiliation in 1996, compared to 6.8 million at the time of census 2001. In both censuses (the last two censuses with the 'religious affiliation' category) approximately one-third of the population indicated that they belonged to conventional or mainline Christian churches. In 2001, a further third of the population indicated that they belonged to one of the independent churches. Amongst those for whom the question was answered, 11.7% stated that they did not belong to any religious group at the time of census 1996, compared to 15.1% at the time of census 2001.

According to the 2001 edition of the World Christian Encyclopedia,[54] in 2000 there were 83 million African Independents and 126 million Pentecostal Charismatics in Africa. Although some of these categories partially overlap,[55] it is possible to define a general clear trend in the continent that differs from South Africa's trends. While Pentecostalism thrives around Africa, especially in West Africa, in South Africa Zionist-Apostolic churches still have a strong mass appeal. In 2001 the overall South African population was 44,819,774 and of those 37.93% belonged to mainline churches.[56] According to census 2001, Anglicans at the beginning of the New Millennium represented 4.8% of the entire population; Methodist 9.2%; Reformed Church 9.0%; Roman Catholic 8.9%; Lutheran 3.2%; PCC 7.6%; AICs 40.8%; 'Other Christian' 12.0%; and Congregationalist/Presbyterian and Baptist (together) were 4.7%.[57] Differently from the rest of the continent in which AICs experienced a growth during the end of colonisation in the 1950s and in the 1960s, in South Africa African Independent Christianity at the beginning of the New Millennium established itself as the biggest Christian denomination while Pentecostal Charismatic Christianity started to overtake several mainline denominations.

A succession of national censuses maps a decline in Anglicanism in relation to the total South African population. Anglicans in 1960 were 12%; in 1970 were 10.4%; in 1980 were 9.0%; in 1991 were 5.7%; in 2001 were 4.8%.[58] In the 2001 census the proportions of Anglicans in relation to the national population across ethnic groups were: Black Anglicans 3.1%; White Anglicans 5.8%; Coloured Anglicans 9%; and Asian Anglicans 0.5%. From a reading of the Church material (online material and ACSA parishes documents) and from the interviews it emerged that more or less in the ten/thirteen years between the last census with data on religion (in 2001) and the present days, the percentage of Anglicans in South Africa did not experience an additional dramatic decrease and membership remained between 3% and 4% of the entire population.[59]

The Anglican Church of Southern Africa reached its highest peak in membership in the 1920s, representing 20% of the South African population, and started to decrease steadily between the 1920s and the 1990s[60] with an arrest between 1991 and 2001 (but still with a slight decrease taking place). In total, Anglicans in 2001 registered 4.8% of the population. On the contrary, the Roman Catholic Church experienced a slow but consistent increase from the 1920s until the 1980s and then a decrease between the 1996 census and the 2001 census. AICs and Pentecostals increased, AICs especially between the 1980s and 2001 while PCCs are going through a steady growth in the last twenty years.

Through an analysis of ACSA's documents and interviews, several internal voices have expressed the opinion that the membership decline in the Church had started to reverse and that Anglicanism was experiencing a re-growth of sorts in South Africa. However, this understanding has not been substantiated with solid detailed datasets and it has not been analyzed in relation to the national population growth and growth of other Christian denominations.

> At the Provincial Missionary Conference that we hold once a year they would say that the membership within the Anglican Church in the region has been growing since the 90s because we have more congregations. But we need to understand those data. For example people are moving to urban areas and although the diocese of Johannesburg has been divided into 4 in 1990 when it experienced a big growth, this does not mean that membership grew at a national level. The country went through changes and the population has moved and changed. While the Anglican membership experience some growth in Johannesburg, for example Sharpeville has lost considerable numbers.[61]

Existing data removes any doubt on the fact that the Anglican Church went through a big decline in the past thirty years. Unlike its European counterparts, though, in South Africa this was not due to a process of secularisation but due to a shift from mainline Christianity to more charismatic forms of religious expression.[62] This shift can be understood in relation to global trends that affected the African continent but also in relation to the specificities of the South African Anglicanism that in a certain way struggled to regain a proper identity in the post-apartheid context and did not develop a strategy to regain its members in the new political dispensation.

One Church, two directions

This section presents and investigates the challenges that Anglicanism faces in contemporary South Africa and it offers an assessment of internal trends that are significantly changing the nature of the institutional approach to membership decline. From an analysis of the Church's documents (especially from the Provincial Synods and Dioceses Synods in the past forty years)[63] and interviews, it emerged that although the Anglican Church feared the decreased numbers in membership, nonetheless they adopted a politics of maintenance more than expansion. In most of the official Synods' documents in the past three decades, there are very limited mentions of membership and issues of growth and decline. As articulated by an Anglican reverend with a strong focus on evangelisation, 'We are experiencing a decline because we are not evangelizing but embracing the "politics of maintaining"'.[64] The politics of maintenance was for example articulated by ex-Archbishop Ndungane on 7 July 1997 in a conversation with Revd. Canon Cyril Okorochat, Director for Mission and Evangelism in the Anglican Consultative Council in London while preparing ACSA's contributions to the Lambeth Conference (1998).[65] Through decades the Church in the Province seems to have maintained the attitude of its origins when Anglicanism was planted in the Cape. Over the years the dominant approach came from the influence of the High Church that did not pose so much emphasis on growing the membership but more on supporting British settlers first and then on promoting social development and justice.

> The Anglo-Catholics in Southern Africa have always been loose on the issue of evangelism. It is part of the history of the church and it is part of the British understanding that you do not talk about religion and politics in public circles. We inherited that understanding of Anglo-Catholicism in Southern Africa but it is not the same in other contexts. You are there to teach your children, you are not there to challenge your neighbor. When you look at [the Church's] documents you won't find anything or very little about growing. Deep down there is a kind of hostility towards evangelism. In fact when we were teaching at the seminary during the 80s, students if they wanted to insult another student, they would call him an evangelist. [. . .] Still today you can talk of growing the Church but we are [Anglicans in general] not comfortable with the term evangelism.[66]

Nonetheless, South Africa experienced charismatic revivals that called for a more active role in growing the membership and evangelisation. Along with other revival movements within mainline churches that were happening with varying degrees of hostility and acceptance in the USA, in the UK and in various ex-British colonies during the 1950s and the 1960s,[67] South Africa produced its own charismatic revival in the 1970s especially under the leadership of Bill Burnett, Archbishop of Cape Town and Primate of Anglican Church of Southern Africa (1974–1981). As Anderson said, 'the presence of Charismatic in South Africa is almost as old as the Charismatic movement itself, which began in Western countries in the 1960s'.[68] The influence of this revival was mainly felt across the white Anglican population and had a limited impact on the overall Church's institutional apparatus and action between the 1970s and the end of the 20th century. As mentioned above, charismatic elements and evangelical attitudes have always been seen with suspicion by the Church's establishment where the focus has been on social change, development and justice with the leadership of the following Anglican Archbishops Philip Russell (1981–1986), Desmond

Tutu (1986–1996), Njongonkulu Winston Hugh Ndungane (1996–2007) and Thabo Cecil Makgoba (2007–present).

The charismatic renewal amongst black South African Anglicans has widely been ignored by the literature and by the Anglican Church establishment.[69] The Iviyo movement, still active in South Africa, is an example of black South African revival. *Iviyo lofakazi baka Kristu*, a Zulu expression that means the Legion of Christ's Witnesses, is a charismatic renewal movement within the Anglican Church of the Province of Southern Africa that started in the 1950s and then spread beyond its place of origins. Like many renewal movements, Iviyo started by individuals responding to local concerns in rural Zululand. The founders were Alpheus Zulu (later Bishop of Zululand) and Philip Mbatha, who initiated the movement following their concerns with the lack of power, energy and enthusiasm in the life of the Church and the institutional incapacity to affect people's life. Iviyo members are committed to recruit at least one new disciple each year.

Changes across the South African Christian spectrum, such as the marked success of Pentecostal Charismatic churches (PCCs) and other forms of charismatic expressions, a less active Anglican membership and changes within the clergy and the leadership (for example, more women, younger leaders, etc.), are all factors that impacted upon more recent trends within ACSA. Trevor Pearce, director of 'Growing the Church' network, said in an interview that 'Archbishop Thabo Makgoba is an Anglo-Catholic but he is behind us and he is supporting the "Growing the Church" initiative'.[70] Overall the sense of a negative attitude and suspicion towards ideas of expansion and evangelisation within the Anglican Church in Southern Africa partially changed in the last ten years. Although the evangelical side in the Anglican community in Southern Africa is still a minority, their initiatives are starting to have a sort of impact that in a few years could influence the Church's membership.

These changes have been initiated from the bottom as well as from the top. For example, several priests started to differentiate services according to the needs and perceptions of the multiple audiences living in the community:

> A huge number of people in the Anglican Church are embracing the charismatic approach and parishes are adapting. Here in St. Mike and All Angels for example we offer three kinds of different services from the High Church style to the more evangelical one. We need to mix up services for not disappointing different communities and expectations. Synods are very traditional and changes start in parishes first.[71]

From a top-down level, in 2003 the discussion around 'Growing the Church' was initiated by the then Archbishop Ndungane at the Synod of Bishops. Ndungane recognised the need to bring several Anglican organisations and synergies together in order to develop a defined and effective strategy for expansion. In June 2005 a report entitled 'Growing the Church' was presented to Provincial Synod that adopted the resolution of initiating a 'Growing the Church Network'. 'Growing the Church' was officially launched at the beginning of 2007 and Revd.

Trevor Pearce was appointed as director. 'Growing the Church' is a network of organisations that engage with Southern African as well as international organisation within the Anglican Communion like Anglican Witness and SOMA (Sharing of Ministries Abroad).[72] Their focus is on expanding the Anglican membership in the Province through the involvement of local leaders and the laity. According to Revd. Trevor Pearce, director of 'Growing the Church', the

> beginning of the network has not been easy but things are changing. Still, many leaders do not understand why we have to go where people are, to a taxi rank or to a coffee shop if we want the Church to grow. But it is changing and there is evidence that the Church membership is growing in the Province.[73]

Revd. Pearce highlighted the numerous challenges that the organisation is facing, along with still existing suspicions from parts of the clergy to financial limitations (only 30% of their activities is funded by ACSA while the rest is through fundraising activities), the vastness of the provincial territory and the difficulties of reaching isolated rural areas, keeping in contact through the use of technology, effectively communicating with Lusophone parishes, and so on. But overall the network had a rich agenda, including Anglican Ablaze, a biannual international conference focusing on Church growth that started in 2012, attracting 1,400 people; in 2014 it attracted more than 3,500 people. Its third gathering was held in Cape Town in October 2016.

Researchers will need more data and an in-depth analysis of a longer period of time in order to understand and assess whether those changes, adopted to increase the Anglican membership in the Province, and in particular in South Africa, are having a successful impact.

A few concluding remarks

A study of the membership of a Christian denomination cannot be detached from an interrogation of the meaning of that membership itself; what does a sense of belonging to a church mean and how has this meaning changed over time?

If, in Alan Andersons's words, it is possible to state 'we cannot understand African Christianity today without also understanding this latest movement of revival and renewal',[74] it is also true that to describe a meaningful pattern of religion in South Africa we need to understand issues taking place in the post-apartheid context such as a more mobile Christian membership that shops around and rationally chooses new churches, new political and economic challenges, a more flexible sense of belonging and different spiritualties.

According to many parish clergy, defining membership and sense of belonging is becoming more and more difficult. They lamented the difficulties of documenting and registering members as well as the 'competition' of the dual (or multiple) sense of belonging and loyalty to different churches and different Christian denominations that many congregants experienced. It is not uncommon to see churchgoers attending alternate services and events accordingly to their changing needs:

> It is an issue of dual spirituality. If they want entertainment they go to a Pentecostal church but if they need a sacrament they go to mainline church. You have people thinking 'this will look good with my friends, with my family'.[75]

And again:

> There is no sense of contradiction to belong to different churches. Sometimes you have people coming to service in the morning, going to another church service in the afternoon and to a bible study in the night in a different church. Yes, it is frustrating. Urban areas have two kinds of churchgoers: church hoppers, that move around different churches; and then you have those ones that remain loyal to the township and their finance remain there too.[76]

If the apartheid era has been defined by Terence Ranger as a time of 'frozen' identities (White, Coloured, Black, Indian but also Zulu, Venda, etc.), when people could not choose what space to occupy, where to move to and where to live, the post-apartheid situation has brought mobility (internal and external with migrants), flexibility and pluralism.[77] And with this plural and mobile society a 'market' of Christian 'churches has started to develop and become more competitive' while membership has started to become a looser and more complex concept not simply identifiable with the 'Church of your parents' as in the past:[78]

> One of our member was sick at the hospital. When I went to visit I saw Pentecostal pastors at the door and the wife told me they called them because they believed they were more powerful in healing. I found it interesting. As an Anglican, I do not have the same view of leadership as perhaps a Pentecostal pastor. I grew up as an Anglican and when I grew up there was no relation with other denominations. Today there is more fluidity and tendency for pastors to talk to each other that would not happen back then. People were not moving around churches.[79]

In the current scenario people can choose accordingly to their needs and vocation (an analogy with analyses produced by the sociology of religion on religious pluralism in the USA can be made here), but additionally South Africa experiences something very peculiar to its own context, something very 'South African'. That is the lack of division and contrast between different Christian denominations; an attitude that perhaps can be traced in the strong ecumenical movement developed during the struggle against apartheid.[80] In the same family it is possible to find members who belong to different churches, who move from one denomination to another in the course of their lives without tension from within but also from without, with no personal perception of a negative contrast or duality and without reprimand from the religious community or the social context. Ironically, the political system built on racial boundaries eroded denominational boundaries.

The natural process of secularisation that was expected in South Africa with the advent of democracy (and for some with the entrenchment of the 'secular' African National Congress in power), as well as in other African contexts with the end of colonisation, did not take place and what we are observing today is not a secularised continent but, on the contrary, a very religious one shaped in part by the many changes in the way religion is expressed and lived and spirituality perceived in everyday life.[81] Mainline churches seem to have struggled to reinvent and recreate a space and a voice in this complex Christian context to the detriment of their membership. This has been particularly true in the case of the Anglican Church of Southern Africa since the 1970s but nonetheless new techniques, reflections and approaches are starting to be developed in order to find new answers to contemporary challenges. The coming years and decades pose challenges and opportunities.

Notes

1 Especially Archbishop Njongonkulu (Winston) Ndungane's collection, AB2582; Anglican Consultative Council, AB1106; Anglican Missionary Association, AB1679. Available at History Papers, Cullen Library, the University of the Witwatersrand, Johannesburg (consulted in February 2014).

2 Fieldwork research in Johannesburg and Pietermaritzburg between February and March 2014 would have not been possible without the generous contribution of the Carnegie Trust through the Small Grant scheme.

3 As Church data is only available for the last decade, the author must acknowledge that figures are not completely precise but that nonetheless are sufficiently reliable when coupled with interviews to provide an understanding of national trends and shifts within the Anglican Church (that nonetheless uses and reconfirms those numbers in its own projections and publications).

4 Categories used in the national censuses changed across years and they are not consistent. Furthermore, political and administrative changes deeply influenced data representation and data collection. As D. Goodhew, 'Growth and Decline in South Africa's Churches, 1960–1991', *Journal of Religion in Africa* 30 (2000): 345 noted,

> during the 1970s South Africa granted a spurious independence to various parcels of its territory, such as Transkei. Consequently, the 1980 and 1991 censuses do not include the people in these areas. The 1991 census was also affected by the fact that the South African state was convulsed by internal conflict, making the collection of data especially difficult. All this means that figures need to be treated with considerable care.

National census data still provides a valuable source in understanding trends and changes over time.

5 For example,

> in my opinion after 1994 the ANC isolated all the organisations that were not the ANC; like IFP, PAC etc. and now we see the marginalisation of churches. At their

> core they were very Marxist . . . they see that they cannot have moral regeneration without churches because South Africa is a religious country. But the state perceives itself as secular; it is distant from religions and they are more and more marginalized.

Interview with Revd. Dr. X, Pietermaritzburg, 16 February 2014.

6 FAQ, question n. 31, Stats South Africa website, available at http://www.statssa.gov.za/census2011/faq.asp.

7 Interview with Bishop X, nearby Johannesburg, 19 February 2014.

8 Interview with Revd. X, Pietermaritzburg, 16 February 2014.

9 Interview with Revd. Y, Pietermaritzburg, 16 February 2014.

10 Fieldwork notes, February 2014.

11 This is in line with a couple of studies on the Anglican clergy in South Africa that highlight how managing high expectations from churchgoers and level of stress caused by social division, economic disparity, crime and injustice in post-apartheid era, accompanied by the lack of clear leadership and strategy from the Central Church, were quite frequently bringing the ordained and laity to depression and alcoholism; see V. Kgabe, 'Abuse of Alcohol by Anglican Clergy: Challenge to Pastoral Care' (Unpublished PhD thesis; Faculty of Theology, University of Pretoria, 2011); D.J.W. Strumpfer and J. Bands, 'Stress among Clergy: An Exploratory Study on South African Anglican Priests', *South African Journal of Psychology* 26 (1996): 67–75.

12 B. Bompani, 'Mandela Mania: Mainline Churches in Post-Apartheid South Africa', *Third World Quarterly* 27 (2006): 1137–49.

13 Available at ACSA website, http://www.anglicanchurchsa.org/.

14 Ibid.

15 Available at http://www.localgovernment.co.za.

16 D. M. Mark, 'The Contribution of the Anglican Church of Southern Africa to Social Development in South Africa and Its Potential Role as a National Partner in Development' (Unpublished Masters dissertation; Department of Social Development, University of Cape Town, 2008). Retired clergy continue to perform pastoral functions; this allows them to generate an income in addition to their pensions provided by the Church (data from ACSA website, diocesan websites, and diocesan offices, consulted in February and March 2014).

17 K. Ward, *A History of Global Anglicanism* (Cambridge: Cambridge University Press, 2006): 141.

18 A. Balcomb, 'From Apartheid to the New Dispensation: Evangelicals and the Democratization of South Africa', *Journal of Religion in Africa* 34 (2004): 11.

19 Balcomb, 'Apartheid'; see also Ward, *Anglicanism*: 153.

20 Balcomb, 'Apartheid': 11.

21 Available at http://cesa.org.za/.

22 Racial classification created by the apartheid regime remains in common use in the current democratic context where, now deprived of any negative connotation, is used to define ethnic belonging. Therefore, this chapter utilises White, Coloured, Black and Indian or Asian to indicate various South African ethnic groups.

23 Balcomb, 'Apartheid': 14.

24 See correspondence between CPSA Cape Town Office and CESA Bishop's office in Archbishop Njongonkulu (Winston) Ndungane's collection, AB2582, Wits Historical Papers Archive.

25 P. Lee, *Compromise and Courage: Anglicans in Johannesburg 1864–1999: A Divided Church in Search of Integrity* (Pietermaritzburg: Cluster Publications, 2005).

26 Ward, *Anglicanism*: 137.

27 R. Elphick and R. Davenport (eds.), *Christianity in South Africa: A Political, Social & Cultural History* (Oxford: James Currey, 1997): 3.

28 J. D. de Gruchy, 'Grappling with a Colonial Heritage: The English-Speaking Churches under Imperialism and Apartheid', in R. Elphick and R. Davenport (eds.), *Christianity in South Africa: A Political, Social & Cultural History* (Oxford: James Currey, 1997): 155.

29 R. Davenport, 'Settlements, Conquest and Theological Controversy: The Churches of Nineteenth-Century European Immigrants', in R. Elphick and R. Davenport (eds.), *Christianity in South Africa: A Political, Social & Cultural History* (Oxford: James Currey, 1997): 32–51.

30 de Gruchy, 'Heritage': 156.

31 Lee, *Compromise*: 14.

32 Already in 1975 the Anglican Church had produced an experimental 'Liturgy 75', but only in 1989 was the official South African Prayer Book published and used in all the languages.

33 R. Elphick, 'Introduction', in R. Elphick and R. Davenport (eds.), *Christianity in South Africa: A Political, Social & Cultural History* (Oxford: James Currey, 1997): 1–15.

34 With 'mainline Christianity' it is intended the group of missionary historical churches that in South Africa includes reformed churches, Anglican, Methodist, Presbyterian, Lutheran, Roman Catholic and Orthodox churches and the United Congregational Church of South Africa.

35 The Catholic Church is the mainline denomination that lost the least number of members after the end of apartheid.

36 Mark, 'Contribution'.

37 Desmond Tutu was enthroned in February 1985 and elected to Cape Town in April the following year, starting his ministry as bishop in September. This followed the first unsuccessful attempt in 1974 when, for the very first time, the Anglican Church nominated a black candidate as bishop. See Lee, *Compromise*: 319.

38 P. Walsh, 'South Africa: Prophetic Christianity and the Liberation Movement', *Journal of Modern African Studies* 29 (1991): 27–60.

39 From Goodhew, 'Growth', and Statistics South Africa (StatsSA) [National censuses from 1996 to 2011], available at http://beta2.statssa.gov.za/.

40 StatsSA, Report No. 03–02–04 (2001).

41 P. Gifford, *Africa Christianity and Its Public Role* (Bloomington: Indiana University Press, 1998).

42 Balcomb, 'Apartheid': 5; P. Gifford (ed.), *The Christian Churches and the Democratisation of Africa* (Leiden: Brill, 1995). For more information on the influence of Christianity on politics see: D. Chidester, J. Tobler, and D. Wratten, *Christianity in South Africa: An Annotated Bibliography* (Westport: Greenwood, 1997).

43 Bompani, 'Mandela Mania'.

44 Interview with Revd. K, Johannesburg, 11 February 2014.

45 The Catholic Church is the historical denomination that lost the least number of members after the end of apartheid.

46 StatsSA, various censuses.

47 Goodhew, 'Growth': 357.

48 J. J. Kritzinger, 'Christians in South Africa: The Statistical Picture', *HTS Teologiese Studies/Theological Studies* 50 (1994): 610–18.

49 Goodhew, 'Growth': 344.

50 StatsSA (1991).

51 M. Prozesky and J. D. de Gruchy, *Living Faiths in South Africa* (London: C. Hurst & Co. Publications, 1995): 237.

52 StatsSA (2001).

53 StatsSA (1980 and 1991).

54 D. B. Barrett (ed.), *World Christian Encyclopedia: A Comparative Study of Churches and Religions in the Modern World* (vol. 2; Oxford: Oxford University Press, 2001).

55 B. Meyer, 'Christianity in Africa: From African Independent to Pentecostal-Charismatic Churches', *Annual Review of Anthropology* 33 (2004): 447–74

56 StatsSA (2001). Please note that affiliation data includes infants, who were assigned to their mother's belief.

57 StatsSA (2001).

58 Various censuses data from StatsSA and literature. According to data provided by the Anglican Church of Southern Africa there are approximately between 3 million and 4 million Anglicans in the Southern Africa province (see http://www.anglicanchurchsa.org).

59 Fieldwork notes, February and March 2014.

60 Please note: this is the time in which the black population started to increase steadily.

61 Interview with Bishop X, nearby Johannesburg, 19 February 2014.

62 S. Bruce, *God Is Dead: Secularization in the West* (Oxford: Blackwell Publisher, 2002).

63 The focus has been in particular on Acts and Resolutions of the Synods of Johannesburg and Cape Town dioceses. Material collected in the Ndungane's collection at Wits Historical Papers and in parishes.

64 Interview with Revd. Z, poor area nearby Johannesburg, 14 February 2014.

65 Wits Historical Papers, AB3347/A, file 2, records 1994–1999.

66 Interview with Revd. Dr. X, Pietermaritzburg, 16 February 2014.

67 Lee, *Compromise*: 349–50.

68 A. Anderson, 'New African Initiated Pentecostalism and Charismatics in South Africa', *Journal of Religion in Africa* 35 (2005): 68.

69 I. Hexham and K. Poewe, 'Charismatic Churches in South Africa: A Critique of Criticism and Problems of Bias', in K. Poewe (ed.), *Charismatic Christianity as a Global Culture* (Columbia: University of South Caroline Press, 1994): 50–69.

70 Interview with Revd. T. Pearce, Johannesburg, 18 February 2014.

71 Revd. Dr. K, Johannesburg, 11 February 2014.

72 For more information, see the Anglican Witness' website at http://www.anglicanwitness.org/ and SOMA's website at http://www.anglicanjoburg.org.za/soma/SharingofMinistries Abroad.aspx.

73 Revd. T. Pearce, Johannesburg, 18 February 2014.

74 Anderson, 'Pentecostalism': 68.

75 Interview with Revd. W, Johannesburg, 14 February 2014.

76 Interview with Revd. Dr. X, Pietermaritzburg, 16 February 2014.

77 T. Ranger, 'Concluding Summary: Religion, Development and Identity', in K. H. Petersen (ed.), *Religion, Development and African Identity* (Uppsala: Scandinavian Institute of African Studies, 1987): 156.

78 R. Stark and L. R. Iannaccone, 'Rational Choice Propositions about Religious Movements', in D. G. Bromley and K. Jeffrey (eds.), *Handbook of Cults and Sects in America* (Bingley: JAI Press, 1993): 241–62.

79 Interview with Revd. Y, Pietermaritzburg, 16 February 2014.

80 Bompani, 'Mandela'.

81 S. Ellis and G. Ter Haar, *Worlds of Power: Religious Thought and Political Practice in Africa* (Oxford: Oxford University Press, 2004): 2.

Asia

8   The Church of South India

Anderson Jeremiah

Introduction

It would not be an overstatement to claim that South India was one of the most important 'modern' missionary destinations since the early 15th century. Missionaries from both Roman Catholic and Protestant traditions from Europe and America established their missionary fields in various parts of South India. As part of an ecumenical spirit, the Church of South India (CSI) was formed in 1947 after a long consultative process. Within this ecumenical movement, space was created for congregations to preserve their own distinct denominational identities and local traditions. This chapter offers a brief historical overview of South India's mission history, an insight into various formative factors in the life of the CSI, concluding with a critical analysis of contemporary issues pertaining to growth and decline.

Mission history in South India

The advent of 'missionary' Christianity, which accompanied the colonial Empires[1] in India, resulted in an interesting interaction between the Gospel as brought by the Western missionaries and the socio-cultural setting of South India.[2] Being the hub of much Christian missionary activity, the southern part of the country proved to be a great laboratory. Despite the existence of a vibrant Orthodox Christian community in the tradition of St. Thomas, dating, it is claimed, from the 1st century, the modern missionary movement provided more diversity because of the number of new converts through mass movements into Christianity.

The Portuguese were the first European colonial power to establish a trading post in India with Goa as the heart of their expansion.[3] Despite an initial cordial relationship between the Thomas Christians and the early settlers from the Portuguese authority, it soon descended into a turbulent relationship with the orthodox community as soon as Goa was seized in 1510 to become the headquarters of political administration of the Portuguese Estado da India, an important centre of Catholic Christianity in the south Asian context. After few decades of collaboration there was a conflict of interest between the Catholic Church and Thomas Christians, eventually ending in an open conflict between these communities.[4] The Portuguese colonial rule did not last very long as the Dutch, Danish and English East India companies came to set up shop in India.

The English East India Company followed the same pattern as the other colonial powers; it prohibited missionary activities within its territories and resisted various efforts by the missionary organisations to allow their presence.[5] However, the English mission organisations continued their efforts and began supporting Protestant missionaries from Europe who were willing to travel to India and other parts of Asia. The Society for the Propagation of Christian Knowledge (SPCK) and the Society for the Propagation of the Gospel (SPG) were the key mission organisations that sent missionaries to British colonies. The English came to the rescue of the Danish settlement in South India to protect them from attacks by local kings. In 1706 two German Protestant missionaries, Bartholomew Ziegenbalg and Heinrich Plutschau, arrived in Tranquebar, Tamil Nadu, inaugurating the Protestant mission activities. To their surprise, they were not welcome in the Danish settlement, were imprisoned and threatened to be sent back home. But once the Danish colonial authorities knew that they were scholars and would be of help for their local governance they were allowed to continue their work.[6] Observing the relationship between the missionaries and the local colonial rulers in the British colonial India, historian Anna Johnston comments,

> The relationship between missionaries and the colonial state was one fraught with complications, ambiguity and extreme provisionality. In different mission fields of the British Empire, this relationship was variously mutually supportive, mutually antagonistic or ambivalent, in short it was highly contingent on local circumstances.[7]

She observes further that as early as 1807, the governors clearly advised the board of directors of the East India Company and others not to interfere in Indian religious tenets, particularly the caste system.[8] When the reform-minded missionaries had difficulty following such an authority and had their own way of evangelising, they too received firm instructions from their own mission directors. Such directives clearly stated that if the missionaries did not obey their strictures and pursued activities that went against the interest of local authorities, it amounted to disobedience on the part of missionaries and became a valid reason for their immediate dismissal. All connections with the mission society would be withdrawn and no further support would be provided for the missionaries concerned.[9] It is in this landscape, underpinned by the encounters between colonial authorities and missionaries, that local Christianity began to take shape.

The roots of the Church of South India: missionaries, denominations and caste

The Catholic missionaries accompanying the colonial power to South India took a pragmatic approach to the caste system. They did not want to get embroiled in caste related conflict, but rather adopted a safer method of non-confrontational attitude.[10] The resourceful missionaries also thought that if they succeeded in getting the 'high caste' converts then it would trickle down to the low caste, making their job easy.[11] But to their dismay, the high caste converts objected to sharing places of worship with low caste Christians, and fearing that negative attitude to caste system would affect their prospect of getting more converts to Christianity, they decided to accommodate caste practices within the church.[12]

The early Protestant missionaries, who were mostly drawn from the pietistic social context in Europe, had a contrasting point of view from that of their Catholic predecessors. They considered that 'caste within the church was an unmitigated evil' and did make genuine efforts to ward off this 'social evil'.[13] For instance the Anglican Bishop of Calcutta, Daniel Wilson, spoke firmly for the elimination of the caste system within the church; he said in a briefing on 5th July 1833, 'The distinction of castes must be abandoned, decidedly, immediately'.[14] But they found it to be too complicated to manage, so they had to yield to the pressure, allowing people from different caste groups to sit in segregated places inside the church.[15] Interestingly, Bishop Heber, a pioneer Anglican bishop, supported the segregated worship practice on the lines of caste and compared it to the situation in America and Europe where Christian masters and slaves worshiped from different places. There were efforts to change such openly discriminatory practices based on caste, but most of them failed, due to the non-cooperation of 'high' caste Christians.[16] Following such open opposition to the efforts of missionaries to check caste-based discrimination within the church, many missionary organisations decided to take up a conciliatory approach to caste practices. Commenting on these historical events, Webster suggests that this 'missionary dilemma' and their decision to take up a conciliatory approach towards caste practices had a significant impact on the history of the South Indian Church.[17] Holding a similar view, Ayub Daniel concludes in an influential and detailed analysis of the Christian missionaries approaches and attitudes to caste system over the past centuries, that they were of three kinds, 'accommodation, rejection and compromise', all of them pursued with an intention of preserving their mission of Christianising rather than emancipating the lives of outcastes, with few exceptions amongst enlightened Protestant missionaries.[18]

Although some of the missionary societies were interdenominational at an organisational level, the majority of missionary societies had strong denominational identities, like the Danish-Halle Mission (Lutheran), Baptist Missionary Society, Church Missionary Society (CMS), the Wesleyan Methodist, the Scottish and American Presbyterians, and the Canadian Baptist Mission.[19] However, they agreed to work and concentrate within particular territories and communities in order to avoid conflicts and confusion. But through a process of consultation and formal conferences, a series of gentleman's agreements were worked out between missionaries and between their mission societies. There was a general agreement not to carry out missionary work in a territory where missionaries of another mission society were already established. The result of such

agreements or treaties would be a more orderly patchwork quilt instead of a
higgledy-piggledy jumble of territorial jurisdictions. What this meant was that
no sheep or shepherd was supposed to stray from one fold to another; nor were
sheep to be surreptitiously stolen.[20] This process of exclusive mission fields gave
impetus to each denominational missionary organisation and churches to assume
distinct geographical identities. But unfortunately, it also had the spin-off effect
in the South Indian context, for these geographical boundaries came to signify
certain caste groups from which the majority of Christian converts were drawn.
Underlining this development Duncan Forrester records,

> The L.M.S in Travancore and some of the C.M.S and S.P.G stations in
> Tinnevelly became known as 'Nadar churches' and converts from other
> castes were not encouraged. In Travancore, the vast majority of Christians
> were L.M.S Christians. Thus, relations between denominations could have
> a caste dimension.[21]

This could be traced as the emergence of a confused identity with the
denominational heritage and caste at their roots. It is also crucial to note that this
method of accommodating and working within the caste framework brought
the missionaries rich dividends in terms of the number of people getting converted into Christianity. But they also had to be very shrewd in not losing the
high caste converts. In some cases, they even had to take special measures to
keep them coming.[22] Those efforts rather had a negative impact on the eman-
cipation of the Dalit converts.[23] One particular caste community meant that
the missionaries did not have to really bother about other cultural issues, which
would distract them from their aim of 'Christianising the heathen'. It can be
attributed to the fact that the missionaries didn't want to give room for inner
and inter-caste conflict within the church, which further strengthened different
communities assuming distinct identities.

There are several studies that document the continuing gap between various Christian groups on the basis of caste differences and the subjugation
experienced by the Dalit Christians within the churches in South India.[24] Particularly, one could trace the roots of caste conflict between various converts
from the days of CMS and London Missionary Society (LMS) missionaries,
who laid the foundation for Anglican churches in South India.[25] Similarly,
other mission organisations, such as the Basel Mission and Scottish Missionary
Society, had to contend with the disruptive nature of the caste system.[26] The
southernmost parts of Tamil Nadu, which were under the Anglican missionary
society's spiritual dispensation, were dominated by converts from the Nadar
community, who preserve their Anglican tradition even today, underlining
their caste identity.[27] In addition, the conflict between Vellalar and Pariyar
Christians assuming an Anglican identity to mask their caste affiliation bears
testimony to this social makeup.[28] Often non–Dalit Christian dioceses look
down upon other dioceses, which constitute members from predominantly
Dalit communities like the northern dioceses, which were either Scottish or

American mission fields. It is also observed that there is very little social commensality between these Christian Dalit and non-Dalit communities. Some of the Dalit pastors are not entertained in some of the congregations and cannot celebrate the Eucharist. Separate cemeteries are kept for Dalit and non-Dalit Christians, deeply embedding the divisions based on caste identities.[29] In Andhra Pradesh, the missionaries predominantly worked among Dalit communities, so inevitably the churches bear a Dalit identity.[30] Members of the present CSI are drawn from the 'Mala' and 'Madiga' communities, two prominent Dalit communities.[31] The historical rivalry between these caste groups results in a strained relationship between the churches which is often played out in public during church leadership elections.[32] This brief survey of the South Indian context offers a background to understand the formation of the CSI as an ecumenical body.

Building on from the complex mission history, an ecumenical movement began to emerge concurrently to the Indian independence movement. As highlighted earlier the Anglican, Presbyterian, Wesleyan Methodist and Congregational missionary movements took to themselves people from various caste communities, especially a large number from the outcastes. Although some of the churches and mission societies chose not to participate in the union, the LMS, CMS, Church of Scotland Foreign Mission Committee, Reformed Church of America and the Methodist Society of Britain all began to work towards a common ecumenical CSI.[33] Capturing the purpose of church union, George, a church historian, says,

> The primary purpose of the formation of the CSI came not from strategy or fear of different brands of Christianity existing in South India then, but from an inner urge and conviction that it is in the will of God such a union should take place.[34]

Even though the CSI was formed with an organic unity in principle, the groups involved in the union continued to preserve their own denominational missionary heritage in the life and ministry of the local congregations, besides safeguarding the caste identity. A CMS pamphlet published in the early days of CSI depicts a clear picture: 'no thought was given to unity on the mission field, Anglicans, Presbyterians, Methodist, Lutherans and a score of others busied themselves building separate churches'.[35] The caste-based segregation masquerading as denominationalism runs deep within the churches in South India; that is evident in congregations who refuse to share the eucharist or pastoral ministry. The preceding discussion showcases that though decades have gone by since the arrival of missionary Christianity, irrespective of the process of ecumenism embodied by the formation of the CSI, factors such as mission heritage, denominational squabbles and caste-based discrimination continue to dictate terms in its existence.[36] A great deal of the attitudes and activities found within the church today stem from this history and continues in order to maintain the status quo and manage the institutional church.

Church of South India: perspectives on growth and change

Before delving into the details of growth and change in the CSI, it would be helpful to get an overview of India during the past four decades (1980–2015). India as a country went through tremendous change during this period. The population doubled in number, going from 650 million in 1980 to 1.2 billion in 2015.[37] This is also the period when India embraced an open market economy and underwent radical liberalisation of the hitherto closed market.[38] It had a profound impact on communities across the country, embracing a new social system driven by the market economy. There was a significant change on the political front as the Indian National Congress party that ruled the country since independence began to lose its grip on the Indian population. Political outfits supported by Hindu right wing groups filled the political vacuum created by the decline of the Indian National Congress.[39] The Bharatiya Janata Party (BJP) first came to power in 1998, proclaiming a new era in Indian democracy. The growth and popularity of the right wing Hindu political party had a great impact on religious minority communities, such as Muslims and Christians, and other cultural minorities (i.e. Dalits), which have become persecuted. To further complicate the social fragmentation of Indian society on the basis of the caste system, the failure to generate social mobility of lower castes and untouchable castes was contributing to serious social strife.[40] Socially disenfranchised people in this landscape found some religions such as Christianity and Buddhism to be vehicles of social change. As discussed earlier, in spite of their limitations, due to the commitment of Christian missionaries towards an equitable living, Christian churches began to flourish as more people embraced Christianity for a better life.

As an independent church, the CSI spread its presence across the five states of South India (Telangana, Andhra, Karnataka, Kerala and Tamil Nadu) and the northern province of Sri Lanka (Jaffna). When it began in 1947, the union of the Church of South India had a membership of little over a million members from the Congregationalist, Presbyterian and Anglican churches.[41] During the formative years, dioceses were formed based on denominational mission boundaries for practical administrative reasons, and not along linguistic or regional boundaries. Often, as discussed earlier, these denominational identities doubled up for caste identity, an organisational process that has left an indelible mark on the life of CSI.[42] According to the latest data,[43] CSI is made up of twenty-three administrative dioceses with fifteen thousand congregations. The total number of people who identify themselves as members of the CSI are estimated around 4.25 million, with little over a million households. The clergy are made up of 3,500 men and more than 200 women priests. There are also 350 permanent deacons and 1,800 lay evangelists. In the past six decades, the membership has grown by over three million, adding about twelve thousand new communicants every biennium.[44] According to the data from 1996, two decades earlier,[45] there were 2.8 million members, spread across twenty-one dioceses, and

10,114 congregations. The clergy accounted for 2,244. When compared with the recent data there is an increase of 1.45 million members and 1,256 clergy. Further, two new dioceses were added and, significantly, there was an increase of almost five thousand new congregations. Recently the CSI made history by appointing its first woman bishop. This is an important growth trajectory for the CSI, given that during the same period other traditional churches (i.e. Roman Catholic, Baptist and Lutheran) and new charismatic churches have also increased in their numbers.[46] This growth within the CSI could be down to a general increase in the population, more members being baptised and new members being welcomed into the church, due to its outreach work in villages and remote rural communities. However, as I will argue later, these numbers could be due to a popular trend in increasing multiple membership of people. To ground this analysis of growth and change in the CSI let us look at a brief study of the diocese of Vellore.

Unpacking the notions of growth: a brief study of Vellore

The diocese of Vellore is one of the youngest among the CSI dioceses. It is located in the region of North Arcot, commonly known as the Vellore district in Tamil Nadu. The diocese of Vellore was carved out of the Madras diocese and formed as an independent diocese on the 26th of January 1976, with an estimated membership of 35,000 people.[47] This region has been home to both Roman Catholic and Protestant mission organisations. According to local historians, Roman Catholic Christianity came to the Vellore region through the Madurai mission in the 17th century.[48] True to its diverse mission history, Vellore also inherited the Anglican mission work and American Arcot Mission of the Dutch Reformed Church in America.[49] It still bears its mission background through the names of various institutions, such as Voorhees, DeValois and Scudder, to name a few. According to the latest data,[50] Vellore diocese has seventy-eight pastorates with eighty priests, of whom five are women. The diocese has approximately 106,320 members spread across more than 610 rural and urban congregations. There were more than five thousand new communicants in 2013–14 alone. Forty-two lay evangelists and seven permanent deacons support ordained priests in the pastoral work. The diocese has more than seventeen educational institutions, eight medical and professional training institutions and more than one hundred elementary schools. Vellore diocese is predominantly a rural diocese and criss-crosses the state boundaries of Tamil Nadu and Andhra Pradesh; this means it is a bilingual diocese speaking Tamil and Telugu languages. More than 90% of the Christians come from the Dalit community. The Vellore diocesan records suggest that in 1996, there were little over sixty thousand people spread across twenty-three pastorates and sixty-seven congregations in the diocese. Comparing it with recent data, one could notice that there was a significant increase in the number of pastorates and congregations. Yet, the same may not be necessarily reflected in the number of members. This could be due to the fact that there must has been significant pastoral reorganisation, whereby new pastorates and congregations were created, and facilitating better pastoral care to remote rural communities. This is an impressive growth for a diocese that in principle began as one small rural congregation with one family in 1861 as part of the American Arcot Mission.[51]

Vellore, the headquarters of the district, is a relatively small city with a population of 186,000, and Christians belonging to different denominations constitute about 4.8%.[52] Vellore functions as a hub of Christian activities and headquarters of the CSI diocese. The city is also home to the Christian Medical College, one of the biggest research hospitals in Asia, drawing many Christians to train, work and receive medical treatment. This dynamic context of a floating population contributes to a larger presence of Christians not accounted for in the national census. The Vellore diocese of the CSI has twelve congregations in the city itself with fifteen priests and a little over six thousand members. Many of these congregations register more than fifty baptisms annually of both existing members and new members. Vellore city has also forty-two registered independent Pentecostal and charismatic churches, with membership ranging from anywhere between twenty-five and six hundred members. Most of the independent Pentecostal churches in Vellore originate in the late 1960s, coinciding with the international Pentecostal movements. Churches like Zion Pentecostal Church and Assemblies of God, which are part of wider national networks, established their branches in the city.[53] Additionally, many churches or fellowships started mushrooming around individual pastors who are able to offer spiritual teaching and prayer support. Some of these independent churches are supported by oversees evangelical groups, particularly from the United States, starting a new phase in the missionary work in South India.

With this background, let us analyse the growth of and challenges for the church in Vellore, which will shed light on the larger growth trajectory of the CSI. According to some of the church leaders in Vellore interviewed during the research, the progress of the diocese can be attributed to two fundamental factors. First is the continuing mission and evangelising approach among the rural and urban communities. The diocese still employs evangelists to travel across the diocesan boundaries to preach and bring new converts to the Christian faith. Many evangelists establish new house groups and congregations in remote villages on a regular basis. These newly formed congregations are often later assimilated into existing pastorates in the nearby area. The diocese then helps the congregations to build small churches where regular worship can take place on Sundays led by a lay evangelist. Clergy from the pastorate take turns to visit these rural congregations on a monthly basis. According to the diocesan statistics, on an average there are about ten congregations per pastorate; attached with them are numerous small house groups in many of the villages across the district.[54] This continuing mission outreach to rural areas contributes significantly to the growth of the diocese. The diocesan officers mentioned that in the last five years more than a hundred new church buildings were dedicated and more are under construction in some of the rural pastorates. Secondly, many of the big urban churches have 'urban mission plans' of planting new churches or establishing sister congregations in new neighbourhoods to facilitate better pastoral care. With the urban expansion in the Vellore district and growth of new residential neighbourhoods, it becomes necessary to develop new parishes and congregations in such neighbourhoods. Some of the members of these newly formed congregations would have been members of already existing urban congregations, but are willing to become founding members of these new sister congregations, along with bringing in new members to them. Interestingly, there is also overlap between the rural and urban missions, whereby some of the urban churches are adopting rural churches to provide pastoral and financial assistance. This missional networking approach appears to be bringing in great dividends for the diocese.

On the other hand, the challenges faced by the church in Vellore could be broadly identified as corruption and failure of leadership, issues with pastoral and spiritual nourishment, and the impact of the popular prosperity gospel advocated by Pentecostal churches. Besides the perennial problem of the caste system within the church, which was dealt with earlier in the chapter, the CSI, like any other institutional church, suffers from over-centralisation of power and hierarchy in its management. Leadership elections have taken on a life of their own in the South Indian churches. The democratic process of electing new bishops, secretaries and other leaders has become a battleground, opening the door to caste identity, corruption and financial irregularities. When all these aspects are played out in the public space, the congregations become weary and look elsewhere for spiritual nourishment. According to many, the number of litigations and other claims of financial irregularities is a stumbling block in their Christian life. It also points to the reality of how institutional churches have become too engrossed in maintaining the church structures, in the process distancing themselves from the congregations and further alienating people. It is in such situations that the 'transparent' approach of independent Pentecostal churches, with less bureaucracy, becomes an attractive alternative. Many people do not want to leave their mother church (CSI) but would like to seek spiritual support from others. Further, the independent Pentecostal churches, with their effective individual pastoral and spiritual care, armed with the prosperity gospel, have made significant impact among traditional Christians. However, as explained earlier, the congregations belonging to the CSI are not necessarily registering any decline. Further, as it could be observed from the Vellore context provided by census data,[55] the overall Christian population has not changed drastically so as to accommodate the growth being shown by the independent churches. This situation points to a rather fluid movement within the various denominational groups, with Christians belonging to the CSI maintaining their membership while also visiting and taking new membership in independent churches and movements.

If we had to analyse the census data of Vellore (Census 2011), there are only about ten thousand Christians belonging to various denominations, but the significant growth of new churches posits an interesting phenomenon: the Christian landscape may have undergone radical changes in terms of denominational reorganisation and accommodating new churches, but the fact is that this change is not necessarily accompanied by numerical growth of new members. As observed earlier, the congregations in the Vellore diocese continue to register growth in terms of baptisms, weddings and new families joining the church, and so are the independent churches. If we add both counts of Christians, attending the CSI and other independent churches, there would be double the number of Christians in Vellore city alone. This is not the case when it comes to the national census report for the Vellore district. The Christian population largely remains the same, keeping in line with the national average in India. It is therefore safe to conclude that, along with other Christian denominations, the CSI is healthy, but not necessarily growing in terms of numbers; similarly it is also not losing any members either. It suggests that all denominations are drawing their members from the same pool of Christians in the city. This process of multiple memberships explains the modest share of Christians in the overall population. But it is important to keep in mind that the growth of new independent Pentecostal and charismatic churches are challenging the monopoly of the institutional churches on Christianity in South India, by becoming the preferred alternative. This process is nothing new, but simply reliving historical precedents in this region, based on the multi-denominational heritage in India presenting itself anew in enabling Christians to embrace new forms of Christian worship without sacrificing their roots. Many Christians express the opinion that they are comfortable with attending various churches, not being limited by their traditional denominations, including the CSI. However, it is inevitable that in the future, those who continue their dual membership in CSI churches and other independent churches might decide to leave the traditional churches for good.

Conclusion

Glancing over the long history of Christianity in South India, it is possible to understand that Christianity is shaped by various socio-cultural and political factors. The harsh realities of historical denominational divisions, punctuated by caste practices, make the CSI a unique case. For many the vision of organic unity is still alive and offers a beacon of hope to the world church. However, the lived reality for many Christians in South India is far more complicated and far from the hope it offers others. Due to its institutional nature, the dioceses within the CSI fold have become victims of corruption, nepotism and failed leadership. As a result, many members of CSI are feeling alienated, leading them to search for alternative sources of spiritual nourishment. The challenges facing church leadership are significant as they have the potential to push the Church into a steady decline.

From an expansive position, if we map the case of CSI onto the wider Anglican Communion, there are compelling similarities. Some provinces within the Anglican Communion may show an increase in numbers as they bring in new members, but others may be either stagnant or in decline. This perception should not be necessarily understood as the eventuality, a dominant European view, rather an adjustment in the landscape of Christianity. Self-identification of

Christians is undergoing a tremendous change for various reasons. But that does not mean they have stopped being Christians, whether Anglicans or Catholics. There is disenchantment among people and lack of appetite for institutional churches, with people preferring less commitment and more involvement, giving rise to multiple memberships. This pattern is not unique to the Western world but could be experienced across the Global South, which has become a comfortable home of contemporary Christianity.

Notes

1 Due to the limited scope of this paper I shall restrict my observations to the British Empire and its missionary connections as it feeds into the formation of the Church of South India. Having said that, it is important to recognise the complexity that existed in the early 18th century with five colonial powers (the French, Dutch, Danish, British and Portuguese) ruling various parts of South India, accompanied by their own bands of missionaries.
2 J. C. Webster, *The Dalit Christians – A History* (Delhi: ISPCK, 1992): 2–5.
3 R. E. Frykenberg, *Christianity in India* (Oxford: Oxford University Press, 2011): 128.
4 Ibid.: 131.
5 K. Koschorke, *A History of Christianity in Asia, Africa and Latin America* (Cambridge: Eerdmans, 2007): 61.
6 Ibid.: 51.
7 A. Johnston, *Missionary Writing and Empire, 1800–1860* (Cambridge: Cambridge University Press, 2003): 72.
8 Ibid.: 73.
9 Ibid.: 75.
10 K. Ballhatchet, *Caste, Class and Catholicism in India 1789–1914* (Surrey: Curzon, 1998): 7.
11 D. B. Forrester, *Caste and Christianity* (London: Curzon, 1980): 14.
12 S. Manickam, 'Mission Approaches to Caste', in V. Devasayam (ed.), *Dalits & Women* (Chennai: Gurukul, 1992): 60–69, 67.
13 Forrester, *Caste*: 42.
14 Koschorke, *History*: 62.
15 Johnston, *Writing*: 67; Frykenberg, *Christianity*: 260.
16 Frykenberg, *Christianity*: 258.
17 Webster, *Dalit*: 37.
18 A. Daniel, 'Approaches of Mission and Church towards the Indian Caste System', *Religion and Society* 42 (1995): 6.
19 Koschorke, *History*: 93.
20 Frykenberg, *Christianity*: 263; C. Graham, *The Church of South India: A Further Stage in Development* (Published on behalf of the appeal committee for women's work in the Church of South India, 1956): 8.
21 Forrester, *Caste*: 84.
22 Ibid.: 136.
23 P. Dayanandan, 'Dalit Christians of Chengalpatu Area and the Church of Scotland', in G. Oomen and J. C. Webster (eds.), *Local Dalit Christian History* (Delhi: ISPCK, 2002): 18–64.
24 N. Koshey, *Caste in the Kerala Churches* (Bangalore: CISRS, 1968); A. Andrews, *The Problem of Caste in the Church: A Challenge to the Praxis of Theology of Liberation with Special Reference to the Church in Tamil Nadu* (Unpublished M.Th thesis; Edinburgh University, 1993).
25 J. W. Gladstone, 'Christian Missionaries and Caste in Kerala', in M. E. Prabhakar (ed.), *Towards a Dalit Theology* (Delhi: ISPCK, 1988): 104–12.
26 G. Shiri, 'In Search of Roots: Christian Dalits in Karnataka and Their Struggle for the Liberation', *Religion and Society* 40 (1993): 28–35; E. Breitenbach, 'Scots Churches and

Missions', in J.M. MacKenzie and T.M. Devine (eds.), *Scotland and the British Empire* (Oxford: Oxford University Press, 2011): 70–72.

27 Forrester, *Caste*: 84.

28 Frykenberg, *Christianity*: 258.

29 M. Azariah, 'The Church's Healing Ministry to the Dalits', in J. Massy (ed.), *Indigenous People: Dalits* (New Delhi: ISPCK, 1994): 320.

30 J.E. Taneti, *Caste, Gender, and Christianity in Colonial India: Telugu Women in Mission* (New York: Palgrave Macmillan, 2013).

31 M.E. Prabhakar, 'Caste-Class and Status in Andhra Churches and Implications for Mission Today: Some Reflections', *Religion and Society* 28 (1981): 9–35.

32 C. Still, 'Caste, Identity and Gender among Madigas in Coastal Andhra Pradesh', *Journal of South Asian Development* 4 (2009): 7–23.

33 On the process of formation of CSI, see the following for a detailed discussion: L. Newbigin, *The Reunion of the Church: A Defence of the South India Scheme* (London: SCM Press, 1979); R.D. Paul, *Ecumenism in Action: A Historical Survey of the Church of South India* (Madras: Christian Literature Society, 1972); B. Sundkler, *Church of South India: The Movement towards Union, 1900–1947* (London: Lutterworth, 1954); A.J. Arangaden, *Church Union in South India: Its Progress and Consummation* (Mangalore: Basel Mission Press, 1947); K.M. George, *Church of South India* (New Delhi: ISPCK, 1998).

34 George, *Church of South India*: 9.

35 CMS Pamphlet, *Travancore: Then and Now* (New College Archives, University of Edinburgh, 1956).

36 George, *Church of South India*: 255.

37 Census 2011, available at http://www.census2011.co.in accessed 10 September 2015.

38 R.S. Sharma, *Rethinking India's Past* (Oxford: Oxford University Press, 2010).

39 C. Jaffrelot, *Hindu Nationalism: A Reader* (Princeton: Princeton University Press, 2007).

40 R. Thapar, *The Past as Present: Forging Contemporary Identities through History* (New Delhi: Aleph Book Company, 2014).

41 George, *Church of South India*: 15.

42 Webster, *Dalit*: 173; S.G. Kurian, 'Kerala: The Christian Dalit's Experience – A Case Study of the Palais Diocese', *Religion and Society* 45 (1998): 11–24.

43 Statistics provided by the CSI general secretary's office April 2015. The data concerning CSI and Vellore Diocese are approximate data, not accurate but moderately reliable. A detailed data collection across the province based on church registers has yet to be conducted. Until such an exercise takes place we have to depend on available data.

44 CSI Statistics 2008–2010, privately circulated in the 32nd CSI Synod.

45 George, *Church of South India*: 273.

46 C.M. Bauman, *Pentecostals, Proselytization, and Anti-Christian Violence in Contemporary India* (New York: Oxford University Press, 2015).

47 There is no proper evidence for this number, but it is a figure widely considered correct according to diocesan officials.

48 Available at http://www.vellorediocese.org/common/history_origin.php accessed 10 September 2015.

49 George, *Church of South India*: 69.

50 Data was provided by the Vellore diocesan office 5 September 2015. Additionally, during 2014–15, the author collected information pertaining to Christians in Vellore. During this data collection period interviews were conducted to provide specific views from people. Their identities are anonymised.

51 George, *Church of South India*: 70.

52 Census 2011.

53 Bauman, *Pentecostals*.

54 According to the national Census 2011, there are more than four thousand villages in the Vellore District.

55 Census 2011.

9 Singapore

Daniel Wee

Anglicanism first arrived in Singapore in 1819 through the settlers from the British East India Company but it wasn't until 1909 that it came into its own as the Diocese of Singapore. In 1966, the Right Revd. Chiu Ban It was consecrated as the sixth bishop of the diocese, and the first local Chinese bishop. Since then, there have been three other bishops – Bp. Moses Tay (1982), Bp. John Chew (2000) and Bp. Rennis Ponniah (2012), all three of whom fall within the span of this study. In 1996, the Diocese of Singapore became part of the newly formed Province of South East Asia, comprising the Dioceses of West Malaysia, Sabah, Kuching and Singapore. Six deaneries were placed under the Diocese of Singapore, and these are Thailand, Indonesia, Cambodia, Vietnam, Laos and Nepal. While there is active missions work in the deaneries, in this study we will only be looking at the growth of the Archdeaconry of Singapore from the 1980 to 2012.

Since the early days of the Anglican work in Singapore, the Church already had a missional view. In 1856, Revd. William Humphrey, resident chaplain of St. Andrew's Church (which later became St. Andrew's Cathedral) preached a Pentecost Sunday sermon in which he expressed the need to reach the locals:

> . . . we continue to have many enquirers, whom we have every reason to believe to be sincere in desiring to enter the fold of Christ. Thus we cannot stop even if we would. We cannot withhold our attention from those who so pleasingly require it; so that the congregation of St Andrew's must, in spite of itself, become a missionary congregation – a centre of diffusing to others the light and comfort and peace of the knowledge of Christ and Him crucified.[1]

By the 1970s, the Anglican churches in Singapore were caught up in the global wave of charismatic renewal that has contributed to a season of sustained growth. This, along with the already evangelical nature of the local Protestant movement, led to an increase in churchgoing Christians.[2] Many of the churches took on a more contemporary flavour, putting in place services with simplified liturgies or non-liturgical ones, often while retaining some traditional elements. The emphasis was less on the form of the service and more on the relational and experiential aspects of their faith. In this sense, it was firmly evangelical in its outlook.

This growth saw the diocese go from 18 local parishes in 1980, to 27 local parishes in 2012. Average weekly attendance rose from about 4,100 in 1980 to over 20,200 in 2012, a growth of nearly 500% over three decades. The Anglicans were not the only ones to enjoy this growth in Singapore as other mainstream evangelical churches saw similar growth throughout this period.[3]

The diocese is predominantly made up of parishioners who are Chinese in ethnicity, reflecting national population trends. They are divided into English speaking and Chinese (Mandarin and other dialects) speaking congregations with a few bi-lingual ones. Apart from that, there are also Indian congregations as a minority, along with several other ministries catering to Filipinos, Indonesians, Myanmarese and so on. This distribution reflects the natural demographic of Singapore's population.

The Anglican Church attendance data used in this study was taken mainly from the 1980 to 2013 annual Synod reports. Whilst information on confirmation and baptism numbers as well as electoral roll membership are available, the average weekly attendance would be a better reflection on the growth performance of the Church for the purpose of this study. There is considerable movement of Christians between churches and denominational loyalty is not an important factor for many Singaporean Christians. As a result, there may be people who have been in the Church for many years and are still not baptised or confirmed. Others may have been baptised and likewise not confirmed until many years later.[4] Electoral roll membership numbers are often far higher than real weekly attendance numbers for a variety of reasons as well. Average service attendance numbers, on the other hand, are usually updated on a weekly basis and represents the most consistent and current metric available to us for this study.

Within these attendance numbers, except for composite figures, we will be looking primarily at the English, Chinese and Indian speaking congregational numbers. The numbers for the other services are relatively small and generally track the trends in the major groups.

Growth of the Anglican Church in Singapore

It is said that a picture paints a thousand words, and the following chart (Figure 9.1) paints in broad strokes for us the story of how the Anglican Church in Singapore has fared over the last three decades. The graph covers the total average attendance at weekend services (inclusive of Saturday services) from the year 1980 to 2013. On the whole, church attendance numbers have grown nearly five-fold when comparing 2013 to 1983. This growth trend is not unique to the Anglican Church in Singapore but is also true of other denominational and non-denominational churches here. Though not reflected in the chart, the growth has picked up considerably since the mid-1970s compared to previous decades. This is ostensibly due to the impact of charismatic Christianity reaching the shores of Singapore.[5]

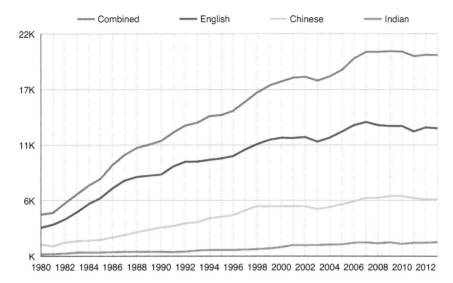

Figure 9.1 Total weekly attendance 1980 to 2013 in the Diocese of Singapore

Source: Annual Synod reports were the primary source of the data. These were manually verified with the churches and corrections made where applicable.

In December 1972, the then bishop of the Diocese of Singapore, Rt. Revd. Chiu Ban It, had a personal charismatic experience – a 'charismatic renewal and baptism in Spirit' while attending the World Council of Churches Assembly in Bangkok.[6] This allowed the charismatic movement to enter into the life of the local Anglican churches with St. Andrew's Cathedral becoming one of the centres for the renewal.[7] By the 1980s, many of the Anglican parishes had already incorporated elements of this charismatic renewal into the life of their churches and in their services.[8] This was especially so for the English speaking congregations who found that they could draw on the English materials and songs that were being imported from the West.[9] The net effect was that the Anglicans found themselves riding the wave of charismatic growth, along with other charismatic churches, in Singapore.

Looking at the graph we see that this growth has several different phases to it, including some years where there had been some declines. Between 1980 and mid-1996, the Church grew fairly steadily and consistently, adding about 3,800 service attendees (14,903 in 1996 to 18,704 in 2000). From 1996 to mid-2000 there was an additional spurt of growth over that four-year period before falling by about 1,300 to 17,406 in 2003. From 2003, there was another surge of growth for the next four years and peaking at 20,795 in 2007. In the last phase, stretching from 2007 to 2013, the numbers plateaued out in a very slight decline, representing the phase with the least growth in average weekend attendance number in the 30-year history of the Anglican Church in Singapore.

In terms of the absolute rate of growth, between 1983 to 1996, the Church added 670 per year to the average weekend attendance. The period of 1981 to 1987 saw some of the fastest growth of 955 attendees per year. Between 1996 to 2000, this rate increased to 950 new attendees per year, but from 2000 to 2003, for the first time since 1980, the attendance declined at a rate of 433 per year. Growth started again in 2003 to 2007 where there was an impressive growth rate of 847 per year. In the final phase from 2007 to 2013, there was a slight decline at a rate of 126 per year.

Baptism figures from 1986 through 2013 declined slightly but was otherwise averaging about 1,400 over the period (see Figure 9.2).

The following chart (Figure 9.3) shows the decadal growth rates (DGR) for the decades of the 1980s, 1990s, and 2000s.

We can see that while there has been growth, the rate of growth itself has been slowing down. Where the English speaking congregations started out with the fastest growth, it is now behind both the Chinese and Indian speaking congregations. The Indian speaking congregations, though smaller than both the English and Chinese speaking ones, showed the most sustained growth rate over the entire period of our study. This pattern of slowing growth was not unique to the Anglican Church but was reflective of the trend of Singaporean churches in general.[10]

This can be partly explained by the fact that the English language was officially introduced into the education policy in 1966 and had become increasingly adopted by the younger generation, often preferring English over their native

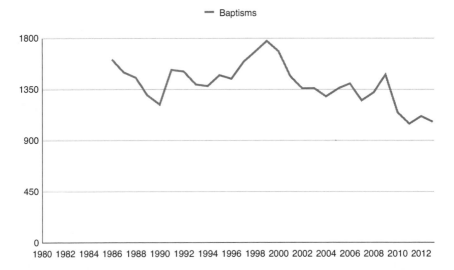

Figure 9.2 Combined baptisms (adult and children) from 1986 to 2013 in the Diocese of Singapore

Source: Annual Synod reports.

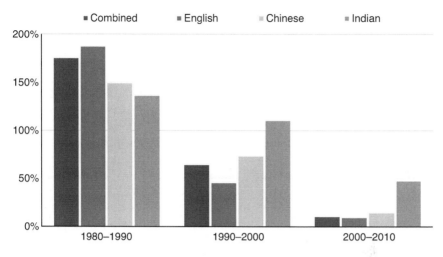

Figure 9.3 Decadal growth rate in the Diocese of Singapore
Source: Calculation based on raw data from the annual Synod reports.

tongue. Whereas dialects have been the dominant languages in the earlier years, English became the preferred language for economic development.[11] English was at the same time the language of the missionaries and Christian literature were available primarily in English as well. As we move into the 1980s, the trend was that Christians tended to speak English. This was true of Chinese, Malay and Indian Christians. There was also a strong correlation of English speakers with economic status as Christianity emerged as the religion of the upper middle class.[12]

In 1978, Singapore also saw one of its largest gospel rallies when Billy Graham held evangelistic meetings for five nights, averaging 65,000 people a night. This event sparked evangelistic fervour[13] amongst churches and gave Christianity some prominence.[14] These initiatives were predominantly in English although some Chinese translations were available. Consequently this gave English speaking evangelical churches, including the Anglican Church, a surge of growth along with a heightened sense of spirituality in the following decade.[15]

In 1984 the government made Religious Knowledge a compulsory school subject which led to secondary school students having to choose either Christianity, Buddhism, Islam or Hinduism as one of their subjects. It has been said that this turned out to be an opportunity for evangelical Christianity and led to many students gaining an acceptance for the faith.[16] Both Christianity and Buddhism saw rapid growth during this period and this led to Religious Knowledge being discontinued as a compulsory subject in 1990.[17]

These and other factors such as the social prestige associated with the language gave English speaking congregations a huge head start over the other languages.

The Chinese language (and dialects), though popular, were increasingly confined to the older generation with English becoming the language of choice for the younger graduates. As can be seen, however, that advantage lasted only up until the 1990s. The DGR for the English speaking congregations fell from a high of 187% in the 1980s to just 10% in the 2000s. At the same time, the DGR for the Chinese speaking congregations fell from 149% in the 1980s to 14% in the 2000s. Indian speaking congregations saw the smallest drop, from 136% to 47% over the same period of time. The sharp drop in the DGR for the English speaking congregations could have been due in part to the change in government and educational policies in response to the growing concern over the growth of Christianity in Singapore.[18] At the same time, nationally, the Chinese speaking churches grew better than the English speaking ones even though both were falling.

The growth of the Anglican Church in Singapore takes place against a backdrop of national growth. In 1980, the resident population was 2.3 million while the total population was 2.4 million. By 2013 the numbers had grown to 3.8 million and 5.4 million respectively.[19] The growth that we see in the Anglican Church has kept pace, or is in keeping with, the growth of the population of Singapore in general as Figure 9.4 indicates. When we examine the national population trends, we find that there is a positive correlation with the average church attendance numbers. The slump in total national population between 2002 and 2007, for example, is reflected as a slump in church attendance during the same period of time.

Demographically, Singapore has a growing number of foreigners, both working and residing there. That percentage has been increasing over the years and

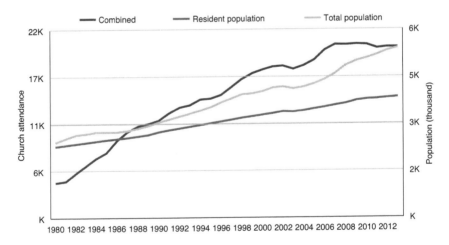

Figure 9.4 Church attendance (left axis) and national population (right axis) in the Diocese of Singapore

Source: Attendance data comes from the annual Synod reports. The national population data comes from the Singapore government statistics website – www.singstat.gov.sg.

some, invariably, have found their way into the local Christian community. We would expect this increase to have had a greater positive impact on the growth of the Church but that has not been the case. While church attendance has surely grown over the last three decades, in the last six years (2008 to 2013) the rate of population growth has outstripped the growth of the Anglican Church. This is especially evident when we look at the attendance numbers as a percentage of the population (Figure 9.5). This means that the foreign influx has largely not found its way into Anglican churches here. In particular, the large influx of mainland Chinese is not reflected in the attendance of the Chinese speaking congregations. By contrast, the non-denominational independent churches seem to have fared much better in this regard.[20]

From this graph we can roughly discern three major phases of the growth/decline of the Anglican Church in Singapore. The first phase, from 1980 to 1988, was marked by remarkably strong growth, continuing the trend that had begun in the mid-1970s. The Rt. Revd. Moses Tay had become the new diocesan bishop in 1982 and was a strong supporter of the charismatic movement, which encouraged the congregations that were evolving in that direction.[21] The 1980s was also marked by a period of great evangelistic fervour in Singapore starting soon after Billy Graham's 1978 evangelistic crusade up through the Luis Palau evangelistic crusade in 1986. Anglican churches were not left out and the majority of the individual parishes saw their strongest growth in this period under Bishop Tay's leadership. He made missions and evangelism a key priority for the diocese.[22]

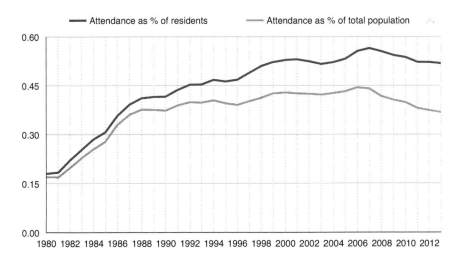

Figure 9.5 Attendance as a percentage of population in the Diocese of Singapore

Source: Calculations based on attendance data from annual Synod reports and national population data from www.singstat.gov.sg.

Probably the biggest impact on growth of the Anglican Church in Singapore in the 1980s (beginning from the mid and late-1970s) was undoubtedly due to the charismatic renewal amongst the churches. While not every parish had adopted a charismatic outlook to ministry, along with more contemporarily styles services, a number did so. Of the 19 or so congregations, not all of which had attained a full parish status, nearly half were open to and embraced the charismatic movement to varying degrees. By 1990, as the decade closed out, the five largest parishes were those who had been the most inclined towards the movement. Their church services tended to be more contemporary and less liturgical though often retaining some elements of traditional worship. In some cases, this meant that there were both contemporary as well as liturgical services being offered. In the contemporary services, it was more likely that they used songs of contemporary Christian worship than hymns. Modern music instruments were also incorporated into these services. At the same time, churches that saw a change in leadership to a more charismatically inclined vicar or priest-in-charge likewise saw a jump in their rate of growth. Conversely, churches that remained more traditional in their ministry outlook saw considerably less pronounced growth. A strong correlation can thus be made for the growth of our Anglican congregations with the degree to which they embraced the evangelical-charismatic-contemporary approach to ministry and services.

Figure 9.3 above also makes a point concerning the development of parishes ordered by language and ethnicity. In particularly, the Indian ministries and churches were still in their infancy and growth was slow during this period. Coupled with the fact that Indians were a minority in Singapore, the decade of the 1980s ended up with the Indian churches being among the smallest in the diocese at that point in time, pointing to the many challenges that faced minority group ministries. As for the Chinese speaking congregations, they tended to be more conservative culturally, and were slower than the English speaking congregations in adopting new forms of worship. The language divide here lined up with the divide between contemporary and traditional approaches to running their services and ministries.[23]

In general, the 1980s was a period of unprecedented growth for the Anglican churches in Singapore. While not all have grown to the same degree, a good percentage of the Church did experience congregation attendance growth. By 1989, however, it seemed that the growth had hit a snag and began to slow down considerably from the early part of the 1980s. The growth trends of some of the individual parishes (Figure 9.6) reveal that different churches experienced periods of growth during the 1980s but for most of them, this growth did not last through 1990. Between the years 1986 to 1990, various churches saw their growth plateauing, and in some cases going into decline. It should also be noted that the vast majority of the churches that experienced significant growth during this season were also those that were open to the charismatic renewal.

By the late 1980s, there were a number of groups that split from the churches to form independent groups. In 1989 a group left Marine Parade Christian Centre to start a ministry that eventually became today's City Harvest Church,

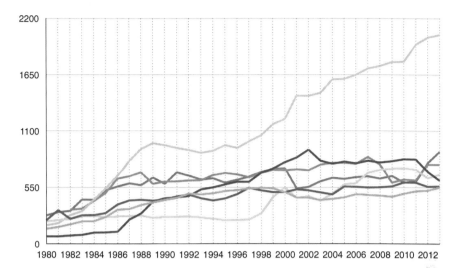

Figure 9.6 Growth of seven of the largest Anglican parishes, excluding the two biggest in the Diocese of Singapore

Source: Annual Synod reports.

one of the largest churches in Singapore. Not too long after that, another group left the same parish to start Cornerstone Community Church, an independent church that is quite sizeable today as well. Another group left Chapel of the Resurrection in 1989 to form Hephzibah Fellowship, also an independent church. In each of these instances, a considerable portion of the existing congregation left, thus impacting the absolute numbers. In these cases, the churches that were growing rapidly saw a loss of members. It turns out that the same charismatic environment that lent itself to enthusiastic growth and evangelism in church also allowed for personality issues to fester to the point where such splits took place. The movement was a double edged sword, and subsequent attempts to put controls in place to prevent runaway groups simultaneously cooled the enthusiasm down which, in turn, led to moderated growth.[24] It is quite possible that after the initial excitement of the charismatic renewal, deeper issues and differences came to the fore. During this same period of time, there were also a number of significant church splits taking place in the national scene – leading to the formation of independent churches, a number of which went on to become today's megachurches.

Some of the problems that stymied the growth stemmed from unhappiness with the leadership of the Church. It was quite common in those days for priests to be rotated in and out of various parishes and congregations. While the change itself does not necessarily lead to decline, in some cases it eventually led to disagreements and divisions. With the growing number of churches in Singapore, and the rise of the megachurches, it was easy for members to resolve the tension by moving elsewhere, often trying out different churches before settling down.[25] At the same time, previously traditional churches that received charismatically inclined vicars or priests to lead them exhibited the propensity for entering into growth. In 1986, one of the Anglican churches moved to a new location – a new residential town – and a new vicar was posted there who was very charismatic, having himself come from a charismatic church. This change led to significant growth that began for that very year.

Collectively, this resulted in an overall slowing down of growth that began around 1990, ushering in the next phase of the growth that continues until about 2007, a period of 17 years in total. It should be pointed out that the call for a 'Decade of Evangelism' by the 1988 Lambeth Conference had virtually no impact on the growth of the Anglican churches in Singapore. During this time, the Church still saw growth but at a reduced rate (combined DGR of 64% in the 1990s compared to 175% in the 1980s). This growth impasse wasn't merely an Anglican phenomenon, but was felt by Christianity in Singapore as a whole.[26]

By 1990, another change was taking place that is seldom discussed. The diocese had 24 parishes at that time but the top five churches made up slightly more than half of the average attendance of the entire diocese. The disparity of the bigger churches continues to grow and by 2000, four of the top churches made up half of the average church attendance for the whole diocese. In the following chart (Figure 9.7), it is apparent that the disparity is great enough that the variations of attendance within the three or four biggest churches are likely to have a larger impact on overall growth trends. We can also see that much of

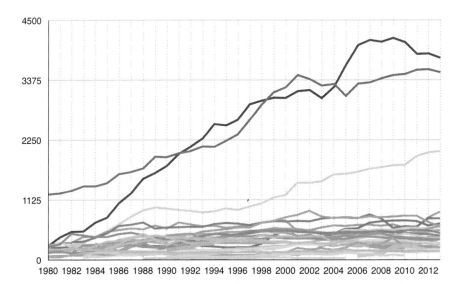

Figure 9.7 Average attendance for all diocesan parishes in the Diocese of Singapore

Source: Annual Synod reports.

the growth was taking place in these larger parishes. Because of this, the overall trends were dominated by factors taking place within these churches.

During the era of the 1990s, much of the initial growth spurt had petered out into more moderate to low levels. The primary changes in congregational attendance during this period were related to leadership issues, whether it is leadership disputes, or changes in leadership. Serious disputes that led to crises in the parishes sometimes led to a change in the leadership of the parish for the purpose of trying to stabilise the situation. There were also more natural reasons for a change in vicars or priests at a parish – such as death, retirements and resignations.

In 2000, Bishop John Chew took over the leadership of the Diocese of Singapore and in the following years, made some changes in the clergy postings. From 1990 to 1999 there were 15 changes of vicars, whereas there were only four in the preceding decade. From 2000 to 2009, there were 24, even more than in the 1990s. Priests, too, were moved around in a similar manner, with three moved in the 1980s, 25 in the 1990s and 51 in the 2000s.[27] Such changes in leadership sometimes have a significant effect on the growth pattern of the Church.[28] In cases where new leadership was brought in to address a crisis, it had the effect of stabilising the congregation and possibly leading to renewed growth. In other cases, the change resulted in an adjustment period that could see a decline in attendance numbers initially followed by subsequent growth. This did not always happen, though, as there were cases where the change led to sustained declines. These clergy movements, along with several leadership disputes in a few parishes, led to a decline in the overall growth from the year 2000 to about 2003. The one inescapable conclusion here is that the person who leads the parish, be it a vicar or a priest, plays a pivotal role in determining if a church grows, sustains or declines. Secondly, when such problems occur in the larger churches, they leave a bigger dent in the overall trend such as what happened in 1989, leading to subdued growth in the 1990s.

The 1990s were not without examples of remarkable growth. One parish, in particular, had languished for many years without growth. In 1997 she received a new vicar who was charismatically inclined. At their church camp that year, there was an outpouring of the Holy Spirit, sparking a revival in the English speaking congregation, which later spread to the Chinese speaking congregation of the church as well. This resulted in three years of unprecedented growth in the history of that church, more than doubling the size of the church from 235 in 1997 to 547 in the year 2000 (see Figure 9.8).

The vigorous growth was curtailed in 2000 as a result of internal issues involving the leadership of the churches, which led to a few years of decline in attendance, as well as a change in the leadership. The change of leadership managed to stem the decline and the parish eventually started growing again in subsequent years. This, again, underscores some of the observations that have been made earlier concerning the nature of charismatic growth with its propensity towards personality centred problems.

In another instance (Figure 9.9), in one of the largest churches in the diocese, growth also stepped up but for slightly different reasons. The church grew well

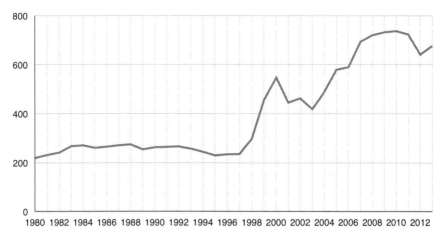

Figure 9.8 Example – impact of a 'revival' or 'outpouring' on growth in the Diocese of Singapore
Source: Annual Synod reports.

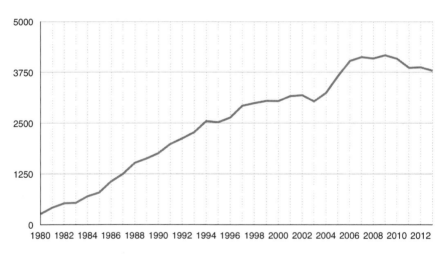

Figure 9.9 Growth trend of the fastest growing diocesan parish in the Diocese of Singapore
Source: Annual Synod reports.

for over 22 years under the leadership of the same vicar. This is one of those rare examples where there was no change of the vicar over the entire span of our study, serving 36 years at the same church. From 1997 to 2002 the growth rate had started to slow down a little even though it still remained the fastest growing parish over the three decades of our study. Its growth contributed to a significant portion of the overall growth of the diocese. In 1980 its average attendance was 263, one quarter of the 1,226 who attended the cathedral which was then the largest parish. By 1991, it had just matched and even surpassed the cathedral, growing over seven and a half times. This remarkable growth can be attributed to the undisrupted leadership, but also to the highly charismatic nature that has been adopted there and the personality of the vicar. It could be said that amongst the more charismatically inclined parishes, this was the most charismatic. The services were contemporary and the spirituality charismatic. In many ways, the experience there would be entirely what would be expected at a typical independent church.

As was pointed out earlier, by 2002 there were signs that the growth was slowing down. The vicar of the church, at this point, embarked on a renewed and strong emphasis on the 'supernatural', focusing on the miraculous and on healings. This did not sit well with some of the parishioners initially and that resulted in some of them leaving the church. Hence the first decline seen in nearly 20 years. What was interesting, however, was that from the next year onwards the church experienced a surge of growth that was stronger than it had seen since 1980. This growth lasted about three years before reaching a plateau. It is interesting that nearly three decades after the charismatic renewal reached the shores of Singapore, emphasis on charismatic ministry was still a significant factor affecting the growth of the church, all else being equal.

When we look at the overall growth of the diocese (Figure 9.1) we can see how the changes in this church impacted the trend. This brings us back to the three phases of growth/decline that we were looking at in Figure 9.5. Starting from about 2006 to the present, there was a moderate decline in the overall attendance numbers. Looking deeper into the individual parish trends, we see that the plateauing and decline in Figure 9.9 may have been a key contributor to this because of its large size. The retirement of a few vicars of large churches at this time (2007, 2011) also resulted in a leadership transition that disrupted earlier growth. It is worth noting that the adoption of cell-group-based strategies by various churches since the 1980s did not seem to have resulted in any significant change in church attendance.

Singapore is a very small city-state that relies heavily on trade and is, for that reason, particularly vulnerable to changes in the global market. Interestingly, however, the 1987 market crash and the 1996 property bubble crash did not seem to have that much of an impact on church attendance. The global financial crisis of 2007 did coincide with the start of this third phase and may have dampened enthusiasm, possibly indicative of an increasingly consumerist spirituality.

From about 2000 onwards, two very prominent independent churches started growing rapidly in Singapore and there were those who flocked to these megachurches for a variety of reasons. While the exact number of Anglicans who have gone over to those churches is not known, it is a commonly cited issue when discussing church growth issues and pastors have acknowledged that they know of such cases happening in their congregations. From the viewpoint of how the Anglican Church fared against other churches, we seemed to have lost some ground in this last phase (Figure 9.10) even though there has been growth.[29] At the same time the independent churches, in particular, were enjoying sky-rocketing in attendance.[30]

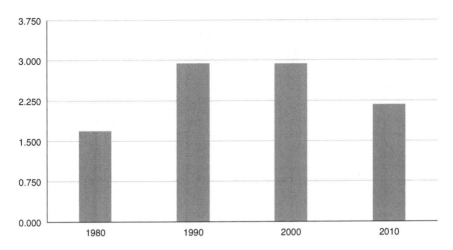

Figure 9.10 Anglicans as percentage of national Christians in the Diocese of Singapore

Source: Calculations based on attendance data from annual Synod reports and national population data from www.singstat.gov.sg.

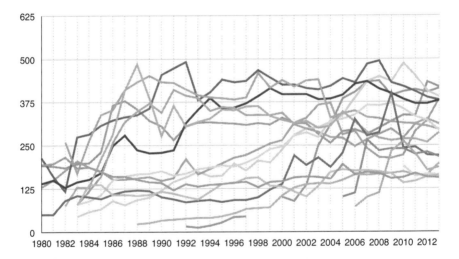

Figure 9.11 Growth trends of smaller parishes in the Diocese of Singapore

Source: Attendance data comes from annual Synod reports and national population data comes from www.singstat.gov.sg.

Whilst there were examples of very encouraging growth, there were also parishes who have not experienced any increase over the years. Putting aside those parishes which grew and then declined as a result of crisis or leadership issues, there were a couple of parishes that seemed to have struggled with growth. On the whole, the growth of the smaller parishes has been a mixed bag and rarely a smooth journey as the following graph shows (Figure 9.11). Various factors,

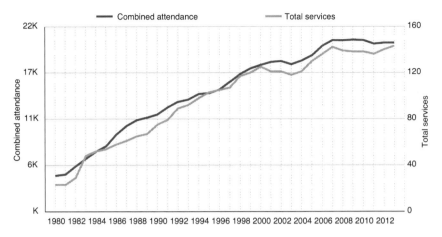

Figure 9.12 Combined attendance compared to number of services held in the Diocese of Singapore

Source: Data came mostly from Synod reports. Other data were directly obtained from the churches in question.

including the premises, style of worship, the leadership, location of the church and so on, feed into these trends that make it very difficult to draw generalised conclusions.

Due to the scarcity and the high cost of land in Singapore, churches are sometimes limited by the availability of space and have to add additional services to accommodate growth or variety. Over the years, the number of separate services offered have grown in tandem with attendance numbers (Figure 9.12).

Conclusion

The Yearbook of International Religious Demography 2014 reported Singapore as the nineteenth fastest growing Christian population in the world in 2014, with an average annual growth rate (AAGR) of 4.12%.[31] At the same time, Christianity in Singapore has grown from 14.6% in 2000 to 18.3% in 2010 while Buddhism and Taoism, the predominant religions, combined have fallen from 51% to 44.2% over the same period of time. This is indicative of a good environment for church growth and the Diocese of Singapore has largely tracked this trend over the last three decades with a steady, though slowing, growth rate. At the same time, the growth of the independent churches, as well as some of the other mainstream denominations, have been better than for the Anglican Church here. We have also started to fall behind in relation to the rate of population growth.

The overall growth trend for the diocese was dominated by the top five or so largest churches which make up about half of the overall attendance numbers. Changes in these few churches often had a non-negligible impact on the combined numbers, and thus much of the growth/decline behaviour can be explained by looking at what happened in the larger churches. That said, there were some common factors at work in both the large as well as the small parishes.

The key factors that have shaped our growth and decline have been the charismatic renewal and evangelical thrust of the 1980s. Among the largest parishes in the diocese today are those who have managed to embrace that charismatic-evangelical spirit. This also correlated to the adoption of more contemporary approaches to ministry and the running of church services. This impetus was not confined to the 1980s but was felt whenever churches experienced charismatic renewals or embarked on strategies along these lines. There was the attendant risk of rapid personality-driven growth leading to personality conflicts and leadership disputes. Our diocese has seen our fair share of such incidents, some of which have resulted in church splits while others have stalled previously strong growth as a result. Nonetheless, the early phase of renewal growth represented the season of the strongest growth during the last 30 years.

This leads to the related factor of church leadership. In many of cases, change in leadership also led to a change in growth pattern. The growth and decline of churches are inextricably linked to the personality and style of the vicars or priests in charge of the parishes and congregations. While there has always been the reminder to not build the ministry around personalities, it remains true that personalities matter, and they often matter a lot to churchgoers. With the increasingly large number of churches in Singapore, Christians here, who have little denominational loyalty, are faced with a wide variety of choices. From the burgeoning megachurches to very small house churches, more often than not, theirs was a decision made with the personality and giftings of the leader in mind. Frequent change in parish leadership seldom resulted in growth, and in most cases came at a cost of temporary declines as the parish transitions and adjusts to a new leader. Such leadership related issues can explain a good number of the individual church trends.

Another significant observation has to do with the strong initial growth enjoyed by the English speaking congregations. This is an example of how government and education policies can influence the growth of the Church, and in this case the English speaking Anglican church. To this day, the youth increasingly prefer English over Mandarin, which corresponds to the age profile of the Chinese churches which tend to have more senior citizens. Similarly, the introduction of compulsory religious studies in secondary schools contributed to evangelistic growth. This is significant since the diocese operates five 'mission' schools here in Singapore. Religious studies have contributed to the growth of those churches based in our mission schools between 1984 to 1990 when the policy changed once again.

Throughout this period, there were various strategic initiatives that one might have expected to be reflected in the statistics. For example, the much vaunted cell-group strategy in the mid-1980s, the Decade of Evangelism in the 1990s, the introduction of the Alpha course (evangelistic programme) in the 2000s, involvement with national Christian movements (such as Love Singapore) and various other initiatives, all seem to have no observable effect either in terms of the overall statistics or even at individual church levels. This comes as a bit of a surprise given how much emphasis was given to some of these initiatives. In fact, it would seem that the factors that solidly contributed to the growth of the Church were often much simpler dynamics that cost little money and operated at the parish level more than it did at the diocesan level.

Similarly, changing economic conditions seem to have relatively little effect, either positive or negative, on overall church attendance. The most recent one, the Global Financial Crisis of 2007, coincided with a decline in the Church's growth but prior to that, the correlation between economic conditions to church attendance was low. This may point to the increasingly globalised nature of Singapore, and Singaporean Christians.

While we have looked primarily at the average church attendance as the metric for our study, the Anglican Church in Singapore has also grown in other areas not reflected in these numbers. There has been considerable expansion in the Anglican social welfare services, hospitals and schools – earning the diocese a good standing with the government and in the public eye. The missionary efforts of our diocese extend beyond the borders of Singapore to the deaneries under our care, and there has been growth in these missionary efforts over the years. At the end of the day, attendance, while an important metric, offers only a single dimensional perspective of the growth of any church or diocese. Only time will tell if the lessons we have gleaned from the past decades translate into effective strategies for growing the diocese in the coming years.

Notes

1 E. H. Gomes, 'W.H.G.', in *An Account of the St. Andrew's Church Mission, from A.D. 1856 to A.D. 1887* (Singapore: The Singapore and Straits Printing Office, 1888): 3.
2 J. Tamney, *The Struggle over Singapore's Soul: Western Modernization and Asian Culture* (New York: Walter de Gruyter, 1996): 52.
3 D. Goh, 'State and Social Christianity in Post-Colonial Singapore', *Sojourn: Journal of Social Issues in Southeast Asia* 25 (2010): 56, 59.
4 K. Hinton, *Growing Churches Singapore Style: Ministry in an Urban Context* (Singapore: Overseas Missionary Fellowship, 1985): 118.
5 J. Koning and H. Dahles, 'Spiritual Power: Ethnic Chinese Managers and the Rise of Charismatic Christianity in Southeast Asia', *Copenhagen Journal of Asian Studies*, 27 (2009): 6.
6 J. Wong, *The Church in Singapore* (Singapore: National Council of Churches of Singapore, 1998): 295–300.
7 M. Poon and M. Tan (eds.), *The Clock Tower Story: The Beginnings of the Charismatic Renewals in Singapore* (revised edition, 40th anniversary edition; Singapore: Trinity Theological College, 2012): 74.
8 L. Eng (ed.), *Religious Diversity in Singapore* (Singapore: Institute of Southeast Asian Studies, 2008): 120.
9 Hinton, *Growing*: 150–1.
10 J. Tay, *A Short History of Indigenous Mission in Singapore* (Singapore: Armour Publishing, 2010): 76.
11 R. Silver, G. Hu and M. Iino, *English Language Education in China, Japan and Singapore* (Singapore: National Institute of Education, 2002): 127, available at http://www.nie.edu.sg/nie_cma/attachments/topic/147e7c6cb6ZG/Silver_Monograph.pdf.

12 Ibid.: 130.

13 K. Eng, *State, Society and Religious Engineering: Towards a Reformist Buddhism in Singapore* (Singapore: Eastern Universities Press, 2003): 265.

14 Goh, 'State': 66.

15 B. Sng, *In His Good Time: The Story of the Church in Singapore 1819–2002* (Singapore: Graduates Christian Fellowship, 2003): 301–2.

16 T. Chong, *Christian Evangelicals and Public Morality in Singapore* (Singapore: Institute of South East Asian Studies, 2014): 6.

17 J. Tan, 'Pulling Together Amid Globalization: National Education in Singapore Schools', in P. D. Hershock, M. Mason and J. H. Hawkins (eds.), *Changing Education: Leadership, Innovation and Development in a Globalizing Asia Pacific* (Hong Kong: Comparative Education Research Centre, 2007): 184.

18 C. Cornbleth, *Curriculum Politics, Policy, Practice: Cases in Comparative Context* (New York: SUNY Press, 2000): 90.

19 'Population and Population Structure, Time Series', available at http://www.singstat.gov.sg/statistics/browse_by_theme/population.html.

20 Goh, 'State': 59, Figure 1.

21 Tay, 'History': 79.

22 M. Tay, *Born for Blessings: An Autobiography of Moses Tay* (Singapore: Armour Publishing, 2009): 57.

23 E. A. Afendras and E. Kuo, *Language and Society in Singapore* (Singapore: NUS Press, 1980): 106–7.

24 The Methodist Church, which was more institutional and slower to embrace and adopt these charismatic influences, also saw growth, albeit at a less intensive rate. They managed, however, to sustain that growth over a far longer period of time without the types of divisions seen in Anglican circles in Singapore. See http://singaporereligion.com.

25 T. Chong and H. Yew-Foong, *Different under God: A Survey of Church-Going Protestants in Singapore* (Singapore: Institute of Southeast Asian Studies, 2013): 67.

26 M. Rice, 'The Emergence of Buddhist Revivalism', *Church & Society* 6, no. 1 (April 2003) (Singapore: Centre for the Study of Christianity in Asia): 13.

27 Clergy movement numbers may not be exact as the data may not be complete or comprehensive. They do serve to demonstrate sufficiently the pattern of the movements. Also note that there has been a significant increase in the number of clergy since the 1980s, as well as the number of parishes. This would naturally lead to clergy movements.

28 Hinton, *Growing*: 166.

29 This is comparing our church size versus national census figures for Christianity in Singapore. See 'Singapore Census of Population 2010: Statistical Release 1: Demographic Characteristics, Education, Language and Religion', available at http://www.singstat.gov.sg/publications/publications_and_papers/cop2010/census_2010_release1/findings.pdf: 11, 13; 'Singapore Census of Population 2000: Statistical Release 2: Education, Language and Religion', available at http://www.singstat.gov.sg/publications/publications_and_papers/cop2000/census_2000_release2/excel/t38–45.xls.

30 Goh, 'State': 59, Figure 1.

31 B. Grim, T. M. Johnson, V. Skirbekk and G. A. Zurlo, *Yearbook of International Religious Demography 2014* (Leiden: Brill, 2014).

10 South Korea

Andrew Eungi Kim

Introduction

The Anglican Church of Korea (*Daehanseonggonghoe* in Korean), which was founded in 1889, has a total membership of about 65,000.[1] The Korean Anglican Church forms a single metropolitical province, comprising three dioceses, three convents, over 120 churches, some 200 clergy, one university, 11 social mission institutions and a publishing house. These figures represent a very small minority in the religious population of South Korea (henceforth Korea) in general and Christian population in particular (see Table 10.1; Figure 10.1). The Church is actively involved in various international church organisations, including the Anglican Communion, the World Council of Churches (WCC) and the Christian Conference of Asia (CCA). Domestically, it is known to espouse the ecumenical movement, as it is a member of the National Council of Churches in Korea (KNCC)[2] as well as the Anglican–Roman Catholic Commission for Unity and Mission. The stated aims of the Korean Anglican Church, at least since the end of the Korean War (1950–1953), have been, among others, to call for social justice and respect for human rights; to engage in social affairs; and, as indicated above, to advocate ecumenical movement and engage in open dialogue with other Christian denominations as well as other religions.

The questions are: What is the history of the Anglican Church in Korea? What are the key historical events in Korea that have shaped the place of Anglicanism in the religious landscape of Korea? What have been its achievements and limitations? Are the factors that account for the rise of Christianity in Korea also applicable to the Korean Anglican Church? There has to date been very limited scholarly attention given to the Korean Anglican Church, as only a handful of books and articles that solely focus on the Church have been published, in both English and Korean.[3] This paper attempts to redress this imbalance by tracing the history of the Korean Anglican Church from its very beginning to more recent developments. The paper outlines major historical events such as the Japanese annexation of Korea, the Korean War and the rapid industrialisation and modernisation that have played important roles in shaping the nature of the Anglican Church in Korea. The paper also discusses how the Church has responded to these challenges and assesses its place in the religious reality of Korean society.

Table 10.1 Religious population in South Korea (in thousands; percentage of total population)

	1985	1995	2005
Buddhist	8,059 (19.9)	10,321 (23.2)	10,726 (22.8)
Protestant	6,489 (16.1)	8,760 (19.7)	8,616 (18.3)
Catholic	1,865 (4.6)	2,951 (6.6)	5,146 (10.9)
Confucian	483 (1.2)	211 (0.5)	105 (0.2)
Won Buddhist	92 (0.2)	87 (0.2)	130 (0.3)
Other Religions	212 (0.6)	268 (0.6)	247 (0.5)
No Religious Affiliation	*23,216 (57.4)*	*21,953 (49.3)*	*21,865 (46.5)*

Note: Total population in Korea in 1985 was 40 million, 45 million in 1995, and 48 million in 2005.

Source: National Statistical Office (1987, 1997, 2006).

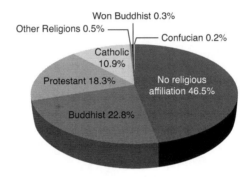

Figure 10.1 Religious population in South Korea
Source: National Statistical Office (2006).

What the paper finds is that unlike other Christian denominations, the Korean Anglican Church has experienced only modest – very modest – growth, maintaining almost a negligible, 'hidden' presence. Also noteworthy about the Church is that its recent membership data are simply nonexistent: while historical data on the Church's memberships are more readily available in published works, the same cannot be said about its more recent membership data.

A history of the Korean Anglican Church

The Anglican Church of Korea began with missionary efforts from England in the late nineteenth century. The first person to plan and suggest Korea as a new mission field was Alexander Croft Shaw, a minister of the Anglican Church of Canada who served as minister to the British Legation in Tokyo and who was a leading figure in establishing the Anglican mission in Japan. In 1880, he sent a Japanese catechist to Korea to learn Korean and appealed to the Society for the

Propagation of the Gospel in Foreign Parts (SPG; now the United Society for the Propagation of the Gospel or USPG) to send a bishop and ministers to Korea.[4] Another impetus for missionary work in Korea came from Archdeacon J. R. Wolfe, the head of the Church Mission Society (CMS) in Fuzhou, China, who visited Korea in 1884 after meeting Horace N. Allen in Nagasaki, Japan. Allen, who was a medical doctor representing the Northern Presbyterian Church of the United States, was on his way to Korea (he became the first Protestant missionary to arrive in Korea in the same year). After observing many 'backward' practices of Koreans during his brief visit to Korea, Wolfe was convinced that the country needed the presence of Christian missionaries. However, his calls for missionary work in Korea were heeded by neither CMS nor SPG, prompting him to begin his 'personal' missionary work by securing funding from Christians in Fuzhou and from Australian friends.[5] He arrived in Busan with two Chinese catechists in November 1885 and they made contacts with the local people. He visited Busan again in February 1887, but there is no record of any convert gained from his efforts. There was, however, one important result. In his wish to secure support for a mission work in Korea, Wolfe published a letter in an Australian missionary newsletter and the publication inspired the Australian minister Revd. Henry Davies to decide to launch Australian missionary work in Korea.[6]

A person who was much more directly responsible for facilitating the launch of missionary work in Korea was Bishop Charles Perry Scott, who was appointed bishop in North China in 1880. Bishop Scott, along with two other bishops based in North China, petitioned the Archbishop of Canterbury to establish a mission field in Korea following the signing of a treaty between Korea and the United Kingdom in 1883.[7] He and Bishop Edward Bickersteth of Japan made further petitions after they visited Korea in 1887.

As a result of these efforts, the English Church Mission (ECM) was founded and the Anglican Church of Korea can be said to have 'officially' begun on November 1, 1889, when a longtime Royal Naval Chaplain Charles John Corfe was appointed as the first diocesan bishop of Korea.[8] Before traveling to Korea, Corfe founded the Korean Missionary Brotherhood, which would later become the Society for the Sacred Mission, in order to recruit and train potential missionaries.[9] He also visited major cities in the United States, Canada and Japan for about a month starting in July 1890 and was able to recruit nine individuals, including two medical doctors, Eli Barr Landis and Julius Wiles, to join him in Korea. Before his departure, Corfe launched a periodical called *Morning Calm* to publicise about, and seek support for, the mission work in Korea.[10]

The first Anglican missionary to land in Korea was Dr. Wiles, who arrived on September 3, 1890, in Jemulpo, present-day Incheon, which is a port city about 30 kilometers west of Seoul. Bishop Corfe (also known in Korea by his Korean name Go Yohan), along with Dr. Landis, arrived in Busan on 23 September en route to Jemulpo, where they arrived on September 29, 1890.[11] Also joining the Anglican mission in 1890 was Mark Trollope, who was to serve as the third bishop of Korea from 1911 until his death from a heart attack in 1930. Six other missionaries arrived over the next few months.

The Anglican missionaries in the beginning largely concentrated on the medical and religious care of foreigners, as

> it was Bishop Corfe's wish that for the first five or six years of the Korean Mission the missionaries should refrain from attempting any direct evangelistic work, and spend the time in quiet preparation, by study of the language, literature, habits, methods of thought, etc. of the people.[12]

During the six-year 'preparation period', the missionaries opened hospitals and dispensaries for both English and Koreans.[13] For example, Dr. Landis opened a hospital in Jemulpo, within a month of his arrival, in October 1890. A report from Dr. Landis shows that the hospital in Jemulpo treated 3,594 patients in 1892 and 4,464 patients in 1894.[14] Also, Dr. Wiles founded a small hospital in Seoul in 1891 and his work was helped by the arrival of a female physician (Lois Rosa Cooke) and a nurse (Gertrude Heathcote) in the same year. The hospital eventually became a hospital for women, a significant development given the fact that a strict separation of sexes was the norm in Korea at the time. Another hospital was opened by Dr. Wiles in Nakdong in 1893. The success of medical missionary work by Anglican hospitals is attested to by the fact that the number of patients treated at the three hospitals up to 1895 exceeded the total of patients treated by hospitals founded by considerably larger missionary groups, such as the Presbyterian Church and the Southern Methodist Church.[15] The arrival of nuns, who were all trained nurses, in the first few years of the Anglican mission proved to be essential in this regard. The nuns of the Sisters of the Community of St. Peter from Kilburn, England, also opened an orphanage in 1893. Another noteworthy achievement for the Anglican mission was the publication of an English–Korean dictionary, the second of its kind, and religious literature, which were made possible in part by bringing over a printing expert and setting up a print shop in 1891 with a printing machine given by the Royal Navy. The Anglican Church, with the leading role played by Mark Trollope, also participated in the translation of the Bible into Korean, which was spearheaded by such renowned Protestant missionaries as Horace Underwood and James S. Gale.

The events marking the end of the period of preparation and the beginning of active mission work were baptism of five orphans, trained by Dr. Landis, and enrolment of six catechumens on Christmas Eve in 1896.[16] In 1897, the first two adult Koreans – Huijun Kim (Mark Kim) and Gunmyeong Kim – were baptised, the first of whom later became the first Korean Anglican priest in 1915. From such modest beginning, the Church began to grow noticeably in the next few years, with the total membership reaching over 200.

> The work among Koreans, which had started with two adult Christians, in 1897, had so developed that in 1904 the number of the baptized was over two hundred, including some hundred communicants. Of these, however, nearly three-fourths were in the Kanghwa stations, the churches in Seoul and Chemulpo having suffered seriously from lack of continuous supervision and encouragement, owing to the constant change of clergy.[17]

There was also a significant change in the Church as Bishop Corfe resigned from his post in July 1904 and returned to England. Bishop Arthur B. Turner became the second diocesan bishop of Korea in 1905. During his tenure, albeit for only five years due to his premature death in 1910, the Church expanded south to Suwon and Jincheon. Also, the first school by the Anglican missionaries was founded in 1908 in Suwon, bearing the name 'Shinmyeonghakgyo' (Faith and Enlightenment schools), followed by the founding of a girls school in Gang-hwa.[18] More schools were established in Jincheon and Budaeri within the next couple of years. An English school was also founded in Incheon. Furthermore, Bishop Turner, along with Methodist and Presbyterian missionaries, played an instrumental role in founding the Korean YMCA in 1903, an important event in the annals of Korean Christianity in Korea. The Anglican Church also began publishing *Jonggoseonggyohoewolbo* (Anglican Church Monthly), Korea's first ever monthly periodical, in 1908.

The Anglican Church during the Japanese Colonial Period (1910–1945)

Modest it may had been, the fruitful beginning of the missionary work in Korea by the Anglican Church entered a new era when the country was annexed by Japan in 1910, which lasted until 1945. The period marked a dark era for all Western religions, including Anglicanism, as all the missionary activities, both direct and indirect, were seriously curtailed by Japanese authorities which viewed the missionaries and their organisations as agents of Western interests. Accordingly, Japanese authorities implemented various anti-Western, anti-church policies, including the surveillance of missionary activities and imposition of strict regulations regarding curricula at missionary-founded schools. Christian leaders were routinely arrested and missionaries were regularly interrogated for anti-Japanese activities. However, most of the missionaries themselves complied with the demands of Japanese authorities.

During this turbulent period, there was a major change in the Korean Anglican Church as well. Bishop Turner died in 1910 and Trollope succeeded as the third diocesan bishop of Korea the following year. Trollope, who became one of the leading Western scholars on Korean culture in the early 1900s, enabled the Anglican Church to enter a new phase of development and growth. In order to train Korean clergy, he founded St. Michael's Theological Institute in 1914, culminating in the ordination of the first Korean priest the following year (the aforementioned Huijun Kim).[19] He also founded in 1925 a convent for Korean nuns, the Society of the Holy Cross (*Seonggasunyeohoe*). In 1922, the bishop spearheaded the construction of a cathedral (Church of St. Mary the Virgin and St. Nicholas), which is noted for its unique mosaic murals and Romanesque architecture, in downtown Seoul, which was completed four years later.[20] From 1923, Trollope also focused on expanding the missionary work to the northern part of the peninsula, i.e., Pyeongan and Hwanghae Provinces. By 1929, the missionary work was expanded nationwide, resulting in the founding of 11 missionary districts with around 60 churches.[21] The number of church members also increased from 4,805 in 1925 to 4,955 in 1929, out of whom 2,893 received the Eucharist.[22] One controversial issue regarding Trollope's work was his intent to extend the ministry of the Anglican Church to both Koreans and Japanese, although Korean services and Japanese services were held on alternate weeks:

> Bishop Trollope realized that the church in Korea must preach to the Japanese as well as to Koreans and so work was begun with this group. Throughout the next years, the Anglican church was the only one in Korea where Koreans, Westerners and Japanese worked side-by-side with equal rights.[23]

Following the death of Bishop Trollope from an accident in 1930, Bishop Cecil Cooper, who had been in Korea for over 20 years as an Anglican priest, succeeded as the fourth diocesan bishop of Korea in 1931. By 1939, there were 30 Korean priests, and churches were formed practically all across the peninsula serving nearly 10,000 adherents (see Table 10.2).[24] However, Japanese authorities implemented even more ruthless laws against missionary activities and missionary-operated institutions in the 1930s, especially following Japan's invasion of Manchuria in 1931. For Japan, the creation of its own state of Manchuria placed Korea in a very strategic place with respect to the defence, communications and economies of the Japanese empire. Japan thus attempted to assimilate Korea and its people through the policy of 'Japanisation' in order to incorporate them as part of the Japanese empire.

The Japanisation efforts became more intense from the late 1930s when, for example, Japanese authorities attempted to obliterate Korean identity by strictly enforcing the use of the Japanese language and ordering Koreans to abandon their Korean family names and adopt Japanese ones. Because admission to government schools and employment were virtually impossible without the Japanese last name, about 80 percent of the Koreans changed their family names by September 1940. The names of churches were also ordered to be changed to bear Japanese titles. Of many measures of the Japanisation programme, however, it was the Shinto shrine issue that became the most challenging and controversial problem for the Church.[25] Shinto worship, popularly known as the worship of the Japanese emperor as the divine descendant of *Amaterasu*,

Table 10.2 Membership of the Anglican Church in South Korea, 1931–1939

Year	1931	1932	1933	1934	1935	1936	1937	1938	1939
Total	6,521	7,092	7,892	7,951	7,402	8,512	9,409	9,566	9,750
Those who received the Eucharist	3,597	3,913	4,280	4,370	4,285	–	5,304	5,426	5,522
Clergy	19	25	27	27	25	–	26	27	30
Evangelists	58	50	53	54	51	–	62	57	44
Churches	64	68	71	78	88	102	108	112	115

Source: Yi, 1990: 205.

Note: These data are extracted from *Morning Calm*.

the sun-goddess, was made compulsory for all Koreans, including Christians, from 1930. Japanese authorities attempted to force the churches to approve and encourage Christian attendance in Shinto shrine ceremonies, which ran counter to Christian teachings against idol worship. In 1935, Japanese authorities also ordered all educational establishments, including Christian schools, to participate in the ceremonies at Shinto shrines, which were instituted in every town. Those missionaries and educators who opposed were summarily dismissed from their posts, some of whom were imprisoned. Churches and schools which opposed participation at Shinto shrine ceremonies were subject to forcible closure. The missionaries and churches were divided over the issue: those who opposed the Shinto shrine obeisance viewed it as a form of idolatry, while those who complied viewed it as an expression of nationalism.[26] After some deliberations, the Methodists, the second largest denomination in Korea at the time, and then the Presbyterians, the largest Protestant group, passed a resolution in 1938 to approve participation at Shinto shrine ceremonies.[27] However, many Christians resisted. Between 1938 and 1945, about 2,000 Protestant Koreans were arrested for noncompliance with Shinto worship and the ensuing incarceration resulted in the martyrdom of up to 50 people.[28] Missionaries who refused to endorse Shinto rituals were summarily deported.

Japanese authorities also attempted to undermine the Korean Church by removing the missionaries from positions of power within the Church and to ultimately deport them.[29] That was because the missionaries as a whole served as an outlet for Korean Christians' contact with the outside world. Beginning around 1937, the Japanese authorities began a campaign warning Koreans not to have contact with foreigners – anyone who had contact with foreigners was considered a spy and faced a possible prosecution. Consequently, nearly 90 percent of the missionaries left Korea by the end of 1940. The remaining missionaries were harassed incessantly by the Japanese government.

The period from the early 1930s to the end of the Japanese colonial rule in 1945 was also challenging for the Anglican Church. In 1941, Bishop Cooper, along with many other Christian missionaries, was expelled, leaving the Church in vacuum and gravely disrupting the Church's medical, educational and social works. St. Michael's Theological Institute and all the hospitals operated by the Korean Anglican Church were also closed down. Another major development in the Church was the appointment of Japanese priest Kudo Yoshio (John Kudo) as the leader the Korean Anglican Church in 1941.

The Anglican Church in post-liberation Korea

Following the defeat of Japan in WWII, Korea was liberated in August 1945. However, grave political and economic instabilities ensued, and the Korean Anglican Church, along with other Christian denominations, was faced with the daunting task of rebuilding. The situation was much worse for the Korean Anglican Church, as it was under great financial duress due to lack of funding from the Church of England. The former also suffered from the shortage of clergy, which was aggravated by the forced closure of the theological institute. Amidst such time of uncertainty, Bishop Cooper returned to Korea in 1946. As of 1946, there were 19 Anglican priests serving the Anglican community of 4,961, a conspicuous drop from the total of 9,750 in 1939.[30]

Just as the Church was making progress with limited resources, signified by, among others, the reopening of St. Michael's Theological Institute in 1949, the Korean War broke out in June 1950. During the war, Bishop Cooper and a number of Anglican missionaries, including Priest Charles Hunt and Sister Maria Clara, were captured and taken to the north by the communists. The latter two died as captives, while Bishop Cooper was released to South Korea following the signing of the armistice in 1953. Four other Anglican priests were martyred during the war, three of whom were executed by the communists in Seoul.

After Bishop Cooper resigned in 1955, Bishop John Daly, who had long served as a missionary in West Africa, including Ghana, arrived as the fifth diocesan bishop of Korea in the following year. In departing from the early missionary efforts that were focused on medical care, education, social work and publishing, Anglican missionary efforts under the tutelage of Bishop Cooper were directed toward industrial and campus missions and toward indigenising the Church by establishing Korean identity. For example, Bishop Daly was a pioneering figure in launching industrial mission, establishing one of the earliest, if not the earliest, industrial missions in Korea in a mining town, providing social work, counseling and education.[31] He also opened Saint Beda Hall in front of Seoul National University for the purpose of carrying out campus mission. Daly also founded a centre for industrial mission in Yeongdeungpo, Seoul, in the 1960s and championed for the workers' rights.[32] He also founded a school with his personal money, Hwangji Middle School, which is still in operation today.

The period from the early 1960s to the late 1980s, which coincides with the country's rapid industrialisation and urbanisation, is characterised by a 'conversion boom', during which a large number of Koreans converted to not only Christianity, both Catholic and Protestant, but also to Buddhism. The Anglican Church of Korea also expanded increasingly across the country during this period, especially since the 1970s, opening new churches across the country and engaging in more social work. Like its Catholic and Protestant counterparts, the Church's involvement in education and social work in particular has played an important role for its growth in Korea. For example, St. Peter's School, a special education school for mentally-challenged children, was founded in 1975, and St. Michael's Theological Seminary was upgraded and expanded as a university (*Seonggonghoedaehakgyo* or Anglican University) in 1994. In addition, during the time of heightened political oppression in the 1970s and 1980s, the Church joined other churches in calling for the respect of human rights and restoration of democracy.

Daly also emphasised the need for indigenising the Korean Anglican Church, stressing the three principles of self-governance, self-reliance and self-propagation.[33] One important element in this regard, he argued, was the consecration of a Korean bishop. In view of this, he sent three Korean priests to study in England, the United States and Australia between 1957 and 1958. In 1965, in marking the 75th anniversary of the founding of Korean mission, the Korean diocese was divided into two dioceses: the Diocese of Seoul and the Diocese of Daejeon in charge of the rest of the country. Cheonhwan Lee,[34] who was the first priest sent abroad, specifically to England, was consecrated as the first Korean bishop and became the first bishop of the Diocese of Seoul,[35] while Bishop Daly was in charge of the Diocese of Daejeon. In 1974, the latter was further divided into the dioceses of Daejeon and Busan, and two new Korean bishops were consecrated. In commemorating the centennial anniversary of the founding of the Anglican Church of Korea on September 29, 1990, the Church reaffirmed its commitment to the spread of the Gospel under the motif of 'Jesus Christ, Life of the Nation', emphasising, among others, the need for peaceful reunification of Korea. It has also joined domestic and international inter-denominational organisations to foster close relationships and to seek ways to improve cooperation in carrying out missionary works.

An even more important development has been the establishment of Korea as an independent province within the Anglican Communion in 1993. Until then, the Church had been under the authority of the Archbishop of Canterbury. In marking the independence, the first Archbishop of Korea, Most Revd. Sungsu Kim (Simon Kim), took over the authority of the Archbishop of Canterbury as Metropolitan (Archbishop in the Church of England) and Primate of the metropolitical province of Korea. Most Revd. Kim has been succeeded by six other Archbishops, including the current Archbishop of Korea, Most Revd. Geunsang Kim (Paul Kim). Under their leadership, the Korean Anglican Church has continued the tradition of active involvement with social affairs, operating various welfare agencies, community welfare centres and food banks. The Church has also engaged in efforts to help develop poverty-stricken areas and to eradicate hunger.

Factors for church growth in Korea and the Anglican Church

Christianity, both Catholicism and Protestantism, is the largest religion in Korea with nearly 14 million adherents, representing about 30 percent of the population. The growth was especially conspicuous from the 1960s to the 1980s during which the number of Christians expanded faster than in any other country, more than doubling every decade.[36] As for the factors for the growth of Christianity, a unique convergence of factors has allowed the new religion to establish its presence in Korea.

The phrase 'human being's extremity is God's opportunity' could not have been more appropriate for the circumstances in Korea at the time of the introduction of Protestantism in 1884 and Anglicanism in 1890. In late nineteenth century Korea, two contextual factors provided a fertile ground from which Christianity experienced considerable success. First, the missionaries arrived in Korea when the country's sovereignty was in jeopardy and the government endeavoured to build a firm relationship with strong Western powers, such as the United States and Britain, by welcoming the missionaries and their religion.[37] King Gojong, the last king of the Joseon dynasty, perceived that salvaging the nation's independence lied in gaining help from the West, especially the United States, which prompted him to accept Western elements, including Christianity. Second, the initial acceptance of Christianity in Korea was closely related to the missionaries' provision of various social services, including medical care and education, which were otherwise unavailable to the masses. In the beginning, indeed, there were largely two groups which warmly responded to the missionaries' efforts: one was the progressive-minded elites who embraced Christian ideals to realise political and social reform, while the other group was the poor farmers and labourers as well as women who received social services provided by the missionaries.

A more recent contextual factor which contributed to the Christianisation of Korea is the rapid industrialisation and urbanisation of the country from the early 1960s to the end of the 1980s.[38] In a span of just one generation, a large number of Koreans who had hitherto lived as farmers in close-knit communities were uprooted from their hometowns and had to live under alienating circumstances. All of this engendered acute feelings of dislocation and dejection. These sentiments became even more intense as the country became more industrialised in the late 1970s and 1980s, as many Koreans felt they were not getting their share of the new riches. The feelings of discontent and deprivation arising from the interminable poverty, widening income gap, inequality of opportunity and the lack of social mobility provided a psychological impetus for a considerable segment of the Korean population to seek a satisfying response in the Christian faith. The promise of liberation from poverty, anxiety, fear and all other types of suffering as well as the idea that all human beings could be saved by the mercy of God attracted the religious imagination of the underprivileged, from which a large majority of the converts were drawn. Furthermore, churches provided a sense of identity and belonging as well as providing support networks, through which Korean Christians found security, trust, cooperation and consolation. We can thus conceptualise the rise of Christianity in Korea not only as a manifestation of people's reaction to the complexity and the rapidity of social changes in modern society but also as an endeavour to regain a sense of community that was lost in urban settings.

The Church's role as an agent of modernisation provided another impetus for the acceptance of Christianity among large numbers of Koreans.[39] From the beginning, the churches as a whole provided the basic tools of modernisation – Western medical science, modern education and technology – and assumed a key role in the economic, political and social modernisation of the country. Many Koreans embraced Christianity as a means of entry into modern society and access to what they believed to be a more advanced civilisation.

There are also religious factors which were instrumental in facilitating the rise of Christianity in Korea. First, when Catholicism was introduced in 1784 and Protestantism in 1884, the country did not have any firmly established organised religion that could have opposed the spread of the new religions.[40] Traditional religious establishments, either because they lacked institutional representation, as in the case of shamanism, or because they were in full decline, as in the case of Buddhism, did not, and could not, put up any opposition to the new religions. This affirms the theory which argues that a new religion is most likely to succeed in areas where there is no strong presence of organised religions. The Korean case is in full agreement with Stark's study, which argues, based on comparative studies of North America, South America and Islamic countries, that rapid conversion to a new religion is more likely to occur in regions where the proportion of the members of traditional religions is low, while the percentage of non-believers is high. That is, a new religion has the best opportunity to succeed in areas where there is no strong presence of, and hence no opposition from, the existing organised religions. The success of Christianity in Korea thus affirms Stark's theory in that most of the converts to Christianity were not members of any traditional religion.[41]

A second religious factor for the warm receptivity accorded to Christianity is the fact that certain Christian doctrines and practices were given selective emphases or syncretised in the image of the basic religious values of Koreans.[42] In an effort to make the imported faith more appealing to a wider audience, Korean clergy accentuated certain Christian messages and doctrines, such as the image of God as the provider of material goods, that are meaningful to the moral fabric and psyche of Koreans. In the process, Christianity made various compromises, stressing the possibility that, much like the underlying motives for practicing shamanism, conversion to Christianity would lead to prosperity, health, longevity and other personal successes. In addition to such emphasis on the utilitarian implications of accepting Christianity, the missionaries and Korean clergy also stressed, in view of the importance of Confucian values to Koreans, the centrality of morality and ethics in the imported faith. In particular, moral values that pertain to the veneration of parents, the most significant socio-cultural imperative governing Korean society, were given special attention. This partly explains why the Korean Church passively accepted the practice of ancestor worship and incorporated memorial services for the dead that partly resemble the Confucian/shamanistic practice of beseeching the ancestors' spirits to bestow material blessings. Through selective emphases on certain Christian doctrines and teachings, therefore, Christian doctrines and practices were made more congenial to Koreans.

Another important factor for the rise of Christianity is the effective church organisation, complete with its innovative strategies and programmes for evangelisation.[43] To become more efficient in ministry, Korean churches expanded Sunday School programmes, initiated various programmes of religious education, institutionalised Bible study, established industrial evangelism and the armed forces chaplaincy, utilised radio evangelism, etc.

The fact that many mainstream, non-Pentecostal churches, including those belonging to Presbyterian and Baptist denominations, absorbed the Pentecostal style of faith, emphasising faith healing, further explains the rise of Protestant

Christianity in Korea.[44] Receiving of the Holy Spirit, faith healing, speaking in tongues and emotional expressions during worship services are all Pentecostal characteristics that are congruent with shamanism, a time-honored religion that has shaped the religious imagination and inclination of Koreans. A Pentecostal denomination which did experience rapid expansion is Full Gospel, which currently comprises 8 percent of the total Protestant population in Korea. And the most prominent Pentecostal church is the world's largest church, Yoido Full Gospel Church, which reportedly boasts one million members. The church began to grow noticeably only since its charismatic pastor David Yonggi Cho began to perform faith healings on people with 'incurable diseases'. In fact, faith healing is identified as the most important reason for the marked growth of the church in its first ten years, which grew from its modest beginning as a tent church in 1958 to a 15,000-member church by 1968.[45] The church's success galvanised many mainstream churches and independent churches, which comprise about 10 percent of the total Protestant population, to follow suit.

In light of the fact that there were nearly 14 million Christians as of 2005, the 65,000-strong Anglican community represents, as mentioned above, a very small Christian group. And the future for the Korean Anglican Church does not look promising. There may be several reasons for this. First, it can be argued that the Anglican Church simply 'lost' in intense competition with other Christian groups in winning Korean converts. That is because the SPG fell far behind its Catholic and Protestant counterparts in terms of human and financial resources, forcing the former to commit a significantly smaller number of missionaries and less funding for its missionary work in Korea. In fact, the Anglican mission in Korea constantly suffered from a serious shortage of personnel not only for evangelistic work but also for various social works. It is also true that Korea was considered a more important mission field by both Catholic and Protestant mission bodies than by the SPG. Second, during the time of heightened missionary work in Korea in the late nineteenth century, various mission bodies working in Korea agreed on a comity agreement to avoid conflicts among the missionaries. However, the agreement allowed the six missionary bodies of the Methodist and the Presbyterian Church to have an upper hand in choosing more desirable areas for carrying out missionary work. Left out of the comity agreement, to a certain extent voluntarily, the Anglican Church, along with other non-participating denominations such as the Salvation Army and the Holiness Church, was disadvantaged in carrying out missionary work, for it could not freely carry out missionary work in more populated areas that were 'chosen by other missionary bodies'.[46] Third, the obscure identity of the Anglican Church, at least from the public perception, may be to blame for the lower receptivity of Koreans to Anglicanism. To begin with, the Korean Anglican Church in Korean, *Daehanseonggonghoe*, has a nonreligious sounding name, like the Salvation Army (*Gusegun* in Korean). Typical Koreans would also have a hard time trying to understand the meaning of the term. Aggravating the terminological obscurity is the lack of people's understanding of how Anglicanism is theologically different from its Catholic and Protestant counterparts. In fact, Koreans tend to vaguely think that there is no significant difference between Anglicanism and Catholicism, except for the fact that Anglican priests are allowed to get married.

Lastly, the relative lack of vitality of the Korean Anglican Church is partly due to the fact that it has largely failed to keep abreast of changing trends in demographics and other social characteristics, all of which required changes in evangelical focus and 'tactics'. To name a few, Korea has experienced rapid urbanisation since the 1960s that lasted for some 40 years. This meant evangelical opportunities not only in urban centres but also in rural areas which largely comprised an older-than-average population. The rise in the number of single and two-person households, including those in their 60s and older, has also rapidly increased. Moving away from the typical extended family structure or nuclear family setting in which children lived together with their parents until marriage, the number of these one- and two-person households has jumped, for example, from 22.8 percent of all Korean households in 1990 to 48.2 percent in 2010.[47] Such changes in households would have meant new challenges and opportunities for churches to expand. Another social change requiring a change in evangelical focus is the rapid rise in the number of foreigners living in Korea. The number of foreigners living in Korea was negligible until the late 1980s, but labour shortage due to Koreans' aversion of manual jobs in small- to medium-sized factories necessitated the importation of large number of migrant workers. The number of migrant workers – and, later, migrant brides – increased substantially over the years, rising to more than a half million by 2005 or 1.1 percent of the total population. The total continued to increase, reaching a total of more than 1.7 million or 3.4 percent of the total population as of early 2015.[48] All of these have represented new opportunities for growth, but the Anglican Church seemed to have not taken advantage of them.

Conclusion

A few observations can be made about the early Anglican missionary efforts in Korea. The beginning of the Anglican Church of Korea would not have been possible without the efforts of Anglican missionaries based in Japan and China. Archdeacon Shaw based in Japan and Bishop Scott of China played instrumental roles in persuading the Anglican Church to establish a mission field in Korea. Also, unlike Japan and China where various Anglican missionary societies participated in launching missionary works, SPG was the only missionary society that was interested in, and ultimately launched, an Anglican missionary work in Korea.

From early on, like their Protestant counterparts, the Anglican missionaries attempted to appeal to the masses by carrying out missionary activities in medical care, education and social work. The Anglican Church of Korea also endeavoured to be a 'homegrown' church in rapport with Korean culture. Such efforts are manifested, among others, in the construction of several Anglican Church buildings which were designed in emulations of the traditional Korean architecture. Some of the early Anglican missionaries also made significant contributions to what can be broadly termed Korean Studies, writing about things Korean and translating Korean writings into English.

The Japanese colonial rule (1910–1945) and the Korean War (1950–1953) brought new challenges for Christianity as a whole and the Anglican Church had its own share of hardships, highlighted by the martyrdom of six clergy during the war. The most opportune time for growth was the period of rapid industrialisation and urbanisation in Korea from the 1960s to the 1980s and this is when the Anglican Church can be said to have experienced a conspicuous growth as well. As a result of such growth, Korea became an independent province within the Anglican Communion in 1993, complete with the consecration of the Most Revd. Sungsu Kim as the first Korean Archbishop of Korea. Since then, six other Archbishops have helped to establish the Anglican Church as one of the most progressive Christian denominations in Korea.

Being progressive, however, has not resulted in growth for the Korean Anglican Church. As evidenced in the last two censuses in 1995 and 2005, all the major religions, except for Catholicism, either experienced no real gains in membership or decline. The absolute number of followers for Buddhism may have grown, but the figure can be seen as a decline if the population growth during the same period is taken into account. Protestantism fared even worse, experiencing a minus growth for the first time in the postwar period. Its membership is expected to fall even further in the new census taken in 2015. The Korean Anglican Church is likely to have suffered a decline in membership in recent years as well. More than its Catholic and Protestant counterparts, however, the Korean Anglican Church is troubled by the fact that it lacks the vitality that can attract new members. It largely remains a 'hidden church', with its presence 'smothered' by much more 'powerful' Catholic and Protestant churches. Due to its relatively small size, its existence is hardly felt by the general populace, e.g., when Koreans are considering a religion for their new faith or a religion to switch to, it is very unlikely that the Anglican Church comes to their minds. The future of the Anglican Church in Korea is thus uncertain at best. The Church now needs to be concerned with survival itself. In an extremely competitive religious market in Korea – there are more than 170 Protestant denominations and 60,000 churches – the idea of expanding its membership seems beyond its reach. The increasing secularisation of Korean society and the projected continuing decline of the religious population mean that there will be more pews to fill for all the churches, but the Anglican Church remains highly uncompetitive, given its limited human and financial resources.

Notes

1 Anglican Church of Korea, *World Council of Churches* (2014). Available from http://www.oikoumene.org/en/member-churches/anglican-church-of-korea accessed 27 December 2014. Detailed data on the number of Anglicans in Korea is very difficult to obtain. It seems that the Korean Anglican Church has not been updating its membership data. I have made inquiries to the central office of the Church in Seoul, but the replies I have received have been the same, that it does not have updated data on its membership. I have

exhaustively looked into census and survey data in Korea but also to no avail. The reason for the lack of data on Anglican membership in Korea is that tabulations of religious population in the country, be it by government agencies or religious organisations, categorise Christians into only two groups – Catholics and Protestants (and its denominations). It is safe to assume that Anglicans are categorised as followers of 'other religions'.

2 The KNCC is a council of six denominations consisting of the Methodist Church, the Anglican Church, the Christ Presbyterian Assembly in the Republic of Korea, the Jesus Presbyterian Church of Korea, the Salvation Army and the Christ Evangelical Church of Korea. Although the council comprises only six denominations, out of more than 170 denominations, its members account for about one-fourth of the total number of Protestants in Korea, i.e., 2 million members out of some 8 million Protestants.

3 C. F. Pascoe, *Two Hundred Years of the S.P.G.: An Historical Account of the Society for the Propagation of the Gospel in Foreign Parts, 1701–1900 (Based on a Digest of the Society's Records)* (vol. 2; London: Society for the Propagation of the Gospel in Foreign Parts, 1901); M. N. Trollope, *The Church in Korea* (London: A. R. Mowbray, 1915); J. B. Whelan, 'The Anglican Church in Korea', *International Review of Mission* 49 (1960): 157–66; C. Jung, 'Hangukseonggonghoeui eojewa oneul' (The Past and Present of the Korean Anglican Church), *Gidokgyosasang* 149 (1970): 99–105; J. Yi, *Daehanseonggonghoe baeknyeonsa* (One-Hundred Year History of the Korean Anglican Church) (Seoul: Daehanseonggonghoe chulpansa, 1990); S. C. Kim, 'Via Media in the Land of Morning Calm: The Anglican Church in Korea', *Journal of Korean Religions* 4 (2013): 71–98.

4 Yi, *Daehanseonggonghoe*: 29.

5 Ibid.

6 A. D. Clark, *A History of the Church in Korea* (Seoul: Christian Literature Society of Korea, 1971): 109.

7 Until 1876, Korea had remained a 'hermit kingdom', maintaining limited diplomatic and commercial contacts only with China. However, after the country was 'forced' to sign a treaty with Japan in that year, it sensed that its sovereignty was in jeopardy, with China and Russia jostling with Japan for the control of Korea. Korea sought help from strong Western powers by signing a series of treaties with Western countries, starting with the United States in 1882. The heightened tension in the region thus forced Korea to accept Western elements, including Christianity.

8 I. P. Joo, *Seonggonghoe, yeollin gyohoeroui chodae: Seonggonghoeui yeoksa, sinang geurigo seongyo* (An Invitation to an Open Church, Anglican Church: The History, Faith and Mission of the Anglican Church) (Seoul: Pureunsol, 2011): 79. The history of Christianity in Korea dates back to 1784 when Catholicism was introduced, although the first Catholic missionary, a Chinese priest, arrived in the country 11 years later. For nearly a century since its introduction, the Catholic Church suffered a series of persecutions, during which as many as 10,000 were martyred (103 of them were canonised as saints in 1984). At the time, Confucianism was the state religion, obliging every Korean to perform an ancestral rite. However, the Catholic Church banned Korean Catholics from performing the rite, as it was considered a form of idolatry. The latter's refusal to perform the time-honored ritual prompted the government to carry out the brutal persecutions. It is thus safe to say that the Protestant missionary work in Korea, including that of the Anglican Church, which began a century later than the Catholic beginning, began under relatively more auspicious circumstances.

9 Yi, *Daehanseonggonghoe*: 33.

10 Ibid.: 34.

11 The date of their arrival was St. Michael's Day, which was why they named their first church, completed two years later in September 1892, St. Michael's Church.

12 Pascoe, *Two Hundred Years*: 715. Cited from G. Paik, *The History of Protestant Missions in Korea, 1832–1910* (second edition; Seoul: Yonsei University Press, 1971): 289.

13 These were not the first modern hospitals in Korea, for Protestant missionaries who arrived a few years earlier started to found hospitals from as early as 1895.

14 Yi, *Daehanseonggonghoe*: 46. Dr. Landis' medical work was short-lived, as he passed away from typhoid fever at the age of 32 in 1898.

15 Ibid.: 47.

16 A. J. Brown, *One Hundred Years: A Story of the Foreign Missionary Work of the Presbyterian Church in the U.S.A.* (New York: Fleming H. Revell Co., 1936): 442; Paik, *History*: 289; Clark, *History*: 129.

17 Trollope, *Church*: 70; cited from Paik, *History*: 290.

18 Joo, *Seonggonghoe*: 79.

19 The theological institute ultimately laid the foundation for what would later become Sunggonghoe University (literally, Anglican Church University) in 1994.

20 As the only one of its kind in Asia, the cathedral stands today as an important historical landmark in Korea and is registered as a 'Tangible Cultural Asset' of Seoul.

21 Yi, *Daehanseonggonghoe*: 201.

22 Ibid.: 158.

23 Clark, *History*: 330–1.

24 This figure represented a small minority among the Christian population at the time (in 1939, there were 141,243 Catholics and 246,779 Protestants in Korea); see S. Kim, 'The Shinto Shrine Issue in Korean Christianity under Japanese Colonialism', *Journal of Church and State* 39 [1997]: 503–21). In proportional terms, however, the figure is significantly higher than the proportion of Anglicans among Christian population in more recent times, especially from 1985 to 2005. For example, Anglicans comprised about 2.45 percent of the Christian population in 1939, but their proportion among Christians fell to a mere 0.38 percent in 2005. Explanations for the 'limited success' of the Korean Anglican Church are given toward the end of this chapter.

25 Kim, 'The Shinto Shrine Issue': 503–21.

26 Japanese Christians had a fundamentally different view about the Shinto shrine controversy. For the Japanese, Shinto is a part of their culture, and hence, attendance at Shinto rituals, whether Christian or non-Christian, meant nothing more than an act of customary ritual and patriotism; see Clark, *History*: 221–32.

27 The Catholic Church was not affected by the Shinto controversy as the Vatican maintained that the shrine participation was merely political and not religious, and that Catholics in Korea had the obligation to observe the laws of the state. This stance, however, was all the more ironic in the light of the strong position taken by the Catholic Church against the ancestor worship in the nineteenth century that led to brutal persecutions.

28 J. H. Grayson, *Early Buddhism and Christianity in Korea* (Leiden: Brill, 1985): 294.

29 R. E. Shearer, *Wildfire: Church Growth in Korea* (Grand Rapids: Eerdmans Pub. Co., 1966): 77–9.

30 Yi, *Daehanseonggonghoe*: 204, 217.

31 J. Jun, 'Bokjisahoewa gidokgyoui gongdongcherosoui yeokhale daehan gochal – Seonggonghoe sahoeseongyohwaldongui yereul jungshimeuro' (A Study on Welfare Society and the Role of Christianity for Community – A Focus on Social Missionary Activities of the Anglican Church), *Gyohoesaeop* 24 (2013): 49–82.

32 Joo, *Seonggonghoe*: 86.

33 Yi, *Daehanseonggonghoe*: 243.

34 Bishop Lee received an honorary CBE from Queen Elizabeth II in 1974. He died in 2010.

35 The Bishop of Seoul is also the Archbishop of Korea and Primate of the Church.

36 S. Kim and K. Kim, *A History of Korean Christianity* (New York: Cambridge University Press, 2014).

37 A. Kim, 'Protestantism in Korea and Japan from the 1880s to the 1940s: A Comparative Study of Differential Cultural Reception and Social Impact', *Korea Journal* 45 (2005): 265–6.

38 W. G. Lee, 'A Sociological Study on the Factors of Church Growth and Decline in Korea', *Korea Journal* 39 (1999): 235–69.

39 A. E. Kim, 'Christianity, Shamanism, and Modernization in South Korea', *Cross Currents* 50 (2000): 112–19.
40 Kim, 'Protestantism': 276–8.
41 R. Stark, 'Church and Sect', in P. E. Hammond (ed.), *The Sacred in a Secular Age* (Berkeley: University of California Press, 1985): 139–49.
42 Lee, 'Sociological Study': 244; A. Kim, 'Korean Religious Culture and Its Affinity to Christianity: The Rise of Protestant Christianity in South Korea', *Sociology of Religion* 61 (2000): 117–33.
43 Lee, 'Sociological Study': 245–7.
44 J. Hwang, 'A Study of the Fundamentalist Tendency in Korean Protestantism: With Special Reference to the Korean Presbyterian Church', *Acta Koreana* 11 (2008): 113–42.
45 J. Byun, *Hangukui osunjeolundongsa* (History of Pentecostalism in Korea) (Seoul: Shinsaenggwan, 1972): 128–31.
46 Institute of Korean Church History Studies, *A History of the Korean Church, Vol. I (16 C. – 1918)* (Seoul: Christian Literature Press, 1989): 218.
47 'Single, 2-Person Households on the Rise', *Korea Herald*, 26 September 2014, available at http://www.koreaherald.com/view.php?ud=20140926000880 accessed 27 January 2016.
48 'Number of Foreign Residents in S. Korea Triples over Ten Years', *Hankyoreh*, 6 July 2015, available at http://english.hani.co.kr/arti/english_edition/e_international/699034.html accessed 30 January 2016.

11 Australia

Ruth Powell[1]

Introduction

This chapter aims to understand and explain the patterns of church growth or decline in the Anglican Church in the contemporary Australian context.

Australia is a stable, democratic and culturally diverse nation. Australia's history is first defined by 60,000 years of habitation by indigenous peoples, with their rich expressions of spirituality integrated with understandings of land. All other Australians are essentially recent migrant arrivals, from 1788 onwards. This island nation of 21.5 million people is physically located in Asia, yet primarily influenced by British and other western history and philosophies. Today, Australia is one of the most multicultural and economically prosperous nations in the world and is highly urbanised with nearly 90% living in urban areas.

The Anglican Church of Australia has descended from the Church of England, which is an important backdrop to the contemporary experience of growth and decline. After describing the sources of information and providing a brief overview of the history of the Anglican Church of Australia, this chapter is divided into the following parts:

- Part 1: Evidence about numerical growth and decline in the Anglican Church of Australia
- Part 2: Factors that impact on the growth or decline of the Anglican Church of Australia
- Part 3: An empirical study of church growth in Australian Anglican churches
- Part 4: Looking to the future: evidence of the five marks of mission

Sources of information

This chapter has drawn from a range of sources. Preliminary interviews with a small selection of senior clergy provided a guide as to the issues that needed to be covered. Writings from historians and missiologists were combined with publicly available reports for governing bodies, such as Synod and Standing Committees, especially documents prepared for the 16th General Synod in 2014.

Empirical data is based on the Australian National Census of Population and Housing, the National Church Life Survey (a collaborative project across 23 Christian denominations), and various sample surveys of the wider population. Estimates of church attendance have been drawn from databases held by NCLS Research, augmented by other sources.

It is important to say something about the National Church Life Survey. The Australian National Church Life Survey (NCLS) is a five-yearly quantitative survey encompassing hundreds of thousands of participants and leaders in thousands of local churches from more than 20 Australian denominations (Catholic, Anglican and other Protestant). The survey covers a wide range of areas of religious faith and practice and social concern, and is the largest, longest running survey of local church life in the world.

The underlying purpose of each NCLS has been to assist churches, at local, regional and national levels, to reflect on their health. Most Anglican dioceses have had some level of participation in each NCLS. While the NCLS is not a full census of all churches, weighting procedures are used at a national level to adjust for non-participating churches.[2]

Where possible in this chapter, data has been presented for the period from 1980 to the most recent date available, with the exception of the NCLS, which commenced in 1991.[3]

A brief history of the Anglican Church of Australia

When English authorities decided to establish Botany Bay as a penal settlement in 1788, most of the new arrivals were nominally Anglican, but the provision of any religious institutional presence was not a top priority. The Church provided essentially a chaplaincy role, held first by Revd. Richard Johnson, and later by Revd. Samuel Marsden. Both men were advocates of the Established Church; however, by 1818, the Church and State were recognised as separate independent institutions. Anglicans had now been joined by Methodists, Presbyterians and Roman Catholics representing other British constituents.[4] The Diocese of Australia was constituted in 1836 under the first Bishop, William Broughton. In the same year, the *New South Wales Church Act* established the equality of the main denominations before the law.

In these early years of colonial settlement, clergy encountered a level of indifference or pragmatism to religious matters that was exacerbated by great distances and hard life of bush pioneers. As Frame describes, 'the Anglican ascendency in New South Wales was secured in, and maintained through, the structures of an English Colonial administration and parochial privilege, with some eventual assistance from missionary organisations, and wealthy benefactors from Britain'.[5] Other Australian states also share similar histories. In short, 'Australia has never experienced Christendom in the way it is found in the UK and North America, but the Anglican Church of Australia has behaved, at times, like an established church in a Christendom culture'.[6]

Part 1: evidence about numerical growth and decline in the Anglican Church of Australia

This first part describes patterns of numerical growth and decline in the Anglican Church of Australia, including Anglican identification or affiliation, weekly church attendance and numbers of congregations and active clergy.

Religious belonging, believing and behaving among all Australians

The following summary indicators within the framework of 'belonging, believing and behaving' demonstrate the changing place of religion in Australian society in the decades prior to 2011.[7] Sources are the five-yearly National Census of Population and Housing and various sample surveys of the Australian population.

- *Belonging:* the overall proportion of Australians who identify with a religion has steadily declined from 96% in 1901 to 61% in 2011.
- *Believing:* 'belief in the existence of God or some kind of higher power' declined from around 78% in 1993 to 69% in 2009.
- *Behaving:* frequent church attendance (at least monthly) declined from 20% in 1980 to 15% in 2009.

Australians who identify as Anglicans

The non-indigenous early settlers largely came from the United Kingdom. The dominance of an Anglican identity among Australians for most of the 20th century can be tracked through the National Census. As Bouma notes, the Census measures 'cultural Anglicans':[8] those who identify with the Anglican Church or associate themselves with the British culture of the Anglican tradition.

From the time of Federation in 1901 until 1947, around 40% of Australians identified as Anglican (or 'Church of England'), peaking in 1921 at 44%. After World War Two, the proportion steadily declined. In 1986, Catholics outnumbered Anglicans for the first time.

Figure 11.1 shows that the proportion of Australians who identified as Anglican declined from 26% in 1981 to 17% in 2011. In contrast, levels of identification with the Catholic Church have remained relatively stable (due, in part, to gains from recent migration), and the proportion who identify with other religious groups has steadily increased. Australians – particularly younger people – have increasingly favoured the 'no religion' identity.

Estimates of attendance growth and decline in Anglican churches

Church attendance is the most commonly used measure of public religious practice in Australia. While some denominations and regions have experienced growth in attendance, the overall trend since the 1950s has been decline. There is no fully reliable source for estimates of Australian Anglican attendance; however, a mix of different methods have been used to build estimates over the 20-year period from 1991 to 2011.

As shown in Figure 11.2, estimated weekly Anglican attendance has declined from 191,600 in 1991 to 155,000 in 2011 (19% decrease). It should be noted

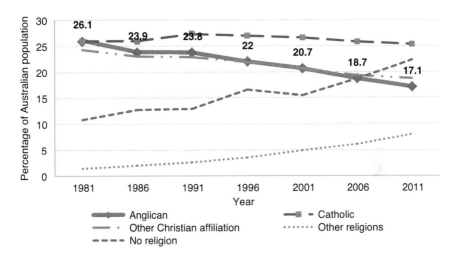

Figure 11.1 The religious identification of Australians: 1981 to 2011

Source: National Census of Population and Housing: 1980–2011, Australian Bureau of Statistics.

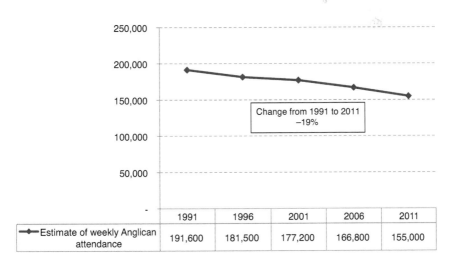

	1991	1996	2001	2006	2011
Estimate of weekly Anglican attendance	191,600	181,500	177,200	166,800	155,000

Figure 11.2 Estimated weekly Anglican Church attendance in Australia: 1991 to 2011

Source: 1991 NCLS, 1996 NCLS, 2001 NCLS, 2006 NCLS and 2011 NCLS augmented with estimates from various church sources.

that the collection using NCLS sources is incomplete and additional information has been sought from dioceses, where possible. In several cases the diocesan
figures have been lower than NCLS estimates, which suggests that this estimation
of decline may be somewhat conservative.

Underlying these figures are differing diocesan patterns. In general,
declines in attendance have been greater in rural dioceses, when compared
to urban dioceses. The Diocese of Sydney experienced growth in attendance
from 1991 to 2011, which has offset the overall trends of decline to some
degree. With reference to patterns of church attendance, these findings confirm assumptions made by commentators about the strong counterpoint that
the Sydney Diocese has historically provided and continues to provide in
Australian Anglicanism.[9]

Number of Anglican congregations and active clergy

The number of Anglican congregations decreased by an estimated 16% between
1991 and 2011. It is likely that many of the closures are in rural areas, and it
is possible that a church presence remains through other congregations in the
parish or neighbouring parishes (see Table 11.1). In contrast, Table 11.2 shows a
19% increase in the number of active clergy between 1981 and 2011, from 2,067
to 2,469 respectively. This different trend may be due to the adoption of team
ministry approaches. It may also reflect the intentional investment in training
and equipping in some dioceses.[10]

Table 11.1 Estimated number of Anglican congregations in Australia: 1991 to 2011

	1991	1996	2001	2006	2011	Change from 1991 to 2011
Estimated number of congregations	3427	3287	3128	2917	2862	−16%

Source: NCLS Research Churches Dataset: 1991, 1996, 2001, 2006, 2011.

Table 11.2 Estimated number of active Anglican clergy in Australia: 1981 to 2011

	1981	1991	2001	2011	Change from 1981 to 2011
Estimated number of active clergy	2067	2160	2302	2469	+19%

Source: C. Reilly, Appendix 2 of 'The Report of the Viability and Structures Task Force', The Sixteenth
General Synod Adelaide June/July 2014 (Sydney: The Standing Committee of the General Synod of the
Anglican Church of Australia, 2014).

Part 2: factors that impact on the growth or decline of the Anglican Church of Australia

What are the factors that lie behind and drive the decline in Anglican identification, attendance and number of congregations? There is a vast amount of commentary from many disciplines addressing this question. From a sociological perspective, we can organise these factors under four broad headings: national contextual, local contextual, national institutional and local institutional factors.[11] This model has been adapted and refined in Australian work.[12]

Contextual factors are forces operating externally to the Church. *National contextual* factors include the socio-structural, economic, political and value commitments of Australian society, and the impact of the physical environment. *Local contextual* phenomena are the immediate neighbourhood influences such as population shifts and neighbourhood changes. Institutional factors are forces internal to the Church itself. *National institutional* factors are seen at the denominational and ecumenical level and include denominational structure, polity, theological orientation, new Church development and mission emphases. *Local institutional* factors are the most important influences on laity satisfaction and include forces internal to the local congregation, such as worship, teaching, leadership, pastoral care and laity mobilisation.

Global and national contextual factors

> Whether Anglicans like it or not, we will have to live with ethnic and religious diversity.[13]

As elsewhere, Australia has experienced extraordinary social and cultural change in recent decades. Global and national factors are drivers of change over which churches have little or no control. Globalisation, a worldwide movement toward economic, financial, trade and communications integration, has had a profound impact on churches. As Bouma notes, 'Even as the churches had no control over the industrialisation, urbanisation and the rise of the middle class that produced the forms of church in the 19th century, so too today they are not in control of the social forces shaping their destinies'.[14]

National cultural factors refer to the changes in the meanings, values, beliefs and sentiments held by the larger population. Much has been written on the broad paradigm shifts by philosophers, social scientists, theologians and others. A few examples include a rising emphasis on individuals, rather than collectives; a shift in the understanding of authority; and values of choice over obligation. These and other cultural factors have all led to a renegotiation of the role of churches in society. While the impact is widespread, the Anglican Church, which historically was significantly integrated with the established power bases in society, has arguably been hardest hit. As Bouma summarises,

> The net effect of socio-cultural changes since about 1960 has been to shift being Anglican from a normal and expected part of Australian life to being one choice among many that people will make on the basis of their perceptions of the costs and benefits of each option. . . . The result is that the likelihood of any person choosing to attend church has decreased.[15]

National social structural forces that have impacted on all Australian churches include: an ageing population, increasing levels of higher education and changing migration patterns. Changing gender roles, marriage and family patterns can be used to illustrate how such social structural factors impact on church life. For example, the role of the family in faith formation is foundational, so there are implications for church life as people marry later, delay family formation and family structures diversify. Increasingly high levels of employment in healthcare, service and retail industries means more people work 'unusual hours' – including Sundays. The increased role of women in the workforce means women are less available as church volunteers than in generations past. General civic engagement has also declined, affecting the fortunes of many voluntary organisations beyond churches.

Over recent decades, the Australian population has changed dramatically in both size and character and these changes are projected to continue. For example, the population is expected to nearly double in the 50 years to 2061.[16] However, this growth is unevenly distributed. The larger cities are experiencing extraordinary population growth, while some rural areas are in decline. This has a direct impact on the resources available to churches in different parts of the nation.

One source of growth is migration, which directly impacts the religious profile of the population. The Anglican Church has not benefitted from the recent waves of migrant inflow in the same way as other religious groups have. Prior to World War II the majority of Australia's migrants came from the United Kingdom; however, after the War, Australia's immigration programme diversified. Recent arrivals to Australia (from 2007 to 2011) were less likely than migrants before 2007 to report an affiliation to Anglicanism (7% and 13% respectively). Between 2001 and 2011, nearly 145,000 migrants who identified as Anglican arrived from a variety of countries, enhancing cultural diversity; however, this has not been sufficient to offset the decline in the churches.

Another feature of population change is increasing social mobility. Just over half (55%) of the Australian population had the same address in 2011 as they did five years earlier[17] – although again, this figure varies across the country. Such high levels of social mobility must create instability in churches, making it more difficult to establish stable leadership structures and pursue longer-term mission and ministry.

Local contextual factors

> The Diocese of North West Australia is nearly the size of Europe.[18]
>
> Rural Australia has changed dramatically. Farming is a corporate enterprise linked to globalisation and international trade. There is lots of innovation and progress with technology in farming, but a smaller population is required, and this will continue. . . . The lure of the city is enormous.[19]

Churches have been and largely remain local institutions, and they are vulnerable to demographic changes in the local community. Small churches are especially vulnerable.

While it is not the only source of growth for a parish, nominal or 'cultural' Anglicans in a local community provide a foundation for potential church attendance. This number varies dramatically across Australian parishes in different settings.

Some Anglican parishes that were primarily Anglo-Celtic in composition have become disconnected as surrounding communities have become dominated by new migrant groups. In other cases, new migrant groups have brought greater numbers, new life and vibrancy to churches. With people moving house at a greater rate, churches may find themselves disconnected from a younger generation of local residents. These kinds of disconnection can then lead to periods of decline. In other settings, there are so-called 'Bible belts' where churches thrive. Some 26% of Anglican parishes who took part in the 2011 National Church Life Survey were either heavily involved (12%) or taking first steps (14%) in ministry towards migrants. This was lower than the Australian average across all denominations (35%); however, this is related to the higher proportions of rural Anglican churches, which are generally less likely to be involved in this kind of ministry.[20]

Compared to most other Australian denominations, the Anglican Church has a disproportionately high number of rural churches. A rural setting presents a greater challenge for church growth. Younger people in rural areas often leave for the cities for education or work and rural populations can shrink with the closure of local industries, resulting in church decline. In some outback parts of Australia, local populations are constantly turning over, resulting in churches with few long-term attenders. Other rural communities are becoming dormitory areas for larger regional centres.

While urban/rural differences are found in other nations, as the earth's sixth largest country in land area, Australia has the additional challenge of its vast size. The tyranny of distance has always been a challenge to the Anglican Church of Australia, with a variety of strategies tried in response. However, issues concerning the ongoing sustainability of such initiatives persist. As the authors of the Report of the Viability and Structures Task Force to the 16th General Synod note, 'The size of Australia will not alter, but the ability to sustain ministry to remote and regional Australia will continue to be a test for our rural dioceses'.[21]

National institutional factors

> While we refer to ourselves as 'The Anglican Church of Australia' and there is widespread perception in the community of the Anglican Church as a unified, coherent entity, the reality is quite different.[22]

National institutional factors highlight aspects of the structures and governance of the Anglican Church, and reflect the impact of the particular history and traditions associated with the Anglican Church of Australia. These factors also partly explain church growth and decline patterns. Indeed, the Viability and Structures Task Force was established at the General Synod in 2010 because of a growing concern about the mission of the Anglican Church and its ability to engage with Australian society.

Picking up the brief historical overview provided earlier, Bishop Broughton was enthroned as Bishop of Australia in June 1836. The Diocese of Tasmania was created in 1842, and then the four dioceses of Sydney, Adelaide, Newcastle and Melbourne were created in 1847. Over the following 80 years the number of dioceses waxed and waned. In 2015 there are 23 dioceses divided into five provinces, with Tasmania being an extra provincial diocese. The creation of the General Synod in 1872, which had representatives from every diocese, meant that Anglicans were amongst the first Australians to establish a national institution.[23] In 1962 the 'Church of England in Australia' was established on a formal constitutional basis. By 1981 the current name 'Anglican Church of Australia' was adopted.

In his outgoing address at the 2014 General Synod, the Primate of Australia (2005 to 2014), Archbishop Aspinall, suggested 'We are being forced to ask ourselves, once more, whether our existing constitutional and organisational arrangements are serving us well and enabling us in the best possible way to minister to Australia in the 21st century'.[24]

A colonial church with an English inheritance

We didn't remove 'Church of England' from our name until 1981![25]
We should have called ourselves 'Church of Australia', but we were too young, too fledgling.[26]

In interviews with a number of Anglican Church leaders, one of the recurring themes was the so-called English captivity of the Australian Church. Interviewees suggested that the Church has not successfully contextualised in ways appropriate for Australian realities, but rather, it has kept looking to England. For a long time key leadership positions were filled from England. It took till 1966 for an Australian-born Archbishop to be appointed (Sir Marcus Loane, Archbishop of Sydney, 1966 to 1982; Primate of Australia, 1978 to 1982). It was not until 1981 that all legal ties with the Church of England were officially terminated and the current name 'Anglican Church of Australia' was adopted.

Institutional governance: a weak federation

The Anglican Church of Australia is often described as a 'confederation of dioceses' with each having its own unique character, Acts of Synod, heritage, ethos and style of operation.[27]
Our constitution is strangling us. We are not able to respond nationally and strategically.[28]

Structural arrangements have given rise to clusters of institutional issues that have impacted on the capacity of the Church for mission. Archbishop Aspinall (Primate from 2005 to 2014) summarised these issues as follows: the different strengths and needs of the 23 dioceses; the roles and powers of dioceses and the General Synod; the composition of the General Synod and the Standing Committee; and the Church's tribunal system and the rights of minorities.[29]

Local autonomy of dioceses: the 1962 Constitution intentionally created a local power structure for dioceses. The strengths of this approach are that local community needs can be given priority in authentic ways. Further, broader decisions cannot be forced onto other dioceses if they are irrelevant or seen as unhelpful. However, at the 2014 General Synod, the outgoing Primate expressed his views bluntly regarding the tension between local autonomy and communion or catholicity.

> At virtually every point, local autonomy has trumped substantial endeavours to express our belonging together, to act together, to provide mutual accountability and support, to plan and organise mission sensibly and to allocate resources where they are needed. That is, the character of the church as catholic has found only the most muted expression in Australia. Local autonomy has trumped catholicity.[30]

Diocesan finances: beyond the large metropolitan dioceses, many other dioceses are in poor financial health and may not be sustainable into the near future. While this is partly related to the changing nature of rural Australia, it is exacerbated by the Church's own governance. The Diocesan Financial Advisory Group (DFAG) has made repeated calls for 'urgent and significant action' regarding the financial and governance challenges. DFAG supports the idea that no less than a revolution is required and that, as a prerequisite, the Church needs to decide whether it is truly a church for the whole nation or not.[31] The way forward remains unclear in 2015.

Child protection: the Anglican Church of Australia shares with other church institutions the tragedy of child sexual abuse. At the 13th General Synod in 2004 an apology was made to all those who have been sexually abused by clergy and church workers. Since then, numerous institutional initiatives have been undertaken to address and improve child protection. In early 2013, the Australian Governor-General of Australia appointed commissioners for a 'Royal Commission into Institutional Responses to Child Sexual Abuse'. While it has been welcomed by church leadership, the Commission has once again placed a harsh spotlight on the Anglican Church. The Royal Commission has also made it evident that more work needs to be done. Diocesan differences in policies, procedures and capacity have made this complex and difficult. Australian bishops continue to collaborate in finding ways forward.[32] However, the ongoing 'ripple effect' of these matters has a far-reaching impact on the capacity of the Church to pursue its mission to proclaim the Kingdom of God.

The influence of theological tradition

> Sometimes there is a fear of evangelicals; it is seen as a 'party'. We are just gospel men and women.[33]
>
> The only issue with a high degree of commonality is mission. If we accept mission as our priority, then we can lead.[34]

Historically, the founders of dioceses emphasised different theological influences: Evangelical, anglo-catholic and liberal or progressive emphases. As bishops were chosen for the newly formed dioceses, '[t]he English clergy selected for these positions reflected the breadth of theological sympathy evident within the Church of England at that time'.[35] Not only was the theological culture reflected in leadership and senior clergy positions, it was also visible in church buildings and architecture. Kaye also makes the case that the democratic, local and pragmatic foundations of the emerging synods in Australia were in line with general moves in society at the time to more democratic and local institutions.[36]

In broad terms, the dioceses continue to reflect the theological emphasis of their first bishops.[37] Sydney, which is the largest diocese, remains largely Evangelical, while other dioceses are characterised by varying degrees of Evangelical, anglo-catholic, Charismatic/Pentecostal and liberal/progressive approaches. Results from the 2011 National Church Life Survey showed that 41% of Anglican attenders identified with an Evangelical or Reformed approach, 27% identified with a Catholic or anglo-catholic approach, 17% identified with a moderate or traditional approach, 10% identified with a Pentecostal or Charismatic approach and only 5% identified with a liberal or progress approach to faith. Some 22% of Anglican attenders claimed that they do not identify with such descriptions. There are diocesan differences in these patterns, with the Diocese of Sydney having the highest proportion of attenders who identified with an Evangelical or Reformed approach (58%). In comparison, other major city dioceses had the following proportions: Adelaide, 33%; Brisbane (Southern Queensland), 43%; Canberra and Goulburn, 30%; Melbourne, 35%; and Perth, 25%. The group of attenders who did not identify with such descriptions is fairly consistent across the dioceses, at 19% to 25%.

An issue that has been subject to decades of debate and continues to divide dioceses is the ordination of women. While the General Synod approved legislation in 1992 allowing dioceses to ordain women to the priesthood, it is up to dioceses to adopt the legislation and a minority have not done so. As of Easter 2015, Australia has two female diocesan bishops.

In summary, at a national and diocesan institutional level, the challenges facing the Anglican Church of Australia are quite undoubtedly extensive. The Viability and Structures Task Force noted that

> From the point of view of government regulation and compliance, it makes for a very complex and at times confusing situation because the Anglican

Church of Australia is not one organic organisation, but 23 organisations. For many years it has been our greatest strength, but in the times ahead it could be our greatest vulnerability.[38]

The way these wider institutional factors are expressed and experienced within specific diocesan contexts will impact on patterns of church growth or decline.

Local institutional factors

There are two keys to effective ministry. The first is good leadership among both ordained and lay people and second is healthy relationships. Strong and vital relationships are the basis on which to build a good and vital congregation.[39]

Intentionality is a keyword. Parish health is linked to the need to be intentionally missionary.[40]

The fourth and final set of factors proposed to impact on church growth is located in the local church. Commentators have dedicated many books and articles to what local churches have done or should do. Spiritual growth and vitality among church attenders is one feature that is emphasised. Churches where attenders report strong levels of personal spiritual growth are also churches which succeed in attracting and retaining newcomers. Observers also point to the style and quality of worship services as important. When the content and presentation of church meetings is not sufficiently compelling, newcomers will not stay. Further, the practices of hospitality matter: welcome, follow-up and ongoing inclusion. Much attention has also been given to the importance of a missional focus and the building of community connections. Leadership is always on the list. The qualities of the local clergy, from their demographic or personality profile, theological orientation, leadership style, to their length of service, are a few of the aspects raised. In addition, the role of lay leadership receives attention, from the professionalisation of church leadership, to theories of collaborative or distributed leadership, or such practical issues as the ratio of staff to attenders.

Nine core qualities of church life

NCLS Research has developed a framework of nine separate but inter-related Core Qualities and three attendance measures that together build a picture of vitality in local churches.[41]

The first three *Internal Core Qualities* have to do with faith in God and relationships within the church community. They focus on the inner life of the community of faith and are often seen as foundational to church life, providing both shape and energy to the other Core Qualities:

- Alive and growing faith
- Vital and nurturing worship
- Strong and growing belonging.

The next three *Inspirational Core Qualities* have to do with leadership and direction and can be catalysts for change in churches. Together they reveal something of a church's openness to change:

• Clear and owned vision
• Inspiring and empowering leadership
• Imaginative and flexible innovation.

The final three *Outward Core Qualities* focus on the interface between the local church and the wider community, in serving others, sharing the faith and assisting others in becoming part of the church:

• Practical and diverse service
• Willing and effective faith-sharing
• Intentional and welcoming inclusion.

Each of these Core Qualities is measured in surveys with multiple questions, focussed on different aspects. The three attendance measures are newcomers without a church background in the church, the retention of youth and overall attendance change.

Table 11.3 contains a set of 'headline indicators' – one per Core Quality – which illustrates trends in the Anglican Church of Australia over a few decades.[42]

Table 11.3 Core qualities of church vitality in Australian Anglican churches: 2001 to 2011

Core Quality	Sample or headline indicator	2001 %	2006 %	2011 %
Faith	I have experienced much growth in faith at my church	27	28	29
Worship	I always/usually experience inspiration during the service here	56	59	64
Belonging	I have a strong & growing sense of belonging here	53	52	53
Vision	I am strongly committed to the vision, goals & direction here	33	34	39
Leadership	Our leaders encourage us to a great extent to use our gifts here	27	23	22
Innovation	I strongly agree our church is always ready to try new things	10	12	12
Service	I have helped others informally in at least three of named ways	55	57	59
Faith-sharing	I invited someone to church here in the last year	42	40	38
Inclusion	Certain I would follow up someone drifting away from church	7	11	11

Source: National Church Life Surveys – Anglican Attender Surveys: 2001, 2006, 2011.

Two indicators have declined between 2001 and 2011: 'inspiring and empowering leadership' and 'faith-sharing'. However, most of these headline indicators have increased in this period, which is a positive sign regarding the increasing vitality of local Anglican churches as perceived by attenders.

Part 3: an empirical study of church growth in Australian Anglican churches

The previous discussion has provided an overview of many of the factors proposed to relate to Anglican church growth or decline, including features of local congregations and the national expression of the Anglican Church, as well as wider contextual factors. While all these factors are certainly related to church growth, what is their relative impact? Does the context primarily determine the fortunes of parishes? Is it all about theological orientation? How much can the local church make a difference? To address these questions, Part 3 describes a limited empirical multivariate study of church growth in 1,089 Australian Anglican churches, whose attenders provided a range of information in the 2006 NCLS. Predictor variables were features of the local community in which the local church is located, the local church's theological tradition and local church health or vitality.

Two outcome measures: church growth and newcomers

While the main focus of this work is to understand numerical growth and decline in churches (defined here as the proportional change in local church attendance between 2001 and 2006), a second measure of 'growth' – newcomers – has been included. The presence of newcomers without a church background is evidence of a parish living out its mission in ways that outsiders can understand and in which they can participate. The ability of some parishes to effectively include newcomers is a reminder that the Church is not merely at the mercy of demographic shifts, but can also contribute to shaping its future. Small changes in the inflows of newcomers locally (defined here as the proportion of attenders who joined their local church in the five years prior to 2006 and were previously not involved in any church) can make significant changes to the shape of the wider denomination.

Assessing the impact of the local demographic context

Previous research using NCLS data on Australian Anglican and Protestant churches has shown that the local demographic context predicts the growth and decline of churches, including the level of newcomers.[43] The current study tests whether these findings apply to Australian Anglican parishes specifically.

'Local community' was defined as the area surrounding each local church within a radius of 2km in urban areas and 5km in rural areas. A selection of measures was made based on what was proposed as important by commentators and what was available from the national census data. For example, population mobility, the community's age profile and levels of religious affiliation have been theorised to be important for church growth. Flows of migration have also been linked to religious engagement, so a measure of the proportion of the local community born in a non-English speaking country was also included. A measure of local context was constructed based on an ABS remoteness category. 'Urban' locations are defined as in major cities of Australia; 'regional' is defined as inner regional Australia; and 'rural' is defined as outer regional Australia/remote Australia/very remote Australia. Further, educational attainment gives an indication of the socio-economic level of a community. See Table 11.4 for a description of each measure.

Assessing the impact of theological tradition

A great deal has been said over the years about the importance of theological tradition in determining whether churches will thrive or struggle (although few have based their assertions on empirical data). For example, Kelley argued that conservative and Evangelical churches would thrive because their clear cut message stands in contrast to the void of meaning that people have increasingly felt as society changes.[44]

NCLS data has provided a rare contribution to this field, with measures of theological tradition based on responses from every available church attender, rather than a select group or a single leader. Previous analyses across all Australian denominations have repeatedly confirmed that theological tradition does indeed play a role in the outcomes of church vitality, with churches influenced by Evangelical and Charismatic/Pentecostal traditions having something of a 'head start' on other groups.[45] The current study tests whether these findings are applicable to Australian Anglican churches specifically.

Each person was asked 'Do you identify with any of the following approaches to matters of faith?' They were able to select up to two options from the following list: Catholic or anglo-catholic, Charismatic, Evangelical, Liberal, Lutheranism, Moderate, Progressive, Pentecostal, Reformed, Traditionalist and 'I do not identify with such descriptions'. The two measures included were the proportion of attenders in local church who self-identified as Evangelical or Reformed and those who self-identified as Charismatic or Pentecostal.

Assessing the impact of local church vitality

While previous NCLS research projects have found that local community context and theological tradition predict church growth patterns, we have also found that the Core Qualities of local church vitality matter. Therefore, it is possible for many churches to break out of the cycle of growth and decline, whatever their theological persuasion or local context. While some churches will inevitably close, there is also much scope for churches to reverse the trends of decline or to start completely new ministries, with good prospects for success.[46] The current study tests whether Core Qualities of church vitality can play a role in predicting church growth and newcomers in Australian Anglican churches after the local context and theological tradition are taken into account.

Two local church vitality measures were aggregated from attenders' survey responses. 'Collective confidence' concerns attenders' evaluations and experiences of their church, whereas 'individual commitment' concerns attenders' religious practices in relation to their own church and more broadly. Confirmatory factor analyses have previously confirmed the structure of these measures.[47] The measures were calculated by averaging the proportions of respondents in the local church who chose the relevant response for each item (see Table 11.4 for descriptions).

Results

Bivariate correlations: Table 11.4 shows how the selected community and church-related indicators correlated with growth and newcomers at the bivariate level. Each correlation was statistically significant (with the exception of Anglican affiliates in the community). That is, the community in which the church is located, the theological tradition of those in the congregation and the vitality of the church are all related to both outcomes: growing in numbers and attracting newcomers. However, the strongest relationship is observed for 'collective confidence'. In churches that are growing, attenders are more likely to describe the church as inspiring, to be growing in their faith and to feel they belong.

Multivariate analyses: linear regression models allowed us to consider a variety of explanatory variables simultaneously in order to identify which had significant effects on each of the two dependent variables, all else being equal. The dependent variable was first, church growth, and then, proportion of newcomers. The results are shown in Table 11.5. These statistics identify relationships but they do not necessarily mean that one factor causes another.

In this study, only one of the proposed community factors is significantly associated with church growth – a growing local population. Having higher proportions of attenders who identify with Evangelical/Reformed traditions is also positively related to growth. Finally, the greater the levels of collective confidence regarding the local church, the more likely the church will be growing. The level of individual religious commitment does not have an impact on growth.

Considering newcomers, results show that the proportion of migrants born in non-English speaking countries in the surrounding community is a positive predictor, whereas the median age of the community is a negative predictor (in other words, churches in older communities are less likely to have newcomers). In terms of theological tradition, having higher proportions of attenders who identify with Evangelical/Reformed or Charismatic/Pentecostal traditions is

Table 11.4 Correlations between growth and newcomers and community/church-related indicators in Australian Anglican churches

Measures	Description	Church growth/decline from 2001 to 2006	Newcomers in previous five years with no recent church background
Local community-related indicators			
Community: population change from 2001 to 2006	Proportional change in the population in a five-year period	0.113**	0.086*
Community: new arrivals from 2001 to 2006	Proportion of all new arrivals to the local community in a five-year period	0.126**	0.102**
Community: university degree	Proportion of the local community with a university degree in 2006	0.112**	0.146**
Community: Anglican affiliation	Proportion of the local community who identify as Anglican in 2006	−0.054	−0.053
Community: median age	The median age of the local community in 2006	−0.123**	−0.207**
Community: non-English speaking migrants	Proportion born in non-English speaking country in 2006	0.145**	0.232**
Community: regional	Based on ABS remoteness category: regional locations are in inner regional Australia	−0.084**	−0.098**
Community: urban	Based on ABS remoteness category: urban locations are in the major cities of Australia	0.126**	0.199**
Local church theological tradition indicators			
Church theological tradition: Evangelical/Reformed theological tradition	Proportion of attenders in local church who self-identified as Evangelical or Reformed	0.215**	0.239**
Church theological tradition: Charismatic/Pentecostal theological tradition	Proportion of attenders in local church who self-identified as Charismatic or Pentecostal	0.102**	0.164**

Local church vitality

Church vitality: collective confidence among attenders	A factor score based on measures of attenders who agree they have grown in faith due to their church; agree leaders inspire them to action, experience inspiration in services, strongly agree church is innovative, and have strong and growing belonging	0.233**	0.328**
Church vitality: individual commitment of attenders	A factor score based on measures of attenders who are in faith-based small groups, practise private devotions frequently, have higher financial giving, place a high importance on God, and are likely to follow up driftouts.	0.161**	0.193**

Source: National Church Life Survey – Anglican Attender Surveys 2006 and Australian Bureau of Statistics, 2006 National Census of Population and Housing.

* Variables with statistically significant effects. *p < 0.01, ** p < 0.001.

Table 11.5 Linear regression for growth and newcomers in Australian Anglican churches

Predictors	Numerical growth	Newcomers
	Beta	Beta
Community-related indicators		
Population change from 2001 to 2006	0.046	0.014
New arrivals from 2001 to 2006	0.114*	0.050
University degree	0.028	0.019
Anglican affiliation	−0.041	0.106
Median age	0.027	−0.090*
Proportion of migrants born in a non-English speaking country	0.005	0.168*
Regional location	−0.019	0.034
Urban location	0.037	0.062
Local church theological tradition		
Evangelical/Reformed theological tradition	0.208*	0.163*
Charismatic/Pentecostal theological tradition	0.043	0.102*
Local church vitality		
Collective confidence among attenders	0.207*	0.282*
Individual commitment of attenders	−0.092	−0.144*

Source: National Church Life Survey – Anglican Attender Surveys 2006 and Australian Bureau of Statistics, 2006 National Census of Population and Housing.

* Variables with statistically significant effects. * p < 0.001.

positively related to levels of newcomers. Finally, when higher proportions of attenders express a collective confidence in the local church, there are more likely to be newcomers. Having faithful, religiously committed attenders is not enough to attract newcomers.

These models account for only a modest amount of the variance in each of the dependent variables. The three sets of variables (community context, theological tradition and church vitality) account for 18% of the variance in newcomers, and 10% of the variance in church growth.

While the variables differ in detail, this overall result regarding the modest prediction of growth aligns with Voas and Watt's Church of England study.[48] Their comments about reasons for this are relevant: while random measurement error (or noise), will be part of the reason, and while it is possible there is some major explanatory variable that has been missed, it is most likely that the sheer diversity of local parish experience is likely to be responsible.[49] Church growth is not simply a matter of following some formula or set of rules.

One difference between the results of the 2014 UK study of growth and this Australian study is the finding about the impact of theological tradition. In the UK study, so-called 'churchmanship' did not relate significantly with growth once other factors were controlled. This inconsistency may be partly due to differences between the character of the UK and Australian context; however, it is most likely to be due to the way that this feature was operationalised in each study.

In summary, local demographic factors do have an impact, but they are neither necessary nor sufficient for growth to occur. Further, theological tradition does make a statistical difference, confirming previous research. However, among Anglican Australian churches, after these other factors are controlled, local church vitality matters. 'Collective confidence' is one of the most powerful predictors of both numerical growth and attracting newcomers. Local church health and vitality is something local churches and leaders – of any persuasion – can impact.

Part 4: looking to the future: evidence of the five marks of mission

> How far does the vision of the local parish extend beyond worship? Are they paying attention to the other marks of mission? Those who focus on others tend to be healthier.[50]

Based on the current trends, what can be said about the future of the Anglican Church? It is evident that significant challenges remain from both within and beyond the Church. What resources does the Church have to draw from? This is not simply a question of the numbers of churches or people. This is about the ongoing health and vitality of local parishes. In Part 4, NCLS data is applied to an Anglican mission framework in order to examine the current capacity of local churches for ministry and mission.

The five marks of mission are an important statement on mission which expresses the Anglican Communion's common commitment to, and understanding of, God's holistic mission:

1   To proclaim the Good News of the Kingdom
2   To teach, baptise and nurture new believers
3   To respond to human need by loving service
4   To seek to transform unjust structures of society, to challenge violence of every kind and to pursue peace and reconciliation
5   To strive to safeguard the integrity of creation and sustain and renew the life of the earth.

Church Life Survey questions can be used to indicate engagement with these aspects of mission in Australia.

First mark of mission: to proclaim the good news of the kingdom

The NCLS asks all participating church attenders about how they speak of faith to their friends and families, whether they invite others to their local church and if they are involved in the evangelistic activities of the church. The proportion of Anglican attenders who felt at ease sharing faith and looked for opportunities increased from 11% in 1996 to 15% in 2011. Further, 25% were regularly involved in the outreach or evangelistic activities of parishes in 2006 and 2011, an increase from 20% in 2001. However, when it comes to inviting family and friends to church, there has been a downward trend since 2001 (see Figure 11.3).

Second mark of mission: to teach, baptise and nurture new believers

While the NCLS doesn't ask individuals to identify themselves as 'new believers', it is possible to focus on the proportion of newcomers to church life, which in Anglican churches was 10% in 1991 and 8% in 2011.

This mark of mission also encompasses the need to build welcoming, transforming communities of faith.[51] The results from three National Church Life Surveys showed that between 2001 and 2011 attenders were more likely to provide a positive assessment of their own growth in faith, experience of vital and nurturing worship, and inclusion of others. Levels of belonging were stable (see Table 11.3).

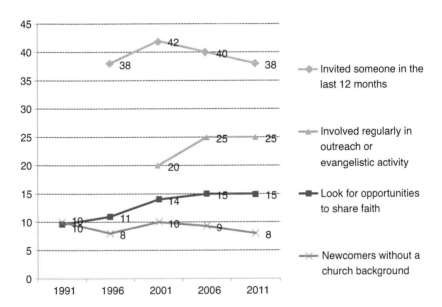

Figure 11.3 Measures of faith-sharing and newcomers in Australian Anglican churches: 1991 to 2011

Source: Australian National Church Life Surveys – Anglican Attender Surveys: 1991, 1996, 2001, 2006, 2011.

Third mark of mission: to respond to human need by loving service

Loving service is a response to the call to feed the hungry, visit the prisoner, care for the sick and so on (Matthew 25). The Anglican Church serves Australian society through national and diocesan agencies which provide community and social welfare services, including aged care, childcare, family, youth, unemployment and disability services. There is also evidence of increased active service from individuals and local churches over time.

Informal acts of service: in the 12 months prior to 2011, 80% of Anglican attenders donated money to charity; 55% visited someone in hospital; 44% helped someone through a crisis; 40% gave possessions to a needy person; 30% cared for someone who was very sick; 23% lent money outside their family; and 19% contacted a parliamentarian or councillor about an issue. The proportion who helped others in three or more of these ways is given in Figure 11.4.

Service by church attenders through community groups: Anglican attender involvement in 'community-based' groups (not connected with the local church) has been relatively stable over 20 years (~25%). Over the same period, involvement in church-based service groups has increased substantially, from 17% in 1996 to 27% in 2011 (see Figure 11.4).

These results show that the way that churches engage with the community is changing. What are the implications of the sharp rise in activities based within local churches? Is this a sign of the Anglican Church in mission in new ways, perhaps trying to build new bridges to their communities?

At the same time, involvement through wider community groups has been relatively stable over two decades, which confirms that connections beyond the Church remain strong. Other research on NCLS data has found that across all Australian denominations there is a positive correlation between hours

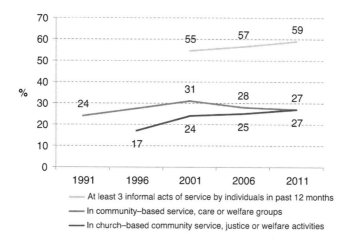

Figure 11.4 Measures of community service in Australian Anglican churches: 1991 to 2011
Source: National Church Life Surveys – Attender Surveys: 1991, 1996, 2001, 2006, 2011.

spent on volunteering within congregations and hours volunteering beyond congregations.[52]

However, it should be noted that previous research based on NCLS data across all Australian churches has found that high levels of service is the quality least associated to outcomes such as attracting newcomers, or numerical growth.[53]

Fourth mark of mission: to seek to transform unjust structures of society, to challenge violence of every kind and to pursue peace and reconciliation

In the 2011 NCLS, a national random sample of Anglican church attenders completed questions about their own social and political views, as well their views on the role of churches on some matters of justice.

Work on changing the structures of society: more than eight out of ten (82%) of Anglican attenders agreed that 'Christians should work to change the structures of society in order to create a more just society'.

Participation in mass campaigns about global justice: seven out of ten Anglican attenders agreed that 'it is a Christian responsibility to take part in mass campaigns designed to address issues of global poverty or injustice (e.g. Make Poverty History, Micah Challenge)'. However, only 9% had been actively engaged in a recent campaign which was among the lowest proportion when compared with other denominations. It is clear there is a challenge for Anglican churches and Christian NGOs to enable those who support campaigning to take action or to remain active.

Involvement by Christians in public policy issues: attenders were asked: 'In your opinion, should Christians be involved in public policy issues in the following ways? Advocacy or lobbying of governments? Public comment?' Compared to attenders from other Catholic and Protestant denominations, the Anglican Church had among the largest proportion of attenders who agreed with Christian advocacy (85% vs 75% overall) and Christian public comment (88% vs 80%).

Church involvement in public policy: in terms of the role of churches in engaging public policy issues, Anglican attenders again demonstrated the strongest levels of agreement with church advocacy (71% vs 63% overall) and church public comment (76% vs 70% overall) compared to attenders from other denominations. A further question asked attenders to select up to four public policy issues from a list of 15 about which their church denomination should be most active. The most commonly selected issues were support for marriage and the family (63%), poverty and disadvantage in Australia (56%) and poverty overseas (42%).

Church commitment to developing countries: in the 2011 Operations Survey audit of local church activity, a representative was asked to indicate specific commitments by their local church to people in developing countries over the previous 12 months. Anglican churches mostly offered financial support (57% vs 61% of all churches), prayer support (53% vs 52% overall) and personal support (38% vs 44% overall). They were less likely than all Australian churches to run campaigns (18% vs 32% overall).

The fifth mark of mission: to strive to safeguard the integrity of creation and sustain and renew the life of the earth

The 2011 NCLS painted a picture of the environmental views and actions of church attenders, leaders and congregations.

Views about Christian environmental responsibility: 83% of Anglican attenders and 87% of senior local Anglican Church leaders indicated that they believed that Christians did have a responsibility to be active about environmental issues. Some 31% of Anglican attenders and 46% of senior Anglican leaders were personally active on such issues (vs 32% of senior leaders in all denominations). Almost three-quarters (73%) of senior local Anglican leaders (vs 67% overall) endorsed the view that caring for the Earth should be an essential part of the mission of the Church. Some 38% of leaders often or sometimes preached about environmental issues, and 35% did so occasionally.

Local church environmental activity: the 2011 Operations Survey included a battery of some 20 items about environmental activities, including in the areas of worship, operations of church buildings and community projects and events. The majority of Anglican congregations (73%) indicated that they recycled. Four in ten churches purchased environmentally friendly consumables and similar proportions had implemented energy savings measures at church buildings, celebrated of a day or a season with an environmental theme and included environmental concerns in worship. Children's activities (20%) and Bible studies/adult faith education sessions (14%) on an environmental theme were much less common.

Age: life stage and generational replacement

When reflecting on the future shape of the Anglican Church, there is one more factor that warrants attention: age. A person's age gives powerful clues about their religious beliefs, attitudes and involvement in church life. In 1966, Hans Mol conducted a landmark study of religion in Australia and concluded that there were no differences in church attendance between different age groups.[54] The intervening years have seen a widening gap between the age profiles of the Australian community and of church attenders. Previously, the expectation was that young people who left the Church would return when they were raising their own children. In Australia, as in other western countries, the young who left the churches in the 1960s and 1970s were the first generation not to return. Now younger age groups are heavily under-represented in Anglican churches (as well as in some other denominations; see Figure 11.5).

There are a number of implications that flow from this ageing profile of the Church. First, it represents the ongoing loss of many loved people, places, buildings, congregations and even ways of doing church that have had meaning for many years. Second, the age group that tends to pick up leadership roles and responsibilities – those in their middle years – is smaller than even 20 years earlier. Third, people of child-bearing age are under-represented, with implications for generational replacement.

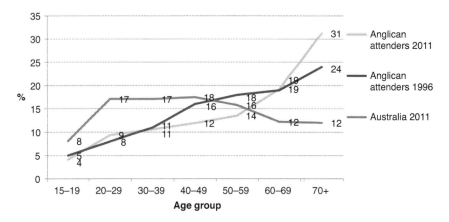

Figure 11.5 Age profile of Anglican adult church attenders and all Australians (15 years+): 1996 and 2011

Source: National Church Life Surveys – Anglican Attender Surveys 1996, 2011 and Australian Bureau of Statistics, 2011 National Census of Population and Housing.

If the focus is numerical growth, then retaining young people is key. We concur with the conclusions of Voas and Watt that the role of the family in passing on faith and nurturing patterns of religious involvement is critical.[55] People who belong to a church in their 20s are likely to continue to attend.

Much has been written about generational (or cohort) differences. In brief, members of cohorts sustain distinctive, shared characteristics due to their shared formative experiences. The 'baby boom' generation is a common example. Other research using NCLS datasets has shown that even among church attenders, different generations approach matters of religion and church life differently.[56]

To some degree, the Anglican Church is in a season of grief at what has or will be lost or perhaps what was never realised. Yet, the effects of the current historical period are widespread and relevant to the experience of every age group, although not necessarily in the same way. Younger generations can be expected to take different approaches to God and the Church into the future. Greater understanding of the differences between generations of Anglicans warrants further attention.

Leadership and vision for the future

> Anglicanism, by its tradition, has had porous boundaries and an outward looking disposition, which is actually the source of vitality and creativity.[57]

Inspiring, empowering and equipping leadership

Leadership is a consistent theme throughout the material collected for this study. When local church attenders describe the local leaders in their congregations,

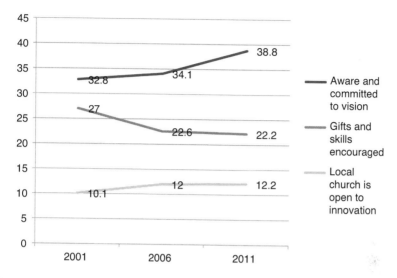

Figure 11.6 Australian Anglican attenders' views on vision, leadership and innovation: 2001 to 2011

Source: National Church Life Surveys – Anglican Attender Surveys: 2001, 2006, 2011.

they generally have a positive perspective. The proportion who agreed with the following statements about the local leadership is shown in parentheses.

There are strong affirmations of local leaders' capacity to communicate well (84%), focus on future directions (81%) and keep the congregation focussed on connecting with the wider community (78%). These strong leadership assets will need to be drawn on as the Church navigates its way into the future. While the percentages remain high (seven out of ten), fewer describe their leaders as able to inspire to action (70%) or to encourage innovation and creative thinking (71%).

The NCLS also looks at whether there is an equipping or empowering culture within the local church. Compared to ten years earlier, in 2011 Anglican attenders were less likely to claim that their gifts and skills were encouraged by the local church leadership (see Figure 11.6). This is an important longer-term trend to watch because it is one of the few indicators that has declined. It potentially also points to an under-utilised resource in churches.

Has the Church become less encouraging? Have local church leaders 'tightened the reins'? Is there less room for a diversity of visions? Or is this more about a change in attenders' perception of what is happening, rather than an actual change in practices? Do more attenders now expect their own contribution to be valued and sought after?

Clear and owned vision for the future

> You need leaders who make decisions after consultation. . . . People want leadership and need to know they can have confidence in their leaders.[58]

The idea that it is important for groups to have a sense of direction, goals or vision for the future, has gained profile among churches in recent decades. Previous research based on NCLS data has consistently found that having a clear and owned vision is important to overall church health and vitality.[59]

Between 2001 and 2011, there was a strong increase in the proportion of Anglican attenders who say they are aware and strongly committed to the vision or directions of their local church (see Figure 11.6). Further, more than three-quarters of Anglican attenders in 2011 were confident that the congregation could achieve the vision, goals or directions it set for itself.

People in churches appear to be finding their footing in the changing tides, attending to questions about their purpose in a given time and place and discovering a shared vision, which evidences a degree of intentionality about the work of local churches in mission. Whether or not the hoped-for outcomes are forthcoming is yet to be seen.

Imaginative and flexible innovation

> I don't mind diversity, but diversity in style must be grounded in the Gospel, shaping life. Whether or not you have communion every week, whether the children are in church, whether it is formal or not: these things are not important. The core must be the Gospel.[60]

Healthy churches are characterised by a culture of openness to new possibilities. Having flexibility to allow innovation is associated with growth in numbers and with higher levels of newcomers.[61]

In 2011, 12% of Anglican attenders strongly agreed that their congregation was always ready to try something new and a further 50% agreed. Attenders assessed their churches as a little more open to innovation than previously. Along with an increased clarity of vision about the future, this suggests churches have a stronger foundation for engagement in effective mission. Yet, the move from potential to actual is challenging.

The final word about hope for future directions comes from attenders in local Anglican Australian churches. When asked what aspects of church life they would most like to see given greater attention in the next 12 months, the four aspects most often selected (from a list of 12) were:

- Encouraging the people in local churches to discover/use their gifts (32%)
- Building a strong sense of community within the congregation (32%)
- Ensuring new people are included well in church life (30%)
- Spiritual growth (for example: spiritual direction, prayer groups) (27%).

Conclusion

This chapter has used interviews, written material and empirical data to explore and explain the patterns of church growth and decline in the Anglican Church of Australia. A brief overview highlighted the intertwined nature of Australia's history and the Church's history. The Anglican Church's role as a 'church for the nation' or as simply another voluntary religious organisation in a diverse landscape remains a point of ambivalence.

In Part 1, empirical evidence was presented that demonstrated a broader backdrop of decline in religious belonging, believing and behaving among all Australians. In recent decades the proportion of Australians who identify as Anglicans has declined as has weekly attendance and the number of Anglican congregations.

Part 2 outlined four sets of factors that impact on the growth or decline of the Church. National and local contextual factors include wider trends, such as globalisation, as well as social and cultural changes sometimes linked with changes in population, and migration patterns. Churches in the rural sectors of Australia have been hard hit by widespread changes that are beyond their control. The vast distances of Australian geography also play their part in terms of contextual effects. The 'weak federation' of dioceses is at the heart of a set of national institutional factors that remain unresolved. Local institutional factors were explored through the framework of the nine Core Qualities and three attendance measures that together build a picture of vitality in local churches. An encouraging note is sounded by the fact that attenders evaluate the vitality of their parishes more highly than previously, with most headline indicators increasing over a ten-year period.

Part 3 contained an empirical study of church growth and newcomers based on 1,089 local Anglican churches. The impact of the local demographic context, local church theological tradition and local church vitality were assessed. Results showed all factors were related to church growth and to newcomer levels. When all the explanatory variables were investigated simultaneously, local demographic factors did have an impact, but it was relatively small. Theological tradition was also related to growth in this study insofar as higher levels of identification with Evangelical/Reformed traditions predicted growth. However, among Anglican Australian churches, after these other factors were taken into account, the health and vitality of the local church added even more explanatory power. Specifically, the factor called 'collective confidence', which highlights the shared beliefs about general ability, capability and effectiveness, was most predictive of growth and newcomers. Confident, mobilised faith communities with a shared sense of purpose and identity are most effective in attracting others.

The final Part 4 was oriented to the future. Data from waves of National Church Life Surveys demonstrated how the five marks of mission are present and changing in local Anglican churches. In terms of proclamation of the Good News, a higher percentage of Anglican attenders now engage in evangelistic activities; however, inviting family and friends to church has trended downward since 2001. The proportion of newcomers has been relatively stable in the 20-year period since 1991. Providing loving service continues to be a strength of Anglican churches, but the way that churches engage with the community is changing. Compared to attenders in other Australian denominations, Anglican attenders stand out as most likely to affirm the need to challenge and transform unjust structures of society; however, there is a gap between attitudes and actions.

Both attenders and local clergy agree Christians should be active about environmental issues, but again there is a gap between intention and action.

This study has covered a wide diversity of factors that can impact the capacity of the Anglican Church of Australia to grow and thrive. As the Church transitions through its current season, perhaps the greatest sign of hope is that Anglican attenders themselves have identified important keys for growth within local churches – such as providing inspiring and empowering leadership, building strong community within the congregation, ensuring new people are included well and nurturing spiritual growth.

> We believe . . . that God has a purpose for the Anglican Church of Australia and the wider Anglican Communion, and equips us with the gifts of grace to face the many challenges that confront us. In a world where so many things are contingent upon another we are called as Christian believers to understand that the new life we have in Christ is contingent on no earthly thing but only on God's free gift of his son Jesus Christ our Lord. No sociological argument or explanation can ever satisfactorily plumb the depths of this truth, no psychological insight reaches to the same vulnerability of the human soul nor can any political ideology ever offer the dignity that is ours in Christ.[62]

Notes

1 I thank the clergy and congregations who took part in this study, NCLS Research team members, Dr. Miriam Pepper and Sam Sterland for the data preparation and analysis work done for this chapter. Production of this chapter would not have been possible without the work of the other members of the NCLS Research team who, at the time of publication, also included: Chandrika Chinnadurai, Chris Ehler, Nicole Hancock, Kathy Kerr, James Schroder, and Amelia Vaeafisi. Direct correspondence to: Ruth Powell, NCLS Research, Australian Catholic University, PO Box 968, North Sydney, NSW, 2059, Australia. E-mail: rpowell@ncls.org.au

2 M. Pepper, S. Sterland, and R. Powell, 'Methodological Overview of the Study of Well-Being through the Australian National Church Life Survey', *Mental Health, Religion & Culture* 18 (2015): 8–19.

3 See, for example: P. Kaldor, [computer file], '1991 NCLS Attender Survey' (Sydney, Australia: NCLS Research, 1991); P. Kaldor, [computer file], '1996 NCLS Attender Survey' (Sydney, Australia: NCLS Research, 1996); K. Castle, [computer file], '2001 NCLS Attender Survey' (Sydney, Australia: NCLS Research, 2001); K. Castle, [computer file], '2006 NCLS Attender Survey' (Sydney, Australia: NCLS Research, 2006); R. Powell, [computer file], '2011 NCLS Attender Survey A' (Sydney, Australia: NCLS Research, 2011).

4 T. Frame, *Anglicans in Australia* (Sydney: University of New South Wales Press, 2007).

5 Ibid.: 51.

6 A. Curnow (ed.), 'Report of the Viability and Structures Task Force', The Sixteenth General Synod Adelaide June/July 2014 (Sydney: The Standing Committee of the General Synod of the Anglican Church of Australia, 2014): 8.

7 A. Kreider, *The Change of Conversion and the Origin of Christendom* (Eugene: Wipf & Stock, 1999).

8 G. Bouma, 'The Church and Socio-Cultural Change' (Melbourne: Report for the Archbishop of Melbourne, 2013).

9   B. Kaye, 'The Strange Birth of Anglican Synods in Australia and the 1850 Bishops' Con-
    ference', *The Journal of Religious History* 27 (2003); M. Porter, *Sydney Anglicans and the
    Threat to World Anglicanism: The Sydney Experiment* (Farnham: Ashgate, 2011); K. Ward, *A
    History of Global Anglicanism* (Cambridge: Cambridge University Press, 2006).

10 Phone interview with Dr. Wayne Brighton, Secretary, General Synod Task Force on Mis-
    sion, Sydney, 30 July 2014.

11 D. Hoge and D. Roozen (eds.), *Understanding Church Growth and Decline 1950–1978* (New
    York: Pilgrim Press, 1979); D. Hoge, B. Johnson, and D. Luidens, *Vanishing Boundaries:
    The Religion of Mainline Protestant Baby Boomers* (Louisville, KY: Westminster/John Knox
    Press, 1994).

12 See, for example: P. Kaldor, *Who Goes Where? Who Doesn't Care?: Going to Church in Aus-
    tralia* (Sydney: Lancer, 1987).

13 Phone interview with The Right Revd. Andrew Curnow, Bishop at Anglican Diocese of
    Bendigo, Sydney, 24 June 2014.

14 Bouma, 'The Church and Socio-Cultural Change': 39.

15 Ibid.: 13.

16 Australian Bureau of Statistics, ABS Australian Demographic Statistics December 2012
    (cat. no. 3101.0). ABS Australian Historical Population Statistics (cat. no. 3105.0.65.001)
    (2012).

17 Australian Bureau of Statistics, Census 2011, Basic Community Profile (cat. no. 2001.0).

18 'Report of the Viability': 14.

19 Curnow, 2014.

20 I. Duncum, N. Hancock, M. Pepper and R. Powell, *Church Involvement in Migrant Ministry,
    NCLS Research Fact Sheet 14008* (Adelaide: Mirrabooka Press, 2014).

21 'Report of the Viability': 14.

22 P. Aspinall, 'President's Address to 16th General Synod 30th June 2014', available at
    http://www.anglican.org.au/News/Pages/GeneralSynodPresidentsAddress.pdf: 2.

23 Available at http://www.anglican.org.au/governance/Pages/governance_introduction.
    aspx.

24 Aspinall, 'Address': 3.

25 Phone interview with The Right Revd. Trevor Edwards, Chair, General Synod Task Force
    on Mission, Sydney, 30 July 2014.

26 Interview with The Most Revd. Dr. Glenn Davies, Archbishop at Anglican Diocese of
    Sydney, Sydney, 26 May 2014.

27 'Report of the Viability': 21.

28 Curnow, 2014.

29 Aspinall, 'Address'.

30 Ibid.: 19.

31 M. Codling (Chair), Diocesan Financial Advisory Group (DFAG), 'Report to General
    Synod Standing Committee' (Sydney: The Standing Committee of the General Synod of
    the Anglican Church of Australia, April 2014).

32 Aspinall, 'Address': 7.

33 Davies, 2014.

34 Curnow, 2014.

35 Frame, *Anglicans*: 58.

36 Kaye, 'Birth'.

37 D. Hilliard, 'Anglicans: Church of England in Australia', in J. Jupp (ed.), *The Encyclopedia
    of Religion in Australia* (Victoria: Cambridge University Press, 2009): 131.

38 'Report of the Viability': 23.

39 Curnow, 2014.

40 Edwards, 2014.

41 R. Powell, J. Bellamy, S. Sterland, K. Jacka, M. Pepper and M. Brady, *Enriching Church Life*
    (second edition; Adelaide: Mirrabooka Press, 2012).

42 NCLS Research, 'Anglican Church Life Profile' (Sydney, Australia: NCLS Research, 2011).

43 See, for example: Powell et al., *Enriching*.

44 D. M. Kelley, *Why Conservative Churches Are Growing: A Study in Sociology of Religion* (New York: Harper and Row, 1972).

45 P. Kaldor, J. Bellamy, R. Powell, B. Hughes and K. Castle, *Shaping a Future: Characteristics of Vital Congregations* (Adelaide: Openbook, 1997).

46 See Powell et al., *Enriching* and Kaldor et al., *Shaping*, for a fuller discussion of these issues in the Australian context.

47 S. Sterland, R. Powell, M. Pepper and M. Dowson, 'Church Vitality – What Lies beneath: Stability of Underlying Factors in Multiple Denominations' (ISSR Conference, Turku, Finland, 2013).

48 D. Voas and L. Watt, 'Numerical Change in Church Attendance: National, Local and Individual Factors' (Church of England: Church Growth Research Programme Reports on Strands 1 and 2, 2014).

49 Ibid.: 100.

50 Brighton, 2014.

51 Available at http://www.abmission.org/data/Publications/2014/6197_PARTNERS_4Nov. pdf.

52 R. Leonard and J. Bellamy, 'The Relationship between Bonding and Bridging Social Capital among Christian Denominations across Australia', *Nonprofit Management and Leadership* 20 (2010): 445–60.

53 Powell et al., *Enriching*.

54 H. Mol, *Religion in Australia: A Sociological Investigation* (Melbourne: Nelson, 1971).

55 Voas and Watt, 'Numerical Change'.

56 R. Powell and K. Jacka, 'Moving beyond Forty Years of Missing Generations', NCLS Research Occasional Paper 10 (2008).

57 B. Kaye, 'Australian Identity and the Anglican Church', Occasional Paper 1, The Australian College of Theology (Kingsford, NSW, Australia, 2005).

58 Davies, 2014.

59 Powell et al., *Enriching*.

60 Davies, 2014.

61 Powell et al., *Enriching*.

62 P. Freier, available at http://www.anglicanprimate.org.au/2015/03/25/primates-introductory-speech-at-anglican-futures-conference/.

The Americas

12 The United States of America

Jeremy Bonner

Shortly after her election as Presiding Bishop of The Episcopal Church (TEC),[1] Katharine Jefferts Schori conceded that her denomination's membership had fallen to 2.2 million, a circumstance she attributed to the fact that 'Episcopalians tend to be better-educated and tend to reproduce at lower rates than some other denominations'.[2] Schori's observation was itself a pithy rendering of the findings of TEC's Officer for Congregational Development, who, just four years earlier, had identified a close correlation between the national birth rate and changes in Episcopal Church membership since the 1950s:

> Not surprisingly, American women with a graduate or professional degree have the lowest birth rate, followed by women with Bachelor's degrees. Also, women in families earning $75,000 or more have very low birth rates, as do women in families earning $50,000 to $74,999. The Episcopal Church has the highest proportion of members among mainline denominations who are college graduates and in households earning $75,000 or more.[3]

In an aging and increasingly childless denomination, Kirk Hadaway concluded, the only way to arrest membership decline was to embrace increasingly creative forms of evangelism calculated to attract not only those from other Christian traditions (something in which TEC historically excelled) but also the unchurched.[4] In the event, however, the first decade of the twenty-first century was to be marked by intra-denominational strife that not only led many Episcopalians to abandon their former church, but also served to characterise The Episcopal Church – rightly or otherwise – as a body more noted for theological controversy than pastoral care.

Discussion of TEC's growth and decline over the past twenty years has been inextricably entwined with arguments regarding its theological trajectory. The departure of a sizable body of North American Anglicans from TEC between 2006 and 2012 has informed a wider discourse that tends to associate theological liberalism with loss of membership, even as the new – and more conservative – Anglican Church in North America (ACNA) insists that its more traditional theology and focused evangelism has resulted in sustained church growth.[5] While the statistical patterns for ACNA are as yet too tentative for definitive conclusions to be reached, it must also be asked whether TEC's demographic contraction is substantively different from that experienced by other mainline Protestant denominations.[6]

Anglicanism long enjoyed an uncertain standing in North America. For the first hundred years of its existence, it sought to live down its reputation as a tool of British interests and eschewed engagement in public life. During the 1880s, however, it experienced significant growth that, in the years prior to the First World War, saw it claim the loyalties of roughly one American in twenty. Promoting its ecclesiastical structures – including the historic episcopate – as the essential basis for Protestant reunion, TEC soon enjoyed an influence out of all proportion to mere numbers and in the immediate aftermath of the Second World War it shared with the rest of the Protestant mainline in the boom in suburban church population.

Such successes were abruptly curtailed by the turmoil of the 1960s.[7] From black civil rights to revision of the Book of Common Prayer and the ordination of women, TEC found itself rocked by debates that revealed critical fault lines among Episcopalians.[8] While the decision to ordain women to the priesthood in 1976 – arguably the most controversial of the decade – ultimately resulted in only small numbers joining the various 'continuing Anglican' sects,[9] overall prospects for future growth appeared bleak, despite the upsurge in Evangelical and charismatic forms of American Anglicanism during the 1960s and 1970s.[10]

Although Episcopalians lack the regional concentration of such groups as the Southern Baptist Convention, the Evangelical Lutheran Church in America or the Church of Jesus Christ of Latter-day Saints, there are certain geographic locations where they are more plentiful. As Figure 12.1 reveals, the areas of greatest Episcopal density are to be found in the Northeast metropolitan corridor extending from Boston to New York, Philadelphia and Washington DC, with subsidiary areas of concentration in southern California and southern Florida. Density is by no means a guarantee of strong congregations; a 2002 study suggested that Episcopal congregations were stronger on average in the South and West than in the Northeast.[11]

While the numerical distribution of Episcopalians is important, so is the extent of TEC's population penetration. As Figure 12.2 demonstrates, TEC is a minor player in both Florida and California and even in the Northeast it constitutes less than 5 percent of the religiously active. Its greatest population penetration is mostly to be found in areas where it historically had a monopoly on Native American missions, such as South Dakota and Alaska.

Any analyst of TEC's changing membership patterns must first take account of the revised definition of membership adopted by the Church in 1986, which required congregations to report not the number of baptised persons in a congregation but the number of persons active in the

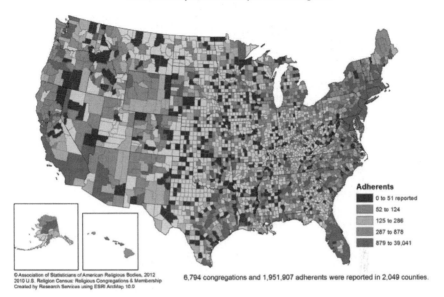

Episcopal Church Adherents in the United States, 2010
Counties Grouped into Five Equal-sized Categories

Adherents
- 0 to 51 reported
- 52 to 124
- 125 to 286
- 287 to 878
- 879 to 39,041

© Association of Statisticians of American Religious Bodies, 2012
2010 U.S. Religion Census: Religious Congregations & Membership
Created by Research Services using ESRI ArcMap 10.0

6,794 congregations and 1,951,907 adherents were reported in 2,049 counties.

Figure 12.1 Number of Episcopal Church adherents in the United States, 2010

Source: Derived from US Religion Census 2010 (available at http://www.rcms2010.org/maps2010. php). Reproduced with the permission of the Association of Statisticians of American Religious Bodies.

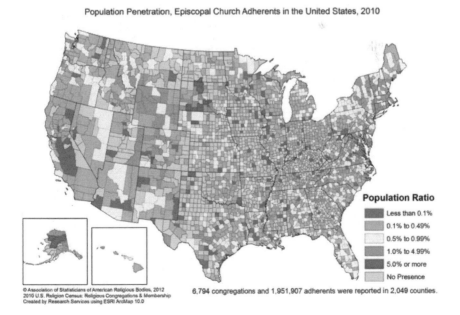

Population Penetration, Episcopal Church Adherents in the United States, 2010

Population Ratio
- Less than 0.1%
- 0.1% to 0.49%
- 0.5% to 0.99%
- 1.0% to 4.99%
- 5.0% or more
- No Presence

© Association of Statisticians of American Religious Bodies, 2012
2010 U.S. Religion Census: Religious Congregations & Membership
Created by Research Services using ESRI ArcMap 10.0

6,794 congregations and 1,951,907 adherents were reported in 2,049 counties.

Figure 12.2 Episcopal Church population penetration in the United States, 2010

Source: Derived from US Religion Census 2010 (Available at http://www.rcms2010.org/maps2010. php). Reproduced with the permission of the Association of Statisticians of American Religious Bodies.

congregation and baptised in the Church.[12] As a result, while TEC lost 175,462 members between 1986 and 2000, on paper it appeared to suffer a 'loss' of 234,815 members (an 8.6 percent one-year decline) between 1985 and 1986. In order to arrive at comparable membership figures for the entire period, a conversion factor of 0.918427 has been applied to TEC baptised membership data for 1980–1985.[13]

Even with this adjustment, TEC lost 227,881 baptised members (8.9 percent) between 1980 and 2000 and the first decade of the twenty-first century proved far worse. From 2001 to 2006 the Church lost 173,663 baptised members (or 7.5 percent of its 2001 membership), while in the Presiding Bishop's first five years it lost a further 231,526 members (10.7 percent of its 2001 membership) (see Table 12.1). The greatest numerical losses in the first part of the last decade were reported in Province 2 (New York and New Jersey) and Province 5 (Illinois, Indiana, Michigan, Ohio, Wisconsin and part of Missouri), while the greatest numerical losses between 2006 and 2011 occurred in Province 8 (Alaska, Arizona, California, Hawaii, Idaho, Nevada, Oregon, Utah and Washington) and Province 3 (Pennsylvania, Maryland and Virginia). Province 5 suffered the greatest overall loss as a proportion of the 2001 provincial population, losing almost a quarter of its members between 2001 and 2011, while Province 4 (covering Alabama, Florida, Georgia, Kentucky, Mississippi, North Carolina, South Carolina, Tennessee and part of Louisiana) reported losses significantly below the national average, particularly in the first half of the decade (see Figure 12.3).

An even more striking decline can be observed in the figures for Average Sunday Attendance (ASA), which fell 97,934 between 2001 and 2006 (11.4 percent of TEC's 2001 ASA) and 102,745 between 2006 and 2011 (13.4 percent of TEC's 2001 ASA), with the highest numerical losses recorded in Province 3 (see Table 12.2). Although generally higher rates of loss were reported in all provinces than for baptised membership, there was less variation between provinces, except for the lower rate of loss reported for Province 4. In the first half of the decade, the worst rates of decline were reported in Province 1 (Connecticut, Maine, Massachusetts, New Hampshire, Rhode Island and Vermont) and Province 3, while Province 7 was the most acutely affected after 2006.

National statistics

By 2010, membership in The Episcopal Church had fallen below two million. One year later, TEC recorded a quarter-century membership loss of 581,461 or 23.2 percent of its 1986 membership, a figure that called into question the viability of many small rural dioceses. From a national church, TEC showed every sign of degenerating into a coastal denomination with minor outposts elsewhere in the nation. The picture is more regionally nuanced than the national figures would have many believe, however, as

Table 12.1 Decline in baptised membership of The Episcopal Church, 2001–2011[14]

	Province 1	Province 2	Province 3	Province 4	Province 5	Province 6	Province 7	Province 8	TOTAL
2001–2006	20,155	27,426	26,671	18,063	26,773	10,891	18,197	25,487	173,663
	(8.6)	(9.4)	(7.2)	(3.5)	(11.9)	(9.5)	(6.7)	(8.4)	(7.5)
2006–2011	25,977	28,646	35,505	28,074	27,168	13,126	31,233	41,797	231,526
	(12.1)	(10.9)	(10.3)	(5.6)	(13.7)	(12.7)	(12.3)	(15.1)	(10.7)
2001–2011	46,132	56,072	62,176	46,137	53,941	24,017	49,430	67,284	405,189
	(19.6)	(19.3)	(16.7)	(8.9)	(24.0)	(21.0)	(18.1)	(22.3)	(17.4)

Provinces of the Episcopal Church
2016-2018 Triennium

Province II Includes:
CONVOCATION OF
EPISCOPAL CHURCHES
IN EUROPE, HAITI,
THE VIRGIN ISLANDS

The Office of the Suffragan Bishop
for Federal Ministries
(Hospitals, Prisons, Armed Forces)
Under the Direction of the Presiding Bishop

The Episcopal Church in Micronesia
Convocation of Episcopal Churches
In Europe
Under the Direction of the Presiding Bishop

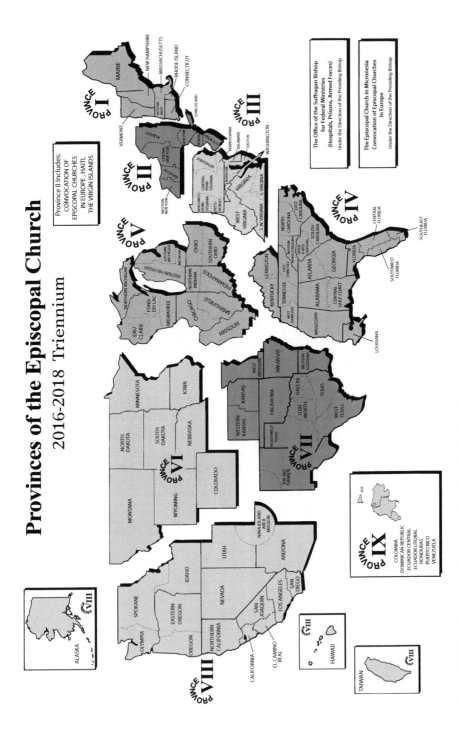

Figure 12.3 Provinces of the Episcopal Church in the United States

Reproduced with the permission of The Office of the General Convention, The Episcopal Church (TEC), New York.

Table 12.2 Decline in average Sunday attendance of The Episcopal Church, 2001–2011[15]

	Province 1	Province 2	Province 3	Province 4	Province 5	Province 6	Province 7	Province 8	TOTAL
2001–2006	10,134	10,842	17,938	16,450	10,639	4,243	10,597	12,397	97,934
	(13.2)	(11.0)	(12.9)	(8.1)	(12.5)	(10.6)	(10.1)	(11.2)	(11.4)
2006–2011	10,114	11,898	19,071	15,988	12,196	5,778	17,011	15,383	102,745
	(15.2)	(13.5)	(15.8)	(8.5)	(16.4)	(16.1)	(18.0)	(15.6)	(13.4)
2001–2011	20,248	22,740	37,009	32,438	22,835	10,021	27,608	27,780	200,679
	(26.4)	(23.0)	(26.7)	(15.9)	(26.9)	(25.0)	(26.3)	(25.1)	(23.4)

Table 12.3 Episcopal Church baptised membership, 1980–2010[16]

Region	1980	1985*	1990	1995	2000	2005	2010
East	999,947	939,423	874,564	832,842	768,702	712,609	627,067
South	580,543	612,336	638,405	661,934	675,744	667,536	618,672
Midwest	482,677	447,299	423,180	398,528	370,821	336,526	291,113
West	493,759	516,900	509,901	511,183	513,778	488,705	415,055
TOTAL	2,556,926	2,515,958	2,446,050	2,404,487	2,329,045	2,205,376	1,951,907

* A conversion factor of 0.918427 has been applied to the raw data to render it compatible with that for 1990 and subsequently.

Table 12.4 Percentage change in Episcopal Church baptised membership, 1980–2010[17]

Region	1980–1985	1985–1990	1990–1995	1995–2000	2000–2005	2005–2010
East	−6.0	−6.9	−4.8	−7.7	−7.3	−12.0
South	+5.5	+4.3	+3.7	+2.1	−1.2	−7.3
Midwest	−7.3	−5.4	−5.8	−6.9	−9.2	−13.5
West	+4.7	−1.3	+0.2	+0.5	−4.9	−15.1
TOTAL	−1.6	−2.8	−1.7	−3.1	−5.3	−11.5

the data contained in Table 12.3 and Table 12.4 illustrate. In these (and subsequent) tables the four defined regions reflect the basic geography of the United States. The East is composed of Provinces One, Two and Three of TEC, excluding the dioceses of Virginia, Southern Virginia and Southwestern Virginia. It covers twelve states in New England and the Mid-Atlantic as well as the District of Columbia, and accounts for twenty-six of the domestic dioceses of TEC. The South consists of Province Four of TEC with the addition of the dioceses of Virginia, Southern Virginia and Southwestern Virginia (from Province Three) and the dioceses of Arkansas and Western Louisiana (from Province Seven). It covers eleven states and accounts for twenty-five of the domestic dioceses of TEC. The Midwest is composed of Provinces Five and Six of TEC, with the addition of the dioceses of Kansas, West Missouri and Western Kansas (from Province Seven). It covers fifteen states and accounts for twenty-five domestic dioceses of TEC. The West consists of Provinces Seven and Eight of TEC, excluding the dioceses of Arkansas, Kansas, West Missouri, Western Kansas and Western Louisiana. It covers twelve states and accounts for twenty-four domestic dioceses of TEC (including the Navajoland Area Mission).

In 1980, almost two-fifths of Episcopalians resided in the East, with the rest more or less evenly distributed between the South, the West and the Midwest. By 2010, less than one-third of Episcopalians were still to be found in the East, while the South was poised to emerge as the region with the largest number of Episcopalians. While both the Midwest and the West continued to undergo a haemorrhage, their rough equivalence in membership in 1980 was gradually undermined by a more precipitate decline in the Midwest, until fewer than one Episcopalian in six still resided in that region by 2010.

From 1980 to 1995, TEC's overall loss of baptised members amounted to 6.0 percent, while from 1995 to 2010 this exploded to 18.8 percent. Both the early 1980s and early 1990s were periods of minimal decline, but losses swelled to 3.1 percent between 1995 and 2000, 5.3 percent between 2000 and 2005 and 11.5 percent between 2005 and 2010. In both the East and Midwest, this membership collapse was sustained and enduring over a thirty-year period, with fewest losses for the Midwest in the late 1980s and for the East in the early 1990s. In the West, an overall gain of 4.0 percent in baptised membership was reported for the period 1980–2000 (though most of this occurred during the early 1980s). After 2000, however, the West began to experience increasingly serious losses, declining 4.9 percent between 2000 and 2005 and 15.1 percent between 2005 and 2010 (the worst performance of the four regions). In the South, by contrast, overall growth of 16.4 percent was reported for the period 1980–2000, though that rate was consistently falling. After a slump of 1.2 per-cent from 2000 to 2005, the South began to fall into line with national trends, reporting a membership decline of 7.3 percent between 2005 and 2010 (though this was still significantly below the national average).

Baptised membership, while a long-accepted metric, can be a misleading measure of church health. The reporting of Average Sunday Attendance (ASA) that began in 1991 has yielded data that speaks more directly to the pattern of active church membership. During the 1990s ASA was relatively stable but by the mid-2000s a marked decline had set in (see Table 12.5).[18] Between 2000 and 2005 the heaviest losses in ASA occurred in the East and Midwest, while the South experienced a much less pronounced decline. In the second half of the decade the rate of loss rose consistently across all regions, with the West actually suffering the highest percentage losses and the South no longer boasting such a dramatically lower rate of decline.

Table 12.5 Episcopal Church Average Sunday Attendance, 2000–2010[19]

Region	2000	2005	2010	Percentage change, 2000–2005	Percentage change, 2005–2010
East	262,696	232,767	191,963	−11.4	−17.5
South	263,265	252,338	220,122	−4.1	−12.8
Midwest	138,310	122,884	101,651	−11.1	−17.3
West	192,308	179,282	144,095	−6.8	−19.6
TOTAL	856,579	787,271	657,831	−8.1	−16.4

A comparison of ASA with baptised membership during the 2000s also yields a very crude measure of member participation.[20] Table 12.6 reveals that the East showed the strongest disparity between membership and participation and the South the strongest affinity, although even the figures for the South were relatively modest. Over the course of the decade, however, the rate of participation has trended downwards, suggesting that, for whatever reason, Episcopalians are less inclined to affirm their faith through sustained corporate worship.

Another measure of church growth is the incidence (or lack thereof) of new baptisms. With its paedobaptist emphasis, Anglicanism has traditionally relied more upon the sacramental admission of infants than the baptism of adults, and the disparity between the two is evident from a comparison of Table 12.7 and Table 12.8. For both groups, however, the rate of baptism

Table 12.6 Episcopal Average Sunday Attendance as a percentage of Episcopal Church baptised membership, 2000–2010[21]

Region	2000	2005	2010
East	34.2	32.7	30.6
South	39.0	37.8	35.6
Midwest	37.3	36.5	34.9
West	37.4	36.7	34.7
TOTAL	36.8	35.7	33.7

Table 12.7 Episcopal Church child baptisms, 1980–2010[22]

Region	1980	1985	1990	1995	2000	2005	2010
East	20,789	21,566	22,123	19,056	15,971	13,195	9,828
South	12,128	13,214	13,562	12,719	12,421	10,989	8,465
Midwest	10,444	9,934	9,102	7,580	7,174	5,760	4,218
West	12,806	13,697	12,075	11,429	11,037	8,736	6,479
TOTAL	56,167	58,411	56,862	50,784	46,603	38,680	28,990

Table 12.8 Episcopal Church adult baptisms, 1980–2010[23]

Region	1980	1985	1990	1995	2000	2005	2010
East	2,244	1,825	2,159	2,190	1,945	1,508	1,060
South	1,701	1,507	2,129	1,991	2,067	1,644	1,118
Midwest	1,392	1,109	1,214	1,005	1,192	940	615
West	2,121	2,177	2,342	2,064	2,027	1,528	979
TOTAL	7,458	6,618	7,844	7,250	7,231	5,620	3,772

has been cut almost in half over a thirty-year period. Child baptisms peaked in the mid-1980s and experienced a precipitate decline beginning in the early 1990s, though with some regional variation. In the East and South the peak came in the early 1990s while the South did not succumb to dramatic decline until after 2000. The overall rate of decline of child baptism of 59.6 percent in the Midwest between 1980 and 2010 compares starkly with the 30.2 percent decline reported for the South and the rates of 52.7 percent and 49.4 percent for the East and West respectively. Even among those raised in the Anglican tradition, the Pew Report offers evidence of significant slippage. While Anglicans outperformed Congregationalists and Presbyterians in terms of retention of adherents from childhood, almost one-third of those raised as Episcopalians either abandoned religion or adopted a non-Protestant form of religious belief in adulthood.[24]

Adult baptism, by contrast, appears to have peaked around 1990. For all the rhetoric of the Decade of Evangelism,[25] adult baptisms declined slightly during the 1990s and precipitately after 2000. While the Midwest reported the worst rate of decline at 55.8 percent, this was not appreciably greater than the 53.8 percent reported in the West or the 52.7 percent reported in the East. The South, once again, had a marginally less poor record with a loss of only 34.3 percent. Interestingly, the South did not actually report the largest number of adult baptisms among the four regions until 2000, indicative perhaps of the less frequent incidence of Christians switching church membership in that region.

Perhaps the most striking statistics of church membership are those relating to marriage (see Table 12.9). While there is a measure of hyperbole in conservative charges that the institution of marriage is no longer valorised in popular culture or within TEC, it cannot be denied that a 70.2 percent decline in the number of marriages, even with a shrinking church population, suggests that the Church is unlikely to repair current losses through natural reproduction. This decline has been most acute in the Midwest (76.3 percent) and in the West (77.7 percent), while the South has suffered a more modest rate of loss (56.3 percent).

Table 12.9 Episcopal Church marriages, 1980–2010[26]

Region	1980	1985	1990	1995	2000	2005	2010
East	14,356	13,809	12,555	9,894	8,253	5,744	4,430
South	7,506	7,362	7,181	6,652	5,912	4,399	3,279
Midwest	7,742	6,119	5,293	4,240	3,559	2,778	1,833
West	9,309	7,837	6,786	6,088	4,717	3,269	2,071
TOTAL	38,913	35,127	31,815	26,874	22,441	16,190	11,613

TEC and the American Protestant mainline

Recent religious surveys, such as the 2008 Pew Forum study of religious affiliation, tend to emphasise the marginality of Anglicanism in the United States. In a nation that only barely identified as majority Protestant (51.3 percent), TEC secured the allegiance of an estimated 1.5 percent of the population. Seven other Protestant groups enjoyed a larger share including relative newcomers such as the Pentecostals (4.4 percent) and nondenominational churches (4.5 percent). Even among mainline Protestant churches (18.1 percent of the US population) the Anglican family was outstripped by the Methodists, Lutherans, Baptists and Presbyterians, while among Evangelical Protestant churches (26.3 percent of the US population) the Anglican share was negligible.[27]

While it cannot be denied that TEC is suffering a very real decline, it is important to consider its performance in relation to other denominations, particularly those in the same mainline Protestant tradition. For this purpose, the reports compiled by the Association of Religion Data Archives are extremely instructive (see Table 12.10). First, it should be noted that the dominant denominational players in American religion are not mainline Protestants. Roman Catholics are present in strength across the continent, with particular concentrations in the Boston-New York-Philadelphia and San Francisco-Los Angeles metropolitan corridors. The Southern Baptist Convention and the Evangelical Lutheran Church in America (ELCA), by contrast, are largely regional bodies, concentrated in the Southeast and the Upper Midwest respectively. Mainline Protestants show less of a tendency to cluster and have a similar distribution to Roman Catholics, with the United Methodist Church and the Presbyterian Church, USA (PCUSA) being among the largest of such bodies. The rise of such outside

Table 12.10 US denominational membership, 1980–2010[28]

Denomination	1980	1990	2000	2010
Roman Catholic Church	47,502,152	53,385,998	62,035,042	58,963,835
Southern Baptist Convention	16,281,692	18,940,682	19,881,467	19,896,279
United Methodist Church	11,552,111	11,091,032	10,350,629	9,860,653
Evangelical Lutheran Church in America	5,379,943	5,226,798	5,113,418	4,181,219
Presbyterian Church (USA)	4,012,835	3,553,335	3,141,566	2,451,980
The Episcopal Church*	2,823,399	2,445,286	2,314,756	1,951,907
Church of Jesus Christ of Latter-Day Saints	2,684,744	3,540,820	4,224,026	6,144,582
Lutheran Church-Missouri Synod	2,622,847	2,603,725	2,521,062	2,270,921
United Church of Christ	2,096,014	1,993,459	1,698,918	1,284,296
Assemblies of God	1,612,655	2,161,610	2,561,998	2,944,887

* The figures for TEC are those listed in the ARDA surveys. The comparable denominational figures are 2,556,926 for 1980 (adjusted to reflect the change in calculating active membership), 2,446,050 for 1990 and 2,329,045 for 2000. The figure for 2010 is identical to that supplied by ARDA.

Table 12.11 Percentage change in US denominational membership, 1980–2010[29]

Denomination	1980–1990	1990–2000	2000–2010	1980–2010
Roman Catholic Church	+12.4	+16.2	−4.9	+24.1
Southern Baptist Convention	+16.3	+5.0	+0.0	+22.2
United Methodist Church	−4.0	−6.7	−4.7	−14.6
Evangelical Lutheran Church in America	−2.8	−2.2	−18.2	−22.3
Presbyterian Church (USA)	−11.4	−11.6	−21.9	−38.9
The Episcopal Church	−13.4*	−5.3	−15.7	−30.9*
Church of Jesus Christ of Latter-Day Saints	+31.9	+19.3	+45.5	+128.9
Lutheran Church-Missouri Synod	−0.7	−3.2	−9.9	−13.4
United Church of Christ	−4.9	−14.8	−24.4	−38.7
Assemblies of God	+34.0	+18.5	+14.9	+82.6

* These figures do not reflect the change in calculating active membership in the 1980s.

groups as the Church of Jesus Christ of Latter-day Saints (LDS Church) and the Pentecostal Assemblies of God since 1980 portends a dramatic reorientation of the American religious landscape, however, in which the relevance of many mainline Protestant groups may be called into question. By 1990, TEC had been overtaken not only by the LDS Church but also by the Lutheran Church-Missouri Synod, a confessional Lutheran body that has never exercised the same social or cultural influence as the ELCA. By 2000, it had fewer members even than the Assemblies of God.

The greatest membership gains of the past thirty years have been achieved by the LDS Church (in 2010 the fourth largest American denomination) and the Assemblies of God, although the Roman Catholics and Southern Baptists both posted respectable gains prior to 2000. Of the five mainline Protestant groups in Table 12.11, TEC performed worst during the 1980s, but this was probably due to the change in the method of calculating membership. During the 1990s, by contrast, only the ELCA lost a smaller proportion of its members, with both the United Church of Christ and the PCUSA posting double digit losses. Between 2000 and 2010, although TEC's rate of decline increased by a factor of three, it actually lost a smaller percentage of its members than did the ELCA. Overall, TEC constitutes a mid-level loser among mainline American Protestant groups, performing less well than the United Methodists or the ELCA but significantly better than either the PCUSA or the United Church of Christ.[30]

Diocesan statistics

The Episcopal Church is a federation of state churches, in which the notion of central authority has always been contested.[31] While regional variations are important, it is the dioceses that constitute the fundamental organising unit of

Table 12.12 Membership of selected dioceses of the Episcopal Church, 1980–2010[32]

Diocese	1980*	1985*	1990	1995	2000	2005	2010
New Hampshire	15,943	15,324	16,223	16,709	16,813	14,725	14,563
New York	69,710	64,828	63,975	62,136	64,301	64,027	60,446
Virginia	71,098	77,844	79,792	82,787	86,211	90,716	79,688
South Carolina	23,415	24,342	24,221	27,142	26,661	30,234	29,196
Fond du Lac	10,313	9,407	9,736	8,887	6,420	6,620	5,859
South Dakota	12,256	12,179	12,086	12,908	11,850	10,830	9,865
Dallas	46,608	31,876**	35,372	34,628	39,376	37,949	31,777
Los Angeles	68,277	74,320	78,235	78,850	72,385	68,241	59,527

* A conversion factor of 0.918427 has been applied to the raw data to render it compatible with those for 1990 and subsequently.

** The Diocese of Fort Worth was formed by a division of the Diocese of Dallas in 1983.

the Church and they demonstrate significant variation in the nature and extent of growth (see Table 12.12). No study of this nature would be complete without some consideration of the particular circumstances of individual dioceses. To this end, the following case-studies (one for each province) seek to provide a degree of perspective on change at the grassroots.

New Hampshire[33]

Although a Congregationalist bastion until the onset of Irish Catholic immigration in the mid-nineteenth century, New England always boasted a significant Anglican minority. Originally part of the Diocese of Massachusetts, the Episcopal Diocese of New Hampshire was erected in 1841, but sprang to prominence in 2003 when it elected Gene Robinson, a priest in an active homosexual relationship, as its ninth bishop.[34] While Robinson's election led Anglican conservatives to predict that it would only accelerate the steady decline in Episcopal membership, the demographic picture for New Hampshire is actually less dire than for TEC as a whole. While the national decline in baptised membership between 1980 and 2010 was 23.7 percent and that for Province 1 reached an alarming 36.5 percent, New Hampshire sustained only an 8.7 percent loss. After a modest decline in the early 1980s, New Hampshire rallied to report a 5.6 percent increase in 1986–90 and a 3.2 percent increase in 1991–96. Membership peaked at 17,281 baptised members in 1997, before entering a ten-year slump that brought New Hampshire to a 14,160-member low in 2007, with declines of 0.5 percent in 1996–2000 and 11.4 percent in 2001–05. Despite a loss of 1,077 members between 2002 and 2003 (a one-year decline of 6.4 percent), which might arguably be attributed to Robinson's election, the diocese has reported modest growth of 1.5 percent in 2006–10, suggesting that it has perhaps reached a membership floor, though another decline of more than 1,000 members (7.0 percent) was reported in 2010–11.

New York[35]

The Episcopal Diocese of York was historically an influential voice in TEC, headed by a cadre of strong-minded bishops that included John Henry Hobart, Henry Potter and William Manning. Initially covering the entire state of New York, it was gradually deprived of territory by the establishment of the Diocese of Western New York in 1838 and the Dioceses of Albany, Central New York and Long Island in 1868, though numerically it has always been among the most populous of TEC dioceses. Despite suffering greater losses between 1980 and 2010 than New Hampshire, New York's 19.1 percent decline in baptised membership was less than half that of Province 2 (40.7 percent). The heaviest losses for the diocese actually occurred in the early 1980s when it experienced a 7.0 percent decline. During the late 1980s and early 1990s this decline continued on a more modest level, with a mere 0.8 percent loss in 1986–90 and a 1.2 percent loss in 1991–96. From 1996 to 2000, the diocese rallied gaining 1,963 new members (an increase of 3.2 percent) and peaking at 65,203 baptised members in 2001. During the 2000s, however, the Diocese of New York entered a period of modest decline, losing 1.8 percent of its members in 2001–05 and 2.7 percent of its members in 2006–10, and falling to 60,446 baptised members in 2010. Such general trends suggested less an abrupt reaction to one single event (there was a loss of only 0.9 percent in 2002–03, for example) than a steady increase in institutional senescence.

Virginia[36]

The Episcopal Diocese of Virginia is one of the few dioceses where divisions between conservative and liberal Anglicans have led to the establishment of extensive rival ecclesiological structures. An influential founding diocese of TEC, Virginia was the centre of Evangelical Anglicanism and home to Virginia Theological Seminary. Portions of the diocese assumed an autonomous status in 1877 (Diocese of West Virginia), 1892 (Diocese of Southern Virginia) and 1919 (Diocese of Southwestern Virginia), leaving the Diocese of Virginia with responsibility for the northeastern portion of the state. As part of the ever-expanding Metro DC corridor, the Diocese of Virginia boasts many wealthy and influential Americans among its members, reinforcing the perception of TEC as a white-collar community. However, the diocese also included a cluster of successful – and culturally conservative – Evangelical parishes that since the 1970s have been committed to active evangelisation. One consequence has been that a straight comparison of the membership trends between 1980 and 2010 reveals the membership of the Diocese of Virginia to have actually grown by 11.9 percent at a time when Province 3's overall losses amounted to 23.4 percent, little different from the national average. The pattern in the Diocese of Virginia has thus been one of steady growth, except for 1991–95 when membership fell by a modest 0.3 percent. The most sustained growth was recorded in 1981–85 when diocesan membership increased by 6.1 percent, but gains of 4.2 percent in 1996–2000, 3.8 percent in 2001–05 and 2.5 percent in 1986–90 were all very respectable, especially when contrasted with the national situation. Indeed, the lowest membership figure recorded since 1985 was in 1987 when the Diocese of Virginia had 76,362 members. Despite a gain of 1.1 percent between 2002 and 2003, however, the Diocese of Virginia lost 11,878 members between 2005 and 2006 (a decline of 13.1 percent in a single year), due to the mass withdrawal of Evangelical parishes to form the Convocation of Anglicans in North America. The overall trajectory of diocesan growth was broken and the Diocese reported only 1.1 percent growth in 2006–10. Worse still, membership declined to 78,358 in 2011, the lowest figure since 1988.

South Carolina[37]

While the Episcopal Diocese of Virginia contained a significant conservative minority in recent years, in the Episcopal Diocese of South Carolina conservatives have been dominant in the diocesan leadership since the early 1980s.[38] One of the first dioceses of TEC, the Diocese of South Carolina gave up territory to permit the erection of the Diocese of Upper South Carolina in 1922. In 1980, South Carolina elected its twelfth bishop, Fitzsimmons Allison, and promptly embarked upon a new era of evangelisation that resulted in sustained growth by the 1990s. Indeed, while Province 4 reported a respectable 10.4 percent membership increase between 1980 and 2010, the increase for the Diocese of South Carolina was 24.7 percent. Until the late 2000s, the diocese followed a pattern of major membership increases alternating with more modest ones, reporting a gain of 7.6 percent in 1981–85 followed by one of 2.2 percent in 1986–90 and a gain of 9.5 percent in 1991–95 succeeded by one of 3.0 percent in 1996–2000. Perhaps its most dramatic success came in 2001–05, when baptised membership grew by 10.5 percent. From a low of 23,359 in 1987, South Carolina crested in 2007 at 31,174, making it the twenty-second largest diocese in the United States and the seventh largest in Province 4. After 2007, however, the diocese underwent a substantial decline in membership, suffering a loss of 6.3 percent between 2006 and 2010. Between 2009 and 2010 it lost a significant 2,188 members, though much of this probably reflected the withdrawal of one particular congregation (St. Andrews, Mount Pleasant), but there was a modest increase of 0.8 percent in 2010–11. In 2012, the Diocese of South Carolina elected to follow the example of dioceses in California, Pennsylvania, Illinois and Texas and withdrew from the national church.

Fond du Lac[39]

Formed in 1874 from the Diocese of Wisconsin, the Diocese of Fond du Lac gave up some of its territory to help establish the Diocese of Eau Claire in 1922. Under Charles Chapman Grafton (bishop from 1888–1912) it was known as a bastion of the heirs of the Oxford Movement. At the heart of the so-called Biretta Belt, it hosted the high church seminary Nashotah House, which trained successive generations of high church clergy to serve parishes across the country. By the late twentieth century, however, much of its diocesan vigour appeared to have been sapped. A 43.2 percent loss in membership between 1980 and 2010 was almost identical with a loss of 42.9 percent for Province 5 as a whole. Much of this decline was sustained during the 1990s, for diocesan membership was effectively static between 1981 and 1985 and increased by 0.3 percent from 1986 to 1990. In 1991–95, however, a 7.3 percent decrease in membership was followed by an even more spectacular decline of 27.2 percent in 1996–2000. The worst year-to-year changes were reported in 1996–97 (a 9.3 percent decrease) and in 1999–2000 (a 16.1 percent decrease). Following this collapse in membership, the Diocese experienced a modest 2.1 percent recovery in 2001–05, only to fall back by a further 10.9 percent in 2006–10. In many ways, Fond du Lac is wholly typical of the general decline in TEC membership across the Midwest.

South Dakota[40]

The Episcopal Diocese of South Dakota is unusual in that it is one of the few dioceses with a significant Native American membership. Organised as the Missionary District of Niobrara in 1871, it became an autonomous diocese one hundred years later. Province 6, to which South Dakota belongs, is the smallest of TEC's provinces, covering six states in the Great Plains and three in the Rocky Mountains, and South Dakota's 19.5 percent membership loss between 1980 and 2010 compares favourably with the 34.2 percent loss suffered by the province as a whole. Until the mid-1990s, the Diocese of South Dakota held its own, with a minimal membership loss of 0.6 percent in 1981–85, gains of 4.5 percent in 1986–90 and 3.6 percent in 1991–95, and a peak membership of 12,908 in 1995. From that point onwards, however, the trajectory has been steadily downwards with losses of 6.5 percent in 1996–2000, 9.8 percent in 2001–05 and 9.6 percent in 2006–10 and a trough membership of 9,865 in 2010. Even more than Fond du Lac, South Dakota has struggled to find a place for itself in a region with a significant Catholic and Lutheran presence.

Dallas[41]

Following the admission of the Diocese of Texas to the General Convention of The Episcopal Church in 1849, a vast jurisdiction of more than 250,000 square miles was subsequently divided into the Dioceses of Texas and West Texas and the Missionary District of Northern Texas in 1874. In 1895, the Missionary District of Northern Texas was organised as the Diocese of Dallas and fifteen years later the Diocese of Dallas itself gave up territory to form the new Missionary District of Northwest Texas (which only attained diocesan status in 1958). In 1980, the Episcopal Diocese of Dallas was the fifteenth largest diocese in TEC, with 50,748 members.[42] Three years later, one-third of the diocese was set apart to form the new Diocese of Fort Worth, with the residual Diocese of Dallas reporting a total of only 34,109 baptised members in 1986. From 1986 to 2010,

Dallas lost only 6.8 percent of its membership, compared to a 17.6 percent loss across Province 7, but for a diocese at the heart of the rapidly growing Sunbelt, this was hardly a reassuring figure. After modest gains of 4.0 percent in 1986–90, Dallas saw its membership decline 2.4 percent in 1991–95, before surging to 12.2 percent between 1996 and 2000. Membership peaked at 39,874 members in 2001, yet the trend since then has been downwards with losses of 4.8 percent in 2001–05 and 8.1 percent in 2006–10 (the latter including the negotiated withdrawal of Christ Church, Plano, in 2006). In 2007, diocesan membership for the first time fell below that reported for 1986 and in 2010 it hit a record low of 31,777. The only slight success in recent years has been a modest 1.5 percent increase in 2010–11, but this was hardly enough to compensate for the vicissitudes of the past decade. Under other circumstances Dallas might well have followed its daughter diocese of Fort Worth out of TEC and its failure to do so may well have cost it more than other dioceses discussed in this chapter.

Los Angeles[43]

In 1895, the Episcopal Diocese of Los Angeles became the second diocese to be erected in California. Despite surrendering territory in 1973 to permit the establishment of the Diocese of San Diego, it remains one of the largest and most liberal dioceses in TEC, reporting 58,822 members in 2011, a figure exceeded only by the Dioceses of Virginia, Massachusetts and New York. It has not entirely escaped the impact of secular decline, though its loss of 13.8 percent of baptised members between 1980 and 2010 was less than the 20.2 percent recorded for Province 8. After an increase of 8.9 percent in 1980–1985, its rate of growth slowed to 1.7 percent in 1986–90 and just 0.4 percent in 1991–95, with membership peaking at 80,074 in 1994. From the mid-1990s onwards a downward trend has been perceptible, with losses of 4.0 percent in 1996–2000, 3.5 percent in 2001–05 and a staggering 12.0 percent in 2006–10. In 2004, diocesan membership for the first time fell below 70,000. Some of these losses can be accounted for by the departure of four large conservative congregations during the 2000s, but like New York, the Episcopal Diocese of Los Angeles has probably been more vulnerable to the growing secularisation of the coastal United States, which has inflicted more damage on mainline Protestant denominations than on more conservative ones.

Conclusion

While it is difficult to draw definitive conclusions from this comparatively cursory view of the data, certain features are evident. There has been a marked increase in the rate of membership loss over the past decade, which clearly owes something to the increasingly public divisions within both TEC and the Anglican Communion. While the wave of secessions in the 2000s has denuded certain geographic areas of large numbers of Episcopalians, however, many of the long-term losses appear to owe more to the secular decline affecting the greater portion of the American Protestant mainline. Bad though TEC's situation may be, it is actually less dire than that facing either the Presbyterian Church (USA) or the United Church of Christ. Where TEC is increasingly pressed, however, is in developing a rationale for its existence as a national denomination, as large swathes of the interior are increasingly characterised by an aging and dispersed population. In metropolitan settings, by contrast, institutional machinery and an affluent membership combine to keep many parishes in working order.

While this chapter lacks the space to deal with the those former Episcopalians who organised the Anglican Church in North America (ACNA) in 2009 in detail, it is instructive to consider such figures as have been made public.[44] Since only about three-quarters of their congregations are currently reporting their membership numbers, the Church has published projections of membership and average principal service attendance, but it has also provided raw data for reporting congregations for 2011 and 2013. While on paper ACNA still has no more than five percent of TEC's current membership, it has reported a 38.6 percent increase in membership and a 59.1 percent increase in average principal service attendance in just two years. While it remains to be seen if such rates of increase can be sustained in the long-term, it is something for leaders of TEC to ponder. It is also worth noting, however, that TEC's losses in membership amounted to roughly 400,000 between 2000 and 2010 yet the Anglican Church in North America today still reports a membership in the order of 100,000. The failure to attract a greater proportion of these Anglican defectors demonstrates the challenge facing the latest iteration of Anglican identity in North America.

Notes

* The author expresses his thanks to the Association of Statisticians of American Religious Bodies, Dr. Kirk Hadaway, Christine Kandic and the Revd. Canon Dr. Michael Barlowe for their assistance.

1 The Episcopal Church was originally known as The Protestant Episcopal Church in the United States of America. For the purposes of this chapter, TEC will be used as the standard abbreviation for the post-1789 Church.

2 *New York Times* Magazine, November 19, 2006, available at http://www.nytimes.com/2006/11/19/magazine/19WWLN_Q4.html.

3 C. K. Hadaway, 'Is the Episcopal Church Growing (or Declining)?' (2004): 13–17 (quotation on 17), available at http://library.episcopalchurch.org/sites/default/files/2004GrowthReport%281%29.pdf.

4 Ibid.: 18.

5 This argument was first advanced in D. M. Kelley, *Why Conservative Churches Are Growing* (San Francisco: Harper and Row, 1972). For critiques of Kelley, see D. R. Hoge and D. A. Roozen (eds.), *Understanding Church Growth and Decline, 1950–1978* (New York: The Pilgrim Press, 1979); D. A. Roozen and C. K. Hadaway (eds.), *Church and Denominational Growth* (Nashville, TN: Abingdon Press, 1993).

6 An interesting feature of the Episcopal contribution to the Faith Communities Today (FACT) survey of 2002 was the tendency of declining congregations to deny their decline. While 40 percent of congregations showed a decline of more than 10 percent according to their parochial reports, only 10 percent of congregations participating in the FACT survey conceded a decline of such proportions. The figures for congregations reporting or claiming growth of more than 10 percent were 36 percent and 35 percent respectively. C. K.

Hadaway, 'A Report on Episcopal Churches in the United States' (April 2002): 59, available at http://library.episcopalchurch.org/sites/default/files/CDR_EpiscFACTreport.pdf.

7   In 2002, Hadaway pointed out that domestic membership peaked around 1966, declined dramatically during the early 1970s, and then plateaued, though his analysis preceded the conflicts of the 2000s. Hadaway, 'Growing': 5–6.

8   K. Kesselus and J. E. Hines, *Granite on Fire* (Austin, TX: Episcopal Seminary of the Southwest, 1995); G. Shattuck, *Episcopalians and Race: Civil War to Civil Rights* (Lexington, KY: University Press of Kentucky, 2000).

9   D. Bess, *Divided We Stand: A History of the Continuing Anglican Movement* (Berkeley, CA: Apocryphile Press, 2006; orig. pub. 2002).

10 On the evangelical/charismatic revival see D. J. Bennett, *Nine O'Clock in the Morning* (Plainfield, NJ: Logos International, 1970); B. Slosser, *Miracle in Darien* (Plainfield, NJ: Logos International, 1979); J. Bonner, *Called Out of Darkness into Marvelous Light: A History of the Episcopal Diocese of Pittsburgh, 1750–2006* (Eugene, OR: Wipf and Stock, 2009): 203–15, 254–72.

11 Hadaway, 'Report': 9.

12 Hadaway, 'Growing': 3–4.

13 This conversion factor was calculated by Dr. Kirk Hadaway.

14 'Baptized Members by Province and Diocese 2001–2011', http://www.episcopalchurch.org/library/document/baptized-members-province-and-diocese-2001-2011.

15 'Average Sunday Attendance by Province and Diocese 2001–2011', http://www.episcopalchurch.org/library/document/average-sunday-attendance-province-and-diocese-2001-2011.

16 Statistics for 1980–2000 derived from scans of church data tables from the *Episcopal Church Annual* provided by Christine Kandic, Congregational Research Assistant, Episcopal Church Center, New York; '2005 Table of Statistics of the Episcopal Church', http://www.episcopalchurch.org/library/document/2005-table-statistics-episcopal-church; '2010 Table of Statistics of the Episcopal Church', http://www.episcopalchurch.org/library/document/2010-table-statistics-episcopal-church.

17 Calculated from Table 12.3.

18 On the trends in ASA during the 1990s, see Hadaway, 'Growing': 6–7.

19 'Average Sunday Attendance by Province and Diocese 2000–2010', http://www.episcopalchurch.org/library/document/average-sunday-attendance-province-and-diocese-2000-2010.

20 Such a figure will obviously overstate the involvement of baptised members, as not everyone attending a Sunday service is a baptised member in good standing.

21 Calculated from Table 12.5.

22 Statistics for 1980–2000 derived from scans of church data tables from the *Episcopal Church Annual* provided by Christine Kandic, Congregational Research Assistant, Episcopal Church Center, New York; '2005 Table of Statistics of the Episcopal Church', http://www.episcopalchurch.org/library/document/2005-table-statistics-episcopal-church; '2010 Table of Statistics of the Episcopal Church', http://www.episcopalchurch.org/library/document/2010-table-statistics-episcopal-church.

23 Statistics for 1980–2000 derived from scans of church data tables from the *Episcopal Church Annual* provided by Christine Kandic, Congregational Research Assistant, Episcopal Church Center, New York; '2005 Table of Statistics of the Episcopal Church', http://www.episcopalchurch.org/library/document/2005-table-statistics-episcopal-church; '2010 Table of Statistics of the Episcopal Church', http://www.episcopalchurch.org/library/document/2010-table-statistics-episcopal-church.

24 Pew Forum on Religion & Public Life, 'Religious Affiliation: Diverse and Dynamic' (February 2008): 31, available at http://religions.pewforum.org/pdf/report-religious-landscape-study-full.pdf.

25 Promoted by the 1988 Lambeth Conference, with the aim of 'making Christ known to the people of his world' (Resolution 43), the 'Decade of Evangelism' had little impact in the Global North provinces.

26 Statistics for 1980–2000 derived from scans of church data tables from the *Episcopal Church Annual* provided by Christine Kandic, Congregational Research Assistant, Episcopal Church Center, New York; '2005 Table of Statistics of the Episcopal Church', http://www.episcopalchurch.org/library/document/2005-table-statistics-episcopal-church; '2010 Table of Statistics of the Episcopal Church', http://www.episcopalchurch.org/library/document/2010-table-statistics-episcopal-church.

27 Pew Forum on Religion & Public Life, 'Religious Affiliation: Diverse and Dynamic': 12, 18. The other 6.9 percent are historically black Protestant churches.

28 Association of Religion Data Archives, US Membership Report,

1980, available at http://www.thearda.com/rcms2010/r/u/rcms2010_99_us_name_1980.asp;

1990, available at http://www.thearda.com/rcms2010/r/u/rcms2010_99_us_name_1990.asp;

2000, available at http://www.thearda.com/rcms2010/r/u/rcms2010_99_us_name_2000.asp;

2010, available at http://www.thearda.com/rcms2010/r/u/rcms2010_99_us_name_2010.asp.

29 Calculated from Table 12.10.

30 See Hadaway, 'Growing': 11–12. Hadaway argues that TEC does as well or better than other mainline Protestant denominations after 1980, but this is based on statistics that end around 2000.

31 The author has served as an expert witness in several court cases, arguing the case that the TEC is not – as a matter of law – a hierarchical church. While there is ample historical evidence to that fact, this view is not held by the current leadership of TEC.

32 Statistics for 1980–2000 derived from scans of church data tables from the *Episcopal Church Annual* provided by Christine Kandic, Congregational Research Assistant, Episcopal Church Center, New York; '2005 Table of Statistics of the Episcopal Church', http://www.episcopalchurch.org/library/document/2005-table-statistics-episcopal-church; '2010 Table of Statistics of the Episcopal Church', http://www.episcopalchurch.org/library/document/2010-table-statistics-episcopal-church.

33 There is no scholarly history of the Diocese of New Hampshire, but see: D. E. Theuner, *Choose Life: A Brief History of the Diocese of New Hampshire: Emphasizing the Years 1952 to 2002* (Concord, NH: Diocese of New Hampshire, 2003).

34 On Robinson and the wider context of his election, see: I. T. Douglas and P.F.M. Zahl, *Understanding the Windsor Report: Two Leaders in the American Church Speak across the Divide* (New York: Church Publishing, 2005); A. Guelzo, 'Bonfire of the Sacristies: To the 2006 General Convention', *Anglican and Episcopal History* 75 (2006): 98–118; E. Adams, *Going to Heaven: The Life and Election of Bishop Gene Robinson* (Brooklyn, NY: Soft Skull Press, 2006); G. Robinson, *In the Eye of the Storm: Swept to the Center by God* (New York: Seabury Books, 2008).

35 J. E. Lindsley, *This Planted Vine: A Narrative History of the Episcopal Diocese of New York* (New York: Harper & Row, 1984).

36 See: E. L. Bond and J. R. Gundersen, *The Episcopal Church in Virginia, 1607–2007* (Richmond, VA: The Episcopal Diocese of Virginia, 2007). Despite extensive research on colonial Anglicanism in Virginia, there is surprisingly little scholarly attention devoted to the recent past.

37 There is no more recent published history of South Carolina than: A. S. Thomas, *A Historical Account of the Protestant Episcopal Church in South Carolina 1820–1957, Being a Continuation of Dalcho's Account, 1670–1820* (Columbia, SC: Bryan, 1957).

38 Confusingly, the body representing Episcopalians in coastal South Carolina today is legally denoted The Episcopal Church in South Carolina, as leaders of the Episcopal Diocese of South Carolina have, thus far, successfully defended their claim to enjoy the authority to withdraw their diocese from the national church in 2012 and, consequently, have retained legal title to the diocesan designation.

39 T. C. Reeves, 'The Anglo-Catholic Movement in Wisconsin', *The Wisconsin Magazine of History* 68 (Spring 1985): 188–98; R. B. Slocum, 'Romantic Religion and the Episcopal Church in Wisconsin: A Consideration of James De Koven and Charles C. Grafton', *Anglican and Episcopal History* 65 (March 1996): 82–111.

40 The only recent account is: R. A. Alexander, *Patches in a History Quilt: Episcopal Women in the Diocese of South Dakota, 1868–2000* (Sioux Falls, SD: Pine Hill Press, 2003).

41 The paucity of material on The Episcopal Church in Texas as a whole and Dallas in particular is striking. L. Brown, *The Episcopal Church in Texas, 1838–1874* (Austin, TX: Church Historical Society, 1963), only deals only with the pre-division Church.

42 This figure is according to the pre-1986 standard for defining membership.

43 There is no most recent published history than: S. C. Clark, *The Diocese of Los Angeles: A Brief History* (Los Angeles, CA: The Committee on Diocesan Anniversaries, 1945).

44 See: A. Gross, 'Congregational Reporting: Churches, Membership and Average Principal Service Attendance', 2013, available at https://c119b78671d19b8aee34-1ab073aa 91389396dfc8b6aabc9b141e.ssl.cf2.rackcdn.com/Congregational_Report_to_Provincial_ Council.pdf.

13 The Anglican Province of South America

Maurice Sinclair and John Corrie

Introduction

Because Latin America is such a vast and varied region of the world, it is necessary to focus our attention in this chapter on Anglican developments in what was until recently known as the Province of the Southern Cone. Since 2014 this part of the Anglican Communion has been re-named as 'The Anglican Province of South America'. It includes the countries of Peru, Bolivia, Paraguay, Uruguay, Argentina and Chile. Also, without implying any difference in the significance of Anglican mission in these different republics, we will give a fuller account of the growth of the churches in Northern Argentina and Peru, and then describe more briefly the evolving situation in the other Dioceses in the Province. Except in our review of earlier history, we make no reference to Anglican mission in Brazil and the other Republics of Latin America. They require separate study.

In our own work we have drawn upon the testimony of Anglicans currently or recently serving in the Province of South America. Their dioceses are relatively new: the oldest established less than 150 years ago and the newest no more than twenty. Institutional development has been interrupted and uneven, and record keeping has been incomplete. Accurate statistics on membership and other data relating to 1980 are in many cases unavailable, and even current figures are not necessarily to hand. Our informants have intimate knowledge of their churches, but where recorded numbers are missing they have given us informed estimates. We quote from relevant published material, but this limited in quantity. The editing and interpretation of the information we have received is of course the responsibility of the authors alone.

Earlier history

With the practical limitations of our work and the specific interest in the period 1980 to 2015, it is still important to describe in outline the earlier history of the Anglican Church in Latin America as a whole.[1] This wider context will help in explaining the issues which the present-day Church has inherited.

The first Anglicans in Latin America were part of the Protestant presence which took advantage of the revolutionary movements of the late 18th Century.

The thrust for independence was challenging both the colonial governments and the Roman Catholic hegemony which had established itself throughout nearly three centuries since the Conquistadores brought Catholicism with them to Latin America at the beginning of the 16th Century. Protestantism was part of the mix of new ideas, and the new republics created opportunities for people such as James Thomson, who was sent by the newly formed British and Foreign Bible Society to distribute Bibles, which he and his agents did with astounding success. Anglicans were part of this missionary zeal, the most famous of whom was Captain Allen Gardiner, who made his first missionary expedition across the Andes in 1838. His pioneering endeavours amongst the southern indigenous communities of Patagonia ended in disaster in 1851 when he and six of his companions met their deaths on the shores of Tierra del Fuego. But his spirit inspired the founding of the South American Missionary Society, which has been so influential in promoting Anglican mission in the Southern Cone. The year 1894 saw the beginnings of mission among the Mapuches of Southern Chile, and the first baptisms in the Paraguayan Chaco occurred in 1898.

Pioneering mission began in this way. Chaplaincies provided the other foundation of Anglicanism in the region. The English came to support the new republics by building railways, mining and other commercial enterprises, and services for English-speaking Anglicans were begun in both Argentina and in Chile in 1825. Soon chaplaincies were established, especially in the major seaports and inland cities, although it took time for them to be accepted by the civil authorities. Some were started in collaboration with Foreign Office Consulates, as in Buenos Aires (1825), Valparaiso (1841), Montevideo (1845), Lima (1849) and three others in Brazil.

The first Episcopal oversight was provided by an intrepid missionary called Waite Hocking Stirling, who was consecrated Bishop of the Falkland Islands in 1869, but whose jurisdiction extended to the whole of Latin America. He urged the chaplains to learn the national and local languages and so reach out beyond the expatriate community. He remained bishop until 1902.

From one, how did today's seven Dioceses of the Southern Cone come into existence? Stirling's administrative base was in Buenos Aires, so it was natural for Argentina to develop a diocesan identity. In 1910 the Falkland Islands came under a new west-coast diocese, so the original one became 'Argentina with Eastern South America'. However, the Edinburgh Conference of that same year famously declared that the cities of Latin America were not an appropriate sphere of mission engagement as they were predominantly Roman Catholic. It was not until the 1958 Lambeth Conference that there was a recognition that South America was a 'neglected continent' and this spurred a move to send forty-five missionaries to Chile, Argentina and Paraguay between 1961–63.[2] A 1968 Lambeth Resolution recognised that rapid social, economic, political and religious changes were taking place and that Anglican Churches should make their 'unique and full contribution'.[3]

Meanwhile, the South American chaplaincies had continued to grow; by 1922 there were nineteen in Argentina alone. However, the number of English-speaking people was soon to be affected by the departure of British companies, and the consequent closure of chaplaincies: a process that accelerated after the Second World War. Throughout this period the main contribution of Anglican mission in the region came through the South American Missionary Society's sustaining work among the Amerindian peoples of the Paraguayan and Argentine Chaco and Southern Chile.

The delay in the full recognition of Latin America as an Anglican sphere of mission had continuing repercussions. Until successive Lambeth Conferences in 1958 and 1968 had indicated otherwise, city-based evangelism and church planting was not open to Anglicans. As a result, in the succeeding decades of the 20th Century the urban development of the Anglican Church remained at an earlier stage in comparison to development in rural areas. Consequently, Latin American urban leaders were slower to emerge and relate to their culturally different Amerindian counterparts. Furthermore, historic hostilities and injustices complicated this relationship. It is significant that the Anglican Church in Chile was the earliest to commit to urban mission and now has the largest overall membership in the Province of South America.

Returning to structural developments, over time separate jurisdictions were created for Brazil and the northern region of Latin America, partnering with the Episcopal Church of the United States. Following the first Latin American Anglican Consultation in Mexico in January 1963 and later that same year a large Anglican Congress in Toronto, the Southern Cone was restructured with a Diocese of Chile, Bolivia and Peru created under Bishop Kenneth Howell, and a separate Diocese for Argentina, Paraguay and Uruguay under Bishop Cyril Tucker. Northern Argentina, with Paraguay still attached to it, became a separate diocese in 1969 headed by Bishop Bill Flagg, while Argentina and Uruguay remained with Cyril Tucker. In 1973 Paraguay separated off and formed its own diocese with an English missionary, Douglas Milmine, as its first bishop. Ordination of nationals was a feature of the 1960s and Northern Argentina was soon to be distinguished in being the first diocese to produce an indigenous Amerindian bishop in Mario Marino, who was consecrated in 1976. Uruguay waited until 1988 to become a separate diocese, with an English missionary William Godfrey as its first bishop.

In 1973 the Anglican Council of South America (CASA) was formed as a provincial umbrella structure with Bishop Bill Flagg as its first presiding bishop. This structure of authority then approved the official inauguration of a Diocese of Peru and Bolivia in 1977 with Bishop David Evans taking over from Bishop Bill Flagg. Brazil was also part of CASA until 1983. In 1983 the Province of the Southern Cone was formally established, and in 1995 Bolivia became a separate diocese with Gregory Venables as its first bishop.

The establishment in this way of Provincial and Diocesan structures served as an integral part of the growth of local churches in the region. Dioceses developed their own structures of authority and administration, training programmes, social engagement and outreach to the indigenous communities. Alongside and supporting this growth in the region as a whole, a number of mission and development agencies have fulfilled a partnership role: USPG; BCMS/Crosslinks; SAMS

USA, UK, Australia, Canada and Ireland; CMS (Australia); TEAR Fund; and Christian Aid. Diversity of ministries such as church planting, Bible translation, struggle for land rights and social justice were made possible by these multiple relationships. However, for the Southern Cone, SAMS UK gave a special continuity of support, and was prominent in providing personnel for urban pioneering.

The following descriptions of Anglican mission in the different Dioceses of the Province of South America will indicate what has resulted from this earlier history of chaplaincies, missionary endeavour,[4] structural development and mission agency support.

The Anglican Church in Northern Argentina

Anglican congregations are spread widely in four of the seven federal states that are included in this Anglican diocese. With surface transport and the lack of a suitably located river bridge it takes two days to reach the churches furthest from the Diocesan Centre in the city of Salta. This geographical scattering is bound up with the identity of members. One of the special features of the Anglican Church in Northern Argentina is its difference in composition from the general population of the region, lowland indigenous people representing a very small percentage. In Anglican membership they are the substantial majority. As noted above, history accounts for this difference. Anglican missionary work dates back to more than a century among the Chaco people, but began in the cities less than fifty years ago. With far fewer British expatriates in the North of Argentina, only one small Anglican chaplaincy church has ever functioned.

By the year 1980 the Anglican diocese had been well established, but its activities were not systematically documented. Information on measures of growth offered here are based largely upon the testimony of the serving bishop, Nicholas Drayson, his colleagues and the memory of fellow church members.

In terms of approximate numbers, the comparison between 1980 and 2015 is set out below:[5]

Table 13.1 Amerindian churches and membership in 1980 and 2015

Amerindian churches and membership	1980	2015
Congregations	50	150
Baptised and confirmed members	4,000	16,000

Table 13.2 Urban churches and membership in 1980 and 2015

Urban churches and membership	1980	2015
Congregations	12	14
Average Sunday Attendance	220	500

For the indigenous churches, other growth indicators include confirmations: between 2009 and 2015, 3,000 new members have been confirmed. In the same period there have been twenty-five ordinations. Set against this has been a similar number of clergy deaths, reflecting the age of the Anglican pastors and the harsh conditions in which many have served. Currently 100 presbyters and 100 deacons minister in the 150 congregations. Between 60 and 100 ordained and lay leaders come together for twice-yearly Bible schools.

The factors which either promote or inhibit growth among these churches are complex but must be taken into account if the bare statistics are to be evaluated properly. First, biological growth must be considered. In the 1960s the ethnic groups in some areas of the Chaco were in danger of extinction, due to exposure to tuberculosis and measles, and because of the neglect of the majority community. A relief and development programme of the Anglican Church played an important part in reversing this trend and was followed by the inclusion of indigenous communities in health care and education provided by the state. With the consequent reduction in infant mortality and child deaths, population increased and with it church membership.

Another factor influencing growth has been Pentecostal renewal, widespread in other parts of Argentina and in Latin America as a whole. With their animistic background the indigenous people are spirit sensitive. The power of the Holy Spirit was crucial in the birth of their churches. Now overtly Pentecostal influence stimulates the Anglican congregations and especially the youth. It may come through the media and be seen to be modern and prestigious as well as spiritual. It may arrive with preachers from other denominations and may result in groups breaking away from Anglican churches. For isolated communities such visits have an understandable impact. An Anglican church may switch to Pentecostal under the influence of revivalists, but then happily become Anglican again when the bishop returns.

This spiritual ferment is accompanied by a process of change catapulting traditional communities into the global culture of the modern world. Increasingly Spanish is the medium of communication, mixed with or replacing the languages of ethnic groups in ordinary conversation and indeed in worship services. Changes in language accentuate the generation gap. With the breakdown of traditional loyalties, other gaps appear. Party politics divides communities; votes are bought with bribes. Numerical growth in the indigenous churches is taking place against a turbulent background which threatens as well as promotes it.

In this context quality of growth becomes critically important. Bishop Drayson in an unpublished paper highlights the question of growth in maturity. In the early decades the Anglican emphasis was upon the indigenous languages for Christian teaching and Christian worship. This respect for the indigenous culture helped in producing a generation of mature leaders, and latterly the translation of the whole Bible in Wichi and New Testaments in Toba and Chorote, the other languages common among the Anglican communities. How then will the increasing use of Spanish affect maturity? In the short-term at least it appears to produce superficiality. In preaching, half understood slogans may replace the thoughtful use of the mother tongue. Long-term, Spanish can provide a door of opportunity for engagement with the wider Church and the wider world. Is there, though, sufficient maturity to maintain Anglican bonds that can hold together widely scattered members in a geographically vast diocese?

Bishop Drayson presses the question further: is Anglican growth transformative? Does it transform the environment? Anglican NGOs are active in the struggle for land rights and the conservation of the Chaco forest currently under extreme threat. However, the participation of church members in these endeavours is mixed. Micro irrigation is transforming some forest gardens. On a larger scale transformation continues in the changes the gospel brings to individual and family lives. One of the most positive evidences of maturity, transformation and quality growth is the success of a new 'Pastoral Familiar' programme: an initiative of women to work with the predominantly male church leadership to establish loving and effective discipline in families.

In interpreting the figures for growth of Anglican congregations in the cities of Northern Argentina, we need to recognise a different dynamic at work. Among the indigenous churches sociological factors have worked in favour as well as against numerical growth. In the urban context Anglicanism is more obviously counter-cultural. At best evangelism and church planting by Anglicans has been undertaken pastorally and biblically. It has spread from towns bordering the Chaco to provincial cities, first to Salta and latterly to Tucuman. People have been converted, lives transformed and close-knit fellowships established. But at the same time the general turbulence affecting the indigenous churches has had a more negative effect upon the urban churches.

Pentecostalism has impacted the Anglican city churches differently. On the one hand, there is the same influence of the media, suggesting that Pentecost style worship is *the* way to worship. But then any attempt to retain Anglican liturgy may produce a split which in the urban situation is more serious. Financial issues are also more divisive. The 'success' of neighbouring Pentecostal churches in the cities may be measured in their ability to pay their pastor a good salary. Few if any Anglican congregations have grown sufficiently to meet the expectations and needs of urban ministers. Money, alongside styles of worship, has become problematic in the development of the Anglican presence in the towns and cities of Northern Argentina. In the eyes of the public Anglican identity depends more upon a recognition of a significant role in the evangelisation and preservation of the indigenous communities than upon a clearly defined urban contribution.

Recognised or not, this contribution is being made and is exemplified by the story of the San Andres congregation in the city of Salta. Its senior pastor, Hugo Vergara, now leads a congregation of more than 120 people: professionals, students, public health workers and the unemployed. They are active socially in a meals service in a deprived area of the city, in the donation of blood, and are currently planting a new congregation. The strength of this local church lies in its biblical teaching, its ministry among young people through 'Youth Encounter in the Spirit', and in a combination of national ordained leadership and expatriate missionary leadership. Founded in 1974, this church has passed though periods of conflict over Anglican identity, moves in location caused by financial crises and lack of continuity in pastoral oversight. Throughout, it has provided a spiritual home for a significant number of Salta people and a focus of Anglican witness and identity in this provincial capital.

Growth, like that of San Andres, there has been, and the potential for growth in the cities remains. Strides in maturity and transformative influence may largely lie in the future. For the present, Anglican churches in the cities of Northern Argentina provide an evangelical expression which relates to both Pentecostal and Roman Catholic churches, enjoys charismatic and ordered worship and retains a capacity for multiplying.

The Anglican Church in Peru[6]

The Anglican Church has been officially present in Peru since 1846, providing a chaplaincy ministry for the expatriate English-speaking community. This focus began to change with the arrival in 1972 of an experienced missionary bishop, Bishop Bill Flagg, whose intention was to plant indigenous churches. When the Diocese of Peru and Bolivia was inaugurated in November 1977 there existed, in addition to the English-speaking chaplaincy, a congregation in one of the Lima shanty towns started three years before. In 1977, the first Peruvian deacon was ordained. Bishop David Evans, who followed Bishop Flagg, was consecrated in May 1978, and began to establish ecclesial structures. The first diocesan synod was held in March 1979. This was a period of evangelism, church planting and rapid growth both in Lima and in the second largest southern city of Arequipa, where a missionary team was established in 1979 and the first church, Christ the Redeemer, consecrated in 1982. By the mid-1980s the middle class areas of Lima (Lima 1) had three Spanish-speaking churches, and in the shanty towns (Lima 2) there were six new congregations.

The intention was to have a social work dimension in each church, supported by a Diocesan social worker, and many projects were set up which were a focus for growth in Lima 2. Evangelistic services were thus complemented by a holistic approach to mission. Lima 1 had a strong ministry with children and young people, and some of these were connected with the burgeoning charismatic movement. The first Peruvian presbyter, Julio Montoya, was ordained in 1980. During this period Anglicans were riding the wave of rapid evangelical growth in Latin America generally. With the growth during the 1980s, it was necessary to ordain ministers as quickly as possible, and although training structures were set up, and SEAN (Study by Extension for All Nations) courses were established, some were ordained with very little theological knowledge and lacking experience. There were varying degrees of commitment to Anglicanism, with some clergy, for example, not committed to infant baptism.

The Vista Alegre congregation in Lima 1 became very 'Pentecostal' in the mid-1980s, and grew rapidly, at one stage to about three hundred people in six months. Many of these were young Roman Catholic charismatics who had left their church and wanted to be part of the action at Vista Alegre. But it could not sustain this growth, partly as the question of Anglican identity became more of an issue, and many left when other charismatic groups became more popular. In the early days the diocese had been informally Anglican, since being 'Pentecostal' engaged with the local culture and all successful churches incorporated charismatic elements. Establishing a distinctively Anglican identity was difficult; there was an issue about baptism, and the international 'Anglican' label was not trusted by Latin American evangelicals who saw it as too associated with Roman Catholicism. Even the use of a clerical collar caused offence! It was agreed to drop the word 'Anglican' in the official title of the diocese and describe it as 'Christian Episcopal'. A creative attempt at enculturation involved the wearing of a Peruvian poncho as a ministerial vestment – cheap, light, transportable – with an Inca rainbow braid. In Peru, Anglicans were accepted by the Roman Catholics as a 'serious' church, but they were not fully accepted by the National Council of Evangelicals of Peru. So although in theory Anglicans were a 'bridge' church between Roman Catholicism and evangelicalism, in practice very little traffic crossed the bridge at this time.

At the end of the 1980s Peru was suffering from a combination of growing terrorism and economic crisis, it was difficult to pay ministerial salaries and the churches of the shanty towns were struggling. The terrorist presence made ministry there very dangerous. However, a programme of soup kitchens, set up in 1990 in response to drastic austerity measures, brought communities together. There were other innovative local initiatives. One involved breeding and selling ducks, and over the years became a most successful income-generating project. Others have included leather workshops, cake making projects, maternity and pregnancy support, a TB programme, student homework projects, medical posts, schools, microfinance, and work with the disabled and deaf. The best projects have come from grass-roots initiatives, although a lot of help has been given by the middle class churches which could provide access to funding, expertise, a social worker and missionary support. The English Chaplaincy Church, which is now the Cathedral of the Diocese, has been a channel for much support to the shanty towns.

In relation to national affairs, the Anglican Church in Peru has often punched above its weight. Bishop Evans was asked to sit on a commission to form a new constitution for Peru. During a visit by the Pope, the Anglican Church had high visibility, and was prominent when the Roman Catholic Church acknowledged the existence and validity of historic churches. Successive bishops have been involved in the Inter-Religious Council and participated with the Ministry of Justice in changing laws on religious freedom. The present bishop is an advisor on religious affairs to the Peruvian government. Anglican influence on the wider stage has been significant.

An English missionary, Alan Winstanley, was consecrated in 1988 to succeed David Evans, and he consolidated the Anglican identity of the diocese, so that during his period there was a growth in maturity, if not necessarily in numbers. Bishop Alan left in 1993 and there followed a period of four and a half years without a bishop in post, although Bishop Gregory Venables of Bolivia provided Episcopal oversight. The process of finding a bishop failed twice, largely because of lack of unity amongst the few pastors. On the initiative of the Province, Bishop William Godfrey, who had been twelve years a bishop in Uruguay, was consecrated in April 1998.

When Bishop William arrived there were three middle class congregations, five churches in poor areas of Lima, four clergy, three foreign missionaries and a regular Sunday attendance of around 320 people. His coming initiated a period of much change and growth, so that the diocese to date reports 51 clergy, 46 of whom are Peruvian, with some 40 congregations located in nine different Peruvian Provinces. The intention is to maintain a balanced identity between 'catholic, evangelical and charismatic'. A strengthening of the 'catholic' dimension has brought with it more formal liturgy, more structures of authority and accountability, and more focus on the weekly Eucharist. This development has considerably shortened the bridge to Roman Catholicism, so that it became possible for former Catholic priests to cross the bridge and join the Anglicans. A two-year process of an 'Ordinariate' was created to provide a period of orientation into Anglicanism. Others from other denominations have also gone through this course of adaptation into Anglican identity. Together these new ministers have contributed to the numerical growth of Anglican churches in recent years.

Partnerships have been established, especially with a Church in Plano, Texas, and a number of American missionaries and teams have brought support, including the Suffragan Bishop Mike Chapman who came in 2010. There has been a partnership since 1992 with the Diocese of Worcester in the UK, and with other Christian organisations. A new administrative centre was built which included a seminary for training clergy, youth ministry and the base for the social work programme. With the diocesan commitment to holistic mission, this has been an important area of growth. Anglicans have responded to humanitarian disasters, such as a major earthquake in 2007 which struck to the south of Lima, and out of these efforts new ministries emerged. Four schools, one secondary and three primary, have been established and are now self-sustaining and income-generating. 'Missions' have been established in many poor areas, often with a focus on work with children and young people; there are now two full-time youth workers, there is a ministry to the disabled run by an English missionary in Lima and a church for the deaf was started in Juliaca. The NGO 'Communion Peru' was created to oversee and strengthen the varied outreach ministries. There has been a significant development of women's ministry established in 1999 called the 'Association of Anglican Women' (AMA in Spanish), which is affiliated with the Mothers' Union, and each church has been encouraged to have a group of members of this association.

Another major change in recent years has been the regionalisation of the work throughout the vast country of Peru. In September 2014 three 'episcopal vicars' were appointed for each of the major regions outside of Lima, and incipient diocesan structures are being created for these areas. The aim has been to have an established church at the hub with 'missions' growing around it, which eventually mature into churches. The churches in Lima and Arequipa and their missions are well established, but in the remoter mountainous areas the new church plants survive with difficulty.

To sustain this ambitious programme of growth, vigorous attempts have been made to develop ministerial training and the indigenisation of leadership. With scarcity of resources, both these priorities remain a challenge. The St Augustine Seminary, opened in Arequipa in 1999 and extended to Lima, developed a four-year training course. The diocese reports that in Arequipa in the year 2000 there was just one Peruvian priest, and to date in that region there are eight priests, four deacons, five lay ministers, four parishes and eight missions. Now there is a relatively small expatriate missionary presence. The move to indigenise has included liturgical development.

Viewed over all, the story of the Anglican Church in Peru, especially in the last forty-three years, is remarkable. From having no more than two congregations in one city in 1976, it has grown to twenty times that number of congregations across the country, with more in formation. Corresponding growth has been achieved in raising leadership, now largely indigenous. Rather than an unruffled progress, this growth has followed a roller coaster pattern, destabilised by tensions over identity, an eruption of terrorism, an economic crisis linked with galloping inflation and a gap in episcopal leadership. Finding financial resources for the work remains a pressing challenge. However, as in other dioceses, the Anglican Church in Peru has been blessed with knowledgeable, experienced and deeply committed bishops, clergy and lay ministers. There has been an openness to the guidance of God's Spirit and numerous testimonies of the Spirit at work in converting and healing power. Here, surely, lies the key to the future.

Anglican churches in urban areas of Chile

For the purpose of this chapter we are giving some indications of the extent and quality of the growth of Anglican churches in the cities in the central region of Chile. Outside our scope is the evangelisation of the Mapuche peoples of Southern Chile, which dates back to the last decades of the 19th Century and has led to the growth of mature churches with indigenous leadership. Currently Bishop Abelino Apeleo heads this important area of evangelistic, pastoral and social ministry, which, though it began in the rural areas, is now equally well established in the cities of the South.

Anglican missionary leaders in Chile were the first to respond to the 'green light' given by the 1958 and subsequent Lambeth Conferences for urban evangelism in Latin America. Early in the 1960s they established an Anglican Centre in Santiago, and, alongside an Anglican chaplaincy in that city and in Viña del Mar, began evangelising and church planting in this central region. A significant step taken subsequent to 1980 was the extension of Anglican churches into the Northern cities of Antofagasta, La Serena and Arica. The earlier extension southwards includes the cities of Conception, Temuco, Valdivia and Punta

Arenas on the Straits of Magellan. This geographical reach makes the Iglesia Anglicana Chilena a truly national church. The Diocesan Bishop in Chile, Hector Zabala, is also the Primate of the Anglican Province of South America.

Two regions of growth can illustrate what by God's grace has been achieved in Chile, and what potential there remains. In 1980 Chilean Anglicans in Santiago numbered about four hundred spread between five congregations and other preaching points. In 2015 one single congregation in the district of Las Condes, under the leadership of Pastor Alfredo Cooper, currently attracts a regular attendance of nine hundred. From this central church seven other congregations and more congregations in formation have been planted. The Santiago experience, reflected elsewhere, is that congregations often fail to grow beyond about fifty members, limited by the level of training of their pastor. The potential of growth beyond this level is great but depends upon the further training not only of the pastor but of a group of lay leaders around him.[7] Among the special ministries that have led to church growth, Marriage Encounter, a weekend of affirmation and healing for couples, has been outstanding. However, the deliberate multiplication of ministers and leaders has been crucial for the advance exemplified in the La Condes District of Santiago.

Valparaiso is the chief port of Chile and British influence in that city came early. The chaplaincy church of San Pablo was founded in 1858. Parallel to urban developments in Santiago, Spanish-speaking congregations began to be planted in the region, among the earliest being the Church of the Resurrection in Gomez Carreño, started in 1968. Current figures for a scatter of ten congregations show a membership averaging ninety-five, and with data limited to the 1990s, there is evidence of a thirty percent increase in growth since that decade. An indication of the potential for further growth is the clarity in the mission statement of the Anglican Church in this region of Chile. Having begun to establish missional communities alongside its congregations, it sets the goal of fifteen such new expressions of church by the year 2020.[8]

The Anglican Church in Central and Southern Argentina

The Anglican Church in this greater part of Argentina has grown out of chaplaincies, as distinct from pioneer missionary work in the north of the country. In 1825 the first Anglican chaplain arrived in Buenos Aires. In the 1860s British immigration into Argentina increased rapidly. In 1869 the Diocese of the Falkland Islands and Eastern South America was created and after some delay Buenos Aires became the base from which Bishop Waite Sterling fulfilled an amazingly extensive ministry. Under his oversight chaplaincy churches were established not only in the Argentine capital but also in the major cities, including Rosario, Cordoba, La Plata and Rosario. The future of this English-speaking church in Argentina must have appeared secure. The years subsequent to the Second World War, however, brought an equally dramatic fall in the numbers of people of English decent. After some closures, seventeen chaplaincy churches remained in 1980, some of which were reduced to a very small and elderly membership.

After having developed the largest chaplaincy ministry in the Southern Cone, this church faced a critical future. Significantly, Richard Cutts, the Anglican Bishop at that time, had recently been profoundly affected by the charismatic movement and began to invite to his diocese those who could be instrumental in bringing renewal to his churches. These visits were accompanied by healings and prophecies of growth. They impacted church members, attracted inquirers and in time raised up new lay leaders and clergy. Dr. Norberto Saracco, a Pentecostal scholar, describes the process of change in this way:

> The Lord has been working in this community of faith so as to transform it from being tied to history and race, and freeing it to become a people open to the Holy Spirit and committed to the mission of God.[9]

Significant developments followed a visit in 1987 from SOMA (Sharing of Ministries Abroad). On-going renewal was promoted by a group chaired by the bishop and called Movimiento de Renovación Anglicana. Its influence spread among the congregations, and especially those in Hurlingham and in Villa Devoto, suburbs of Buenos Aires. Events such as Marriage Encounter and Youth Encounter in the Spirit were both the fruit of deeper faith and the means of extending it. Alpha courses also brought in substantial numbers of new members. This outreach has touched business people through lunch time services in the Anglican Cathedral in the heart of Buenos Aires. Youth has been included in the renewal, evidence for which is provided by a recent Villa Devoto camp with more than one hundred young people.

Writing in his book celebrating the centenary of his church, Agustin Marsal identifies the factors that have spurred the growth of his congregation and that of others: miracle in answer to prayer, art and culture enhancing worship, social solidarity, the wealthy helping the poor and unemployed, one church reaching out to others. In all that is new there is respect for the old: a key perhaps to the Anglican way of gospel advance.[10]

The Anglican Church in Paraguay

An influx of new settlers, following the terrible loss of population in the War of the Triple Alliance, brought an Anglican chaplain to Paraguay to minister to them in the 1870s. In 1888 Bishop Waite Sterling, whose vast diocese included Paraguay, sent an Anglican missionary, Wilfred Barbrooke Grubb, to evangelise the tribes of the Chaco region with whom there had been no previous peaceful contact by the Paraguayans. Barbrooke Grubb's pioneer labours were instrumental in bringing to birth a church of the Enxet and Sanapana peoples.[11]

In 1913 an Anglican chaplaincy church was consecrated in the capital, Asunción. However, the main focus of Anglican ministry remained the support of the indigenous Chaco churches. It was not until the 1960s that an attempt was made to establish congregations among urban Paraguayans. Early in that decade an

Anglican school was founded, and has subsequently developed as an important Christian influence in Paraguayan society.

A separate Anglican diocese was formed for Paraguay in 1973 under the oversight of Bishop Douglas Milmine. By the year 1980 the churches based in specific ethnic groups were centred upon the original mission of Makthlawaiya and distributed among as many as twenty widely scattered ranches. In that year one English-speaking congregation and four Spanish-speaking urban congregations were worshipping in Ascunción and one in Concepción.

In the 1970s the future of the ethnic communities was increasingly threatened by the enclosure of their traditional lands by Paraguayan ranchers. At the request of leaders of ethnic communities the Anglican Church responded to this situation with a project for land settlement and land purchase. Three tracts of land were eventually secured: Sombrero Piri (1980), La Patria (1983) and El Estribo (1985). Anglican congregations in the Chaco are now concentrated on land on which the people have shared property rights. These Enxet- and Guarani-speaking churches now number twenty-four and their total membership is approximately one thousand, though with communities that are still semi-nomadic membership is hard to quantify. Parallel with this development of the Chaco churches, the urban congregations have increased from five to seven in Asunción and from one to three in Concepción. Linked with the Anglican school there is now an accredited faculty for teacher training.

The quality of Anglican work and witness is also reflected in the translation of the Bible into the Enxet language. Both in urban and rural areas evangelistic and pastoral ministry is matched with social engagement in the context of poverty. Anglican witness and influence spans the wide social spectrum in Paraguay. The further training and multiplication of ordained and lay ministers will be crucial for its future.

The Anglican Church in Uruguay

Within thirty years of an abortive invasion of Montevideo by a British fleet and army in 1806–7, a large number of British civilians were settled in Uruguay and engaged in developing its infrastructure. In 1841 a group of these residents asked for the provision of Anglican Church services. Two years later the first Anglican chaplain was appointed. As early as 1845 Holy Trinity Church was built on a prime site in the city.

In the years prior to the Second World War, when the English-speaking community was still numerous, there was, however, a constant struggle to maintain a regular ordained ministry, though the Church remained a vital resource. Subsequent to 1945 the number of English-speaking residents in Uruguay progressively declined. Even so Anglican bishops based in Buenos Aires gave oversight and appointed chaplains for Holy Trinity for periods of years. In 1977 help came from the Episcopal Church in Brazil and Anglican services were begun in Spanish.

A decisive step towards founding an indigenous church came in 1987 with the appointment of William Godfrey as bishop and with the inauguration of the Anglican Diocese of Uruguay in 1988, the original chaplaincy church becoming the cathedral. Bishop Godfrey initiated a remarkable ministry among homeless people, linked with the regeneration of the area around the cathedral. Important social engagement began in this way, together with the formation of Spanish-speaking congregations. This development was continued under Bishop Miguel Tamayo, a Cuban, who succeeded William Godfrey in 1998. The present bishop, Michele Pollesel, came to Uruguay from Canada in 2013. The diocese has a Uruguayan assistant bishop, Gilberto Porcal.

The period between 1980 and 2015 has marked a transformation of the Anglican presence in Uruguay. In 1980 there existed in the country one English-speaking congregation. In 2015 there are eleven congregations, ten of which are Spanish-speaking. In this period the number of clergy has increased from one to ten, and average church attendance from a total of 40 to 180. Educational, medical and other social projects have multiplied. The outreach of the Church has related largely to less privileged Uruguayans. The generation of financial support for its pastoral ministry remains a serious problem.

Uruguay has the reputation of being the most secular republic in South America. The population is largely urban. Initial responses to the gospel are often muted. The churches in Uruguay, including the Roman Catholic Church, receive few government privileges, a situation which favours solidarity among denominations. The Anglican Church, with its strong ecumenical sympathy, has a special opportunity in this respect. If it can find a sustainable way of under-girding its work financially, it will continue to have much to offer in terms of pastoral care, social outreach and as a contributor to Church unity.

The Anglican Church in Bolivia

No Anglican congregation existed in Bolivia prior to an invitation in 1979 from the Bolivian Evangelical Assembly. Anglican missionaries serving in Peru responded and came to La Paz to work among students and professional people. In 1984 a similar beginning was made in Santa Cruz, and in the 1990s a single missionary was instrumental in planting a church in Cochabamba. The newest Anglican initiative has focused on the city of Tarija.

This pattern of growth took place under the supervision from Peru of Bishop David Evans. In 1993 Gregory Venables was consecrated as an assis-tant bishop to give oversight within Bolivia itself. Two years later Bolivia was made a separate Anglican diocese under the leadership of Bishop Venables. He was instrumental in strengthening the Anglican identity, affirming its historic and catholic nature as well as its evangelical and charismatic qualities. After Gregory Venables moved to Buenos Aires, a North American, Frank Lyons, was made bishop in 2001 and served until 2012. His successor is a Singapor-ean, Raphael Samuel, who as a missionary had established the Anglican work in Santa Cruz.

Bearing in mind that the Anglican Church in Bolivia is perhaps the newest expression of Anglicanism in the world, its growth since 1980 is especially significant. This way of being Christian has a proven appeal to middle class as well as less privileged Bolivians. It is capable of creating flourishing congregations. Women play a key role in these. In 2015 a woman was ordained as presbyter, the first in the Province of South America. With such advantages, five congregations were established in four major cities, each with an outreach into less privileged districts. Active Anglican membership is currently reckoned to be five hundred. At its peak, however, total membership was substantially higher and the congregations numbered seven. The recent losses can be attributed to superficial loyalties of some local leaders and scarcity of resources in maintaining a work with such a wide geographical spread.

Bishop Raphael Samuel currently speaks of growth in the Anglican Church in Bolivia as plateauing. The path for resumed growth is, however, becoming clearly defined. A key commitment is 'intentional discipleship', the nurture and equipping of members to fulfil their potential in service and leadership. The four cities are to become centres for regional development with national leaders and mission partners exercising team ministry and responding to a common vision. Even for this small minority denomination the aspiration is to impact the life of the nation. The central Anglican congregation in Santa Cruz is strategically situated in a university district of the city and the aim is to develop further Church-based student ministry. 'Intentionally discipled' students will graduate to contribute Christianly in business, caring professions, government and in Church leadership.

Under God, this vigorous but tiny Bolivian Anglican church has big ambitions. Its realisation is in Bolivian hands but also requires partners: a missionary presence integrated into the life and witness of the local congregations in the different regions, and a relationship with mission agencies and sister churches that respond to the Bolivian priorities. The story of growth now focuses upon potential. The nation is at a point of change. Chronic instability, unrelieved poverty and pervasive corruption may give way to something different. An outpouring of God's Spirit upon the churches, including the Anglican, could indeed lead to national renewal.

Conclusions about the growth of Anglican Churches in this region

A denomination with its origins in England does not have an entirely natural entrance into South America. British colonialism, the dubious ally of mission, has not operated significantly in this sub-continent. Immigration of English-speaking people has risen and fallen. Chaplaincies have certainly been significant building blocks for the Anglican Church in the Southern Cone, but the dynamic for its growth has its source in the Evangelical Revival and latterly in the charismatic movement. The pioneers, both foreign missionary and national, have been shaped and inspired by the gospel, and many of those who have followed them have been dramatically renewed by the Holy Spirit. At intervals throughout the history leaders have emerged with outstanding gifts and tenacious faith in the redeeming and transforming power of God. Whereas at the beginning of the 19th Century there were no Anglican churches in the region, by 1980 there were approximately 150 congregations distributed in major cities and remote rural areas in five republics of the Southern Cone. Today the number of congregations large and small is approaching four hundred in six republics.

The missionary impetus lies behind this growth in numbers and gives a basis of Anglican identity, making it an evangelical church with a catholic and reformed history and open to renewal movements. In a region where Catholicism and evangelicalism are expressed in other ways, this Anglican identity may have no immediate recognition or appeal. Yet paradoxically, a biblical combination of evangelical and catholic traditions is what the Latin American Church most needs and which Anglicanism, the product of the moderate 'Cranmerian' Reformation, can demonstrate and offer. Actually, in a part of the world that retains a religious sense, the potential for Anglican witness is great, and, where confidently expressed, has the proven results described in this chapter: church growth, a remarkable variety and degree of social engagement and influence beyond its size as a minority church. An outstanding example of this impact has been the development of SEAN International, 'Study by Extension for all Nations'. What began forty years ago as an Anglican theological training programme in remote villages in the south of Chile now serves churches in one hundred different countries, with courses translated into seventy different languages. They have a pastoral emphasis, and good quality of pastoral care is another feature of Anglicanism at its best, and adds significantly to the value of the Anglican presence in areas where bigger churches may lose members as fast as they gain them.

Authentic Anglican identity makes for an Argentine, Chilean or Amerindian church. There has been a high level of commitment to the ethnic groups as well as the national languages, reflected in four major Bible translation projects in recent decades. Liturgies and choruses express the local genius. Anglicans identify with the aspirations and longings of communities and nations. Indigenisation can thus be linked with strategy in mission. Anglican mission has included a focus upon students and professional sectors where these have been relatively neglected and unchurched. The Anglican experience is sensitive to the fact that cultures are not static. There is a growing generation gap in South America and ministry among children and young people must meet this challenge.

Impetus, identity, indigenisation and strategy are Anglican assets. What of its structure and its resources? The formation of dioceses and of the Province has over the years provided a necessary framework for growth. Episcopal oversight is an integral part of Anglicanism. However, the traditional Anglican diocesan structure has a financial cost hard to carry in the South American context. There has been heavy reliance upon overseas partner agencies and churches. Radical attempts are being made at self-sustainability, but sheer lack of money clouds the future.

Human resources are of course more important than material resources, although the two are inter-related. There is a huge priority for in-depth training of leaders for mission and ministry but this has a generally unaffordable cost if conducted on a traditional residential basis. Where pastors have not received the necessary level of training, congregations reach only a low ceiling of growth. To overcome this limitation, a significant new approach to formation and training not only includes extension methods, but an intentional discipleship and multiplication of lay leaders within congregations, with the aim of developing team ministry and eventual new church plants. The essential and very great potential of women in this developing teamwork is increasingly being appreciated and valued. Such recognition and approach depends upon the availability of gifted and visionary senior pastor presbyters, and the periodic input of specialist teachers.

For the sake of growth, the need to localise training also relates to the need for regionalisation. Even within republics, distances between major cities and concentrations of churches in rural areas are very great. Growth depends upon cohesion between congregations that have geographical proximity and the possibility of frequent contact. Isolation, on the other hand, has been a serious hindrance of growth. Isolated leaders can and do fail in ministry and abandon their charges. Discontinuity is disruptive and a serious hindrance. Continuity in leadership is a great advantage and is favoured by supportive regional and local fellowships.

In trying to make an assessment of the growth and decline of Anglican churches in these republics, it may be more appropriate to speak of great potential and significant limitation, inherent strength and current weakness. The potential is in the gospel, joyfully received, appropriated and expressed. The strength is in a tradition which at best is evangelical, catholic and charismatic in a truly biblical sense. In spite of external and internal crises, the Anglican Church in this region of the world has by God's grace grown in size and maturity. We can believe that its remaining fragility will be outweighed by God-given inner strength.

Notes

1 Information on this section has been derived mainly from D. Milmine, *La Comunión Anglicana en América Latina* (Santiago, Chile: Banka Grafika, 1993); D. Milmine, *The Anglican Communion in Latin America* (Tunbridge Wells: South American Missionary Society, 1993); K. Ward, *A History of Global Anglicanism* (Cambridge: Cambridge University Press, 2006): 102–11.
2 *The Lambeth Conference 1958* (London: SPCK and Seabury Press): Section 2:71.
3 *Lambeth Conference 1968* (London: SPCK): Resolution 64:45: 'The Conference recommends that the member Churches of the Anglican Communion should place prominent emphasis upon Latin America in their missionary education, their prayers, and their commitment to world mission'.
4 In should be noted that even in the pioneering period the missionary initiative was by no means confined to expatriates. Local leaders were prominent in the spread of the gospel, having made the good news their own.
5 Both sets of table data are based on the personal knowledge and estimates of the serving Anglican bishops of Northern Argentina in the corresponding periods. Complete written records of church membership have not been kept.

6   Information in this section on Peru is drawn from diocesan sources and personal knowl-
    edge of the church and region.
7   The ordination of women as presbyters is a local option in the Province of South America.
    The Diocese of Chile does not currently pursue this option.
8   Defined in a statement of the Iglesia Porteña Anglicana in *Las Tablas*, 4 October 2014.
9   Quoted by A. Marsal, *El Buen Pastor* (Argentina: M. Lafitte Ediciones, 2014): 7. Quotation
    translated from Spanish original.
10 Ibid.: 205–16.
11 Milmine, *La Comunión Anglicana en América Latina*: 33–4.

England

14 The Church of England

David Voas

Times have been hard for the Church of England, as for most major churches in the developed world. The culture has become markedly less Christian over at least the past few decades and arguably much longer.[1] The impact can be seen in the number of churches, clergy, members, attenders, baptisms, confirmations, religious weddings and funerals. The numerical change is described below, followed by an explanation of the decline as the product of generational replacement.[2]

Infrastructure

Every corner of England belongs to a parish of the Church. Although parish boundaries are comparatively ancient, the set of parishes is not completely fixed. Some churches have been closed, and some parishes have been merged with others. In 1980 there were 16,806 churches in 13,663 parishes; by 2013 the numbers had dropped by about a thousand, to 15,799 and 12,557 respectively. According to Statistics for Mission 2013, the figure for churches 'includes 128 churches with no buildings'. Deducting these ethereal churches from the total would make the drop in church and parish numbers almost identical.

While in absolute terms the loss is clearly substantial, the fall of 6% in the number of churches is considerably less than the decline in full-time stipendiary clergy (30%), members on the electoral roll (41%) or usual Sunday attendance (37%) over the period 1980–2013. A key problem for the Church of England is the inertial drag of the large stock of under-used churches and sparsely populated parishes. One can debate what the right number of churches might be; what is hard to dispute is that the existing churches are not where one would ideally want them to be.

Stipendiary clergy are assigned to a 'benefice', which may be a single parish or (increasingly) multiple neighbouring parishes. Unsurprisingly, the number of benefices is similar to the number of full-time stipendiary clergy, and both contracted by about 28% between 1980 and 2012. The trajectory of these two quantities has not been identical, however. While the number of benefices declined steadily over the past three decades, clergy numbers were initially fairly stable, bolstered in part by the ordination of women as deacons from 1987. The stock of diocesan clergy started to fall in 1994: women were first ordained as priests in that year, but initially they were outnumbered by men leaving in protest. Of more significance in the medium and long-term were the resource constraints that resulted from the sharp downturn in the value of the Church's investment portfolio at the beginning of the decade and the continuing erosion of electoral rolls.[3]

Clergy

Figure 14.1 shows the evolution of full-time stipendiary diocesan clergy numbers by age and gender. The total numbers changed little between 1980 and the early 1990s, but declined from around 10,800 in 1993 to 7,800 in 2012. Particularly in the past decade, much of that gap has been filled by self-supporting clergy.

Ordained ministry was reserved for men at the beginning of the period, but the ordination of women as deacons (starting in 1987) and then priests (from 1994) has led to a growing contribution of women to the total. Although the numbers of male and female candidates for ordination have been fairly similar over the past decade, men remain considerably more likely than women to become stipendiary diocesan clergy. Women are disproportionately represented in chaplaincy and also self-supporting ministry. Nevertheless it seems very likely that gender parity will be achieved among Anglican incumbents, and it not hard to imagine a time when the parochial clergy, in common with other caring professions, is predominantly female.

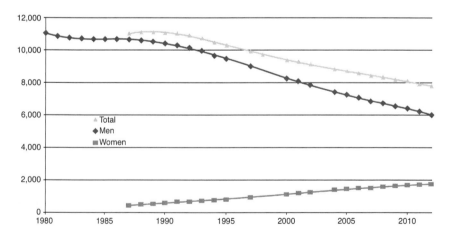

Figure 14.1 Full-time stipendiary diocesan clergy by gender, 1980–2012, in the Church of England

Source: Church of England published and unpublished statistics, assembled by the author.

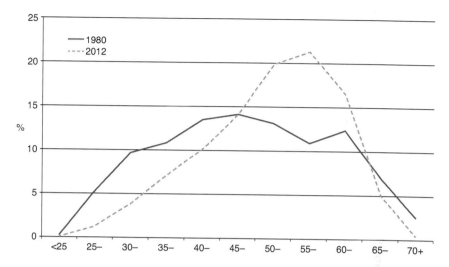

Figure 14.2 Age distribution of full-time stipendiary diocesan clergy, 1980 and 2012, in the Church of England

Source: Church of England published and unpublished statistics, assembled by the author.

There will be a large amount of turnover in the decades ahead. Figure 14.2 shows the age distribution of full-time stipendiary clergy in 2012 compared to 1980. The age of ordained ministers is now strongly skewed; only 23% are younger than 45, compared with 40% in 1980. The Church is interested in recruiting younger adults as ordinands, but the majority of candidates are still aged 40+. There is little difference between ordained men and women in average age, but most of the younger ordinands are male.

The ethnic profile of the clergy remains less diverse than the congregations being served. An estimated 97% of ordained ministers are white; even among curates, the figure is 95%.[4]

Overall participation in the Church of England

Every parish maintains an 'electoral roll', so called because it lists the lay people entitled to vote in Church elections. For practical purposes it can be regarded as a register of members aged 16 and over. To be on the roll one must live, or be a regular worshiper in, the parish. Every six years the roll is renewed, and between these revisions its size tends to creep up as names are added but not deleted. The graph of the total count therefore follows a sawtooth pattern (Figure 14.3).

For all its deficiencies, the electoral roll provides some approximation of the number of adults in the country who consider themselves to be part of the parish. The total has fallen by 41% between 1980 and 2013, from about 1,815,000

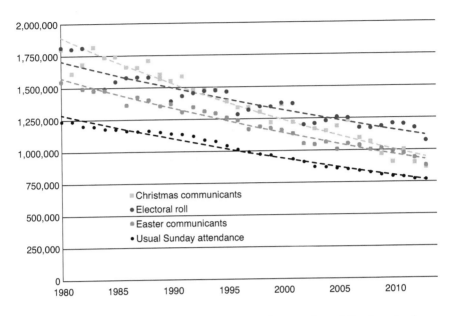

Figure 14.3 Change in electoral roll, Easter communicants and usual Sunday attendance, 1980–2013, in the Church of England

Source: Church of England published and unpublished statistics, assembled by the author.

to 1,076,000. (The Diocese of Europe is excluded here and throughout this chapter.)

Attendance at worship services has been in gradual decline for decades. Parishes have long been asked to estimate their 'usual Sunday attendance' (uSa), and the total has fallen by 37% between 1980 and 2013, from about 1,240,000 to 775,000. The decline has been fairly steady over the period, though it was most rapid during the decade to 2003, when the losses were twice as high as in the periods before or since.

The major festivals of Christmas and Easter bring many people to church. Christmas in particular attracts much larger numbers of irregular or non-attenders than other services (bar occasional offices). More than a third of adults in the country go to church at some point during the Christmas season, if only for choral concerts or nativity plays. The Church had 2,352,000 people attending for Christmas (Eve and Day) in 2013, compared with 1,255,000 at Easter. The Christmas turnout at parish churches in England is three times what one would find on a usual Sunday.

In the cities, the holiday produces only a modest boost to attendance. Christmas lifts church attendance in both rural and suburban areas, but the causes are different. In the country it is a matter of usual churchgoers making a point of attending at Christmas, even if ordinarily they only turn up every couple of weeks. In the suburbs, by contrast, the influx consists of people who do not usually go to church.

Two pieces of evidence give us reason to suppose that these people are – to be blunt – consuming a little religious theatre for the holidays. The first is that a lower proportion of people in suburban areas take communion at Christmas than elsewhere, suggesting that they do not regard themselves as belonging (though perhaps the churches are more focused on carols than communion). Moreover, fewer than half the people in Anglican churches in southern England at Christmas will be there again when Easter comes around. People who see themselves as churchgoers, even if just occasional ones, will make a point of attending at Easter.

Of course these people may think of themselves as Christian or as being 'spiritual', even if they are not normally churchgoers. Nevertheless it seems likely that what motivates many of them to attend at this particular time of year is nostalgia for a real or imagined past. In their search for the magic of Christmas they embrace traditions of every sort, from the secular (listening to the Queen's speech, going to the panto, making mince pies) to the religious (carols, nativity plays, church services). Still, Christmas attendance gives us some notion of the reach of the Church in society and culture.

The number of Christmas churchgoers has been comparatively resilient during the past decade. Whereas average Sunday attendance fell by 10% between 2005 and 2011, Christmas attendance was only 6% lower in 2011 (Christmas fell on a Sunday in both years, which makes them suitable for this comparison). The number of people taking communion at the holiday has fallen rapidly, by about 3% per annum compared to 1% per annum for Christmas attendance. This contrast implies that Christmas services or attenders or both are less orientated towards the Eucharist than previously.

Going back before 2000, we only have statistics on Christmas communicants. The figures show a relatively steep drop from 1980 to the present. It is hard to be sure, but judging from the past decade the decline may be more in the religious character of the participation than in the number of participants.

For Easter, the gap between the attendance and communicants counts is much smaller than for Christmas, and the two series have been basically parallel over the past decade. It is likely, therefore, that the change in the number of Easter communicants since 1980 serves as a good index of the change in overall Easter attendance. The rate of decline matches that for the electoral roll and usual Sunday attendance: the total dropped by 43% between 1980 and 2013.

To summarise, the statistics on the electoral roll, Easter communicants and usual Sunday attendance follow parallel tracks from 1980 to the present. The decline has been basically linear, but it is probably more accurate to draw a trendline that shows a constant rate of decline (as in Figure 14.3) rather than to calculate an absolute annual loss. The rate of change over this period has been −1.6% per annum. If that rate persists, participation as measured by membership, usual Sunday attendance or Easter attendance, will drop by a quarter over 18 years and by half in 43 years.

It is worth pointing out that the population of England has not been stationary over the past few decades. It increased by 15%, or seven million people, between the census years of 1981 and 2011, with nearly four million coming since 2001. That means that the Anglican declines (described above in absolute terms) have been even more severe when considered relative to population. Likewise, however, it does seem apparent that population growth has moderated the losses. The rate of decline over the past decade has been approximately 1% per annum rather than the 1.6% seen for the whole period since 1980. New arrivals from around the world have boosted religious activity in England, though for both political and economic reasons it seems unlikely that immigration will continue at previous levels.

Attendance

A substantial number of people attend on days other than Sunday, and uSa has fallen out of favour in the Church of England. In 2000 the Church introduced a new set of measures based on attendance counts conducted during October. The average weekly attendance (aWa) is taken to be representative of participation in a typical week. The average weekly attendance (including midweek attendance, and based on the October counts) is about 30% higher than uSa; in 2013 it was a shade less than one million. Average Sunday attendance (as calculated from the counts) is also approximately 8% higher than usual Sunday attendance (as estimated by the person completing the parish return). The reasons for this difference are unclear. In dioceses where the financial contribution expected from the parish is a function of uSa, there is an incentive to avoid setting the figure too high. It is also possible, however, that harvest festivals in October mean that the average seems higher than usual, and hence the parish returns provide a lower figure for uSa.

For present purposes our interest is less in the absolute level of participation than in the pattern of growth or decline over recent decades. The historical data on ordinary attendance is the 'usual Sunday attendance' count; the question is whether the trend in uSa is representative of overall participation. In preparing Statistics for Mission 2012, the Research and Statistics Unit of the Church of England produced a fully revised set of indicators for the period 2003–12. These figures show identical declines in average Sunday attendance and uSa. Adult and child attendance fall by about 1% and 2.5% per annum respectively, for an all-age decrease of 1.33% per annum. It seems reasonable to suppose, therefore, that the uSa time series from 1980 accurately reflects the change in Sunday attendance.

Midweek attendance has increased since 2003, however, and it seems likely that the growth began considerably earlier. For adults the increase is comparatively modest: an average of several hundred attenders a year, for an annual uplift of about 0.7%. (There was a much larger increase – of 6,000 people, or 5% – from 2012 to 2013.) For children, more substantial numbers were being added to the midweek count each year to 2011; 'Messy Church' and other 'fresh expressions of Church' that involve children are probably behind most of this increase. There has been concern that some parishes were including school services in the counts, and in 2013 the annual statistics form asked for such figures to be recorded separately. Probably as a result, child midweek attendance was halved from 80,000 in 2011 to 41,000 in 2013. The comments in the next few paragraphs refer to the statistics up to 2012, prior to the explicit exclusion of school services.

For adults, the Sunday losses are about ten times as high as the midweek gains. Even for children they are twice as high, but here the midweek services do make a substantial contribution to moderating the decline in average weekly attendance. The question that needs to be addressed is whether Sunday and midweek attendance provide similar levels of religious instruction.

The pattern of children's attendance is changing substantially. Usual Sunday attendance can be broken down between adults and children since 1986; during the following two and a half decades children's share of the total fell from 22% to less than 15%. A growing proportion of children's attendance comes during the week.

The 2011 census of population tells us that there are about 23 children under the age of 16 for every 100 adults in England. Interestingly, the Statistics for Mission 2012 report produced by the Church gives a marginally better ratio for average weekly attendance. The national totals are 204,000 children and 839,300 adults attending (either Sunday or midweek), or nearly one child for every four adults. If those children continued to participate in adulthood, weekly attendance at worship would be maintained at current levels. It needs to be noted that the Sunday figures are less favourable; with midweek services excluded, the ratio is closer to one child for every six adults.

The gap between weekly and Sunday attendance is important. For adults, average weekly attendance is only 15% higher than average Sunday attendance; for children it was 60% higher in 2012 (for 2013 figures, see Table 14.1). A substantial proportion (37%) of children were only counted midweek, and these services may be their only exposure to church. Midweek worship offers considerable scope for innovation, as well as real opportunities to reach children from non-churchgoing families. The cautionary note for the Church is that some of the events – particularly those at schools or in playgroups – may not be especially effective in producing an enduring connection to religious activity.

Table 14.1 Sunday and weekly attendance in 2013 for adults and children in the Church of England

	Adults	Children
Average Sunday attendance	713,600	122,900
Average weekly attendance	831,600	163,900

Source: Church of England published and unpublished statistics, assembled by the author.

Another implication is that the point at which most young people are lost to the Church comes during youth and early adulthood rather than childhood. Although connections may be weak if children are not attending Sunday school or Sunday services, a large number still have some association with the Church. Generational replacement is breaking down at the point where young people are making their own decisions about what to do.

Attender versus attendance trends

One challenge in interpreting the numbers is that they tell us about attendances, not attenders. Users of the 1851 Census of Religious Worship have always faced the difficulty that many Victorians attended both morning and evening services, so attendance counts must somehow be scaled down in estimating the number of churchgoers. Today the problem is the reverse: many 'regular' churchgoers do not attend every week.

If everyone goes to church weekly or not at all, then one million attendances in a given week translates directly into one million attenders. If people attend just once a month, then a weekly attendance count of one million would suggest that there are four million churchgoers. Thus any estimate of the number of churchgoers is sensitive to the assumptions we make about attendance frequency.

One solution is to maintain a register for several weeks in a sample of churches so that we can identify who has or has not come previously. One of the best known studies of this sort was carried out in the diocese of Wakefield in 1997.[5] The results of the survey are surprising and, to be frank, hard to believe. Of all individuals attending at least one service during an eight-week period, more than half came only once. Very few came every week, so that the one-time attenders outnumbered the every-week attenders by more than 12 to 1. There is a completely uniform distribution of people coming 2, 3, 4, 5, 6 or 7 times during the eight weeks. It is very hard not to suspect that measurement error has had major effects; one wonders how many people were entered multiple times on the registers. Ignoring the single visits, the investigators suggest that the number of churchgoers is about 40% higher than usual Sunday attendance, which seems reasonable. Unfortunately we still do not know whether this ratio is constant, rising or declining.

A common conjecture is that even regular attenders now appear more sporadically than in previous decades. Church leaders sometimes argue that the fall in average weekly attendance exaggerates the decline in the number of churchgoers, because fewer people are coming every week. The conjecture is plausible and deserves investigation (using more than anecdotal evidence).

Some evidence can be found in church statistics. Over the past few years the diocese of Leicester has asked parishes to enumerate joiners and leavers with the aim of estimating the size and growth of the 'worshipping community'. The figures imply that there has been growth of 15% over the four years from 2009 to 2012, while attendance showed little change.[6] This method is now being attempted across the country, and all parishes were asked for figures on joiners and leavers in the 2013 return. The results do not inspire confidence. According to these reports, there are one and a half times as many joiners as leavers. Many more people come for the first time than drop out because of death or illness (31,000 versus 17,000); residential moves produce more gains than losses, and 25% more people returned to church than left.

The problem is that it is very difficult to count losses to the worshipping community. Decades of experience with many denominations have taught religious statisticians that it is easier to count people on the way in than on the way out. The stock is easier to assess than the flow, however, and the estimates of the size of the worshipping community provided in the 2013 returns are plausible. The figures suggest that it is 25% larger than average Sunday attendance.

The argument that declining attendance is the product of declining frequency rather than declining numbers of attenders can be made, but much more evidence will be needed to make it convincing. The evidence from social surveys does not support the hypothesis that churchgoers are attending less often. We can use the British Social Attitudes survey to compare the past few years with the situation 25 years earlier. In the mid-1980s, 42% of people in England said that they regarded themselves as belong to the C of E; the figure has dropped to 25%. Self-described Anglicans report virtually the same frequency of attendance now as in the past, however. In fact, it appears from Table 14.2 that the proportion attending at least weekly is slightly higher now (though half never go at all).

As is well known, the attendance frequencies that people provide on social surveys are often inaccurate. Churchgoers who aim to attend weekly may claim to do so, whatever their degree of success. A degree of exaggeration does not matter to the comparison between past and present, however, unless people were formerly less likely to overstate their attendance than they are now.

Another test is to compare attendance at Easter with that in an ordinary week. The theory would be that all churchgoers still make a serious effort to attend

Table 14.2 Frequency of attendance for self-identified Anglicans in Great Britain

	1983–86	2008–11
Once a week or more	7.3	8.6
Once every two weeks	2.8	2.6
Once a month	7.2	7.2
Twice a year	17.8	14.3
Once a year	10.2	8.7
Less often	9.2	7.2
Never or practically never	45.0	50.5
Varies too much to say	0.6	0.9
Total	100.0	100.0
N	3,201	3,388

Source: British Social Attitudes Survey.

on the holiest day in the Christian calendar, even if the importance attached to regular weekly attendance has diminished. Some of those in church at Easter will be visitors or infrequent attenders, but one might assume that they are balanced by churchgoers who are unavoidably absent. If so, Easter attendance is arguably a reasonable proxy for the total number of churchgoers (defined as people who go at least once a month).

If the ratio of average weekly to Easter attendance has diminished over time, it implies that the decline in weekly attendance has been more rapid than that in the number of churchgoers. There has been no discernible trend over the past several years, during which Easter attendance has been about 25% higher than average weekly attendance. All Easter attenders have only been counted since 2001, however; to go back several decades, we have statistics only for Easter communicants (i.e. participants in Holy Communion). These figures are usable for our purposes if we can assume that the proportion of Easter attenders who take communion has held up.

It seems unlikely that a diminishing proportion of attenders are taking communion at Easter: if anything the reverse should be true, as clergy have become increasingly permissive about eligibility for the Eucharist. It also seems unlikely that churchgoers are becoming more casual about attending at Easter. Given these assumptions, the theory that churchgoers are now attending less often than previously receives little support from the statistics. Usual Sunday attendance was about 80% of the number of Easter communicants in the early 1980s, and it is slightly higher now; indeed, it reached 88% in 2013. The ratio crept up very slightly and then fell back in the middle of the period, but overall the relationship between the Easter and usual Sunday figures has been relatively stable. By implication, the trend in uSa is a reasonable index of the change in the total number of churchgoers over the past few decades.

The story is the same if we take the electoral roll rather than Easter attendance as a proxy for the total number of active Anglicans. Usual Sunday attendance was two-thirds of the electoral roll figure at the beginning of the 1980s, just before the revision of 1983; it was the same in the years prior to the revision of 2013. The ratio has gone up and down during the intervening period (rising when the roll is cleaned and then falling in the years that followed), but overall it is far from clear that members are attending less often. Looking only at the years when a new roll was compiled, we can see signs of a tapering off in uSa relative to the Anglican total, but it is rather slight, and the ratio in 2013 is the same as at the last revision in 2007.

Occasional offices

Baptisms

Before the Second World War nearly everyone was baptised (unless they were Jewish or from some other religious backgrounds). Nearly three-quarters of infants were baptised in the Church of England.[7] Over the past 75 years, christening has gradually ceased to be so prevalent and is now practised by a minority in England.

A small part of the relative decline is the result of the rapid growth in the Muslim, Hindu, Sikh and Buddhist groups. According to the 2011 census, 12.2% of children aged 0–4 belong to one of these four religions, up from 7.9% in 2001. We can use these and other figures to estimate the number of births in England that are to people of Christian heritage. The percentages discussed below use this adjusted total as the base, so that the changes described are not the product of post-war immigration.

Since 1987 the Church has counted baptisms in three categories: infants (under one year of age), children (between 1 and 12) and adolescents/adults. Previously the division was between infants and others, but young children were typically counted as infants. The exact breakdown for the early 1980s therefore depends on estimation.

Infant baptism is much less common now than even a few decades ago. In 1980, almost 40% of infants were baptised in the Church of England; by 2012, it was no more than 14% of 'eligible' (i.e. Christian heritage) infants. A small part of the gap is simply the result of timing: some children are being baptised later. In the early 1980s, an additional 4% of children were baptised when aged 1–12 rather than in their first year of life; the figure is now about 8%. Juvenile and adult baptisms also add to the total. These numbers fell in the early part of the period, but since the mid-1990s they have slowly strengthened and now contribute another 1.5–2% to the fraction baptised in each birth cohort. The net result is that the Anglican baptised share in each year of birth has fallen from an estimated 45% in 1980 to about 23% now (although many of the baptisms for children born recently have not yet occurred).

As a reminder, non-Christians have been excluded from these calculations. Taking the entire population as a base, the baptised Anglican share of recent birth cohorts will be around 20%. At the beginning of the millennium baptised Anglicans were still a majority in England; that is no longer the case, and generational replacement will produce a steady decline in the Anglican share of the population.[8] The established status of the Church is increasingly likely to be questioned in the decades ahead.

To end on a more positive note for the Church of England, infant and child baptisms have not dropped in recent years, with the Anglican share of each birth year remaining steady between 2007 and 2013. Adult baptisms have gone up over the past decade, albeit from a small base. Time will tell whether this interruption in the long-term pattern of decline is temporary or enduring, but at least for the moment the Church is holding its own with this key rite of passage.

Confirmation

The number of confirmations has fallen sharply, from not quite 98,000 in 1980 to slightly more than 19,000 in 2013. As the number of baptisms declines, it is not surprising that confirmations should follow suit. The ratio of confirmations to baptisms (lagged by 13 years) has also been dropping, however. In the 1980s, almost a quarter of the baptised were subsequently confirmed. In recent years the proportion has fallen to one in eight. In consequence the decline in confirmations has been twice as rapid as the decline in baptisms.

The gender differences are substantial and persistent: the female confirmation counts are about 50% higher than the male totals, and there has been very little narrowing of that gap. By contrast, the age pattern has changed significantly. What especially stands out is the collapse in the traditional norm of confirmation in early adolescence (ages 12 to 15). In 1980 exactly half of those confirmed were in this age group; the proportion is now a quarter. In absolute terms the numbers have gone from 49,000 per year to about 5,000 per year. There has been a slight shift towards earlier confirmation, but the major change has been in the proportion of adults (aged 20+). Although these numbers have also fallen (from more than 25,000 to less than 9,000), adult confirmation has held up better than teenage participation, and adult women now contribute almost half of the female total.

It is tempting to suppose that the admission of baptised but unconfirmed persons to Holy Communion (approved by the General Synod of the Church in 1996) has had an effect. After all, if baptism is accepted as the only qualification needed to receive the Eucharist, the incentive to become confirmed is reduced. There is some variation between dioceses and parishes in the implementation of the guidelines, but there has been a general lowering of barriers.

It is clear, though, that the steep decline in the number of young people seeking confirmation pre-dated this change. Excluding people aged 20 and older, the number of confirmations fell by half in the 1980s, by 40% in the 1990s and by a further 40% in the first decade of the new millennium. These very steep declines must call into question the viability of confirmation as a traditional rite of passage.

Marriages

The Church of England carried out a third of marriages during the 1980s. The fraction fell steeply in the several years following the Marriage Act 1994, which allowed weddings to be conducted in 'approved premises' other than churches and register offices. The Church's share of all marriages has been largely stable over the past decade, standing at slightly more than one in five in 2012.

In absolute terms the Church solemnised only half as many marriages during the decade to 2012 as in the 1980s. The Church has maintained its position relative to other religious organisations, however. It accounted for two-thirds of marriages with religious ceremonies in the decades since 1980, and in the past few years the proportion has crept up to three-quarters.

Funerals

In 2013, the Church of England conducted 159,000 funerals or services in crematoria and cemeteries, compared to about 132,000 baptisms, 19,000 confirmations and 50,000 weddings. Funerals therefore account for a large share of occasional offices, a reflection both of the higher levels of adherence in the oldest generations and the perceived suitability of religious solemnity to mark the end of a life.

Not even funerals have been exempt from numerical decline, however. In 2003, 43% of deaths in England led to Anglican funerals or services; in 2013 it was 33%, or about 57,000 fewer. The decline has been most marked with services at crematoria/cemeteries rather than in church funerals. The latter dropped from 20% to 18% of all deaths between 2003 and 2013, the former from 23% to 15%. It may be that non-religious options are increasingly available at places of cremation and burial.

The proportion of deaths that were marked by Anglican funerals or services varies by diocese, ranging from London at 16% to Hereford at 64%. In a few dioceses (Carlisle, Gloucester, Norwich, Sodor and Man) around half of deaths are followed by a Church of England funeral or service.

The geography of church participation

Numerical growth must be distinguished from the level of participation, and the socio-demographic context is important to both. Often attendance is highest as a proportion of the population in rural areas where growth is hard to achieve; growing churches are often found in cities where relatively few people are active Anglicans. Middle class suburbs with church schools, or inner city parishes with Christians arriving from overseas, offer great opportunities; rural districts and areas of industrial decline can be far more challenging. One of the difficulties for the Church of England is that its traditional rural strongholds and its new centres of urban growth are so different. The Church is faced with a strategic challenge: the question is whether the focus should be on supporting areas of existing strength or on developing churches that are growing but not yet as significant in absolute terms.

The comparatively low attendance levels found in towns and cities are in part the legacy of urban decline that began many decades ago, though it is now potentially being reversed. Village churches have more participants relative to population, but they are often struggling to maintain their numbers. Elderly, rural, white congregations are important but becoming comparatively less so. Vitality is easier to find in areas with younger, urban, ethnic minority attenders.

There is a clear urban/rural divide in Anglican churchgoing. In towns and cities, 2% of adults (aged 16+) will attend services in a parish church on a usual Sunday. In villages the corresponding figure is 4.5%. The difference has two components: religion is comparatively stronger in the countryside than in the cities, and the Church of England has a smaller share of the actively religious population in urban areas. Not only are cities home to many followers of non-Christian faiths, they also offer a large number of independent churches.

Levels of Church of England attendance are highest in rural parishes where the population is predominantly Christian and white British, with older people well represented. For growth, however, it is a different story. Unsurprisingly, population growth is linked to increased church attendance, just as rises in the percentage of the people identifying with no religion on the census are associated with decline. Areas with substantial Christian ethnic minority populations – which of course tend to be urban – are most likely to see church growth. Higher education is also associated with growth. It should be noted, though, that these factors account for only a very small fraction of the overall variation in church growth. Demographic change makes a difference, but it is not remotely necessary or sufficient for growth to occur.

At a local level, people moving into an area can make a difference. New housing will bring in new people, some of whom will transfer from other churches. The arrival of retired people or Christian immigrants can be a boost to growth. In most of these cases, of course, the growth is not produced by making new Christians but through drawing in existing ones.

Demography is more frequently mentioned as a cause of decline. Young people move out of parishes where houses are expensive or from rural areas where there is little work. Where many houses in a parish are holiday homes, attendance will be affected. In very small parishes there are few new people available to attract in any case.

Some problems are especially acute in cities. In some instances elderly members of the congregation tend to retire out of the area. Populations are relatively mobile, with the result that people do not stay long enough to develop enduring ties in the local church. And of course the growth of non-Christian minority groups may mean that the pool of Christians is smaller. In some instances the composition of a parish has changed significantly. Growth in the number of new immigrants from a Christian background can provide a boost, but some of the new attenders move away from relatively deprived areas as soon as they are able to do so.

Diocesan trends

Attendance in the Church of England varies substantially from one diocese to another. Some of this variation is influenced by the proportion of people who belong to other faiths or have no religion. We can use 2011 population census data to limit our attention to self-identified Christians in each diocese. If attendance at Easter provides a reasonable estimate of the number of active Anglicans, then the concentration varies from a high of 8% of Christians in Hereford to a low of 2% in Durham (Table 14.3).

The strength of the Church of England in the rural west – especially the dioceses of Hereford, Gloucester, Salisbury and Bath and Wells – is immediately apparent. Nearly all of the dioceses in the top half of the table are in the province of Canterbury. From the province of York, only Carlisle (which makes it into the top ten) does better than mid-table. The same pattern is seen in tables of other measures of adult participation, whether based on usual Sunday attendance, average weekly attendance or the electoral roll.

If we look at change rather than the stock, London was the one diocese to show growth in Easter attendance over the past decade; Southwark was in second place (Table 14.4). The diocese of London covers most of Greater London north

Table 14.3 Anglican Easter attendance per 1,000 Christians by diocese, 2011, in the Church of England, 2011

Diocese	Province	Easter attendance/ 1,000 Christians
Hereford	C	79
Salisbury	C	76
Gloucester	C	70
Bath & Wells	C	68
St Edmundsbury & Ipswich	C	67
Chichester	C	64
Truro	C	63
Carlisle	Y	63
Winchester	C	61
Exeter	C	61
Guildford	C	58
Oxford	C	55
Norwich	C	53
Ely	C	52
London	C	49
Canterbury	C	48
Peterborough	C	47
Portsmouth	C	46
Rochester	C	44
Ripon & Leeds	Y	42
Coventry	C	42
St Albans	C	41
Leicester	C	41
Bristol	C	39
Southwark	C	39
York	Y	39
Blackburn	Y	38
Chester	Y	38
Bradford	Y	36
Newcastle	Y	35
Derby	C	35
Lincoln	C	33
Worcester	C	33
Southwell & Nottingham	Y	33
Lichfield	C	32
Chelmsford	C	32
Birmingham	C	29
Manchester	Y	27
Wakefield	Y	27
Sheffield	Y	26
Liverpool	Y	25
Durham	Y	21

Source: Church of England published and unpublished statistics, assembled by the author.

Table 14.4 Annual growth in Easter attendance by diocese, 2003–2013, in the Church of England

Diocese	Province	Annual growth
London	C	0.58
Southwark	C	−0.13
Oxford	C	−0.21
Ely	C	−0.31
Bristol	C	−0.47
Durham	Y	−0.49
Coventry	C	−0.57
Peterborough	C	−0.58
Sodor & Man	Y	−0.66
Leicester	C	−0.68
Chelmsford	C	−0.74
Sheffield	Y	−0.79
Derby	C	−0.82
Birmingham	C	−0.85
St Albans	C	−0.93
Chester	Y	−0.93
Guildford	C	−0.94
Ripon & Leeds	Y	−0.96
Carlisle	Y	−0.97
Manchester	Y	−1.06
Lichfield	C	−1.12
Winchester	C	−1.17
Rochester	C	−1.22
Canterbury	C	−1.24
Bradford	Y	−1.24
Chichester	C	−1.35
Newcastle	Y	−1.45
Southwell & Nottingham	Y	−1.48
Salisbury	C	−1.49
Gloucester	C	−1.49
Hereford	C	−1.53
York	Y	−1.56
Portsmouth	C	−1.57
Bath & Wells	C	−1.63
St Edmundsbury & Ipswich	C	−1.73
Wakefield	Y	−1.95
Blackburn	Y	−2.01
Exeter	C	−2.02
Liverpool	Y	−2.14
Norwich	C	−2.19
Lincoln	C	−2.36
Truro	C	−2.52
Worcester	C	−2.59

Source: Church of England published and unpublished statistics, assembled by the author.

of the River Thames; Southwark includes most of Greater London south of the river, plus eastern Surrey. London and Southwark also take the top two places for change in adult usual Sunday attendance (again, marginal growth in London, slight decline in Southwark); for child usual Sunday attendance, they rank third and second respectively (decline in both). In addition, these two dioceses are among the handful to show growth in the electoral roll between 2003 and 2013.

A good deal has been written about the relative success of London, often crediting episcopal leadership and diocesan policy for the recent growth. The main explanation is likely to lie, more prosaically, in immigration. Between the censuses of 2001 and 2011, the populations of the dioceses of London and Southwark grew by 16% and 12% respectively, or in absolute terms by more than half a million and more than a quarter of a million. The UK-born population was unchanged during that period. A substantial proportion of the new arrivals are Christian. They compensate for the continuing loss of Christians among the UK-born, the numbers of whom fell by 21% in London and 17% in Southwark over the decade. The result is that (according to the 2011 census) 40% of Christians in London, and 30% of Christians in Southwark, were born outside the country.

Francis, Laycock and Village examined change in a basket of indicators across dioceses during the 1990s, which had been billed a 'decade of evangelism' by the Anglican Communion.[9] London grew, but there was decline in all of the other dioceses, ranging from 12% in Salisbury to 30% in Durham on their aggregate measure. The correlation between change during the 1990s and the years 2003–13 is generally low; there is little association between the Easter count trends for the two decades, for example, apart from the position of London at the top of the table. Usual Sunday attendance is more similar; in addition to London, five out of the ten dioceses that declined least in the 1990s remained among the best performers in the more recent decade (Ely, Coventry, Oxford, Salisbury and Derby). Lincoln fared worst in both periods.

Academics refer to the 'golden triangle' of Oxford, Cambridge and London; intriguingly (and perhaps coincidentally) there is an equivalent in recent church statistics. The four dioceses that have done best at maintaining Easter attendance in the past decade are London, Southwark, Oxford and Ely (which includes Cambridge); for child uSa the top positions are filled by Ely, Southwark, London and Oxford (in that order), and for adult uSa the list is London, Southwark and Ely, with Oxford in sixth place.

The generational pattern of decline

The future need not be the same as the past, but it is important to understand what is happening. Three common ideas about churchgoing appear to be incorrect:

1   Attendance decline occurs as busy adults drift away from regular practice.
2   The young may find worship dull, but when people marry, start families, see their children leave home, or reach retirement, an interest in religion returns.

3   There is a reservoir of faith waiting to be tapped; the Church just needs to reawaken its dormant constituency of people who are 'believing without belonging'.

We can test these ideas using major national surveys, in particular the British Social Attitudes survey from 1983 onwards. What emerges is that the large decline in attendance has not happened because many adults have stopped going to church. The decline has happened because more and more adults never start attending in the first place.[10] The change that leaders have to worry about, in other words, goes on not within any particular generation, but from one generation to the next.

We tend to suppose that people become more religious with age, perhaps when they start families or become widowed. If so, today's partygoer might be tomorrow's churchgoer. A significant number of adults do become more observant, but they are balanced by others who move away from religion. Most of these changes seem to occur for personal reasons that are not systematically related to having children or reaching old age. On average such life events have only slight effects.

Social forces are not making each of us gradually less religious. On the contrary, the evidence suggests that on average people experience little change in their religious beliefs and practices once they reach their early 20s. What secularisation does is to change the environment in which children are raised and the likelihood of effective religious upbringing. Each generation comes to be less religious than the one before.

While many individuals do enter or leave the Church as adults, net change within any given generation has historically been small. If people belong in their 20s, they will probably stay for the rest of their lives – but if they don't, it will be hard to bring them in.

The obvious conclusion is that the Church must retain its young people if it is to thrive. The Church of England has not done well in keeping the children and grandchildren of its members. For each successive year of birth over the 20th century, a smaller and smaller proportion of people regard themselves as belonging to the Church.

It is sometimes argued that the decline in churchgoing in Britain is simply one instance of a more general drift away from participation in voluntary organisations.[11] Trade unions, political parties and many other associations have lost ground in recent decades. The problem is that people are still interested in working conditions, current affairs and a host of other issues; it is less evident that they still feel religious. Topics of concern and modes of participation change as society changes; it may be that modernisation causes problems not just for religion but for some other forms of collective activity as well. The real question, though, is whether people are still inclined to believe even if not to belong, and the answer appears to be 'no'.[12]

It should not be forgotten that there are 4,774 Church of England schools, a fifth of state schools in England. A quarter of state primary schools and one in 16 state secondary schools are Church of England schools; they are slightly smaller than average, and hence 18% of all primary and 5% of all secondary pupils in England attend these schools. The Church's influence extends beyond the state sector; indeed, around 1,000 of the 1,300 independent preparatory and secondary schools in England have a Church of England ethos.[13]

The advance of secularity has been slowed by the arrival of millions of immigrants, many of whom are more religious than the British average. Only half of the new arrivals are Christian, however, and only a minority of the Christians come to worship in Anglican churches. Nevertheless the contribution made by African and other ethnic minority groups to the health of the Church of England is indisputable. The question is whether this infusion will continue, and whether the second and third generations will be more like their parents or their white peers in religious participation. The ethnic composition of the laity is changing rapidly, while the leadership is still largely old and white (if increasingly female).

Young people and the Church

The situation seems paradoxical. For decade after decade, children have become less religious than their parents. To put it another way, there are many families in which parents continue to identify themselves as belonging to the Church and to attend services while their adult children do not. (There are some families, but far fewer, where the reverse is true.) If parents regard religion as important – and one presumes that they do – why have they failed to pass it on to their offspring? One key question is whether we are seeing the effects of value change among young people or of value change among parents. It is possible that parents have simply become less committed to religious involvement by their children. As the value attached to autonomy has increased, adolescents are increasingly allowed to avoid church.

The European Values Study allows us to investigate this issue. There is a battery of items introduced as follows: 'Here is a list of qualities that children can be encouraged to learn at home. Which, if any, do you consider to be especially important? Please choose up to five'. Eleven qualities are listed: good manners; independence; hard work; feeling of responsibility; imagination; tolerance and respect for other people; thrift, saving money and things; determination, perseverance; religious faith; unselfishness; obedience.

The sample included 505 respondents who identified themselves as Anglicans. Religious faith was by a considerable margin the quality that was mentioned least often by this group as something that children ought to acquire. It was included as a priority by only 11%, as compared to good manners by 94%, tolerance and respect by 83%, independence by 47% and even imagination (the second-least popular) by 27%. On average, people who call themselves Anglican seem unconcerned about transmitting religion to the next generation.

Perhaps, though, things change if we exclude nominal Anglicans. We might naturally suppose that people who say that religion is very important in their own lives would include religious faith in their list of qualities that are especially important for children to learn at home. In fact, however, only 36% do so. Of the much larger number who say that religion is 'quite important' to them, a mere 10% mention faith as something important for their children to acquire. Among Anglicans who say that they attend services at least once a month, the figure is 28%. In other words, even religious Anglicans seem surprisingly reluctant to make inculcation of religion a priority in child-rearing.

The key finding from analysis of the full dataset (for many countries and denominations) is that institutional involvement in a religion, including respect for the role of religious organisations, is the crucial characteristic in distinguishing between respondents who do or do not make religion a priority in raising children.[14] It is not enough to regard religion as important, or to be 'spiritual': without some tie to an institution – past or current involvement in church, or a high regard for its functions – people tend not to make religious transmission a priority. The religiously unaffiliated and people who say 'I have my own way of connecting with the divine' are unlikely to see transmission as important, even if they regard religion as important in their own lives. By contrast, churchgoers or members of religious organisations, and people who say that the church answers moral and family problems, do want to see children raised in a faith. Being connected to church makes one significantly more likely to see religious faith as important for children.

Secularisation cannot be explained solely in relation to the intergenerational transmission of beliefs and values, of course. Secular activities (including television, music, the internet, games and so on) compete with religion for time and attention. Geographical mobility may have positive or negative effects on churchgoing. These and other factors are important, but ultimately religion depends on the commitment of one generation to pass it on to the next.

Counter-currents

It is worth addressing three topics that appear to offer better news for the Church of England than the trends discussed above: the substantial increase in giving, the rise in attendance at cathedral services, and the growth of 'fresh expressions of Church'.

The total amount of direct giving (planned giving plus church collections and boxes) doubled in real terms between 1980 and 2000. Expressed per person on the electoral roll, the amount tripled over this period, from £1.80 to £5.40 weekly (in 2012 pounds). The sum then continued to rise gradually, but fell off after the onset of the recession; the level (in constant pounds) in 2012 was the same as in 2002.

There has been considerable interest in recent years in the vitality of cathedrals.[15] While no simple explanation for growth in attendance has emerged, it is arguably attributable to the popularity of weekday choral evensong in the southeast of England. The evidence is available in Holmes and Kautzer, though the interpretation is my own.[16]

All of the growth in cathedral attendance has been in midweek services (p. 17). It is unevenly spread, and most growth has been in London and the Southeast (the increases for St Paul's, Chichester, Ely and Norwich can be found on pp. 21, 23). In most cathedrals, choral evensong 'was identified as the most consistently well attended weekday service' (p. 28). It seems clear that the majority – and possibly nearly all – of the total attendance gain has been at these services. The phenomenon is consistent with the Christmas pattern described above, where middle class people in the Home Counties turn out in force for carol services and midnight mass. For people fond of the English choral tradition and attracted by a high church setting, choral evensong in a cathedral offers something available nowhere else. In any event it seems likely that cathedrals are a special case, and that any lessons would not be readily transferrable to ordinary parish churches.

It is reasonable to end with a movement that shows the Church responding innovatively to contemporary conditions. The Church of England has encouraged the development of new forms of collective worship, targeted at people who are not members of traditional congregations. These so-called 'fresh expressions of Church' typically combine activities that are attractive to the unchurched with elements of Christian teaching and accessible worship. At the same time as offering something to the broader community, they help to create 'a new, large, relationally based fringe'.[17]

Parishes are asked for the number of participants in 'fresh expressions of Church' (fxC), and these counts are included in attendance statistics. A good deal of uncertainty arises as a result. Three particular problems are:

1   The vicar or church warden completing the form may overlook fxC groups that should be included. The Church Army research unit has found evidence of undercounting.
2   The vicar or church warden completing the form may count some groups as fxC that do not in fact qualify as such (for example because they are not 'fresh' initiatives or should not be regarded as 'church'). In conducting a major study on this topic, the Church Army research unit asked parishes to identify fxC; on closer examination nearly half (46%) were found not to meet the definition.
3   The participants in cafe church, Messy Church (orientated towards young children) or other popular fxC may be more interested in the secular than the religious content of the activity. Although the groups might count as new congregations in the eyes of the Church, the people themselves may not see their presence in the same way. At a minimum it seems unlikely that they are as committed on average as attenders at conventional services.

The net effect on the statistics is hard to judge. It is very likely that many fresh expressions are not being counted; it is also likely that some things are being counted that should not be. And in addition to these concerns about accuracy and reliability, we will increasingly have to grapple with issues of validity. The new forms and places of worship extend the reach of the Church of England, but within this enlarged penumbra will be people who might be surprised to find that they contribute to reported church attendance.

Unfortunately we have little information on the interests and commitment of people who come along to fxC. One is reminded of the Kendal study on alternative spirituality led by Paul Heelas and Linda Woodhead, on the basis of which they claimed that a 'spiritual revolution' is underway – one that may displace congregational religion.[18] Their evidence is basically the same as that provided on fxC: there is rapid growth in what they called the holistic milieu, where the activities are defined as spiritual by the providers. The problem is that yoga, aromatherapy, etc., like Messy Church, café church, etc., may be viewed very differently by the leaders and the consumers. Some participants may have their minds on higher things, and some might be led that way, but arguably most are just attracted by the activity.[19] Similarly, it's hard not to suspect that most fxC attenders are there for the 'expressions' and not for the 'church'. The question of how many end up with real commitment remains to be answered.

Supporters of 'fresh expressions of Church' will readily admit that we are dealing with apples and oranges, but argue that new forms of church community deserve to be counted just as much as traditional congregations. Sceptics suggest that including fxC in the attendance figures amounts to counting apple seeds as apples and masks the extent of numerical decline. It may be years before the issue is resolved.

Notes

1   C. Brown, *The Death of Christian Britain: Understanding Secularisation, 1800–2000* (second edition; Abingdon: Routledge, 2009); H. McLeod, *The Religious Crisis of the 1960s* (Oxford: Oxford University Press, 2007).
2   The data for this chapter come from the official records of the Church of England. Its Research and Statistics Unit produces annual reports that can be downloaded from the Church website: https://www.churchofengland.org/about-us/facts-stats/research-statistics. aspx and in the pre-internet era were published in the Church of England Yearbook. The author also intends to make statistics available at British Religion in Numbers (www. brin.ac.uk). The Research and Statistics Unit kindly supplied more complete versions of some time series to the author as part of the work undertaken for the Church Growth Research Programme, conducted during 2012–14.
3   A. Chandler, *The Church of England in the Twentieth Century: The Church Commissioners and the Politics of Reform, 1948–1998* (Suffolk: Boydell Press, 2006).
4   Church of England, *Statistics for Mission 2012: Ministry* (2013): Table 14.6.
5   S. Cottrell, 'Better Than Average – Understanding the Changing Patterns of Church Attendance', *Ministry Today* 18 (2000), available at https://www.ministrytoday.org.uk/magazine/issues/18/.
6   But see the detailed analysis and critique in M. Wigglesworth, 'A Critical Evaluation and Theological Reflection on "Worshipping Community"' (Unpublished MA dissertation; St John's College, Durham, 2014).
7   D. Voas, 'Intermarriage and the Demography of Secularisation', *British Journal of Sociology* 54 (2003): 83–108.
8   Voas, 'Intermarriage'.

9 L. J. Francis, P. Laycock and A. Village, 'Statistics for evidence-based policy in the Church of England: predicting diocesan performance', *Review of Religious Research* 52, no. 2 (2010): 207–20.

10 D. Voas and A. Crockett, 'Religion in Britain: Neither Believing nor Belonging', *Sociology* 39 (2005): 11–28; A. Crockett and D. Voas, 'Generations of Decline: Religious Change in Twentieth-Century Britain', *Journal for the Scientific Study of Religion* 45 (2006): 567–84.

11 G. Davie, 'Praying Alone? Church-Going in Britain and Social Capital: A Reply to Steve Bruce', *Journal of Contemporary Religion* 17 (2002): 329–34.

12 Voas and Crockett, 'Religion in Britain'.

13 According to the Independent Schools Information Service.

14 D. Voas and S. Doebler, 'Secularization in Europe: An Analysis of Inter-Generational Religious Change', in W. Arts and L. Halman (eds.), *Value Contrasts and Consensus in Present-Day Europe* (Leiden: Brill, 2013): 231–50.

15 L. Barley, 'Stirrings in Barchester: Cathedrals and Church Growth', in D. Goodhew (ed.), *Church Growth in Britain: 1980 to the Present* (Farnham: Ashgate, 2012): 77–90; Theos and The Grubb Institute, *Spiritual Capital: The Present and Future of English Cathedrals* (London: Theos and The Grubb Institute, 2012); J. Holmes and B. Kautzer, 'Cathedrals, Greater Churches and the Growth of the Church', Church Growth Research Programme Report, 2013, available at http://www.churchgrowthresearch.org.uk/progress_findings_reports.

16 See Holmes and Kautzer, 'Cathedrals'.

17 Church Army, 'An Analysis of Fresh Expressions of Church and Church Plants Begun in the Period 1992–2012', Church Growth Research Programme Report, 2013, available at http://www.churchgrowthresearch.org.uk/progress_findings_reports: 22.

18 See P. Heelas and L. Woodhead, *The Spiritual Revolution: Why Religion Is Giving Way to Spirituality* (Oxford: Blackwell, 2005).

19 D. Voas and S. Bruce, 'The Spiritual Revolution: Another False Dawn for the Sacred', in K. Flanagan and P. Jupp (eds.), *A Sociology of Spirituality* (Surrey: Ashgate, 2007): 43–62.

Conclusion

David Goodhew

Christianity is never as weak as it appears, nor as strong as it appears.

Philip Jenkins[1]

Numbers are not the only thing that matters in the Anglican Communion, by any means. The Christian faith started with just one person, in a tomb. The numerical strength or weakness of a community is not a referendum on its actual worth. Churches should see themselves in terms of their growing or diminishing spiritual depth and their growing or diminishing capacity to serve the communities in which they are set. Churches should also see themselves against the backdrop of the wider history of Christianity, a history which has seen once vibrant areas shrink drastically (such as Asia Minor) or 'backwaters' which have become highly strategic (such as the USA). In all comments about growth and decline, it cannot be overstressed that generalised comments about a particular nation or region are generalisations which obscure much fine detail. Overall growth in a country, region or diocese conceals significant areas of decline and *vice versa*.

But numerical growth or decline *does* also matter. It matters intrinsically[2] and also because numerical growth deeply moulds the narratives which churches tell about themselves. Churches, like individuals, live out of the narratives they tell themselves. Individuals, congregations and entire provinces of Anglicanism see themselves as major or minor players, identities reinforced by whether they see themselves as growing or shrinking. The stories churches tell of themselves may reflect reality, but often such stories are based on past realities and do not face what is now happening. This study has shown how rapidly the Communion has changed since 1980, making the danger of living out of past narratives and failing to face the changes that have happened all the more likely.

Modern Anglican narratives exist within the overarching secular narrative which assumes that Christianity is in decline.[3] Yet, as Johnson and Zurlo show in chapter 2 and as the other chapters confirm, Anglicanism has roughly doubled in size since 1970. In 1970 around 47 million self-identified as Anglicans worldwide. In 2010, that figure was around 86 million and is almost certainly higher now. The phrase 'Anglican Communion' is routinely paired with words such as 'crisis' or even 'collapse' in the media and elsewhere. But reports of the death of Anglicanism have been greatly exaggerated. The Anglican Communion has major troubles, notably serious divisions about theology and ethics, but these have not prevented its marked expansion in recent decades. A major reason why Anglicanism's divisions have been so problematic is because its rapid growth has globalised such divisions.

For several decades Anglican narratives have spoken of the shift in the Communion 'from the west to the rest'. This narrative is correct, but still often understated. The chapters of this book show the twin movements of the dramatic decline in many (not all) parts of the west and the rapid expansion of Anglicanism in many (not all) parts of the 'Global South'. Taken together, these twin movements mean that, whilst Anglicanism in 1980 was swinging numerically towards the 'Global South', now it is overwhelmingly a 'southern' faith. Anglicanism in Africa, Asia and Latin America was 19% of global Anglicanism in 1970. Now it is 60% or more. North American Anglicanism was 9% of global Anglicanism in 1970. By 2010 it had dropped to 3% and is now smaller still.[4]

Beyond this, the generalisation that the bulk of Anglicanism's growth is in the 'Global South' obscures the highly differentiated nature of that growth. Chapters 4, 5, 6, 9 and 13 of this volume show how Nigeria, Congo, Kenya, Singapore and parts of South America have grown rapidly since 1980. However, areas such as Ghana, South Africa, South Korea and the Church of South India have not grown or have grown much more slowly than their population or other churches in those nations (chapters 3, 7, 8 and 10). Likewise, the narrative that western Anglicanism is mainly in decline obscures the highly differentiated nature of that decline. As chapters 11, 12 and 14 on Australia, the USA and England show, the rate of decline in western Anglicanism varies markedly from precipitate to modest. These chapters also show how Anglicanism is stable or even growing in a limited number of parts of the west.

Many narratives of Anglicanism are incomplete because they omit unexpected areas of recent growth.[5] In 1980, the number of Anglican congregations across Indonesia, Vietnam, Cambodia, Thailand and Nepal could be counted on the fingers of one hand. In 2015, the number of Anglican congregations in these countries reached approximately 100. In 1980, the trajectory across Indonesia, Vietnam, Cambodia, Thailand and Nepal appeared, if anything, downwards, with the sole Anglican congregation in Vietnam having closed in 1975 and other countries seemingly hostile or indifferent 'soil' for the planting of congregations. The expansion of Anglicanism in this region has mainly occurred since 1990 and there is considerable likelihood that further expansion in these countries will happen in the coming years.[6]

Indonesia, Vietnam, Cambodia, Thailand and Nepal are not, at first sight, obvious places into which the Anglican Communion seemed likely to expand and have received minimal attention in recent studies of the Communion.[7] Yet the recent trajectory of Anglicanism in these countries is a salutary reminder to expect the unexpected. Recent decades have seen many areas which were seen as 'key' in sharp decline, whilst areas which appeared 'poor soil' for Anglicanism have recently grown into significant centres.

This volume's chapters in Anglicanism in Congo, the Province of South America and Singapore show how they have grown into significant centres of Anglicanism since 1980. However, a case could be made for looking at other areas of the Communion – such as Ethiopia – which previously had small Anglican communities, yet are expanding.[8] The Anglicanism of the early 21st century has radically changed from the Anglicanism of 1980, let alone that of the early 20th century.

Conversely, parts of western Anglicanism are in severe decline. Chapters 11 and 12 show that the most serious decline is found in many rural dioceses in the USA and Australia. And the experiences of Canada and Wales fit this pattern.[9] The continued viability of Anglicanism in such areas is being, or may soon be, called into question. But it should not be assumed that Anglicanism *per se* is on the way out in the west. There are significant areas of resilience and a few areas of growth. Notably, some major cities seem less prey to secularisation than other parts of the west. A wider issue, beyond the scope of this volume is the extent to which congregational decline in western Anglicanism is part of a much wider decline in communal activity in the west. Compared, for example, to the membership of British political parties, membership of the Church of England has held up rather well.[10]

Crucial for western Anglicanism is whether it is able to adapt to the changing demographics of the west. Cities such as London, New York and Sydney are changing fast. London's population has risen by c. 50% since 1990. As recently as 1970 the population of London was 86% 'white British'; it is now heading towards one-third 'white British'.[11] In this light, the growth of the diocese of London offers hope for western Anglicanism, where many urban centres are expanding and becoming markedly more diverse. But the diversifying cities do not automatically mean expanding Anglican dioceses. Churches which do not adapt to such demographic shifts will be left behind by such shifts.

A sensitive research area is growth and decline in Anglicanism in the USA, complicated as it is by recent divisions. Nonetheless, the comparative trajectories of the Episcopal Church (TEC) and the Anglican Church in North America (ACNA) constitute a research nettle that needs grasping, but in a way that avoids being drawn into culture wars, not least because such research will help us to see through the fog generated by such wars. Jeremy Bonner's valuable work in this volume needs following up with further studies that include all shades of Anglicanism in the USA and which provide a more fine-textured picture of a denomination changing before our eyes.

Substantial areas of the world beyond the west are shrinking or experiencing minimal growth or growing less than the rate at which their populations are growing – i.e. even if they are growing as an absolute number, they are shrinking as a proportion of their respective countries. Chapters 3, 7, 8 and 10 on Ghana, South Africa, South India and South Korea show churches which are both substantial and which also have a certain fragility. However, the trajectory of Anglicanism elsewhere and the experience of other denominations in those countries show that they also have considerable capacity to grow. Their future trajectory is therefore particularly hard to plot with certainty.

Anglicanism offers a stimulating context for discussions about secularisation. Anglicanism both confirms and refutes secularisation theories. Its wide (albeit uneven) geographical spread is a valuable corrective to (usually) western academic debates which too easily assume that what happens in the west is of the greatest significance or, even worse, that sooner or later everyone else 'will become like us'. The burgeoning religiosity of London and Singapore raises the possibility that the opposite may be happening and that the west may become more like 'the rest'.[12] There is a significant, though not automatic, correlation between the world's 'trade routes' and Anglican growth. Overall, the marked growth of Anglicanism worldwide since 1980 is an important correction to academic and media narratives which assume the inevitability of secularisation. John Wolffe's insightful survey of London's religious shifts shows how religion in London initially declined and then later grew during the 20th century. Wolffe cogently argues that we should view contemporary shifts in faith in terms of 'religious change', rather than in terms of 'religious decline'.[13]

This said, the dramatic decline of parts of Anglicanism, often coupled with shifts towards 'no religion', agnosticism and atheism in parts of the west, suggests a further stage in their secularisation. In parts (*not all*) of white British, North American and Australasian culture, the coming decades may test just how low religiosity can go. There is some evidence of secularisation impacting upon parts of the developing world, but whether this becomes a major phenomenon and whether the developing world secularity looks like western secularity remains to be seen.

This volume offers partial answers, which require further research to clarify and develop. Discussions of growth and decline within Anglicanism in recent decades have often previously depended on limited data and sometimes debatable assumptions. The contributors to this volume have substantially extended the data available for global Anglicanism and refined the terms of the debate, but there is much more to do. Following the admirable strapline of Grove Books, this volume is, in some ways, the first word in a much larger debate; it is certainly not the last word. The rest of this conclusion consists of observations on future areas for research.

The first and most crucial area for further research is data. The chapter authors in this volume have worked with data sets which vary from the highly detailed to the highly challenging. The meaning they have derived from such data has been hard won and often depends on comparing one form of evidence with others. Where multiple quantitative measures can be used and where they can be checked against smaller case studies and qualitative work, conclusions are most secure. Conclusions are more qualified where the data is less sturdy, although much can still be said, if care is taken. Therefore, a crucial research task is to gather further data and refine what data currently exists. A linked task is to provide a greater range of data. In particular, case studies of growing regions, dioceses and individual parishes would be of huge value in discerning the precise nature of rapidly growing Anglican provinces. It should be noted that the data from much of western Anglicanism, including the Church of England, is also far from ideal and cannot bear overly detailed analysis. Data refining is no less needed in the west to sort the wheat from the weeds.

Second is the nature of growth and decline. It is a cliché in some circles to suggest that some developing world church growth is a mile wide and an inch deep. This is a problematic phrase, partly because of its condescension towards the developing world, partly because the issue of 'inch-deep faith' is found just as much in the developed world. This said, deeper studies of what numerical growth and decline consist of would be of great value. Case studies, again, have much to offer, but so too do comparative studies. Comparing the nature of Anglican growth, stability and decline in, for example, a range of African or Asian cities would be highly illuminating. Likewise, comparative studies of Anglicanism in various rural areas across the west will have much to offer.

Third, there is the obvious need to map growth and decline in those parts of the Anglican Communion not covered in this volume. Those many areas not covered in this book were omitted not because they were less significant, but because it was impossible to cover all that deserves to be covered. In particular, it would be hugely valuable to look at less researched areas of Anglicanism, such as the previously mentioned growth in Indonesia, Vietnam, Cambodia, Thailand and Nepal. Detailed studies of such regions and many others would be of great value and may uncover further areas of Anglican growth of which the wider Communion is unaware. Conversely, there would be merit in studying areas of Anglicanism mainly, but not exclusively, in the west, which have been in lengthy and steep decline. The introductory chapter cited the diocese of Quebec, which estimates that two-thirds of its congregations will shortly close or have to amalgamate with others.[14] What is causing such secularisation and how it compares with secularisation elsewhere greatly deserves study.

Fourth, why are churches growing or declining? This is a huge and partially unanswerable question. A wide range of researchers have posited theories.[15] Their views should be considered, but treated with caution. One of the most striking shifts in global Christianity is the way that some major cities evidence striking religious vitality – a vitality evident in Anglicanism, in Christianity more widely and in other faiths. For many decades, cities were depicted as the epicentres of secularisation. Recent research, depicting vigorous urban religiosity across a range of cities, calls that assumption into question.[16] Equally, the ecclesial snobbery sometimes seen in the west which assumes church growth must in some sense be 'dodgy', or the assumption sometimes found in developing world Anglicanism that western decline must be the result of theological error, should be treated with considerable caution.[17] What certainly will help are researchers who take pains to sift the data, to challenge assumptions both of secularisation theorists and over-optimistic/over-pessimistic church leaders alike.

The question of how theological tradition and church growth and decline relate to one another was summarised in the opening chapter.[18] The 'pentecostalisation' of many parts of the Communion has fed into their growth. Alongside this, provinces rooted in the evangelical tradition have also tended to grow. Those rooted in the anglo-catholic tradition have been less likely to grow, although there are significant exceptions to this trend. The years between 1980 and the present have seen significant decline in many parts of the western church which lean towards a liberal theology. However, whether this is because of, or despite, such a theology remains to be seen. At the same time, liberalism's intellectual strength allows it to punch above its numerical weight. How – or whether – this will continue depends much on the trajectory of new centres of theological education arising in the Anglicanism of the 'Global South'.

Fifth, how does numerical growth link or not link with spiritual growth and growth in service of the wider community? This question is hardest of all to answer but hugely pertinent to Anglicanism as it seeks to grow in every sense of the word 'grow'. It would be a serious mistake to assume that areas which have seen marked numerical growth are unconcerned about spiritual growth or growth in service of the wider community. There is much evidence that one form of growth feeds into another.[19] This said, the 'pentecostalisation' of significant parts of the Communion sometimes involves linkage with notions of 'prosperity gospel' which deserves to be questioned.

A wider question is how the poverty and affluence of a society impact on Anglicanism's growth and decline. There is a rough correlation between affluence and church decline and poverty and church growth, as scholars such as Norris and Inglehart have argued. Globally, the areas where Anglicanism has struggled most have tended to be the most affluent and, as McLeod showed in his study of the 1960s, the challenge of secularity increased markedly from the 1960s as consumerism spread across the west.[20] Conversely, the tragic recent history of Sudan, South Sudan and Congo show that severe socio-economic crisis is no bar to marked church growth and may even fuel it. But correlation is not causation. There are many exceptions that do not fit this pattern and there is the question of what happens to church growth/decline when previously affluent societies experience austerity and previously poor societies become more prosperous.[21] A related theological question is how to explain suffering in human life (theodicy), which is sometimes used in popular discourse as an argument against faith. These are profound matters, but it cannot be overlooked that this question is being asked most strongly in the more affluent societies and appears less prominent in poorer societies.[22]

Narratives matter. The narratives told of the Anglican Communion depend heavily on assumptions made about its numerical growth or decline. This volume is a contribution towards more accurate and more comprehensive narration. The Anglican Communion has seen dramatic growth *and* decline since 1980, depending on where you look. Overall, the Communion has roughly doubled in size in recent decades and the large majority of its members are now from the developing world. Some areas which previously seemed marginal have grown markedly. Areas well outside British influence or which do not even use the English language have seen new Anglican churches arising. Some major cities, supposedly the most secular of modern spaces, have moved from decline to growth. Alongside this, areas previously seen as pillars of Anglicanism have declined in absolute terms, or in relation to their growing population. In a few such places where decline has been severe, Anglicanism could be reduced to a small remnant in the coming decades. But, as those selling financial products sometimes say, it would be a mistake to assume past trends were a guarantee of future performance. Just as Anglicanism grew and declined in many surprising ways between 1980 and the present, so it will in the future. The decades since 1980 have seen more dramatic expansions and contractions within Anglicanism than at any point in its history. Who is to say that the coming decades will be any less eventful.

Notes

1 Jenkins adapted a saying of Bismarck about Russia in making this comment. See: P. Jenkins, *The Next Christendom: The Coming of Global Christianity* (revised edition, New York: Oxford University Press, 2007): 261.

2 For a discussion of why seeking numerical growth is intrinsic to the practice of Christianity, see: D. Goodhew (ed.), *Towards a Theology of Church Growth* (Farnham: Ashgate, 2015).

3 C. Taylor, *A Secular Age* (Cambridge, MA: Harvard University Press, 2007).

4 T. M. Johnson and G. A. Zurlo, 'The Changing Demographics of Global Anglicanism, 1970–2010', in D. Goodhew (ed.), *Growth and Decline in the Anglican Communion, 1980 to the Present* (Abingdon: Routledge, 2017): 37–8.

5 For a discussion of how recent studies of the Anglican Communion omit unexpected areas of growth, see: D. Goodhew, 'Growth and Decline in the Anglican Communion', in D. Goodhew (ed.), *Growth and Decline in the Anglican Communion, 1980 to the Present* (Abingdon: Routledge, 2017): 7.

6 Available at http://www.anglican.org.sg/index.php accessed 200516.

7 They are largely absent from, for example: W. Sachs, *The Transformation of Anglicanism from State Church to Global Communion* (Cambridge: Cambridge University Press, 1993); K. Ward, *A History of Global Anglicanism* (Cambridge: Cambridge University Press, 2006); B. Kaye, *An Introduction to World Anglicanism* (Cambridge: Cambridge University Press, 2008); I. S. Markham, J. Barney Hawkins IV, J. Terry, and L. N. Steffensen (eds.), *The Wiley-Blackwell Companion to the Anglican Communion* (Chichester: Wiley Blackwell, 2013); M. Chapman, S. Clarke, and M. Percy (eds.), *The Oxford Handbook of Anglican Studies* (Oxford: Oxford University Press, 2015); A. Day (ed.), *Contemporary Issues in the Worldwide Anglican Communion* (Abingdon: Routledge, 2015).

8 Available at http://dioceseofegypt.org/explore/horn-of-africa/ accessed 26 May 2016.

9 See: Goodhew, 'Growth and Decline': 15.

10 G. Davie, *The Sociology of Religion* (London: Sage, 2007): 92–3.

11 B. Judah, *This Is London* (London: Pan Macmillan, 2016): 203. The demography of London is charted in detail in: E. Kaufmann, 'The Demography of Religion in London since 1980', in A. P. Cooper and D. Goodhew (eds.), *No Secular City: London's Churches, 1980 to the Present* (Oxford: Oxford University Press, forthcoming).

12 The striking growth of Christianity in contemporary London is being charted by the forthcoming volume: Cooper and Goodhew (eds.), *No Secular City.*

13 J. Wolffe, 'Towards the Post-Secular City? London since the 1960s', *Journal of Religious History*, forthcoming.

14 Goodhew, 'Growth and Decline': 15.

15 For a survey of theories on growth and decline from an academic perspective, see: Davie, *Sociology of Religion*: 46–158.

16 There is now considerable evidence that faith is thriving in some late modern cities, rather than being submerged by secularity. See, for example: T. Carnes and A. Karpathakis, *New York Glory: Religions in the City* (New York: New York University Press, 2001);

B. Tah Gwanmesia, *Blessings under Pressure: The Work of Migrant Churches in the City of Rotterdam* (Rotterdam: SKIN, 2009); M. Gornik, *Word Made Global: Stories of African Christianity in New York City* (Grand Rapids: Eerdmans, 2011); P. Brierley, *Capital Growth: What the 2012 London Church Census Reveals* (Tonbridge: ADBC, 2013). See also: Cooper and Goodhew (eds.), *No Secular City*.

17 For a survey of western 'theology of decline', see: D. Goodhew, 'Towards a Theology of Church Growth', in D. Goodhew (ed.), *Towards a Theology of Church Growth* (Farnham: Ashgate, 2015): 27–36.

18 Goodhew, 'Growth and Decline': 20–2.

19 For example, the diocese of Singapore combines deep social concern with concern to share the Christian faith. See: D. Wee, 'Singapore', in D. Goodhew (ed.), *Growth and Decline in the Anglican Communion, 1980 to the Present* (Abingdon: Routledge, 2017): 175.

20 H. McLeod, *The Religious Crisis of the 1960s* (Oxford: Oxford University Press, 2007): 102–23.

21 For analysis of the debate about how affluence and poverty impact on growth and decline, see: Davie, *Sociology of Religion*: 104–6.

22 For a discussion of how concern over theodicy fits with wider patterns of western thought, see: Taylor, *A Secular Age*.

Afterword

Graham Kings

Introduction

In his prophetic book on ecology, published 40 years ago, *Enough Is Enough*, John V Taylor argued against 'any conjectural projection of present trends into the future without allowing for unforeseen change of a radical kind'. He wrote:

> By plotting a graph of the expansion of the monasteries throughout the Middle Ages we might easily have concluded that nine-tenths of the British people were celibates today. But such a calculation would not have allowed for such a change as the dissolution of the monasteries.[1]

This warns against projection of trends. None of us knows what is round the corner. However, this book has taken such a warning to heart and is careful not to claim too much.

The editor, and all the authors, are to be congratulated. In chapter 1, David Goodhew helpfully points out what is special about this book: the question of data quality is addressed in each particular chapter. He goes on to add, 'at times, conclusions are limited by the limitations of the data', and continues later:

> It is striking how, in all but one case, the conclusions of demographers Todd M. Johnson and Gina A. Zurlo chime with the detailed work of the individual case studies.

I have greatly enjoyed the statistics and ruminations of these chapters. The editor's summary comment in chapter 1 is perceptive:

> churches that intend to grow tend to grow and churches that do not intend to grow tend not to grow.[2]

What are we make of all this? Let us consider the words of Jesus, the Apostle Paul, an evangelical Anglican Kenyan Archbishop, David Gitari, and a catholic Anglican Franciscan writer, Martin Laird, before concluding with Chou En Lai and Archbishop Thomas Cranmer.

1. Jesus

Jesus' words to his disciples in Samaria, after the woman at the well had gone to pass on the good news to her neighbours, are significant for our topic:

> Do you not say, 'Four months more, then comes the harvest'? But I tell you, look around you, and see how the fields are ripe for harvesting. The reaper is already receiving wages and is gathering fruit for eternal life, so that sower and reaper may rejoice together. For here the saying holds true, 'One sows and another reaps.' I sent you to reap for that which you did not labour. Others have laboured, and you have entered into their labour.
>
> (John 4:35–38)[3]

These chapters have helped us to 'look around us', at different parts of God's worldwide Church. Rather than a response of 'Oh well, that works for them over there but it could not happen in our country', it may be worth considering whether in our own context 'the fields are ripe for harvesting'. We are closely related, and interwoven, across the universal Church in this generation.

Over the decades covered in this book, the growth described has built on previous hard work. Bible translation and publishing is one example. Often the fruit of this is not seen immediately but much later.[4] We are closely related, and interwoven, across the universal Church in time, back through the ages.

2. Paul

When Apollos, full of the Holy Spirit following the teaching of Priscilla and Aquila at Ephesus (Acts 18), crossed the Aegean Sea and went to Corinth, the church there experienced a crisis of leadership and possible splits. Some Christians at Corinth, according to Paul, said:

> 'I belong to Paul', or 'I belong to Apollos', or 'I belong to Cephas', or 'I belong to Christ'.
>
> (1 Cor 1:12–13)

Paul wisely focused on the cross, rather than on personalities, rhetoric and eloquence and went on to comment:

> What then is Apollos? What is Paul? Servants through whom you came to believe, as the Lord assigned to each. I planted, Apollos watered, but God gave the growth.
>
> (1 Cor 3:5–6)

His emphasis on God giving the growth is heartening.

In Ephesians 4:15–16, Paul[5] exquisitely mixes his metaphors in writing about the whole body:

> But speaking the truth in love, we must grow up in every way into him who is the head, into Christ, from whom the whole body, joined and knit together by every ligament with which it is equipped, as each part is working properly, promotes the body's growth in building itself up in love.

Writing from prison (Ephesians 3:1), his mind soars beyond the four walls enclosing him. In our mutual encouragement, across dioceses and provinces of the Anglican Communion, we also need to 'speak the truth in love'. A recent example of this, on various topics, was at the Primates' Meeting in Canterbury in January 2016[6] and the Anglican Consultative Council in Lusaka, Zambia, in April 2016.[7] A key feature of both was an emphasis on intentional evangelism and discipleship.

We are called to grow up into Christ our head. The growth comes from him. The image of being 'knit together' is powerful about our relationships across the Anglican Communion today. Since it is echoed in the Collect for All Saints' Day in *The Book of Common Prayer*, it also resonates for the Communion of Saints:

> O Almighty God, who has knit together thine elect in one communion and fellowship in the mystical body of thy Son . . .

Again, catholicity in space and time.

When 'each part is working properly', then there is organic growth in numbers and 'in love'.

3. David Gitari

I remember David Gitari, when he was Bishop of Mount Kenya East, before he became Archbishop, drawing on the growth of Jesus as a young boy and applying it to holistic growth in his diocese.[8] The 12-year-old boy was apparently lost and eventually found by Mary and Joseph in the temple at Jerusalem 'sitting among the teachers, listening to them and asking them questions' (Luke 2:46). After they returned to Nazareth:

> Jesus grew in wisdom and in stature, in favour with God and with people.
> (Luke 2:52)

Gitari expounded this as Jesus growing in 'wisdom' (his mind); 'stature' (his body); 'in favour with God' (his spirit); and 'in favour with people' (in his community). He asked why, in his diocese, each child and community should not be able to grow in these four ways. So he worked tirelessly to promote education (mind), development (body), evangelism (spirit) and justice (community).

The following statistics, from diocesan records in the archive of St Andrew's College, Kabare, bear witness to the phenomenal growth in his diocese. Between 1975 and 1990 the number of parishes rose from 19 to 93, the number of vicars rose from 30 to 120, of deaconesses from 0 to 20, community health workers from 0 to 308. Sixty-seven church buildings were consecrated, including Embu Cathedral; about 150,000 people were baptised and about 90,000 confirmed. Two missionaries were sent to other countries, to Zaire and West Germany.

Episcopal leadership in mission, which is intentional in holistic growth, is clearly a significant feature of growth in the chapters of this book. We see this in the example of David Gitari.

4. *Martin Laird*

In his profound book *Into the Silent Land: A Guide to the Christian Practice of Contemplation*, the American Anglican Franciscan, Martin Laird, discusses the difference between 'techniques' and 'skills':

> Techniques are all the rage today. They suggest a certain control that aims to determine a certain outcome. They clearly have their place. But this is not what contemplative practice does. The difference may be slight but it is an important one. A spiritual practice simply disposes us to allow something to take place.
>
> For example, a gardener does not actually grow plants. A gardener practices certain gardening skills that facilitate growth that is beyond the gardener's direct control. In a similar way, a sailor cannot produce the necessary wind that moves the boat. A sailor practices skills that harness the gift of wind that brings the sailor home, but there is nothing the sailor can do to make the wind blow. And so it is with contemplative practice, not a technique, but a skill. The skill required is interior silence.[9]

The diverse chapters of this book have subtly manifested some skills which may be developed for further Church Growth in the Anglican Communion. These should be distinguished from 'techniques' and from any idea that skills automatically produce growth. God in his beneficence provides growth for the flowers, wind for the boat and the growth for his Church worldwide.

One of the key 'skills', intending to grow, emanates organically from the delight in growing, in numbers and in depth.

Conclusion

At the Primates' Meeting, the Lambeth Conference of 2020 was discussed, decided upon and announced at the press conference.[10] The Primates were cognisant of the importance of the centenary of the Lambeth Conference of 1920.[11] This issued the famous 'Appeal to All Christian People'[12] which encouraged

Christian unity through discussions about the mutual recognition of ministries. The ecumenical setting of the growth and decline in the Anglican Communion is substantial. An example of this is Latin America, traditionally Roman Catholic and increasingly Pentecostal. As preparations are made for Lambeth 2020, it may be worth pondering Paul's key words 'with all the saints' in this passage:

> I pray that you may have power to comprehend, with all the saints, what is the breadth, and length, and height, and depth, and to know the love of Christ that surpasses knowledge, so that you may be filled with all the fullness of God.
>
> (Ephesians 3:18)

David Goodhew points out in the first chapter:

> The power of the English nation may have waned, but the potency of the English language and English-speaking cultures is fundamental not only to the modern world, but to modern religion – a factor which will influence significantly the future trajectory of the Anglican Communion.[13]

This intriguing matter of the power of the English language in the internet age is important for developments of the post-denominational churches in China. This needs weighing against the following quip, quoted by John V Taylor:

> The shrewdest attitude towards both the past and the future is that taken by Chou En Lai [Chinese Prime Minister 1949–76] who, when asked how he assessed the French Revolution, replied, 'It's a little too early to judge.'[14]

We end with Cranmer and a famous prayer. In an earlier book, edited by David Goodhew, *Towards a Theology of Church Growth*, Ashley Null contributed a chapter full of insight, and with a wide hinterland in Reformation studies, 'Divine Allurement: Thomas Cranmer and Tudor Church Growth'. He concludes:

> Cranmer's favourite word for evangelism was 'allurement'. . . . Clearly, Cranmer thought that the inherent drawing power of divine free forgiveness was the root of all evangelism. Consequently, in his revisions for the 1552 *Book of Common Prayer*, he decided to insert the Comfortable Words immediately before the *Sursum corda*. Thus, he put his twin means of moving human affection heavenward – scriptural rumination and cultural contextualisation – at the very heart of Tudor worship. The mission, vitality and expansion of the church today would be well served by doing likewise for our own time.[15]

The interweaving links between prayer, evangelism and Church growth are foundational. The Prayer of St Chrysostom in the *Book of Common Prayer* services of Morning and Evening Prayer, includes grace, unity, petition, promise, numbers, desire and the key phrase 'as may be most expedient for them', before mentioning truth and life eternal:

> Almighty God, who hast given us grace at this time with one accord to make our common supplications unto thee; and dost promise that when two or three are gathered together in thy Name thou wilt grant their requests: Fulfil now, O Lord, the desires and petitions of thy servants, as may be most expedient for them; granting us in this world knowledge of thy truth, and in the world to come life everlasting.
>
> (Amen)

Notes

1 J. V. Taylor, *Enough Is Enough* (London: SCM Press, 1975): 13.
2 D. Goodhew, 'Growth and Decline in the Anglican Communion, 1980 to the Present', in D. Goodhew (ed.), *Growth and Decline in the Anglican Communion, 1980 to the Present* (Abingdon: Routledge, 2017): 8, 6.
3 Bible quotations are taken from the New Revised Standard Version (Anglicised edition).
4 See L. Sanneh, *Translating the Message: The Missionary Impact on Culture* (Maryknoll, NY: Orbis Books, 1989 and 2009).
5 I am content to follow the cumulative case for the Pauline authorship of Ephesians made by G. B. Caird, *Paul's Letters from Prison: Ephesians, Philippians, Colossians, Philemon in the Revised Standard Version* (Oxford: Oxford University Press, 1976).
6 Available at http://www.primates2016.org/.
7 Available at http://www.anglicannews.org/news/2015/11/let-love-lead-the-anglican-communion-childrens-prayer-at-launch-of-acc-16.aspx.
8 I worked in the Diocese of Mount Kenya East, at St Andrew's College, Kabare, 1985–91. For an obituary of David Gitari, see G. Kings, 'Archbishop David Gitari 1937–2013: Evangelist, Prophet, Liturgist and Bridge-Builder' on Fulcrum https://www.fulcrum-anglican.org.uk/articles/archbishop-david-gitari-1937–2013-evangelist-prophet-liturgist-and-bridge-builder/. For his use of the Bible, see G. Kings, 'Archbishop David Gitari: Biblical Interpretation in Action in Kenya' on Fulcrum https://www.fulcrum-anglican.org.uk/articles/archbishop-david-gitari-biblical-interpretation-in-action-in-kenya/.
9 M. Laird, *Into the Silent Land: A Guide to the Christian Practice of Contemplation* (Oxford: Oxford University Press, 2006): 3–4. Laird is Associate Professor of Theology at Villanova University.
10 Available at http://www.primates2016.org/articles/2016/01/15/communique-primates/. See also G. Kings, 'The Centre Holds: Primates 2016 in Canterbury', available at http://www.missiontheologyanglican.org/interweavings/the-centre-holds-primates-2016-in-canterbury-/.
11 Available at http://www.archbishopofcanterbury.org/pages/lambeth-conference.html.
12 For the text of Resolution 9, The Appeal to All Christian People, scroll down at http://www.methodist.org.uk/downloads/ec-1920-Lambeth.pdf.
13 Goodhew, 'Growth and Decline': 19.
14 J. V. Taylor, 'The Future of Christianity', in J. McManners (ed.), *The Oxford Illustrated History of Christianity* (Oxford: Oxford University Press, 1990): 665.
15 A. Null, 'Divine Allurement: Thomas Cranmer and Tudor Church Growth', in D. Goodhew (ed.), *Towards a Theology of Church Growth* (Farnham: Ashgate, 2015): 215.

Index